DOS and Windows™ Protected Mode

Programming with DOS Extenders in C

AL WILLIAMS

Andrew Schulman
Series Editor

Addison-Wesley Publishing Company

Reading, Massachusetts   Menlo Park, California
New York   Don Mills, Ontario   Wokingham, England
Amsterdam   Bonn   Sydney   Singapore   Tokyo   Madrid
San Juan   Paris   Seoul   Milan   Mexico City   Taipei

Many of the designations used by manufacturers and sellers to distinguish their products are claimed as trademarks. Where those designations appear in this book and Addison-Wesley was aware of the trademark claim, the designations have been printed in initial capital letters.

The author and publisher have taken care in preparation of this book, but make no expressed or implied warranty of any kind and assume no responsibility for errors or omissions. No liability is assumed for incidental or consequential damages in connection with or arising out of the use of the information or programs contained herein.

Library of Congress Cataloging-in-Publication Data

Williams, Al, 1963-
    DOS and Windows protected mode : progamming with DOS extenders in
C / Albert A. Williams.
      p.   cm.
    Includes index.
    ISBN 0-201-63218-7
    1. Operating systems (Computers) 2. MS-DOS (Computer file) 3. PC
-DOS (Computer file) 4. Microsoft Windows (Computer file) 5. C
(Computer program language) I. Title.
    QA76.76.063W553 1993
    005.4'469--dc20   92-37101
                                                    CIP

Series Editor: Andrew Schulman
Managing Editor: Amorette Pedersen
Production Editor: Andrea G. Mulligan
Line drawings: Jennifer Noble
Set in 11-point ITC Galliard by Benchmark Productions

1 2 3 4 5 6 7 8 9 -MU- 9695949392
First Printing, December 1992

CONTENTS

Part III—Big Problems, Big Solutions   301

Chapter 16—Welcome to the Real (Protected) World   303

Chapter 17—A DOS Extended Mutant Turtle   309

ACKNOWLEDGMENTS

Books of this size and scope would not be possible without the efforts of many people. Thanks, of course, to Andrew Schulman for his valuable advice, help, and encouragement. I'd also like to thank Andrea Mulligan, Amy Pederson, Andrew Williams, Chris Williams, and all the other people at Addison-Wesley and Benchmark for their efforts. I appreciate what my friends at all the DOS extender firms have done to help, too. Finally, thanks to my family for their patience and understanding—I won't start another book for at least a month!

Versions of Copy Builder, FPM32, and TURTLE have appeared in *Dr. Dobb's Journal* and are used with permission (thanks to Jon Erickson).

INTRODUCTION

My DOS is Not Dead. Sorry About Yours.

PC software isn't what it used to be. Today's users demand sophisticated software—the kind once found only on expensive workstations. Despite the best efforts of many, MS-DOS (DOS) is still the preeminent operating system for PCs. Unfortunately, DOS was never meant to support these huge programs.

Tied to the original 8086 and 8088 processors, DOS can only address 1 megabyte (1M) of memory. Normally, less than 640 kilobytes (640K) of that is available for application programs. Modern PCs, with 286, 386, and 486 processors are much more capable—the limiting factor is real-mode DOS.

Of course, there are newer operating systems that don't suffer from these limitations. Still, the market favors DOS/Windows, and will for the foreseeable future. While OS/2 2.0 and Windows NT battle for market share, their combined user base is only a small fraction of the DOS market. And even these new systems run DOS programs. Clearly, DOS programs still have the largest market potential.

DOS extenders allow programs to tap the power of these sophisticated machines without switching to a new operating system. In particular, extenders allow DOS programs to easily access large amounts of memory. A 32-bit extender also abolishes the 64K segment limit inherent in 16-bit DOS programs. A few of the commercial products that rely on DOS extenders include:

- Windows 3.0 and 3.1 (Microsoft)
- Lotus 1-2-3 Version 3.X (Lotus Development)
- AutoCAD/386 (AutoCAD)
- Paradox/386 (Borland)
- Mathematica (Wolfram Research)
- IBM Interleaf Publisher (Interleaf)
- Borland C++ (Borland)

Why Not 32-bit DOS?

You may wonder why Microsoft (or some other enterprising company) doesn't simply produce an extended DOS operating system. Unfortunately, advanced systems like OS/2 or Windows that run multiple DOS programs can't directly provide a single DOS program with access to more than 1M of memory. True, you can run many programs at once, but each suffers from the same DOS memory limitations.

DOS architecture is not suitable for protected mode. DOS depends heavily on segment arithmetic for memory management, and has little provision for shared resource management. Worse, DOS assumes 64K segments and direct access to physical addresses. Even if DOS were widened to 32 bits, no existing application programs would be able to run without extensive modifications.

Will DOS ever catch up to the protected-mode world? It already has. DOS extenders provide just the protected-mode interface to DOS we desire. As you would expect, of course, most programs need a recompile (or relink) to work, and require some modifications.

Consider a typical PC running DOS and Windows. Windows programs are 16-bit protected-mode programs—they can access much more memory than DOS programs. Windows can also run regular DOS programs. This is truly protected-mode DOS. Regular DOS programs execute with few surprises in the Windows DOS "box." However, behind this DOS interface is a DPMI (DOS Protected Mode Interface) server. A sophisticated program can make a call to the server and open up a wealth of protected-mode services.

DOS extenders take most of the pain out of dealing with DPMI directly. In addition, they allow your programs to run even when Windows (or DPMI) is not present. You can also get extenders that allow you to write true 32-bit Windows programs. Still, the underlying base is Windows, and below that, DOS. So while you have never opened a box that says, "Protected Mode DOS," in some ways, you probably have—you just didn't realize it. The question is: Can you write programs for this "new" DOS?

Why This Book Is for You

This book will show you how to apply your C programming skills to the DOS extender environment. We will cover DOS extender fundamentals and work up to complete, practical example programs for protected-mode DOS and Microsoft Windows. (Don't forget—Windows is a DOS extender.) To get the most from this book, you should be a proficient C programmer. It also will be helpful—but not necessary—if you understand PC programming and assembly language. On the other hand, most of the Windows programs in this book don't require any special Windows programming knowledge.

How to Use This Book

This book contains two parts. Part 1 looks at protected-mode DOS programming and products. Part 2 contains several large programming examples, case studies that illustrate the practical techniques and real-world problems associated with building extended applications.

This book examines several different DOS extenders and their related tools. Each chapter stresses concepts that apply to all DOS extenders and highlights differences and similarities among extenders. Many chapters illustrate these ideas with example programs. Most chapters contain tables that show how different extenders implement the functions the chapter covers. If you already own an extender (including Microsoft Windows), these tables will help you relate the material in the chapter to your extender. If you don't own an extender yet, the tables will help you see the differences among extenders.

The Example Programs

If you want to compile any of the example programs, you must have the DOS extender and compiler that the specific example requires (and the hardware those tools require, of course). Some examples will work with multiple extenders; others require a particular one. The companion disk has a free copy of Phar Lap 286 Dos Extender Lite to get you started. The examples cover these compilers and extenders:

- Microsoft Windows 3.x (with the Windows SDK or Borland C)
- Intel 386/486 Code Builder
- Phar Lap 286 | DOS Extender (with Microsoft C or Borland C)
- Phar Lap 386 | DOS Extender (with MetaWare or Watcom C)
- Rational DOS/4GW (with Watcom C)

Conventions

Since this book covers protected mode exclusively, the term PC refers to a computer with an Intel or Intel-compatible (such as AMD) 80286 (286), 80386 (386), or 80486 (486) processor. An XT is a PC with an 8086 or 8088 processor, which can't run in protected mode. For the purposes of this book any reference to a 386 (meaning a PC with an 80386 processor) also applies to a 486.

A 0x precedes hexadecimal numbers (as it does in C and C++). Alternatively, an H may follow hexadecimal numbers (as in assembler). Numbers separated by colons (0040:0010, for instance) are also in hex. All other numbers are in decimal unless noted otherwise.

A byte is 8 bits wide, a word contains 16 bits (even in 32-bit code), and a double word has 32 bits. This follows the convention from conventional real-mode DOS programs. A paragraph, which is a real-mode construct, consists of 16 bytes of memory starting at an address evenly divisible by 16 (paragraphs are important when interfacing with DOS). K, as in 16K, is short for 1024 bytes (or 1 kilobyte) and M is 1024K (a megabyte). G represents 1024M (a gigabyte).

By convention, bit 0 of a binary number is the least significant bit. Therefore, bit 7 is the top bit of a byte; bit 31 is the top bit of a double word.

A DOS extender is any program that allows DOS-like programs to run in protected mode. These programs (DOS extended programs) can use conventional interrupt 0x21 and BIOS interrupts to request system services (such as memory allocation and I/O).

A 16-bit (or 286) DOS extender allows programs to use features found on 80286 processors. A 32-bit (or 386) DOS extender enables programs to make full use of 80386/80486 processors. Of course, a program built with a 286 DOS extender will run on a 286, 386, or 486 PC. The 286 designation pertains to the minimum processor the program requires.

The term Windows refers to Microsoft Windows 3.0 or 3.1, unless otherwise noted. Windows/NT refers to the 32-bit Microsoft Windows operating system. Win32 refers to the 32-bit Windows API, implemented in Windows NT, or perhaps on top of Windows 3.1 (Win32s).

A Personal Note

Several years ago, I bought a shiny new 386 PC and wondered what it could do. What started out as a few protected-mode experiments quickly grew into a full-fledged DOS extender (see "PROT" in the book *DOS 5: A Developer's Guide*). Things have changed quite a bit since then. What I want to show you in *DOS and Windows Protected Mode* is that protected mode isn't unusual or exotic. Today's PC programmers are writing protected-mode code—even if they don't always know it.

Before Windows, DOS extenders were already well on the way to becoming a common tool in the modern programmer's arsenal. Windows 3.0 (and later 3.1) accelerated this process tremendously. Windows development is a significant portion of the PC programming pie—and every Windows 3.1 program is a DOS extended program. With more and more users joining the Windows bandwagon and Windows NT right behind, PC programmers must embrace protected mode.

Once you get used to programming without memory constraints, without the dreaded 64K limit, and without the other baggage imposed by the real-mode PC/MSDOS juggernaut, you will wonder how you will managed to write real-mode DOS code at all. Protected-mode programming is wonderful—come in and join the party!

Al Williams (CIS 72010,3574)

Part I:
Introduction to DOS Extenders

CHAPTER ■ 1

What's a DOS Extender, Anyway?

MS-DOS, and the programs that run under it, can only directly address 1 megabyte (1M) of memory. DOS machines use the first 640K for RAM memory. The PC reserves the remaining 384K for I/O devices and the ROM BIOS.

Modern PCs that use Intel (or Intel compatible) 80286, 80386, or 80486 Central Processing Units (CPUs) can operate in at least two different modes: real mode and protected mode. Real mode matches the MS-DOS programming model—the processor acts like a fast 8086 CPU and can only address 1M of memory under normal circumstances.

Protected mode allows access to many advanced programming features. The most visible feature is the availability of more memory. A 286 can address a maximum of 16M; 386 and 486 processors can handle 4096M (4 gigabytes, or 4G). (Chapter 4 covers protected-mode features in detail.)

Programmers using protected-mode operating systems (like Unix or OS/2) can easily make use of these advanced programming features. Of course, switching to these operating systems means abandoning the enormous DOS market. DOS and Windows programmers must turn to a special mini-operating system—a DOS extender. DOS extenders come in two flavors: 16-bit and 32-bit. A 16-bit (or 286) DOS extender will work with

3

286, 386, or 486 CPUs. A 32-bit (or 386) extender can only run on a 386 or 486.

Microsoft Windows has a built-in DOS extender—any Windows program that runs in standard or enhanced mode is already an extended program. Standard mode uses an integrated 286 extender (DOSX.EXE); enhanced mode uses a 386 extender (DOSMGR built into WIN386.EXE). Windows 3.1 only allows these two modes. Earlier versions of Windows supported real mode—the mode that does not use an extender. Since Windows programs require plenty of memory and multitasking support, Microsoft dropped real mode starting with version 3.1.

For compatibility, the Windows 386 extender runs normal Windows applications in a 16-bit environment. However, Windows uses many of the 386 features to support better memory management and multitasking transparently to the program. Windows also can accommodate 32-bit extended programs.

Programming with DOS Extenders

Programming with a DOS extender is similar to working with unadorned DOS. C programs usually don't require many, if any, changes work with work in the DOS extended environment.

Consider the program in Listings 1-1 and 1-2 (DFIT.C and DFIT.H). This program reads any number of files into memory, and writes them to floppy disks. DFIT attempts to pack the files on the least number of floppies possible. DFIT lacks sophisticated error handling and other nice touches, but it is more than adequate to expose some important weaknesses of real-mode DOS.

Listing 1-1 depends on two functions to do most of the real work: read_file() and write_files(). Listing 1-3 on page 10 contains a DOS implementation for these functions (DFITDOS.C). Compiling the program is simple. For the Borland compiler use

```
bcc -ml -DHUGE=_huge -F OF00 dfit.c dfitdos.c
```

For the Microsoft compiler, use

```
cl -AL -DHUGE=_huge dfit.c dfitdos.c
```

The read_file() function allocates a block of memory to hold the entire file. It uses halloc() instead of malloc() to create this block. The halloc() function creates _huge pointers—pointers that can reference blocks larger than 64K. Of course, the pointers that reference the file data must also be _huge. Since DFIT may not always need huge pointers, it uses HUGE instead of the _huge keyword. The -DHUGE=_huge option on the command line has the same effect as

```
#define HUGE _huge
```

Under real-mode DOS, the read() and write() file I/O calls can only handle 64K or less. Therefore, both read_file() and write_files() must break larger files up into 64K blocks.

Listing 1-1. DFIT.C

```
/* DFIT.C - Disk fit program
   Compile with:
-DOS-
Borland:    bcc -ml -DHUGE=_huge dfit.c dfitdos.c
Microsoft:   cl -AL -DHUGE=_huge -F OFOO dfit.c dfitdos.c

-EMS-
Borland:    bcc -ml -DEMS dfit.c dfitems.c
Microsoft:   cl -AL -DEMS -F OFOO dfit.c dfitems.c

-286-
Borland: bcc286 -DHUGE=_huge dfit.c dfitdos.c
Microsoft:
286|DOS Extender pre-2.5
   cl -AL -Lp -G2 -DHUGE=_huge -F FOO
      dfit.c dfitdos.c llibpe.lib
286|DOS Extender 2.5 and later:
   cl -AL -Lp -G2 -DHUGE=_huge -F FOO
      dfit.c dfitdos.c
```

```
-386-
Watcom: wcl386 -DHUGE= -ldos4g dfit.c dfit386.c
*/

#include "dfit.h"

/* info about files */
struct file_entry *files, read_file();

/* number of entries in files[] */
int nrfiles,maxfiles;

/* target drive */
char drive;

void main(int argc, char *argv[])
  {
  int i;
  if (argc<2) help();
  drive=toupper(argv[1][0]);
  if (drive<'A'||drive>'Z') help();
/* if no files on command line, prompt for them */
  if (argc==2)
    printf("Enter an empty line to begin copy\n");
  while (argc==2)
    {
    char fn[_MAX_PATH],*p;
    printf("File name or spec? ");
    fgets(fn,sizeof(fn),stdin);
    if (*fn=='\n') break;
    p=strchr(fn,'\n');
    if (p) *p='\0';
/* process them */
    proc_files(fn);
    }
/* if files on command line, process them */
  if (argc!=2)
    {
    for (i=2;i<argc;i++)
      proc_files(argv[i]);
    }
```

```
/* write the files out some indefinite number of times */
  do
    {
    write_files();
    } while (prompt("Write files again? (Y/N)","NY")=='Y');

  exit(0);
  }

/* Instructions for malformed command line */
void help()
  {
  printf("DFIT by Al Williams\n"
         "Usage: DFIT drive [file.....]\n"
         "Wildcards are allowed.\n");
  exit(1);
  }

/* compute free space on target disk */
unsigned long freebytes()
  {
  struct diskfree_t frees;
  _dos_getdiskfree(drive-'A'+1,&frees);
  return (unsigned long)frees.bytes_per_sector*
         frees.sectors_per_cluster*
         frees.avail_clusters;
  }

/* print prmt, wait for a key in valid -- shifts key
   to upper case */
int prompt(char *prmt,char *valid)
  {
  int c;
  printf("%s\n",prmt);
  do
    {
    c=getch();
    if (!c)
      {
      getch();
      continue;
```

```
    }
  c=toupper(c);
  } while (!strchr(valid,c));
 putchar(c);
 putchar('\n');
 return c;
 }


/* process files (maybe wildcards) */
proc_files(char *spec)
  {
  int n=0,stat;
  struct find_t info;
  char drive[_MAX_DRIVE],sub[_MAX_DIR],
       file[_MAX_FNAME],ext[_MAX_EXT];
/* spit file apart */
  _splitpath(spec,drive,sub,file,ext);
/* search for matching files */
  stat=_dos_findfirst(spec,_A_NORMAL,&info);
  while (!stat)
    {
/* found a file, rebuild complete name */
    char path[_MAX_PATH];
    char *ext=strchr(info.name,'.');
    if (ext) *ext='\0';
    _makepath(path,drive,sub,info.name,ext?ext+1:"");
    if (ext) *ext='.';
/* read file in */
    printf("Reading %s\n",path);
    read_file(path,info.name,info.size);
    n++;
    stat=_dos_findnext(&info);
    }
  return n;
  }


/* error messages */
static char *errfmt[]=
  {
  "Out of memory\n",
```

```
    "Can't open %s\n",
    "Read error on %s\n"
    "Write error on %s\n"
    };

/* error routine */
void errabt(int nr,char *string)
  {
  putchar('\n');
  printf(errfmt[nr],string);
  exit(nr+2);
  }
```

Listing 1-2. DFIT.H

```
#include <stdio.h>
#include <conio.h>
#include <ctype.h>
#include <dos.h>
#include <stdlib.h>
#include <string.h>
#include <io.h>
#include <sys\types.h>
#include <sys\stat.h>
#include <fcntl.h>

#ifndef HUGE
#ifndef EMS
#error Must define HUGE=_huge or HUGE= or EMS
#endif
#endif

/* info about files */
extern struct file_entry
  {
/* name of file -- no directory */
  char name[13];
/* size of file in bytes */
  unsigned long size;
#ifdef EMS
/* starting page number (EMS only) */
```

```
   int pageno;
#else
/* pointer to start of data -- non-EMS */
  char HUGE *data;
#endif
/* set to 1 when written out */
  char write;
  } *files, read_file();

/* number of entries/maximum entries in files[] */
extern int nrfiles,maxfiles;

/* target drive */
extern char drive;

struct file_entry read_file(char *path,char *name,
      unsigned long siz);
void write_files(void);
void help(void);
unsigned long freebytes(void);
int prompt(char *prmt,char *valid);
int proc_files(char *spec);
void errabt(int nr,char *string);
```

Listing 1-3. DFITDOS.C

```
#include "dfit.h"
#include <malloc.h>

struct file_entry read_file(char *path,char *name,
      unsigned long siz)
  {
  unsigned long bufp=0;
  int handle;
  struct file_entry ret;
/* make room for new entry */
  if (maxfiles<nrfiles+1)
    {
    if (!files)
      {
```

```
        files=(struct file_entry *)
             malloc(sizeof(struct file_entry)*10);
        }
      else
        {
        files=realloc(files,(maxfiles+10)*
                      sizeof(struct file_entry));
        }
      if (!files) errabt(0,"");
      maxfiles+=10;
      }
/* store info */
   strcpy(ret.name,name);
   ret.size=siz;
/* allocate space */
   ret.data=(char *)halloc(siz,1);
   if (!ret.data) errabt(0,"");
/* open file */
   handle=open(path,O_RDONLY|O_BINARY);
   if (handle==-1) errabt(1,path);
/* read data in 64K (or less) chunks */
   while (siz)
      {
      unsigned long bsize=(siz<0x10000)?siz:0x10000;
      if (bsize!=0x10000)
         {
         if (read(handle,ret.data+bufp,(unsigned)bsize)==-1)
           errabt(2,path);
         }
      else
         if (read(handle,ret.data+bufp,0xFFFE)==-1||
             read(handle,ret.data+bufp+0xFFFE,2)==-1)
               errabt(2,path);
      bufp+=bsize;
      siz-=bsize;
      }
   close(handle);
   files[nrfiles++]=ret;
   return ret;
   }

void write_files()
```

```
  {
  char fn[_MAX_PATH];
  int remaining=nrfiles,i;
  unsigned long dremaining, total_size=0L;
/* reset statistics */
  for (i=0;i<nrfiles;i++)
    {
    files[i].write=0;
    total_size+=files[i].size;
    }
/* assemble output file name prefix */
  fn[0]=drive;
  fn[1]=':';
  do
    {
    struct file_entry *max;
    printf("%lu bytes remaining\n",total_size);
    prompt("Insert disk in the destination drive "
           "and press <SPACE>"," ");
    dremaining=freebytes();
    do
      {
/* find largest file that will fit... */
      max=NULL;
      for (i=0;i<nrfiles;i++)
        {
/* skip file that has already been written */
        if (files[i].write) continue;
        if (!max&&files[i].size<=dremaining)
          max=files+i;
        else if (max&&files[i].size<=dremaining
                &&files[i].size>max->size)
              max=files+i;
        }
/* if file found */
      if (max)
        {
        unsigned long siz=max->size,bufp=0;
        int handle;
/* make output file name */
        strcpy(fn+2,max->name);
/* open file */
```

```
      handle=open(fn,
              O_WRONLY|O_CREAT|O_BINARY|O_TRUNC,
              S_IWRITE|S_IREAD);
      if (handle==-1) errabt(1,fn);
/* write it in 64K (or less) chunks */
      printf("Writing %s\n",fn);
      while (siz)
        {
        unsigned long bsize=(siz<0x10000)?siz:0x10000;
        if (bsize!=0x10000)
          {
          if (write(handle,max->data+bufp,
                  (unsigned)bsize)==-1)
            errabt(3,max->name);
          }
        else
          if (write(handle,max->data+bufp,0xFFFE)==-1||
              write(handle,max->data+bufp+0xFFFE,2)==-1)
                errabt(3,max->name);
        bufp+=bsize;
        siz-=bsize;
        }
      close(handle);
/* update statistics */
      total_size-=max->size;
      remaining--;
      dremaining=freebytes();
      max->write=1;
      }
    } while (max);
  } while (remaining);
}
```

Although DFIT is straightforward and simple to compile, it doesn't work well. The problem isn't with DFIT, but with DOS (or, more precisely, with real mode). DFIT performs poorly under unaugmented DOS, since it often requires more memory than DOS can supply.

Notice that DFIT stores each file in memory. This allows it to read files from multiple floppy disks, and makes it unnecessary for it to reread files.

Obviously, DFIT will require plenty of memory when reading many large files.

At most, a DOS program has around 600K of memory available. Extreme memory management techniques (using memory managers to fill unused video memory, etc.) might yield as much as 700K, but that is rare. Since DFIT's purpose is to pack files on multiple floppy disks, it must be able to fill more than one floppy disk. With 360K floppies, DFIT can probably collect enough files to fill two disks. For larger disks, DFIT is useless. Even with 700K free, DFIT couldn't fill a 720K disk.

DOS Alternatives

When DOS programmers need more available memory, they traditionally turn to one of these techniques:

1. Disk-based memory (overlays, temporary files, etc.).
2. Expanded memory (EMS).
3. Extended memory (XMS, or a variant).

All three of these methods supply memory that is only indirectly accessible to DOS programs (see the sidebar *DOS Extender Alternatives*). The program must copy or map portions of the additional memory to areas that it can address. This additional overhead considerably complicates the read_file() and write_files() functions.

DOS EXTENDER ALTERNATIVES

DOS programs have only a few options for acquiring additional memory. Broadly speaking, DOS programs can access the following types of memory:

- Conventional Memory—The memory below 640K.
- Upper Memory—Additional memory between 640K and 1M.

continued

continued

- Extended Memory—Memory above 1M (including the small High Memory Area or HMA).
- Expanded Memory—Not memory at all, but a protocol for accessing external storage. This storage could be dedicated memory (an EMS board), extended memory (see above), or a disk drive.

Windows programs don't usually distinguish between conventional and extended memory since Windows contains a DOS extender. For backward compatibility with older versions of Windows, Windows 3.x programs can also use expanded memory.

DOS does not provide memory management for memory above 1M (DOS versions prior to DOS 5 would not manage memory above 640K). Instead, programs must agree on a protocol to share extended and expanded memory.

Expanded memory always relies on a driver to manage memory requests. The driver may access a special hardware device (like an Intel AboveBoard or an AST Rampage), or convert extended memory or disk space into expanded (EMS) memory. Of course an EMS driver for an AboveBoard or a Rampage won't work with extended memory.

Extended memory is more complicated since there isn't a single standard for accessing it. The Extended Memory Specification (XMS) protocol is by far the most prevalent. However, if an XMS driver is not present, a program can locate and reserve extended memory itself. There are two very different methods in common use to do this: the VDISK method and the INT 15H method. (If you would like to know more about these techniques, look in the bibliography.)

continued

continued

Neither EMS nor extended memory protocols provide directly usable memory. In each case, the program must copy or map memory into conventional memory before using it (see Listing 1-4, DFITEMS.C). As a special case, the XMS driver can provide direct access to almost 64K of extended memory (the High Memory Area, or HMA) to one DOS program at a time. However, this isn't enough memory to make much difference to most programs.

Many XMS drivers can also relocate portions of extended memory into unused areas above 640K (but below 1M). Ordinarily, this region contains video RAM, BIOS ROMs, network buffers, and other system-related memory. However, few systems use all of this space. These relocated chunks of extended memory are Upper Memory Blocks (UMBs). Although they are directly addressable by DOS programs, they are usually quite small, and their size (and even presence) will vary from machine to machine.

Many 386/486 memory managers support both EMS and XMS. For example, Microsoft's EMM386, Quarterdeck's QEMM or Qualitas's 386Max use extended memory to provide EMS, XMS, UMBs, and an HMA. These programs also provide special interfaces (VCPI and DPMI, discussed later on) that allow them to cooperate with DOS extended programs. ■

Expanded memory, or EMS, is a common choice to provide DOS programs with additional memory. An EMS driver supplies additional memory in 16K pages, and reserves a 64K page frame below 1M. Expanded-memory pages are not directly addressable by DOS, but the driver can place any four 16K pages into the page frame on demand. Since DOS programs can access the page frame, this allows them to read and write EMS memory.

Listing 1-4, DFITEMS.C, shows file functions for DFIT that use EMS memory. As you can see, the 16K page size and the four-page limit combine to complicate significantly matters. While the code is complicated, at least compiling DFIT with EMS support is simple—just useBorland C++

```
bcc -ml -DEMS dfit.c dfitems.c
```

or Microsoft C/C++

```
cl -AL -DEMS dfit.c dfitems.c
```

Programs that use EMS must perform the following steps (the function names refer to functions in Listing 1-4):

1. Ensure that an EMS driver is present (see ems_init()).
2. Ask the driver for the page frame's address (see ems_init()).
3. Request the required amount memory from the EMS driver; the driver returns a handle the program uses to refer to the memory (see ems_alloc()).
4. As required, instruct the driver to map pages from the EMS handle into the page frame. Once in the page frame, the program can read and write data as usual (see ems_map()).
5. Release the EMS pages before termination (see ems_close()).

When the EMS version of DFIT terminates via a Control-Break or critical error, it doesn't reach step 5 to return the EMS pages it is using. This prevents other programs from using them until you reboot the computer. Practical programs must intercept these events and free the EMS memory. This makes genuine EMS programs even more complicated than DFITEMS.

Listing 1-4. DFITEMS.C

```c
#include "dfit.h"
#include <malloc.h>

/* EMS variables */
static init=1;
static int ems_handle=0;
static long lastpg=0L;
char far *page_frame;
union REGS r;
```

```
void ems_call(union REGS *);
void ems_err(int,int);
void ems_init(void);

/* terminate EMS processing */
void ems_close(void)
  {
  /* free EMS handle */
  if (ems_handle)
    {
    r.h.ah=0x45;
    r.x.dx=ems_handle;
    ems_call(&r);
    }
  }

/* generic EMS call */
void ems_call(union REGS *r)
  {
  int cmd=r->h.ah;
  int86(0x67,r,r);
  if (r->h.ah) ems_err(cmd,r->h.ah);
  }

/* start EMS transaction */
void ems_init()
  {
  FILE *driver;
  init=0;
  /* check for EMS */
  driver=fopen("EMMXXXX0","r");
  if (!driver) ems_err(0,0);
  fcloG   16
se(driver);
/* get EMS status */
  r.h.ah=0x40;
  ems_call(&r);
/* get version # */
  r.h.ah=0x46;
  ems_call(&r);
/* must have EMS 4.0 */
```

```c
  if (r.h.al<0x40)
    {
    printf("EMS 4.0 or better required.\n");
    exit(9);
    }
  /* get & store page frame address */
  r.h.ah=0x41;
  ems_call(&r);
  FP_SEG(page_frame)=r.x.bx;
  FP_OFF(page_frame)=0;
  /* register ems_close */
  atexit(ems_close);
  }


/* map siz bytes starting at page into page frame */
void ems_map(int page,unsigned siz)
  {
  int i;
  unsigned total=0;
  /* map 4 consecutive pages into pfa */
  for (i=0;i<4;i++)
    {
/* don't go past size request */
    if (total>=siz) break;
    r.h.ah=0x44;
    r.h.al=i;
    r.x.bx=page+i;
    r.x.dx=ems_handle;
    ems_call(&r);
    total+=16384;
    }
  }

/* print EMS error message */
void ems_err(int cmd,int code)
  {
  printf("EMS error #%x(%x)\n",cmd,code);
  exit(10);
  }

/* allocate EMS pages */
```

```c
long ems_alloc(unsigned long siz)
  {
  long pg=lastpg,pgs;
/* calculate # of pages required */
  pgs=(siz+16383)/16384;
/* init handle if req'd */
  if (!ems_handle)
    {
    r.x.ax=0x5a00;
    r.x.bx=0;
    ems_call(&r);
    ems_handle=r.x.dx;
    }
/* reallocate to contain required # of pages */
  lastpg+=pgs;
  r.h.ah=0x51;
  r.x.bx=lastpg;
  r.x.dx=ems_handle;
  ems_call(&r);
  return pg;
  }


struct file_entry read_file(char *path,char *name,
        unsigned long siz)
  {
  unsigned bufp=0;
  int handle;
  struct file_entry ret;
/* start up EMS routines */
  if (init) ems_init();
/* make room for new entry */
  if (maxfiles<nrfiles+1)
    {
    if (!files)
      {
      files=(struct file_entry *)
            malloc(sizeof(struct file_entry)*10);
      }
    else
      {
      files=realloc(files,(maxfiles+10)*
```

```
                    sizeof(struct file_entry));
      }
    if (!files) errabt(0,"");
    maxfiles+=10;
    }
/* store info */
  strcpy(ret.name,name);
  ret.size=siz;
/* allocate space */
  ret.pageno=ems_alloc(siz);
/* open file */
  handle=open(path,O_RDONLY|O_BINARY);
  if (handle==-1) errabt(1,path);
/* read data in 64K (or less) chunks */
  while (siz)
    {
    unsigned long bsize=(siz<0x10000)?siz:0x10000;
/* map EMS chunk */
    ems_map(ret.pageno+bufp,(unsigned)bsize);
    if (bsize!=0x10000)
      {
      if (read(handle,page_frame,(unsigned)bsize)==-1)
        errabt(2,path);
      }
    else
      if (read(handle,page_frame,0xFFFE)==-1||
          read(handle,page_frame+0xFFFE,2)==-1)
            errabt(2,path);
    bufp+=4;
    siz-=bsize;
    }
  close(handle);
  files[nrfiles++]=ret;
  return ret;
  }

void write_files()
  {
  char fn[_MAX_PATH];
  int remaining=nrfiles,i;
  unsigned long dremaining,total_size=0L;
/* reset statistics */
```

```
    for (i=0;i<nrfiles;i++)
      {
      files[i].write=0;
      total_size+=files[i].size;
      }
/* assemble output file name prefix */
  fn[0]=drive;
  fn[1]=':';
  do
    {
    struct file_entry *max;
    printf("%lu bytes remaining\n",total_size);
    prompt("Insert disk in the destination drive "
           "and press <SPACE>"," ");
    dremaining=freebytes();
    do
      {
/* find largest file that will fit... */
      max=NULL;
      for (i=0;i<nrfiles;i++)
        {
/* skip file that has already been written */
        if (files[i].write) continue;
        if (!max&&files[i].size<=dremaining)
          max=files+i;
        else if (max&&files[i].size<=dremaining
              &&files[i].size>max->size)
            max=files+i;
        }
/* if file found */
      if (max)
        {
        unsigned long siz=max->size;
        unsigned bufp=0;
        int handle;
/* make output file name */
        strcpy(fn+2,max->name);
/* open file */
        handle=open(fn,
              O_WRONLY|O_CREAT|O_BINARY|O_TRUNC,
              S_IWRITE|S_IREAD);
        if (handle==-1) errabt(1,fn);
```

```
/* write it in 64K (or less) chunks */
        printf("Writing %s\n",fn);
        while (siz)
          {
          unsigned long bsize=(siz<0x10000)?siz:0x10000;
/* map in EMS chunk */
          ems_map(max->pageno+bufp,(unsigned)bsize);
          if (bsize!=0x10000)
            {
            if (write(handle,page_frame,(unsigned)bsize)==-1)
              errabt(2,fn);
            }
          else
            if (write(handle,page_frame,0xFFFE)==-1||
                write(handle,page_frame+0xFFFE,2)==-1)
                  errabt(2,fn);
          bufp+=4;
          siz-=bsize;
          }
        close(handle);
/* update statistics */
        total_size-=max->size;
        remaining--;
        dremaining=freebytes();
        max->write=1;
        }
      } while (max);
    } while (remaining);
  }
```

The functions in DFITEMS.C are complex since they must keep track of which EMS pages are in the page frame and which are not. XMS programs have similar problems—they must copy the regions they want to work with to a buffer below 1M. In short, EMS and XMS can provide a DOS program with more memory, but access to the memory is far from transparent.

Protected Mode to the Rescue

Instead of EMS, DFIT could use a 286 (16-bit) DOS extender. The extender allows the program to directly access up to 16M of memory (assuming the computer has that much). In some cases, a 16-bit extended program (which can run on a 286, 386, or 486 PC) may have access to virtual memory—the PC's disk can transparently supplement main memory.

There is no additional listing for a 286 version of read_file() and write_files(). The DOS versions in Listing 1-3 will work nicely with most 286 extenders. The 16-bit extender provides a much larger pool of memory via the DOS interrupt 0x21 memory management calls. This allows DFIT's calls to halloc() to use up to 16M of memory transparently. DFIT uses this memory directly—there is no need to map or copy areas of memory as there is under EMS or XMS.

Converting DFIT to use a 286 extender doesn't require much work. You use the the same compiler—you could even use the original .OBJ files, if you wish. The key is how the program is linked.

Some extenders (like Ergo's OS/286) require you to process the .EXE file after linking; others (Phar Lap's 286|DOS Extender, for one) require special options for the linker. In either case, you may have to link with special libraries depending on the extender. The DFIT286.EXE program on the companion disk for this book uses the Phar Lap 286 | DOS Extender and Microsoft C.

Since only the link step is different, compiling the 286 version of DFIT is straightforward. With Phar Lap, you can use Borland C++:

```
bcc286 -DHUGE=_huge dfit.c dfitdos.c
```

or Microsoft C/C++

```
cl -DHUGE=_huge -AL -G2 -Lp -F 0F00 dfit.c dfitdos.c
```

Not all programs are as easy to convert as DFIT. However, most programs require little work to port to the 16-bit environment. In later chapters, you will learn where any problems arise and how to deal with them.

Note that _huge pointers are still required. Although a 16-bit program can address up to 16M, segments still can't exceed 64K. On the other hand, this is why conventional DOS compilers still work with 16-bit extenders. As long as you use _huge pointers, the C compiler will take care of the details for you.

While the 286 version of DFIT is an improvement, it isn't perfect. If you experiment with it, you will find you can exhaust DFIT's memory by storing many small files. You will run out of memory even though the total number of bytes DFIT stores is much less than available memory. In this case, you have not run out of memory, you have run out of segments.

Depending on the DOS extender, halloc() may only be able to create 2,000 to 4,000 64K blocks (or blocks smaller than 64K). For example, if you use halloc() to allocate a 300K region and two 30K buffers, you would consume seven blocks. At this rate, you can quickly run out of blocks. We will see in Chapter 4 why protected mode imposes an upper limit on the number of segments a program can allocate.

Of course, you could manage memory more efficiently to avoid this problem. For example, DFIT could use halloc() to reserve all available memory at once. Then DFIT would parcel out memory from this large block for each file.

386 Simplifications

You also can compile DFIT with a 386 (32-bit) extender. These extenders are similar to their 286 counterparts, but operate only with 386 and 486 processors. Unlike 286 systems, a 386 extender requires a special 32-bit compilers such as WATCOM C, MetaWare High C, or Zortech C++. DFIT.C and DFITDOS.C will compile under many of these compilers. (You may need to replace the call to halloc() with a call to malloc(); with a 32-bit extender these functions are equivalent.)

DFITDOS.C will work with a 386 extender without modifications. However, some easy-to-make modifications will simplify the program and take better advantage of 386 features. Extenders for the 386 have several advantages over the 286 variety. One benefit a 386 extender provides is potential access to much more memory—up to 4G. Nearly all 386 extenders also support virtual memory, further increasing available memory. DFITDOS.C automatically uses these features via the halloc() or malloc() library call. Although the amount of available memory may increase dramatically, the access to it is still transparent.

Most importantly, with a 386 extender, integers and pointers are 32 bits wide by default. Most DFITDOS operates under the 16-bit limit, it must read and write files in 64K chunks. But a 32-bit program can read and write each file as one unit (at least, up to 4G).

The 386 allows segments to be practically any size (up to 4G). This reduces or eliminates segmentation concerns (including segment starvation) in most programs. DFITDOS.C has to use huge pointers to handle arrays greater than 64K. A 386 program doesn't need huge pointers.

DFIT386.C (Listing 1-5) shows the 386-specific versions of read_file() and write_files(). Notice how simple the functions are without the 64K read and write limits, and without the need for huge pointers. As an added benefit, these functions can use real and virtual memory up to 4G. Compilation is simple. With the WATCOM C compiler, for instance, you can use

```
wcl386 -DHUGE= -ldos4g dfit.c dfit386.c
```

Of course, there are some disadvantages. A 386 extender requires you to use new compilers, linkers, and debuggers. Also, the final program will only run on a 386 or 486 PC.

Listing 1-5. DFIT386.C

```
#include "dfit.h"

struct file_entry read_file(char *path,char *name,
        unsigned long siz)
  {
  int handle;
  struct file_entry ret;
/* make room for new entry */
  if (maxfiles<nrfiles+1)
    {
    if (!files)
      {
      files=(struct file_entry *)
           malloc(sizeof(struct file_entry)*10);
      }
    else
      {
      files=realloc(files,(maxfiles+10)*
                  sizeof(struct file_entry));
```

```c
      }
    if (!files) errabt(0,"");
    maxfiles+=10;
    }
/* store info */
  strcpy(ret.name,name);
  ret.size=siz;
/* allocate space */
  ret.data=(char *)malloc(siz);
  if (!ret.data) errabt(0,"");
/* open file */
  handle=open(path,O_RDONLY|O_BINARY);
  if (handle==-1) errabt(1,path);
/* read data in one fell swoop */
  if (read(handle,ret.data,ret.size)==-1) errabt(2,path);
  close(handle);
  files[nrfiles++]=ret;
  return ret;
  }


void write_files()
  {
  char fn[_MAX_PATH];
  int remaining=nrfiles,i;
  unsigned long dremaining,total_size=0L;
/* reset statistics */
  for (i=0;i<nrfiles;i++)
    {
    files[i].write=0;
    total_size+=files[i].size;
    }
/* assemble output file name prefix */
  fn[0]=drive;
  fn[1]=':';
  do
    {
    struct file_entry *max;
    printf("%lu bytes remaining\n",total_size);
    prompt("Insert disk in the destination drive "
           "and press <SPACE>"," ");
    dremaining=freebytes();
    do
```

```
      {
/* find largest file that will fit... */
      max=NULL;
      for (i=0;i<nrfiles;i++)
         {
/* skip file that has already been written */
         if (files[i].write) continue;
         if (!max&&files[i].size<=dremaining)
           max=files+i;
         else if (max&&files[i].size<=dremaining
                &&files[i].size>max->size)
             max=files+i;
         }
/* if file found */
      if (max)
         {
         int handle;
/* make output file name */
         strcpy(fn+2,max->name);
/* open file */
         handle=open(fn,
             O_WRONLY|O_CREAT|O_BINARY|O_TRUNC,
             S_IWRITE|S_IREAD);
         if (handle==-1) errabt(1,fn);
/* write file with one call */
         printf("Writing %s\n",fn);
         if (write(handle,max->data,max->size)==-1)
            errabt(3,fn);
         close(handle);
/* update statistics */
         total_size-=max->size;
         remaining--;
         dremaining=freebytes();
         max->write=1;
         }
      } while (max);
   } while (remaining);
  }
```

DFIT386.C contains the simplest file I/O calls of all. Take special note of the "read data in one fell swoop" code in read-file, and the "write file with one call" code in write-files. The 32-bit extender frees DFIT from memory management concerns and allows the program to concentrate on its primary task—copying files.

What About Windows?

Windows programs—which are really 16-bit DOS extended programs—can also transparently access large amounts of memory. Listing 1-6 has a simple Windows code fragment that can allocate up to 8M on many PCs. In 386 enhanced mode, the program can usually allocate more memory than you actually have—thanks to virtual memory. In enhanced mode, a single allocation can be as large as 16711680 bytes (16M-64K). (Some sources (including the *Window's Programmer's Guide*) incorrectly state that the limit is 64M.)

Listing 1-6. WINMEM.C

```
/* Try to allocate 8 Meg from Windows -- this may take
   awhile. */
#include "winpmode.h"
#include <windows.h>

#define MEGABYTE 1048576L

char result[64];

char *test()
  {
  HGLOBAL h;
  DWORD siz=8*MEGABYTE;
/* Try 8 Meg first. If that doesn't work keep trying
less and less in 1 Meg decrements */
  while (siz&&!(h=GlobalAlloc(GHND,siz))) siz-=MEGABYTE;
  if (h) GlobalFree(h);
  sprintf(result,"Allocated %ld megabytes",siz/MEGABYTE);
  return result;
  }
```

For now, don't try to compile Listing 1-6. You will see how to compile simple Windows programs in Chapter 5. Just realize that Windows programs are nothing more than DOS extended programs which also can use a big library of graphics and windowing calls (the Windows API).

Review

DOS extenders are mini-operating systems. They execute protected-mode programs and provide a DOS-like (for example, interrupt 0x21) interface. Your program continues to make DOS calls that allocate memory, read files, and write to the screen, but the extender greatly enhances these functions.

A 16-bit extender will run on 286, 386, or 486 processors. A 32-bit extender, which is more powerful than a 286 extender, will only run on 386 or 486 machines. One of the most popular 16-bit extenders is Microsoft Windows. In standard mode, it is a classic 286 (or 16-bit extender). In 386 enhanced mode, it is still a 16-bit extender, but it takes advantage of advanced 386/486 features to provide better multitasking, increased memory, and virtual memory.

CHAPTER ■ 2

DOS Extenders: Under the Hood

A DOS extender truly is a miniature operating system. It executes under MS-DOS, which in turn executes protected-mode programs. While there are many functions an extender must perform, the most important one is interrupt handling. DOS extenders emulate most DOS and BIOS interrupts. DOS extended programs still use interrupt 21H, for example, to read and write files. DOS extenders also supply some special functions to alter the extender's operation, or to take advantage of special features.

Some DOS and BIOS calls change slightly under a DOS extender. For example, with most 386 extenders you can read a 1M (or larger) block from a file. The ordinary DOS read call (interrupt 21H function 3FH) allows you to read a maximum of 64K at once.

Interrupts

The PC is highly dependent on interrupts. For example, when you press a key, the keyboard generates a hardware interrupt—interrupt 9. Other I/O devices (the mouse, disk drives, etc.) also cause interrupts. In addition, programs request services from DOS and the BIOS by issuing software interrupts.

Extenders must intercept hardware interrupts and process them using the original real-mode DOS and BIOS interrupt handlers (or duplicate the original handler's behavior). If the extender didn't do this, vital system components like the clock and the keyboard would be almost useless. Extenders are also responsible for processing software interrupts to provide services to programs.

When a DOS extender detects a software or hardware interrupt, it may do one of three things:

1. Raise an error—the extender does not support the interrupt.
2. Perform some internal action—the extender may completely replace some DOS or BIOS calls (for example, setting interrupt vectors).
3. Send the interrupt to the real-mode handler this is called *reflecting* the interrupt (for example, file I/O).

Interrupt Reflection

DOS extenders use different methods to accomplish interrupt reflection. Most extenders temporarily return to real mode, reissue the interrupt, and return to protected mode. This requires several steps (see Figures 2-1a on page 33 and 2-1b on page 34). On a 286, the switch to real mode requires the processor to reset—a potentially time-consuming operation.

A few commercial 386 and 486 extenders (the one in Windows Enhanced mode, for example) use virtual 86 (V86) tasks to execute DOS and BIOS calls instead of switching to real mode. The CPU behaves much like an 8086 in V86 mode. Certain instructions and events (like interrupts, for example), generate faults that cause the CPU to return to protected mode.

Switching to real mode to handle interrupts is faster than using V86 mode. Still, switching to real mode interferes with some protected-mode features (notably multitasking). It also makes interrupt processing more complex—some interrupts can occur in either real or protected mode.

Figure 2-1a. DOS Extender Interrupt Handling

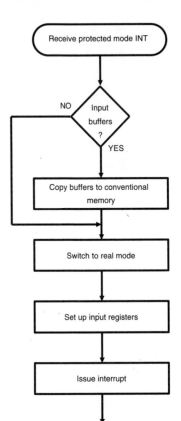

continued in Figure 2-1b

In Chapter 4 we will study DOS extender operation in greater detail. For now, keep the following key points in mind:

- DOS extenders run programs in protected mode.
- Extenders must handle software and hardware interrupts.
- Extenders allow protected-mode programs to access DOS and system services transparently.

Figure 2-1b. DOS Extender Interrupt Handling

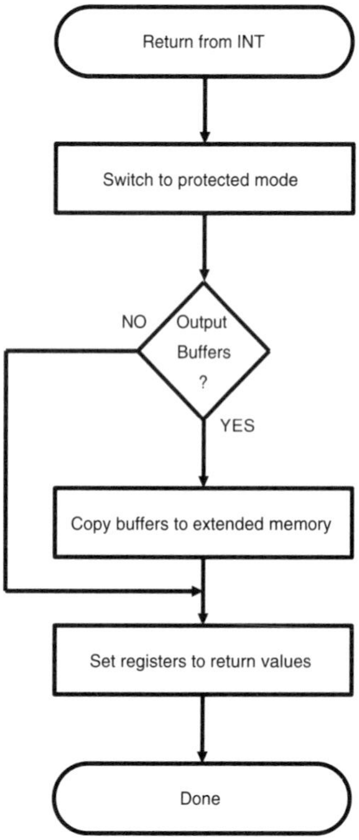

```
        ┌─────────────────────────┐
        │     Return from INT      │
        └─────────────────────────┘
                     │
        ┌─────────────────────────┐
        │  Switch to protected mode │
        └─────────────────────────┘
                     │
        NO      ╱ Output ╲
      ◄────────  Buffers
                  ╲   ?   ╱
                     │
                    YES
                     │
        ┌─────────────────────────┐
        │ Copy buffers to extended memory │
        └─────────────────────────┘
                     │
        ┌─────────────────────────┐
        │  Set registers to return values │
        └─────────────────────────┘
                     │
        ┌─────────────────────────┐
        │          Done            │
        └─────────────────────────┘
```

Chapter 4 will discuss some of the issues DOS extenders must address to do these three important steps. If you are a die-hard hacker, there are at least two DOS extenders that come in source code form: my own PROT (from the book *DOS 5: A Developer's Guide*) and the extender that comes with the GNU C/C++ for DOS package (see Chapter 3). PROT and the GNU extender use completely different methods to accomplish the same goals, so they are interesting to contrast (more about that in Chapter 4).

Pros and Cons

DOS extenders allow you to write giant-sized programs that can access large amounts of memory. Still, there are many benefits to using a DOS extender. Many extenders support other protected-mode features, such as:

- Virtual memory
- Flat (nonsegmented) memory model (386/486 only)
- Flexible segmentation (386/486 only)

In addition, using the 32-bit architecture on a 386 or 486 can provide a significant performance boost to programs that are computationally intensive (such as mathematics, scientific, engineering, and CAD programs). Some 386/486 extenders (and their compilers) simplify porting Unix programs. Some 286 extenders emulate the OS/2 programming interface, which can simplify portability between DOS and OS/2 programs.

Of course, DOS extenders can have some drawbacks. An extended program that makes many DOS or BIOS calls will execute more slowly than a comparable nonextended program. Also, using a DOS extender prevents your program from running on an 8086/8088-type computer (or even 286-based computers, if you use a 386 extender).

Compatibility

Another potential problem with extended programs concerns compatibility with other protected-mode programs. The problem results when a DOS extender attempts to switch the processor's mode while it is already in protected mode.

Before the appearance of industry standards, this was especially true of 386/486 PCs using memory managers such as Quarterdeck's QEMM, Qualitas's 386MAX, or Microsoft's EMM386. In 1987, industry leaders developed the Virtual Control Program Interface (VCPI) specification. VCPI allows programs to share protected-mode resources. A later, somewhat similar specification is the DOS Protected Mode Interface (DPMI).

When a program like QEMM or EMM386 keeps the processor in protected mode, it provides a VCPI (or DPMI) interface. Other programs can use this interface to allocate memory, switch processor modes, and perform other protected-mode tasks. Remember, VPCI and DPMI are not DOS extenders. They are simply standards that define protected-mode services. One protected-mode program (the host) provides these services, while other protected-mode programs (clients) use them.

Many modern DOS extenders can cooperate with protected-mode programs that use VCPI or DPMI. Of course, extenders can always run when no other protected-mode programs are running. A problem can arise if your extender only supports one protocol (say, DPMI), and the PC is running software that supplies another protocol. Later, we will examine VCPI and DPMI in more detail. For now, remember that VCPI and DPMI are standards that allow protected-mode programs to work jointly, and that most, but not all, extenders can utilize either interface.

Tools

Some vendors sell DOS extenders complete with a full set of tools: C compiler, symbolic debugger, etc. Others only package the DOS extender with a minimum set of tools (usually an assembler, linker, and a simple debugger).

Most 286 DOS extenders work with regular DOS or OS/2 1.x compilers (like Microsoft C or Borland C++). Some emulate OS/2 to some extent so that the compiler simply generates OS/2 executables which are then run under MS-DOS with the aid of the DOS extender. Other 286 extenders link with special libraries (or patch existing ones) to produce protected-mode programs.

A 386 extender won't work with a 16-bit DOS or OS/2 1.x compiler. However, many companies offer 32-bit compilers that produce programs for DOS extenders. These compilers often strive to maintain compatibility with PC standards usually Microsoft C.

Many developers like to buy everything from one vendor. Others are more comfortable using their existing compilers, or using another that closely mimics it. Luckily, there is a wide range of choices for both preferences. With so many companies producing DOS extenders and tools (see Chapter 3), you should have no trouble finding something that suits your taste.

Don't confuse compilers that generate protected-mode code with compilers that run in protected mode. You can use Microsoft C 6.0, running in real mode, to produce programs for a 286 DOS extender (you could even do this on an XT). Conversely, if you were running out of memory during compiles, you could run the protected-mode OS/2 compiler (using Phar Lap's 286 extender; see Chapter 3) and generate code for regular DOS. Not all compilers that run in protected mode generate protected-mode code. By the same token, not all compilers that create protected-mode code run in protected mode, and some can run in both modes.

Executing Programs

DOS can't execute protected-mode programs. DOS executes the extender; the extender loads and runs the protected-mode program. Most extenders allow you to bind the extender with your program. Binding places a copy of the extender in the same file as your program. The user types your program's name, but the extender starts instead. Then the extender automatically executes your program. This is transparent to the user.

Other vendors cause your program to load the extender automatically when it starts. In this case, the extender must be accessible on disk in a separate file.

During development, most extenders let you skip the binding process. Instead, they generate non-DOS executables. You must explicitly invoke the extender to run these programs. For example, the command

```
RUN286 myxprog
```

starts a 286 extender (RUN286 from Phar Lap), and tells it to execute the program named myxprog.

Practical Considerations

When you distribute an extended program to end users, you also must distribute the extender in some form. Some vendors allow you to distribute programs with no restrictions. Others charge a license or royalty fee that varies depending on how many copies you will distribute. Even if the extender is bound with your program, you must still be certain you have the legal right to distribute the extender.

In Chapter 3, you will find a list of companies that sell DOS extenders and their policies for redistribution. However, distribution license polices change frequently, so be sure to check with the manufacturers for the latest information.

The DOS Extender Choice

While PC hardware gets more and more sophisticated, real-mode DOS continues to restrict performance. DOS extenders are the key to writing powerful programs that can use modern PCs to their full potential. If you develop DOS or Windows applications that could use more memory, faster execution, and simplified addressing then you must be prepared to switch to protected mode.

CHAPTER ■ 3

The DOS Extender Tool Box

The DOS extender market can be loosely grouped into two categories of vendors: those that produce DOS extenders, and those that develop tools htat work with DOS extenders (such as C compilers). Many tool companies license extender technology from others and sell complete packages.

Most 286 extenders use development tools that produce DOS or OS/2 1.x programs. There may be an extra library to link with, or patches to existing libraries, but the compilers are the same familiar tools you use everyday. You may not even need to recompile a program to make it work with a 286 extender. If the program doesn't violate any protected-mode constraints (we'll look at those in a later chapter), you can simply relink with the new libraries.

Most 32-bit compilers and assemblers produce a 32-bit object format known as Easy-OMF. A 32-bit linker can transform an Easy-OMF object file into a protected-mode executable. However, the libraries you will need are closely tied to the compiler and the DOS extender. You can't compile and link for one DOS extender and expect the executable to work with a different brand of extender. If you plan to buy a DOS extender and a compiler from different companies, be sure they are compatible.

The remainder of this chapter provides a brief overview of the major DOS extender products available at the time this was written (the companies are in alphabetical order). Of course, the field is rapidly changing—companies announce new products, capabilities, and licensing arrangements frequently. (A complete list of these companies, with their addresses and phone numbers, appears in Appendix C.)

DOS Extender Manufacturers

Ergo   Ergo (formerly Eclipse; A. I. Architects prior to that), has four DOS extender offerings. Their OS/286 extender is 16 bit, and the OS/386 extender is 32 bit. They also sell the DPM16 DOS extender; a 286 DPMI extender; and DPM32, a 386 DPMI extender. The OS/286 and DPM/16 extenders allow you to use regular DOS compilers like Microsoft C. You compile the program as you would for real-mode DOS, and include a few extra libraries in the link. After the linker generates an executable, you run Ergo's post-processing program on it to generate a protected-mode executable. You can't use regular DOS debuggers to look at these protected-mode programs; Ergo supplies a simple debugger.

The OS/386 extender requires a third-party 32-bit C compiler like WATCOM C). The interface is similar to the regular DOS programming interface.

DPM16 is more like OS/2 than DOS, although the DOS interface is still present. DPM16 uses the OS/2 executable format (NE files). It supports dynamic link libraries (DLLs) and multiple (but not asynchronous) execution threads. However, DPM16 doesn't emulate OS/2; you still use regular DOS compilers and a custom debugger from Ergo. You do have to use a linker that can create OS/2 executables (most linkers do, since Windows uses the same NE file format).

Programs for DPM16 and DPM32 will coexist with VCPI and DPMI. OS/286 and OS/386 only support VCPI. All except DPM16 can also support virtual memory. You must purchase a special license to distribute programs you build with Ergo's tools.

Flash-Tek   Flash-Tek offers a 386 extender that is very similar to the Zortech 386 extender (see Symantec, below). Unlike the Zortech extender, the Flash-Tek offering supports debugging, virtual memory, and both Zortech and WATCOM compilers.

IGC   IGC doesn't sell DOS extenders directly to end users or developers. Instead, they license their X-AM DOS extender to other vendors (notably Intel, see Tool Manufacturers on page 36). X-AM is one of the few DOS extenders that executes DOS and BIOS calls in V86 mode instead of switching to real mode. This is advantageous for multitasking, but degrades performance considerably.

Phar Lap   Phar Lap produces both 286 and 386 extenders. Their 286|DOS Extender product works with Microsoft or Borland C and C++. It supports the traditional DOS call interface, and a subset of the OS/2 1.x API. The Phar Lap extender uses conventional 16-bit compilers and debuggers. Programmers also can make good use of the OS/2 API. You can use dynamic link libraries (DLLs), and multiple threads that work like their OS/2 counterparts. Some versions of the Borland C++ compiler include a limited version of this extender (286|DOS Extender Lite). The *DOS and Windows Protected Mode* companion disk also has a free copy of 286|DOS Extender Lite for Borland and Microsoft C and C++. See Appendix E, *286|DOS Extrender Lite User's Guide,* and the README.LIT file on the companion disk for more information.

Phar Lap also markets 386|DOS Extender, which comes with an assembler, linker, and a simple debugger. You can purchase a C compiler from a third party, or Phar Lap will sell you the extender and the MetaWare High C/C++ compiler (see below). Phar Lap provides a rich set of functions for working with the 386 and controlling the extender. An optional package (VMM|386) allows 386|DOS Extender to exploit virtual memory. Phar Lap's latest 386 extender (TNT) provides a subset of the console-oriented Windows NT WIN32 interface and uses the NT compiler and tools to create 32-bit programs (see Chapter 14 for more about WIN32).

Applications built with Phar Lap's extenders will work under the VCPI or DPMI environments. Phar Lap requires you to buy a special license to distribute programs built with their DOS extenders.

Rational Systems   Rational Systems manufactures two DOS extenders: DOS/16M (a 16-bit extender) and DOS/4G (a 32-bit extender). The Rational 386 extender employs split mapping—the memory below 1M is accessible to protected-mode programs and real-mode programs. Your protected-mode code and data load into extended memory. This split model reduces segmentation concerns. This simplifies programming, but it subverts protected mode's inherent safeguards against improper memory access. Dereferencing a NULL pointer, for example, should be no catastrophe in protected mode. A segmented extender will catch the offending reference and generate an error message that includes the address of the guilty instruction. A split or flat model extender will allow many NULL pointer references to pass unnoticed until they crash the system.

Both DOS/16M and DOS/4G can support virtual memory and can work in VCPI or DPMI environments. DOS/16M works with regular DOS compilers. DOS/4G requires a 32-bit compiler. WATCOM (see below) includes a limited version of the DOS/4G extender with their 32-bit C compiler.

Rational also markets BigWin, a system for creating 32-bit Windows applications with Windows 3.x. This product, which requires a 32-bit compiler, is a regular Windows program (the supervisor) that attaches to your 32-bit program. The 32-bit program makes Windows-like calls to the supervisor, which translates them into regular 16-bit Windows functions. Windows returns to the supervisor, which translates the results for the 32-bit program.

Tool Manufacturers

Intel   Intel sells the 386/486 C Code Builder Kit. This bundle contains a C compiler, a linker, a source-level debugger, a librarian, a Make utility, and a DOS extender that supports virtual memory—everything you need, except an assembler. Code Builder's best feature is its licensing agreement. Intel allows you to distribute Code Builder programs freely. This is a deciding factor for many developers.

Intel uses a licensed variant of IGC's X-AM DOS Extender. The extender works with DPMI. It won't actively use VCPI, but it can coexist with VCPI servers. Since IGC executes DOS calls in V86 mode, Code Builder (like other V86 extenders) is often much slower than extenders that switch to real mode to process interrupts.

Code Builder uses a flat-memory model exclusively—there are no segments to worry about. With its lack of segments, and its 32-bit integers and pointers, Code Builder is a good choice for porting Unix software to the PC. Of course, with flat-memory model, you lose many benefits of protected mode—in particular, an errant program can destroy any portion of memory (see the discussion of Rational's split model extender on page 36).

Intel's C compiler and library are highly compatible with Microsoft C. Unfortunately, Code Builder doesn't allow much manipulation of the 386 environment. It is essentially a 32-bit Microsoft C clone. If you want an easy-to-use, easy-to-learn system, this is an advantage. If you want to directly manipulate the 386's advanced features, it is a disadvantage.

MetaWare   The MetaWare High C/C++ compiler is a very capable 32-bit compiler for use with 386 DOS extenders (it also can create AutoCad/386 applications), with a rich set of language extensions. For example, MetaWare allows C functions to declare local functions, much as in Pascal (see Listing 3-1). While using these features may help you organize your code, it also will lock you into using MetaWare C. MetaWare does provide an option to compile code that is more similar to ANSI C and Microsoft C.

If you avoid using the extensions, you shouldn't have many problems with portability (see Chapter 15). If you start with existing DOS code, you will definitely want to avoid the extensions. MetaWare's non-ANSI extensions are not compatible with the *de facto* Microsoft standard.

The MetaWare compiler comes with an abundance of tools: an editor, linker, some Unix-like utilities, and several additional libraries. Both a source-level debugger and a profiler are also available. MetaWare also resells the Phar Lap 386|DOS Extender with some of its compilers.

MetaWare also produces the Windows Advanced Development Kit (ADK), which allows the Metaware High C/C++ compiler to produce 32-bit applications for Microsoft Windows. It is similar to Rational's BigWin (see page 42).

Listing 3-1. Function Nesting in MetaWare C

```
/* Example of Function Nesting in High C
   compile: HC386 LIST31.C */

#include <stdio.h>

main()
  {
  /* nested function */
  void sayhello()
    {
    printf("Hello\n");
    }
  sayhello();   /* references local sayhello() */
  external();
  }

void sayhello()
  {
  printf("Howdy!\n");
  }

external()
  {
  sayhello();  /* references global sayhello(); */
  }
```

MicroWay   MicroWay produces NDP C 386, a globally-optimizing C compiler and DOS extender. MicroWay is best known for their FORTRAN products, and NDP C 386 can link with NDP FORTRAN.

Silicon Valley Software   Silicon Valley Software (SVS) markets the C^3/C compiler package. It includes an ANSI/Microsoft-compatible compiler, a source debugger, the usual development tools, and a 32-bit DOS extender licensed from Intel. The extender is a variant on the IGC extender, and is practically the same extender found in Code Builder. Like Code Builder, SVS's extender is royalty-free.

Symantec   Symantec acquired Zortech C++ in 1991. The Zortech package includes a C++/C compiler, debugger, and royalty-free (although somewhat limited) 286 and 386 DOS extenders. Zortech can also produce programs for regular DOS, 16-bit Windows, OS/2, and several third-party DOS extenders (Flash-Tek, Phar Lap, and Rational, for example).

WATCOM   The WATCOM C/386 32-bit compiler is highly Microsoft compatible, and is well known for its sophisticated code optimization. The WATCOM package includes a version of the Rational DOS/4G 386 extender and a 32-bit Windows supervisor. It also generates code for most popular extenders.

WATCOM ships a source-level debugger, a profiler, a linker, a librarian, and several libraries with their C compiler. The WATCOM compiler also can create AutoCAD/386 applications using the AutoCAD Development System (ADS).

Other Resources

GNU C++   The Free Software Foundation's GNU project distributes a C/C++ compiler for Unix systems. This compiler is also available for 386 protected mode, and is free (or nearly free) from a variety of sources.

The 386 package (ported by D. J. Delorie) contains an extender that supports virtual memory and VCPI. It comes with several utilities including an assembler, a symbolic debugger with minimal source support, and a profiler. The extender is not compatible with DPMI.

The GNU package is an inexpensive way to experiment with DOS extender technology. However, it isn't a substitute for commercial products. Since programs running with the GNU extender are not compatible with DPMI they aren't practical in a production environment. There is no support for signals or C interrupt handling. Also, the lack of serious debugging tools is a major obstacle. If you discover a bug or problem with the package, it can be a problem, because there is no consistent support for free software (though it does come with source code you can hack). Another drawback is that there are several restrictions on distributing code built with GNU C++.

On the other hand, the GNU package is free (or almost free) and comes with source code. It is available from several on-line services and disk distributors such as the Austin Code Works (see Appendix C for a list of resources).

Non-C Resources

While most protected-mode programs use C and C++, many vendors support other languages as well. Lahey, MicroWay, Phar Lap, SVS, and WATCOM all support FORTRAN, for example. Many mainframe FORTRAN programs require so much memory that protected mode is the only way to bring them to the PC. MetaWare, and SVS also have DOS extended Pascal compilers.

Selecting a DOS Extender

DOS extenders, like many things in life, are not "one size fits all." You might want to consider the following questions:

Do I need a 386 extender?

A 386 extender is more powerful than a 286 extender, but using one will prevent your program from operating on 286 computers. While most developers have 386 or 486 machines, there are still many 286 machines in the hands of end users (see the sidebar, *Why 286 Extenders?*). Another factor is that 286 extenders work with development tools you probably already own. Not only is this convenient, but also it can simplify compiling existing DOS code.

WHY 286 EXTENDERS?

Many programmers find the existence of 16-bit extenders puzzling. With the spotlight on newer processors, the 286 seems woefully out of date. Yet new 286 extenders keep appearing, and there is a high demand for them.

Though 386 extenders have many benefits, there are good reasons to consider a 286 product:

- A 286 extender works with conventional compilers that you probably already own.

- DOS code usually requires fewer changes to work with a 286 extender.

- There is still a large segment of the market using 286 processors. This is especially true of the international market, where 386 and 486 PCs may be very expensive or unavailable. Of course, 286 extended programs can still run on 386 and 486 PCs.

In general, if your program doesn't need special 386 features (32-bit integers, linear addressing of up to 4G, and efficient virtual memory), you should certainly consider a 286 extender. Of course, if you know your software will only run on 386 or 486 PCs, you might as well use a 386 extender. But if a broader market potential is important to you, don't ignore the many 286 users out there. ■

Am I willing to pay royalties?

Many DOS extenders require you to pay royalties (or a license fee) on copies you distribute.

Do I need virtual memory?

Some extenders don't support virtual memory. If you need more memory than your users will have, you must select an extender that uses the disk to provide virtual memory.

Is the extender compatible with industry standards?

You should only consider extenders that can coexist with VCPI, DPMI, and XMS. Almost every PC user with a 386 uses a VCPI memory manager or HIMEM.SYS (an XMS driver); Windows and many new memory managers supply a DPMI environment.

Is there adequate compiler and debugger support?

Be certain that the extender you select will work with the current version of the compiler you want. You can expect this when buying an extender and compiler in one package. And remember that good debugging support is essential for productive programming: make sure the DOS extender package will let you debug your protected-mode program.

CHAPTER ▪ 4

Protected Mode: The Inside Story

Some C programmers think they don't need to understand the underlying machine, but most programmers eventually do. In particular, knowledge of protected mode will help you debug programs, exploit special features, and select a DOS extender. This chapter will examine protected-mode architecture in detail.

On the other hand, if you find all these details confusing, don't worry. You can write many protected-mode C programs without knowledge of the internal architecture.

Although this chapter discusses many protected-mode features, there are a few things it won't cover (for example, how to switch to protected mode—your DOS extender handles that for you). Only issues that affect DOS extender programming appear in this chapter. If you would like more details about general protected-mode programming, see the bibliography at the end of this book.

The architecture of the 486 and the 386 appear nearly identical to programmers. The 286's protected mode is very similar, but not identical, to the 386's. The 386 and 486 can both execute 286 protected-mode programs.

Remember, a DOS extender is a small protected-mode operating system. For the purposes of this chapter, the terms DOS extender and operating system are interchangeable.

Architecture

Figures 4-1a and 4-1b (on pages 51 and 52) shows the 286 register set. Most of the 386/486 registers appear in Figures 4-2a (page 52) and 4-2b (page 53). Notice that the 386 general-purpose registers are twice as wide as the corresponding 286 registers. Only the segment registers are the same size (16 bits). Normally, when you run a 16-bit (real or protected mode) program on a 386/486, you waste the upper 16-bits of the registers. Of course, if you know you are running on a 32-bit processor you can use the extended registers even in 16-bit real- or protected-mode code. For an example of this, see the FPM32 Windows program in Chapter 15.

The 386 has three control registers, CR0, CR2, and CR3. These registers control the operation of the CPU. For example, bit 0 in CR0 determines if the processor is in real or protected mode. The 286 MSW (Machine Status Word) register is the same as the first 16 bits of CR0.

Privileged Segments

Selectors

Segmentation is the key to understanding protected mode. A protected-mode segment register holds a 16-bit segment selector (see Figure 4-3 on page 54). Unlike segments in real mode, this selector value has nothing to do with the segment's location in memory. Rather, it is an index into a table of segment descriptors. Each descriptor defines one segment. The descriptor is what determines the segment's location in memory, its size, type (e.g., code or data), and other important parameters.

Notice in Figure 4-3 that the selector contains three fields. The two bottom bits (RPL in Figure 4-3) indicate the privilege level (described later). Two selectors that differ only in their RPL fields reference the same segment. That is, selectors 10H, 11H, 12H, and 13H all point to the same segment descriptor.

Figure 4-1a. 286 Registers

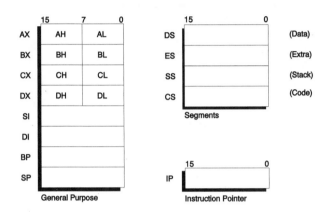

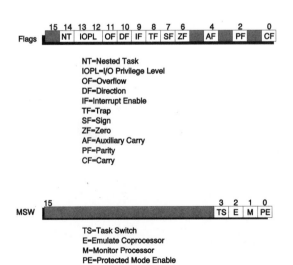

Figure 4-1b. 286 System Registers

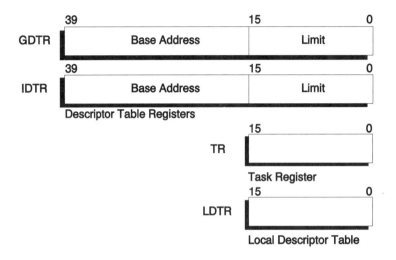

Figure 4-2a. 386 Registers

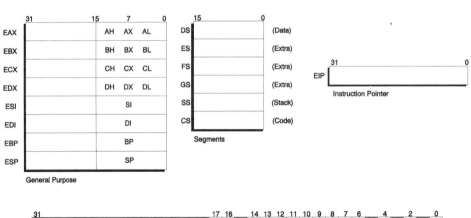

Figure 4-2b. 386 Registers

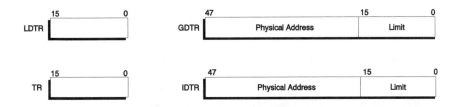

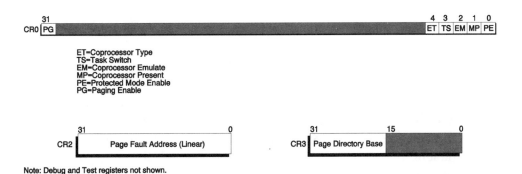

Note: Debug and Test registers not shown.

Bit 2 (TI) determines which table of descriptors defines the segment. There are three segment descriptor tables: the global descriptor table (GDT), the local descriptor table (LDT), and the interrupt descriptor table (IDT). If TI is 0, segment's descriptor is in the GDT. If it is 1, the LDT contains the descriptor. Segment selectors never refer to the IDT.

Descriptor tables can't exceed 64K, and each descriptor is 8 bytes long, so each table can hold up to 8,192 segment descriptors. The 13 index bits (bits 3 to 15) in the selector determine which descriptor to use in the table specified by the TI bit. This upper limit of 8,192 descriptors is responsible for the upper limit on the number of segments in protected mode, which was mentioned in Chapter 1.

Figure 4-3. Protected-Mode Segment Selector

TI=Table Indicator
RPL=Requestor Privilege Level

The Tables

The GDTR and IDTR determine the location of the GDT and IDT, respectively. On the 386, each register contains a 32-bit address, and a 16-bit limit (a total of 48 bits). (The 286 uses a 24-bit address.) The limit is one less than the length of the table in bytes. The address is a linear address—not a segment/offset pair. This linear address is simply a 32-bit number from 0 to 4G that represents the segment's starting location. If memory management is not active (more about that later), a linear address corresponds to the actual physical memory location. When memory management is active this may not be true.

The processor reserves the first GDT descriptor. Any attempt to access memory via this descriptor is invalid. GDT selectors with an index field of 0 (i.e., selectors 0, 1, 2, and 3) are null selectors. This means that in protected mode, far NULL pointers are truly illegal. In real mode, a NULL pointer actually references linear address 0. While you usually don't mean to use a NULL pointer in real mode, it isn't illegal (and is occasionally correct).

The GDT, as its name implies, is global—even when the processor is running multiple programs (or tasks) together, the GDT does not change. This is also true of the IDT—each task uses the same table. If one task changes the GDT or IDT, it affects all tasks.

Each descriptor in the IDT defines the response to one of the 256 possible interrupts. In protected mode, the IDT is used instead of the real-mode interrupt vector table at address 0000:0000. Like the other descriptor tables, the IDT can contain up to 8,192 descriptors, but the processor only uses the first 256.

The LDTR holds the location of the LDT. Each task can have its own LDT. Unlike the GDTR, the LDTR does not contain an address/limit pair. Instead, the LDTR holds a segment selector that must point to a special entry in the GDT that points to the LDT. The GDT can contain pointers to many different LDTs. Some protected-mode environments use multiple LDTs, and some don't; the meaning of "task" also differs from one protected-mode environment to the next. In Windows Enhanced Mode, for example, each DOS box gets its own LDT, while all Windows programs share a single LDT and, from this perspective, together all look like a single "task."

Table 4-1 shows the fields in a basic descriptor table entry. Figure 4-4a on the next page shows the layout of specific protected-mode descriptors. There are many special descriptors that don't define segments. For example, Figure 4-4b shows the descriptor that defines LDT.

Table 4-1. Common Descriptor Table Entry Fields

Field	Meaning
Present Flag	Set if segment is present in memory
Base Address	Starting location (not necessarily physical) of segment in memory
Limit	Maximum legal byte offset (or minimum for stack)
Type	Type of segment (code, data, stack, etc.)
DPL	Segment's protection level (0=highest, 3=lowest)

How can a 32-bit descriptor specify a segment from 1 byte to 4G long? After all, the limit field is only 20 bits wide. The G bit (bit 55) works with the limit field to make large segments possible. If G is 0, the limit field corresponds to the segment's maximum legal byte offset (one less than its length). For example, if selector 0x30 refers to a segment where G=0 and the limit field is 0xFF, then addresses 0030:0000 0000 to 0030:0000 00FF are legal. Trying to use addresses larger than 0030:0000 00FF (0030:0100 0000 or 0030:0000 F000, for instance) will cause an error. Note in particular that, while reading a byte at 0030:00FF is legal, reading a word from the same location is not.

Figure 4-4a. Code and Data Segment Descriptors

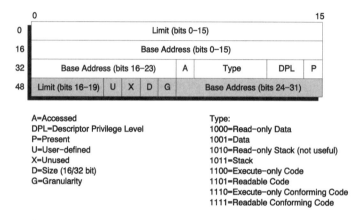

A=Accessed
DPL=Descriptor Privilege Level
P=Present
U=User–defined
X=Unused
D=Size (16/32 bit)
G=Granularity

Type:
1000=Read–only Data
1001=Data
1010=Read–only Stack (not useful)
1011=Stack
1100=Execute–only Code
1101=Readable Code
1110=Execute–only Conforming Code
1111=Readable Conforming Code

Shaded areas are 386/486 only. These fields must be zero on the 286.

Figure 4-4b. LDT Descriptor

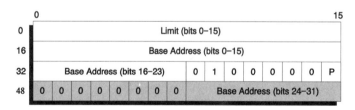

P=Present

Shaded areas are 386/486 only. These fields must be zero on the 286.

When G is 1 the 386 shifts the limit field left 13 places (the same as multiplying it by 0x1000), to make a 32-bit limit. The 386 sets the bottom 12 bits of the 32-bit limit to 0xFFF. If a descriptor has a limit field of 1, and G is 1, the actual limit is 1FFFH. When G is 1 and the limit field is 0, the limit is FFFH.

This allows you to specify a 32-bit segment of any size up to 1M in length. You also can specify segments up to 4G long in 4K steps. When G is 0, the segment can range from 1 byte to 1M long. When G is 1, the segment can range from 4K to 4G in length. In psuedo C, you could duplicate the 386's logic like this:

```
if (G==0)
   max_offset=limit;
else
   max_offset=limit*0x1000+0xFFF;
```

The 286 is not as flexible as the 386. A 16-bit segment can't exceed the dreaded 64K limit. The 286 can create segments of any length up to 64K. Even though the 286 can address 16M of memory, you still must access it 64K at a time. Of course, 16-bit code running on a 386 or 486 has the same limitations.

A stack segment's limit field is different. It represents the *lowest* possible offset. A 16-bit stack segment always begins at offset 0xFFFF; a 32-bit stack starts at 0xFFFFFFFF. Using offsets less than the limit will cause an error. This is handy when you run out of stack space and must expand the stack. By changing the limit, you (or the protected-mode system you're running under) can make the stack grow without relocating it.

There is nothing to prevent the creation of two descriptors that point to the same area of memory. In fact, this capability is essential. A DOS extender, for example, might load a file into a data segment, and then jump to a code segment that starts in the same place. This process is known as *aliasing*. The operating system must have some way to modify the GDT and other system tables. Therefore, the operating system will often have a data segment alias to the GDT.

Some 386 extenders set up a data segment that covers all 4 Gs of linear memory (we'll examine linear memory in the section on memory management on page 62). Then tables (like the GDT) can be written directly via that data segment.

Don't worry if you don't understand all the bits in the descriptor. Things will become clearer as you learn more about protected-mode's privilege mechanisms.

Protected-Mode Privilege

In protected mode, each program has a privilege level from 0 to 3. Programs at privilege level 0 (PL0 or ring 0 programs) are the next most privileged and can execute any instruction and access any data. Programs at PL3 (ring 3 programs) are the least privileged, and can't execute certain instructions. They also can't access data that belongs to more privileged programs (that is, with *lower* privilege levels). Each segment descriptor has a descriptor privilege level (DPL) that the CPU uses for protection. The processor can alsocontrol an application's use of I/O and interrupt instructions.

DOS extenders (and operating systems) can use privilege protection to prevent faulty programs from disturbing the operating system or other tasks. However, some DOS extenders effectively subvert the protection mechanism—in those cases, program bugs can place you at risk of corrupting the system, just as in regular DOS. This can simplify programming in some situations, but it prevents the CPU from effectively protecting the system and other programs from an errant program.

The privilege hierarchy also allows device and interrupt virtualization. PL0 programs (such as the operating system or a DOS extender) can intercept interrupts and I/O requests from non-PL0 programs. The PL0 program can elect to allow the request, or it may simulate the I/O (or interrupt). For example, a multitasking operating system might intercept I/O requests to the video display. Instead of passing these on directly to the video hardware, the operating system would manipulate a virtual video display and update a window on the system's true video display. This is how Windows Enhanced mode's Virtual Display Device (VDD) manages windowed DOS boxes.

A program's privilege level can be determined by examining the RPL field of the selector in the CS register. The RPL value is the current privilege level, or CPL. In assembly:

```
mov ax,cs
or  ax,3   ; AX now equals privilege level
```

You can't directly modify the CS register to change the RPL, yet there are ways to call higher- or lower-privileged code (via the call and task gates discussed later in this chapter, for example).

Table 4-2 shows the instructions that only PL0 programs can execute. If a PL3 program could, for example, reload GDTR, privilege protection would be meaningless. By allowing only PL0 programs to do this, the DOS extender or operating system has the option of exercising complete control over lower-privilege programs. PL3 programs can examine GDTR and other privileged registers, but can't modify them.

Table 4-2. PL0-Only Instructions

Instruction	Action
HLT	Halt processor
CLTS	Clear task switch bit
LGDT	Load GDTR
LIDT	Load IDTR
LLDT	Load LDTR
LTR	Load TR
LMSW	Load MSW
MOV	Move from/to control/debug/test registers (386)

Data Access

Every time your program loads a segment register, the CPU performs several sanity checks on the selector value. Failing any of these tests will result in an error. For example, if you try to load an execute-only segment selector into the DS register, an error occurs. Privilege violations can also cause errors. Each descriptor has a descriptor privilege level (DPL). When a program loads a data segment register (DS, ES, FS, or GS), the CPU checks the DPL against the program's CPL and the selector's RPL. First, it compares the CPL to the RPL. The largest one becomes the effective privilege level (EPL). If the DPL is greater than or equal to the EPL, the CPU loads the segment register. If the DPL is less than the EPL, an error occurs. (If you can't keep these CPLs, DPLs, EPLs, and RPLs straight, don't worry. Nobody else can either.)

The CPU performs additional checks when you *use* a selector. For example, if selector 0x0030 is read-only, you can load it into DS. Trying to write to the segment however, will cause an error. For example:

```
mov ax,0030H  ; read-only
mov ds,ax     ; no error
mov [100],cx  ; error!
```

It is always legal to load a null selector (0x00 to 0x03) into any segment register. Any attempt to access memory via the null selector will cause an error. For instance:

```
xor ax,ax          ; ax=0
mov es,ax          ; OK -- no error
mov ax,es:[100]    ; Error!
```

I/O Access

The IOPL field in the EFLAGS register allows a PL0 (ring 0) program to control the privilege level required to perform IN, OUT, and related operations (see Table 4-3). For each attempted I/O operation, the CPU compares CPL to IOPL. If CPL is less than or equal to IOPL, the operation proceeds. Otherwise, the processor raises an error. If IOPL is 0, only ring 0 programs can use the IOPL-sensitive instructions. If IOPL is 3, all programs can execute I/O instructions.

Not all privilege violations are real errors, however. Some systems (Windows, for one) deliberately cause IOPL errors to call the operating system. As an example, consider the STI and CLI instructions (these correspond to _enable() and _disable() in C). When a user program issues one of these instructions, the ring 0 operating system receives an "error." However, it may simply set a flag and restart the program. When interrupts occur, the PL0 program will examine the flag to determine if it will send the interrupt to the PL3 program or handle the interrupt itself.

Table 4-3. IOPL-Sensitive Instructions

Instruction	Action
CLI	Disable interrupts
STI	Enable interrupts
IN	Input from port
INS	Input string from port
OUT	Output to port
OUTS	Output string to port

Only a PL0 program can set the IOPL field. When other programs modify the flags, IOPL doesn't change. For example, assume this code is running with CPL=3 and IOPL=0:

```
MOV AX,0FFFFH    ; Set all bits
PUSH AX          ; Load flags with AX via stack
POPF
```

After this code fragment executes, IOPL will still be 0. Even if a program's privilege level doesn't allow it to access an I/O port, there is another way that it might be allowed to do so. You will see how this works later in the chapter during the discussion of tasks.

Privilege Level for Code Segments

Programs often change the CS register via a jump, call, or return instruction. The processor will not load a selector into CS unless the segment is of executable type, and present. Also, the DPL of the segment must equal the CPL.

A special type of code segment doesn't have the CPL requirement. A conforming code segment uses the CPL of the program that calls it (or jumps to it). These segments do have a DPL—it just doesn't become the CPL. Still, the DPL of a conforming code segment must be numerically less than or equal to the CPL of the calling program. In other words, you can't transfer control to less-privileged conforming code segments. If you could, a malicious program (Trojan horse) could manipulate the return address of a conforming code subroutine and force the processor to return to an arbitrary address in a higher privilege level.

Since you can't execute code in a segment with a different privilege level, how does privilege change? There are several methods available. The CPL can change involuntarily when an internal or external interrupt occurs (we will cover interrupt handling later in this chapter). A special type of segment, a call gate, can also change CPL. When we learn about tasking (coming up next), you'll see that switching to a new task might also change CPL. Under Windows, and many DOS extenders, the most common way to change CPL is by deliberate generation of an error (fault). This turns out to be much faster than call gates and task switching. Other DOS extenders avoid the problem altogether, by not bothering with multiple privilge levels. However, since tasks are important in all CPL changes, we will return to our discussion of code privilege after we learn more about multitasking.

Multitasking

In protected mode, task state segments (TSSs) support multitasking. They also can support interrupts service routines and coroutines. A TSS descriptor (Figure 4-5) points to a special data structure in memory (see Figure 4-6). This structure must be at least 44 bytes long (104 bytes on the 386), but it can be longer.

Programs cannot access a TSS with the TSS selector; the CPU uses it internally. When the operating system fills in a TSS, it must use a data segment (either an alias, or one that allows it to access all memory). TSS selectors always appear in the GDT.

Most of the fields in the TSS hold registers for the task while it is inactive. Before a new task resumes (or begins) execution, the processor updates most of the old task's TSS fields (the shaded ones in Figure 4-6). The operating system sets the other fields when it creates the TSS. The processor then loads the registers with the values in the entire TSS. The TR register holds the current task's TSS selector.

Near the end of the TSS there are fields that contain SS and SP (or ESP) values for PL0, PL1, and PL2 programs. When a task changes CPL, it must use a separate stack for each level. The processor uses these stacks when CPL changes, as we will soon see.

Figure 4-5. TSS Descriptor

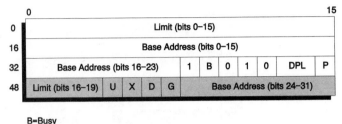

B=Busy
DPL=Descriptor Privilege Level
P=Present
U=User–defined
X=Unused
D=Size (16/32 bit)
G=Granularity

Shaded areas are 386/486 only. These fields must be zero on the 286.

You can transfer control to a TSS by jumping to it or calling it. Task gates (Figure 4-7) can also pass control to a task. In real-world DOS extenders, these methods are not used since they are very slow (even one of Intel's manuals suggests avoiding them). Most of the TSS structure is unused, except for the PL stacks and the I/O permission bitmap (see Figure 4-6 on the following page).

It is not unusual to find TSSs larger than the minimum size. The extra space can hold information specific to the operating system or DOS extender. For example, the system may store information about the task's open files in the TSS. Operating systems often store coprocessor state information in the TSS if multiple tasks may use it.

Another use for extra space in a 386 TSS is the I/O bitmap. The TSS field at offset 66H contains a pointer to the optional I/O bit map. Since the 16-bit field is relative to the start of the TSS, the bitmap must be nearby. Several TSSs can share a bitmap, if they are all within 64K of it.

Figure 4-6. Task State Segment (TSS)

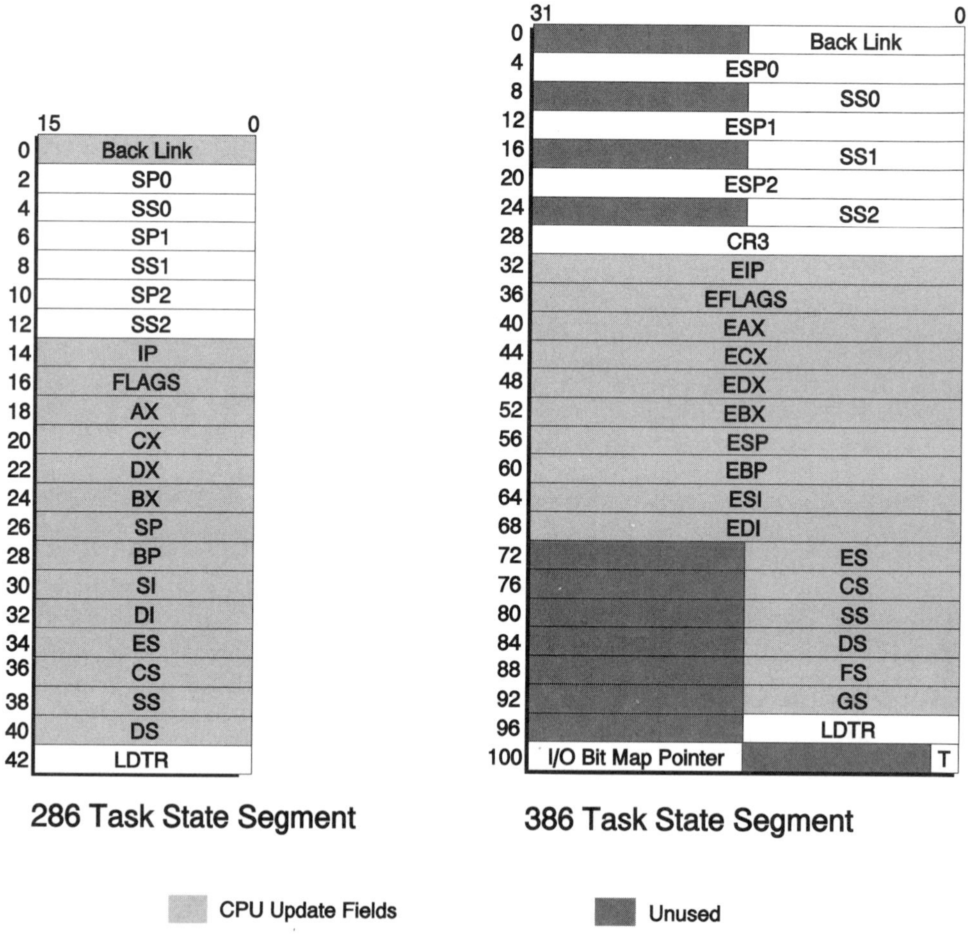

286 Task State Segment   386 Task State Segment

[CPU Update Fields]   [Unused]

Each bit in the I/O map represents one port. If a task attempts to execute an I/O instruction, the 386 will compare the task's CPL to IOPL. If CPL is less than or equal to IOPL, the I/O proceeds. If CPL is greater

Figure 4-7. Task Gate

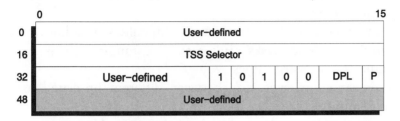

DPL=Descriptor Privilege Level
P=Present

The shaded field must be zero on the 286.

than IOPL, the CPU checks the I/O bitmap. If the bit that represents the specified port is 0, the I/O operation may continue. If it is set, or if the I/O bitmap is not present, the processor denies access.

When the processor forbids access to an I/O port, an error occurs. The system may terminate the offending task or return an error. Sophisticated 386 systems can use this error to simulate I/O devices. It may do this because the device doesn't exist, or to allow multiple tasks to use the same device (for example, many tasks sharing the screen). There is of course a performance penalty for this I/O port virtualization, as any user of Windows Enhanced mode will testify.)

A full 386 bitmap is 8K long, but it can be shorter. The processor considers any entries past the end as 1s. The bitmap should always end with FFH.

More on Code Segments

Now that we understand the TSS, we can look at CPL changes again. When the CPU loads a TSS, the CPL changes to the value in the TSS's CS image. A TSS (or task gate) is loadable if its DPL is greater than or equal to the calling program's EPL.

If a TSS has a DPL of 3, any task (even a PL3 task) can jump to it. This doesn't violate any protection rules. The old task can't affect the new task's registers or its private memory.

Using tasks for function calls presents many difficulties (in addition to their poor performance). Since tasks can't easily communicate, it is awkward to pass parameters or return values.

TSSs are better suited to switching between different unrelated programs. Tasks can communicate via memory they share in the GDT, or via a segment of memory that both tasks define in their LDTs. However, tasks usually don't communicate at all. Most often, tasks are separate entities and the operating system handles any required communications.

Call gates (Figure 4-8) are more suitable for function calls between CPLs (although they too are slow). Each call gate, a special descriptor table entry, defines a function. A far call instruction may use the call gate selector in lieu of a segment. In OS/2 1.x, many kernel functions used call gates.

When the processor detects a call to a gate, it verifies the gate's accessibility. To verify a call gate, the processor computes the EPL (the larger of the RPL and CPL). If the EPL is less than or equal to the gate's DPL, the gate is accessible. In any case, the new segment's DPL must be less than or equal to the current CPL. Call gates can't reduce the privilege level. For example, a PL0 program can't call a PL3 subroutine via a call gate.

Figure 4-8. Call Gate

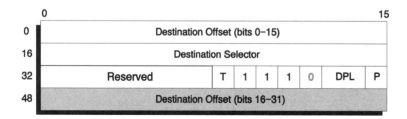

T=Type (0=Call Gate, 1=Trap Gate)
DPL=Descriptor Privilege Level
P=Present

The shaded field must be zero on the 286.

If the gate is accessible, the processor ignores the call's offset. Instead, execution will transfer to the location specified by the segment and offset in the call gate. This way, the call gate, not the calling program, determines the new execution address.

When a call gate doesn't change the CPL, it acts like a normal far call. If CPL does change, the processor reloads the stack segment and pointer from the current TSS (indicated by the TR register). There are six fields in the TSS that contain pointers to a PL0, PL1, and PL2 stack. The CPU loads the stack pointer and segment from the appropriate fields. It then pushes the old stack segment and pointer on the new stack.

Some functions expect arguments on the stack. The CPU will copy the number of parameters indicated by the WC (word count) field from the old stack to the new stack. A 16-bit call gate copies 16-bit words, and a 32-bit call gate (386 only) copies 32-bit words. The CPU places the parameters after the old stack pointer, but before the return address on the stack.

For calls with a fixed number of arguments, the WC mechanism can move the actual parameters from one stack to another. Calls that support varying arguments (C's printf(), for example) require a little more work. Commonly, the caller passes a pointer to the argument list. Since the pointer's length is constant, the WC mechanism works.

What happens when a call gate subroutine returns? If the CPL changed, the processor reverses the above steps to restore CPL. If WC is not zero, the subroutine must use a return that removes the parameters (i.e., RETF 2). The return instruction removes the parameters from both stacks. To prevent protection violations, the processor clears any segment registers that contain selectors of the subroutine's privilege, but are more privileged than the calling program.

Although call gates allow CPL switches, they are relatively slow. Most extenders simply use interrupts or cause errors to call the operating system, or do not bother with different privilege levels in the first place.

Interrupt Processing

The IDT can contain up to 256 task, trap, or interrupt gates. Each gate corresponds to one exception or interrupt. Internal and external events can cause interrupts. The CPU can generate many internal interrupts to signal a variety of error conditions. External interrupts in protected mode are similar to those in real mode. I/O devices such as the keyboard generate hardware interrupts when they need attention.

Intel divides internal interrupts into three classes: traps, faults, and aborts. A fault indicates a correctable error. For instance, trying to load a segment when its present bit is clear causes a fault. The operating system can load the segment, mark it as present, and restart the instruction. Traps occur for software interrupts (the INT and INTO instructions), and some 386 debugging interrupts. Traps are not restartable. Aborts are severe errors, they are not restartable. Most systems will terminate a program that generates an abort.

Table 4-4 lists the protected-mode internal exceptions. Several exceptions push an error code on the stack. For most exceptions, the error code is the selector involved in the error. Only exception 0x0E (the 386 page fault) uses a different error code. If the code is 0, the null selector caused the error, or the CPU could not decide which selector was responsible.

Table 4-4. Protected-Mode Exceptions

Name	INT	Error	Code Type	Possible Causes
Divide	0	No	Fault	DIV or IDIV
Debug*	1	No	N/A**	Hardware Debug
Break	3	No	Trap	INT 3
Overflow	4	No	Trap	INTO
Bounds	5	No	Fault	BOUND
Opcode	6	No	Fault	Bad instruction
No NPX	7	No	Fault	Coprocessor
Double	8	Yes (always 0)	Abort	Two faults
NPX over	9	No	Abort	Coprocessor
Bad TSS	10 (0xA)	Yes	Fault	Bad TSS
Segment	11 (0xB)	Yes	Fault	Not present segment
Stack	12 (0xC)	Yes	Fault	Stack error
GP	13 (0xD)	Yes	Fault	General protection
Page*	14 (0xE)	Yes	Fault	MMU problem

Table 4-4. Protected-Mode Exceptions (cont.)

Name	INT	Error	Code Type	Possible Causes
Divide	0	No	Fault	DIV or IDIV
NPX	16 (0x10)	Yes	Fault	Error from coprocessor
Alignment***	17 (0x11)	No	Trap	Unaligned memory access

*386 only
**The 386 debug interrupt (INT 1) is sometimes a trap, and sometimes a fault.
***486 only

When IBM designed the original PC, the internal exception interrupts were reserved by Intel, but not used. IBM used many of them for hardware and BIOS interrupts, causing much difficulty when the 286 arrived. For example, the PC BIOS uses INT 10h for video services, while, as Table 4-4 shows, Intel has defined it to be a math coprocessor exception. DOS extenders and other protected-mode systems must take special measures (like relocating the hardware interrupts or examining the value of CS at interrupt-time) to prevent confusion. The DPMI specification distinguishes interrupts from exceptions, and it is up to a DPMI server to keep straight which one, for example, an INT 10 is. Luckily, this is normally transparent to the programmer.

Trap and interrupt gates (Figure 4-9) are very similar to call gates. These gates don't have a WC field, since interrupts don't pass arguments on the stack. Although trap and interrupt gates have a DPL, you should usually set them to 3. If an interrupt occurs while the CPU is executing PL3 code, and the gate is not PL3, the processor will be unable to process it.

Trap gates and interrupt gates operate identically, except for their handling of the IF flag. When an interrupt gate transfers control, it clears the IF flag. This disables hardware interrupts (except NMI). Trap gates don't modify IF.

Interrupts also can initiate a task switch if the corresponding IDT entry is a task gate. This is sometimes useful for handling hardware interrupts. Using a task switch forces the processor to save all registers on entry and restore them before exiting. This relieves the interrupt routine from this job. Unfortunately, the task switch usually takes too long to be practical.

Figure 4-9. Trap/Interrupt Gate

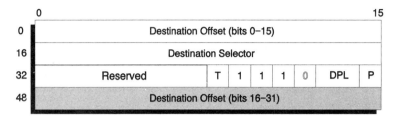

T=Type (0=Call Gate, 1=Trap Gate)
DPL=Descriptor Privilege Level
P=Present

The shaded field must be zero on the 286.

If you handle interrupts with task gates, remember that tasks are not reentrant. If the interrupt occurs again while the task is still running, a general protection fault will occur.

The General Protection Fault

Exception 0x0D is the general protection (GP) fault. The processor generates it as an all-purpose exception (most Windows unrecoverable application errors—UAEs—are GP faults). While the other exceptions have well-defined meanings, the GP fault is nonspecific. Some possible causes are:

- Writing to a read-only segment
- Using the null selector
- Loading CS with a non-executable segment
- Trying to access a segment with an offset greater than the segment's limit
- Loading any segment register (except CS) with an execute-only segment
- Switching to a busy task
- Attempting I/O when CPL is greater than IOPL

Some common DOS programming practices will cause GP faults in Windows and other protected-mode programs. Microsoft's int86x() library call, for example, writes code on the fly into an array. It then jumps into the array to execute the code. In protected mode, this causes a GP fault since you can't load CS with a data segment selector. However, you can still use the same basic idea: you simply have to generate a code-segment *alias* for the data segment. In Chapter 5, you will see a replacment for Microsoft's ill-mannered int86x() call that does just that.

An operating system or DOS extender may not treat all GP faults as errors. For example, if a ring 3 program executes an input instruction when IOPL is 0, a GP fault will occur. The operating system may examine the instruction causing the fault, and perform the read on the PL3 program's behalf. If the operating system was simulating the device, it would return an appropriate value to the program. One caveat: A simple instruction that causes a GP fault may actually cause tremendous amounts of ring 0 code to execute. A simple instruction like STI might take *much* longer to complete than you would expect, because the instruction is possibly being simulated in software.

Memory Management

The 386 and 486 support advanced memory management via a built-in Memory Management Unit (MMU). The MMU provides support for at least five programming techniques:

- Virtual memory
- Sparse segmentation
- Process separation
- Page protection
- Address translation

The MMU is a very powerful part of the 386's architecture. To activate the MMU, a PL0 program sets bit 31 of CR0. Only PL0 programs can activate and configure the MMU, allowing other programs to manipulate the MMU would defeat the purpose of privilege protection. Use of the MMU is optional, some protected-mode systems never activate the MMU. (See Figure 4-2b.)

The MMU deals with memory in 4K byte pages. For each 4K page, the MMU tracks three basic pieces of information:

1. Whether the page is present in memory
2. The page's physical address (when present)
3. The page's access level (see page 60)

Virtual Memory

Virtual memory systems can use the MMU's present bit. If a page is not present when a program tries to access it, the 386 generates an error (exception 0xE; see Table 4-4). The operating system can then load the page from disk.

Systems that provide virtual memory on the 286 must swap entire segments. When a memory fault (exception 0xB) occurs, the operating system must load the segment in memory (possibly swapping out other segments), mark it as present, and restart the operation.

Segment swapping is usually less efficient than working with 4K pages. The system may be forced to swap many small segments to make room for incoming segments. Worse, a large segment (say, 64K) could take significantly longer to swap in and out than a 4K page. In 32-bit protected mode, segment swapping is impractical. Few systems could afford the overhead required to swap a 4G segment.

Sparse Segmentation

There is another reason that segment swapping is impractical in 32-bit mode. A segment-based virtual memory scheme must fit an entire segment in memory at once. This prevents creating segments larger than the machine's physical memory.

Why would you want segments larger than physical memory? Consider Figure 4-10, which shows an imaginary DOS extender's logical memory map (or operating system memory map, if you prefer). Notice that user programs start at address 0 and can grow to the top of the stack. The stack starts at 3G and grows down. The operating system starts at 3G and grows up. This has several advantages.

Figure 4-10. Sample 386 Memory Map

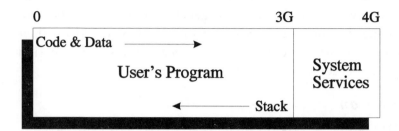

As the program loads, the extender allocates 4K pages for it. It also creates additional stack pages as needed. The space between the program and the stack doesn't exist in physical memory. Instead, physical pages fill the space as the program needs it.

This memory scheme also simplifies the system service routines. When the user program calls a system service, it may need to pass a pointer to a data buffer. With the memory map in Figure 4-10, the system services will use a data segment that has the same base address as the user's data segment. However, its limit will be 4G instead of 3G. This allows the system services to access its private data and user data without recalculating the supplied offsets or switching between segments.

Process Separation

Assume that our hypothetical system (in Figure 4-10) allows multitasking. The MMU allows each task to have its own memory map. Each program would start at its own address 0. Even if it wrote to every byte of memory in its space, it couldn't write over another program's code or data.

Of course, the MMU can map one or more 4K pages into multiple address spaces. For example, many system service pages could be mapped into every task's address space. Common shared pages also can allow tasks to communicate with each other.

Page Protection

A page can have an access level that identifies it as a system page or a user page. Any program can use a user page, but. PL3 programs can't access a system page. Even if a page is a user page, the MMU can prevent PL3 programs from writing to it by controlling the page's R/W (Read/Write) bit.

This protection is in addition to that provided by segmentation. Programs use logical addresses (a segment and an offset). The 386 adds the base address of the segment to the offset to generate a linear address. Programs can only generate linear addresses in certain ranges, based on their access to segments. The MMU converts these linear addresses to physical addresses. The MMU's access bits protect linear addresses.

Address Translation

The MMU uses two types of tables to translate addresses. The page directory contains physical pointers to page tables (see Figures 4-11 and 4-12). Each table has 1,024 four-bytes entries (4K bytes). A page directory entry (PDE) corresponds to 4M of contiguous memory; a page table entry (PTE) corresponds to a 4K page.

When a program uses a segment selector and an offset (a logical address), the CPU finds the base address of the segment (from its descriptor) and adds the offset to create a linear address. If the MMU is inactive, this linear address is the physical address. That is, the CPU uses it directly to address memory. When the MMU is active, it translates the linear address to a physical address.

Figure 4-11. Page Directory Entry

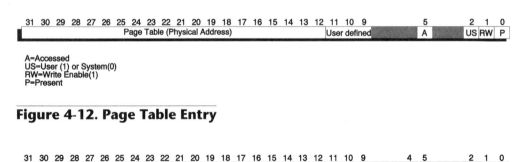

31 30 29 28 27 26 25 24 23 22 21 20 19 18 17 16 15 14 13 12	11 10 9	5	2 1 0
Page Table (Physical Address)	User defined	A	US RW P

A=Accessed
US=User (1) or System(0)
RW=Write Enable(1)
P=Present

Figure 4-12. Page Table Entry

31 30 29 28 27 26 25 24 23 22 21 20 19 18 17 16 15 14 13 12	11 10 9	4 5	2 1 0
Page Table (Physical Address)	User defined	D A	US RW P

D=Dirty
A=Accessed
US=User (1) or System(0)
RW=Write Enable(1)
P=Present

To translate a linear address, the MMU divides it into three fields. The first field (bits 31 to 22) selects one PDE. That PDE points to a page table (via a physical address). The second field (bits 21 to 12) selects one PTE from the page table. The physical address's bottom 12 bits are from the third field (bits 11 to 0 of the linear address). The remaining bits come from the selected PTE.

The page directory base register (the PDBR field in CR3) contains the physical address of the current page directory. Since the page directory holds 1,024 entries, and each entry corresponds to 4M, the directory spans the entire 4-G address range. Each task may have its own CR3 register in its TSS (see Figure 4-6).

Process separation is possible because of these independent CR3 registers. However, many operating systems (including Windows) maintain one page directory and set every task's CR3 register to that value. This effectively subverts the process separation mechanism, in exchange for better performance and simpler operation.

There is a cache (the translation-loakaside buffer, or TLB) which the processor uses for linear-to-physical translation, to avoid the overhead of accessing page tables on every memory read and write. Reloading CR3 invalidates this cache.

Each PDE has a set of protection bits. If the system bit is zero, the entire 4M range is inaccessible to PL3 programs. The PDE's R/W bit also affects the entire 4M range. The MMU ignores the PTE bits if the PDE protects a page.

Handling Page Faults

The MMU generates exception 0x0E when a page fault occurs. Attempting to access a page when any of the following conditions are true will cause a page fault:

- The PDE's present bit is clear
- The PTE's present bit is clear
- A PL3 task tried to write to a read-only page
- A PL3 task tried to access a system page

The error code on the stack (see Figure 4-13) identifies the cause. Also, the CR2 register (see Figure 4-2b) will contain the linear address of the fault. The operating system uses this address to locate the page in virtual storage. When the present bit is 0, all other bits in the PTE or PDE are available for the operating system's use. This allows the operating system to store data about the absent page table or page (for example, a disk address).

Absent PDEs can reduce the amount of memory the MMU requires. Let's take one last look at our hypothetical DOS extender. It allows each task a virtual memory space of 4 Gs. The MMU tables alone for each task would require more than 4M of storage. A 4M overhead would make our extender prohibitive for most computers. Yet, most tasks probably don't use the entire 4 Gs of space, and certainly none use it all at once. A task can start out with a 4K page directory with no present entries. When it accesses a page, the operating system can create the corresponding page table. If the task uses many page tables, they can be swapped to and from disk by manipulating the present bits in the page directory (note that page tables are 4K in size, just like pages).

Figure 4-13. Page Fault Error Code

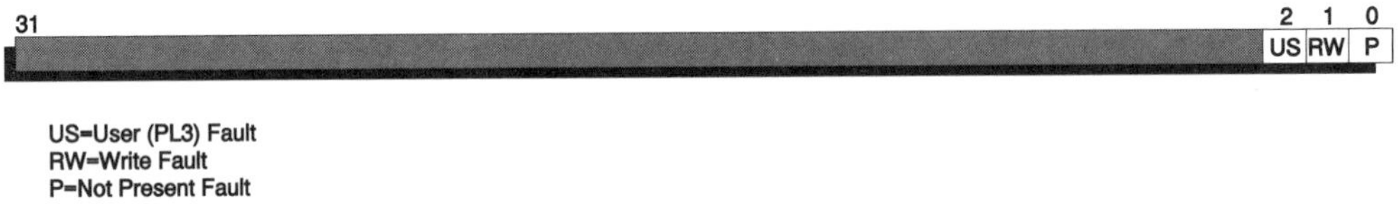

US=User (PL3) Fault
RW=Write Fault
P=Not Present Fault

Addressing Review

Let's review how programs form protected-mode addresses. Programs specify addresses via a segment and an offset (a logical address). Then the following algorithm computes the required physical address:

1. The CPU locates the segment descriptor that corresponds to the specified selector.
2. The processor forms a linear address by adding the segment base address (from the descriptor) and the program-supplied offset.
3. The MMU uses the top 10 bits of the linear address to select a page directory entry. This entry points to a page table.
4. The MMU uses the next 10 bits of the linear address to select one page table entry.
5. The MMU forms the physical address by concatenating the 20-bit page address from the PTE and the last 12 bits in the linear address.

Of course, this algorithm assumes that all PTEs are present. Real systems must also swap in PTEs when required. Also remeber that all linear addresses are in fact first checked in the TLB—otherwise, every memory read or write would require two more reads, to the page directory and page table!

On the 286, the linear address is the same as the physical address—there is no MMU. The same applies when the 386 MMU is inactive (see bit 31 of CR0).

Of course, paging (and the other features we have discussed) won't work until the CPU is in protected mode. Your DOS extender takes care of this for you, but it is still useful to learn a little about the required steps.

Mode Switching

When the processor is reset, it begins in real mode. Switching to protected mode involves, at minimum, the following steps:

1. Detect a CPU capable of running in protected mode
2. Detect any protected-mode environment (DPMI or VCPI)
3. Build an IDT
4. Build a GDT

5. Disable interrupts (including NMI, the motherboard supports NMI disable))

6. Load GDTR

7. Set IDTR

8. Set bit 0 of MSWR (CR0 on the 386/486)

9. Flush instruction prefetch queue (near JMP)

10. Load segment registers

11. Enable interrupts

If DPMI or VCPI is present, they will handle the details of switching to protected mode—the other steps are not strictly required. The extender will use the APIs these environments provide to perform the switch.

Of course, there are other steps you might perform while switching modes (build an LDT, set up MMU tables, enable the processor's A20 address line, or reprogram hardware interrupts.). If you would like to learn more about the actual steps required to switch to protected mode, refer to the bibliography (or read on to find out where to get the source code to several complete extenders).

Once the 286 switches to protected mode, only a processor reset can return it to real mode. This is a problemfor DOS extenders, which often need to switch between protected and real mode. The AT motherboard has special circuitry that provides a solution that became famous during the days of OS/2 1.x. When a protected-mode program wants to return to real mode, it places a special signature in a reserved location in the motherboard's CMOS RAM. It also stores the address where real-mode execution is to resume.

When the AT BIOS gains control after a reset, it examines the CMOS RAM. If it finds the signature, it recognizes that the reset originated from a protected-mode program that wants to return to real mode. It then transfers control to the address specified in the CMOS RAM.

Luckily, the 386 and 486 can switch from protected to real mode. A protected-mode program can return to real mode by performing the following operations:

1. Disable interrupts (including NMI, if possible)

2. Disable paging (if paging was on)

3. Set data segment registers to pseudo-real-mode selectors

4. Reset bit 0 of MSWR (CR0 on the 386/486)

5. Flush prefetch queue (near JMP)

6. Set IDTR to 0000:03FF

7. Enable interrupts

A pseudo-real-mode selector is a code or data segment that has a 64K limit, byte granularity, is present, and is writeable. If you fail to load the segment registers with pseudo-real-mode selectors, your real-mode code will behave erratically or fail. (Look up SEG4G in *DOS 5: A developer's Guide* for a way to exploit this "mistake.")

Further Study

If you want to learn more about protected mode, you'll need the Intel manuals on the CPUs you are interested in programming. *The Programmer's Reference Manual* is designed for application programmers and the *Operating Systems Writer's Guide* covers the rougher topics (see the bibliography for a complete listing). There are also at least two DOS extenders that you can easily obtain the source code for. One is PROT, the DOS extender that appears in my book *DOS 5: A Developer's Guide*. This extender uses V86 mode to handle interrupts and supports multitasking. GNU C/C++ for DOS comes with a mode-switching DOS extender in source code form (see Chapter 3).

Part II:
DOS Extenders and Windows in Detail

CHAPTER ■ 5

Dipping into DPMI

The DOS Protected Mode Interface (DPMI) allows DOS extended programs to cooperate with each other and with operating environments like Microsoft Windows. If a DPMI host is present, a DOS extender must use it instead of other methods to switch to protected mode, allocate protected-mode memory, and manipulate protected-mode interrupts. While DPMI provides important functions, don't think that DPMI is a DOS extender. The extender must still translate addresses, copy data for DOS calls, and provide important APIs to control operation.

Although you will usually access DPMI indirectly (via the Windows API or your extender), there are times when you may need to use some DPMI services explicitly. This chapter will examine methods for accessing DPMI. You will see specific DPMI functions used throughout this book.

With the overwhelming acceptance of Windows in the PC marketplace, you can't afford to ignore DPMI compatibility. If the extender you are using won't coexist with DPMI, your protected-mode programs won't be able to run in the Windows enhanced mode DOS box (there is no DPMI support for DOS boxes in standard mode). Many other operating systems (like OS/2 2.0) also support DPMI while still other systems plan to support it in the future.

Protected-mode programs that use DPMI services are DPMI clients. A program, like Windows, that supplies DPMI services is a DPMI server or host. Clients communicate with the host via interrupts (primarily interrupt 0x31).

Windows programs in standard and enhanced mode can always call DPMI functions. If your DOS extender is DPMI compliant, your DOS-extender programmay be able to make DPMI calls to allocate memory, execute real-mode code, and perform other useful tasks. Some DPMI extenders offer no alternatives to these calls. When no external DPMI host is present, the extender assumes the role of the host (however, some do not support a complete DPMI interface). Table 5-1 shows a summary of the most common DPMI calls. You can find a more complete list, along with details about calling these functions, in Appendix B.

Table 5-1. Common DPMI Calls

Function	Description
0x0000	Allocate descriptor
0x0001	Free descriptor
0x0003	Get selector increment value
0x0007	Set segment base address
0x0008	Set segment limit
0x0009	Set segment access rights
0x0100	Allocate DOS memory block
0x0101	Free DOS memory block
0x0102	Resize DOS memory block
0x0200	Get real-mode interrupt vector
0x0201	Set real-mode interrupt vector
0x0202	Get processor exection handler vector
0x0203	Set processor exection handler vector
0x0204	Get protected-mode interrupt vector
0x0205	Set protected-mode interrupt vector
0x0300	Simulate real-mode interrupt
0x0301	Call real-mode procedure (far return)

Table 5-1. Common DPMI Calls (cont.)

Function	Description
0x0302	Call real-mode procedure (IRET return)
0x0303	Allocate real-mode callback
0x0304	Free real-mode callback
0x0400	Get DPMI version information
0x0500	Get free memory information
0x0501	Allocate memory
0x0502	Free memory block
0x0503	Resize memory block
0x0600	Lock region
0x0601	Unlock region
0x0900	Get and disable interrupt state
0x0901	Get and enable interrupt state
0x0902	Get interrupt state

The DPMI Connection

When a DOS extender begins execution, it examines the system to find any protected-mode environments that are already present. If it finds a DPMI (or VCPI) host, the extender must use it to manage protected-mode execution. If no host is present, the extender may load its own host, or use its own methods to switch modes, allocate memory, etc.

DPMI comes in several flavors. Version 0.9 is the earliest and by far most widely available. However, not all extenders and hosts support the entire standard. Also, some 0.9 hosts (like Windows) support selected version 1.0 features. Avoid using host-specific features—you should not assume the program will always run with the same host.

Detecting and Calling DPMI

Never directly call DPMI to do anything your extender can do for you. That way, the extender can determine if DPMI is present or not and act accordingly. Before you directly call DPMI, you must ascertain that a DPMI host is active.

Some extenders (Rational's 4G/W, for example) allow you to call a subset of the DPMI interface even when no DPMI host is present (i.e., the extender provides a subset of INT 0x31 services). Others (like Windows or Ergo DPM/16) provide a full DPMI host. In these environments, you may safely request supported DPMI services without checking for a host. Remember, Windows in standard mode only supplies DPMI for Windows programs. DOS programs that run in a Windows DOS box should still check for a DPMI host.

Detecting DPMI from real mode is simple. You can use interrupt 0x2F function 0x1687 to find if DPMI is present and learn some details about the host. Listing 5-1 shows a short real-mode program that illustrates this interrupt. Some programs use another DPMI function (interrupt 0x2f, function 0x1686) to detect a DPMI host. The function determines the CPU mode if a DPMI host is present. The function returns 0 in the AX register if the CPU is in protected mode. Calling this function from a protected mode program should yield a 0 if DPMI is present. While this usually works, the DPMI specification warns against it. Interrupt 0x2F is shared by many TSR programs and DOS. Some unknown program could erroneously respond to the call and give you false results.

Listing 5-1. DPMI.C

```
/* Real mode program to detect DPMI
   Borland: bcc dpmi.c
   Microsoft: cl dpmi.c
*/
#include <stdio.h>
#include <stdlib.h>
#include <dos.h>


void main()
  {
  union REGS r;
  struct SREGS s;
  segread(&s);
```

```c
/* use INT 0x2F function 0x1687 to detect DPMI */
  r.x.ax=0x1687;
  int86x(0x2f,&r,&r,&s);

/* if AX non-zero, no DPMI */
  if (r.x.ax)
    {
    printf("DPMI not present.\n");
    exit(1);
    }

/* DH and DL contain the version number */
  printf("DPMI version %d.%d detected.\n",r.h.dh,r.h.dl);

/* if bit 0 of BX is set then 32-bit else 16-bit */
  if (r.x.bx&1)
    printf("32-bit support detected.\n");

/* CL contains code for processor type */
  printf("Processor=%s.\n",
      r.h.cl==2?"80286":
        (r.h.cl==3?"80386":
        (r.h.cl==4?"80486":"Unknown")));

/* DPMI hosts may require a private data area for its
   own purposes. The size of this area in paragraphs
   (16 bytes) is in SI */
  printf("This host requires %d "
      "paragraphs of private data.\n",r.x.si);

/* Entry point in ES:DI -- calling this address will switch
   you to protected mode */
  printf("Entry point =%04X:%04X.\n",s.es,r.x.di);
  exit(0);
  }
```

Your DOS extended program can't directly call interrupt 0x2F to detect DPMI—the call is only valid from real mode. However, you can issue a real-mode interrupt using one of the services described in Chapter 10. Listing 5-2 shows how to detect DPMI under Phar Lap's 286 extender.

Listing 5-2. DPMIT.C

```
/* Detecting DPMI with Phar Lap 286|DOS Extender
   Borland: bcc286 dpmit.c
   Microsoft: cl -AL -G2 -Lp dpmit.c

   Note: Some DPMI hosts turn off when they detect
   the Phar Lap extender start up to prevent conflicts.
   (QDPMI does this when its XCHK flag is set, for example).
   In these cases, it will appear that DPMI is not present
   unless you disable this behavior in the host.
*/

#include <stdio.h>
#include <phapi.h>
#include <string.h>

void main()
  {
  REGS16 r;
/* zero out registers */
  memset(&r,0,sizeof(REGS16));
/* set AX to 0x1687 and issue real mode INT 0x2F */
  r.ax=0x1687;
  DosRealIntr(0x2f,&r,0,0);
/* return status in AX */
  if (r.ax)
    printf("No DPMI host detected\n");
  else
    printf("DPMI present\n");
/* See DPMI.C for more info on return values */
  }
```

Extenders that never switch to real mode (Intel Code Builder, for example), will never detect DPMI using interrupt 0x2F. Instead, they must provide a call or flag that you can test. For Code Builder, you can test the GDA_DPMI flag in the gda_env member of the _gda structure. Here is a code fragment that will do the trick:

```
#include <extender.h>
extern _GDA *_gda;
main()
```

```
{
if (_gda->gda_env&GDA_DPMI) dpmi_exists();
   .
   .
   .
```

You call most DPMI functions via interrupt 0x31 from protected mode. The AX register contains a function code; other registers may hold parameters, depending on the function. Various extenders provide a C language interface for some functions, but you can always use the int86() or int86x() functions, too.

DPMI and Windows

Windows programs rarely need to call DPMI directly. Instead, you can use the Windows API to allocate and lock memory, reserve DOS memory, and so on. Microsoft documents seven DPMI functions that you may have occasion to call from a Windows 3.1 program (see Table 5-2). However, you can (and eventually will) call other DPMI functions. If a Windows API function duplicates the DPMI call, it is usually easier to use the Windows API. For Windows 3.0 programs, you may need to resort to DPMI more often. Some of the DPMI-like functions in the Windows API were undocumented in Windows 3.0. Of course, you can use the undocumented functions if you know how (see *Undocumented Windows* in the bibliography).

Table 5-2. DPMI Calls for Windows Programs

Function	Description
0x0200	Get real-mode interrupt vector
0x0201	Set real-mode interrupt vector
0x0300	Simulate real-mode interrupt
0x0301	Call real-mode far procedure
0x0302	Call real-mode interrupt procedure
0x0303	Allocate callback
0x0304	Free callback

Integral to the Windows DPMI host is the Windows DOS extender (DOSX.EXE for 16-bit and the DOSMGR VxD inside WIN386.EXE for 32-bit). The Windows DOS extenders support most, but not all, standard DOS calls. Table 5-3 shows the DOS calls Windows does not support in protected-mode. Most of these are outdated calls that you should avoid, anyway. Windows does support interrupt 0x21 functions 0x25 and 0x35 (these set and read interrupt vectors). However, under Windows, these functions operate on the protected-mode interrupt table, not the real-mode vectors. You will need to use DPMI functions 0x0200 and 0x0201 to manage real-mode interrupts (see Chapter 9 for more about interrupts).

Table 5-3. Windows Unsupported Interrupt Functions

Interrupt	Function	Description	Comments
0x20	N/A	Terminate program	Use interrupt 0x21 function 0x4C
0x21	0	Terminate program	Use interrupt 0x21 function 0x4C
0x21	0x0	FCB file open	Use handle I/O instead of FCB functions
0x21	0x10	FCB file close	
0x21	0x14	FCB sequential read	
0x21	0x15	FCB sequential write	
0x21	0x16	FCB file create	
0x21	0x21	FCB random read	
0x21	0x22	FCB random write	
0x21	0x23	FCB file size	
0x21	0x24	FCB set random record number	
0x21	0x27	FCB random block read	
0x21	0x28	FCB random block write	
0x25	N/A	Direct disk read	

Table 5-3. Windows Unsupported Interrupt Functions (cont.)

Interrupt	Function	Description	Comments
0x26	N/A	Direct disk write	
0x27	N/A	Terminate and stay resident	

An Example

Calling any DPMI service from a protected-mode program is as simple as issuing an interrupt 0x31 with the proper numbers in the registers. Real-mode programs can't use DPMI (except to detect its presence as shown in Listing 5-1). Listing 5-3 is a simple Windows program (MEMINFO.C) that uses DPMI services to learn about the current state of protected-mode memory.

Listing 5-3. MEMINFO.C

```
/* Use DPMI to learn Windows memory statistics
Compile with:
Borland:
BWINCOMP MEMINFO

Microsoft:
MWINCOMP MEMINFO
*/

#include <dos.h>
#include "winpmode.h"
struct
  {
  unsigned long maxfree_block;
  unsigned long unlock_max;
  unsigned long locked_max;
  unsigned long lin_size;
  unsigned long unlock_total;
  unsigned long free_total;
  unsigned long physical;
```

```
   unsigned long lin_free;
   unsigned long pgfile_size;
   char reserved[12];
   } meminfo;

char *test()
   {
   union REGS r;
   struct SREGS s;
   char _far *buffer=(char _far *)&meminfo;
   segread(&s);
   r.x.ax=0x500;
   s.es=FP_SEG(buffer);
   r.x.di=FP_OFF(buffer);
   int86x(0x31,&r,&r,&s);
   win_printf("Free Memory Information",
      "Largest Free Block: %lu (bytes)   Free Pages: %lu",
      meminfo.maxfree_block, meminfo.free_total);
   win_printf("Virtual Memory Information",
      "Number of pages in page file=%lu",
      meminfo.pgfile_size);
   win_printf("Linear Memory Information",
      "Linear Address Size: %lu (pages)  Free: %lu (pages)",
      meminfo.lin_size,meminfo.lin_free);
   return "Done";
   }
```

MEMINFO.C uses PMWIN.C (Listing 5-4) and PMWIN.H (Listing 5-5) to deal with Windows specifics. WINPMODE.H (Listing 5-6) is a header that programs like MEMINFO use to pick up PMWIN's prototypes. Many of the example programs later in this book use PMWIN.C. You will find PMWIN handy for your own experiments, too. See the sidebar, *Compiling and Running the Windows Examples* for more details about PMWIN.

PMWIN.C ensures that your program is in protected mode, so MEMINFO doesn't need to check for a DPMI server. If you want to use DPMI from a normal Windows program that might run under Windows 3.0, you should check for protected mode, too. This is easily accomplished with the GetWinFlags() function that Windows provides. The WF_PMODE flag will be set when the processor is in protected mode. Windows 3.1

always runs in protected mode, so if you know you are running under Windows 3.1, you don't need to make the protected-mode check.

MEMINFO uses DPMI function 0x500 to obtain information about the DPMI memory system. From there, it is a simple matter to read the contents from the buffer and display them. The win_printf( ) function that PMWIN.C provides displays the results.

DPMI 1.0

The newest version of the DPMI specification, version 1.0, has better support for virtual memory, multitasking, and resident programs and it is backward compatible with DPMI 0.9 programs.

Two obvious changes to version 1.0 are simple improvements to the 0.9 host. All 1.0 functions return error codes in the AX register when they fail. The 0.9 host sets the carry flag when an error occurs. While you still need to check the carry flag, the error code now gives you more information about the failure.

The other elementary difference is the way a 1.0 host treats client programs. Under DPMI 1.0, each protected-mode program has its own LDT and IDT. The 1.0 host provides functions to allocate and manipulate shared memory allowing you to communicate with other DPMI programs.

Windows 3.1 implements DPMI 0.9—aa this book is being written there are no DPMI 1.0 hosts commercially available. Still, if you understand DPMI 0.9, you will have no problem when a 1.0 host finally appears.

DPMI and You

Today, programmers can't afford to ignore DPMI. Protected-mode programs that will run under Windows (even if they are not Windows programs) must cooperate with DPMI. You can think of interrupt 0x31 (DPMI) as the standard interface to protected-mode DOS, just as interrupt 0x21 is the way to talk to real-mode DOS.

COMPILING AND RUNNING THE WINDOWS EXAMPLES

Most of the Microsoft Windows examples in this book use the PMWIN framework (see Listings 5-4 through 5-11) allowing the programs to focus on protected-mode specifics rather than Windows user interface issues.

To compile a program named EXAMPLE.C, use one of the following command lines:

Borland:

```
BWINCOMP example
```

Microsoft:

```
MWINCOMP example
```

Listings 5-10 and 5-11 contain BWINCOMP.BAT and MWIN-COMP.BAT.

Pick the "Run Program" selection (see Figure 5-1) in the File menu to run the example program. You can run the program as often as you wish; then exit from the File menu, or with the system close box.

Use PMWIN to try your own programs out, too. The program must supply a function, test(), that PMWIN will call when you select the "Run Program" menu item. The test() function takes no arguments and returns a character pointer. PMWIN displays the string that test() returns. The WINDOSX.H file (Listing 5-7) contains the definitions your program needs.

If you need to do other input or output during your experiment, use the win_printf() and win_input() functions. The win_printf() functions's first argument is a window title. PMWIN will displays this title on the window used to show your output. The remaining arguments work exactly like a normal printf().

continued

continued

The win_input() routine takes the same arguments as win_printf(). PMWIN uses the output as a prompt string, and allows you to enter text in a dialog box. The return value of win_input() is a character pointer to a static buffer that contains the input string.

Both win_input() and win_printf() use small static buffers for work space. Therefore, do not let any strings you use with these functions exceed 512 bytes.

If you are a Windows programmer, you might be interested to know that win_printf() uses a simple call to MessageBox() so that Windows does most of the dirty work. The win_input() routine is slightly more complicated—it uses a custom dialog. PMWIN programs are not as well behaved as normal Windows programs (they only yield while calling win_input() or win_printf()), but they have the virtue of simplicity.

Microsoft's int86x() function does not work for Windows programs; Borland's does. Microsoft users must use MSCINT.C (Listing 5-6) to replace Microsoft's int86x() function. MSCINT.C relies on small model, assumes that DS is always the program's default data segent, and does not properly handle interrupts 0x25 and 0x26 (these interrupts do not clean up the stack properly). Since all of the Windows programs in this book, this poses no problem.

If you examine Microsoft's int86x() code, you will see that it dynamically constructs a subroutine on the stack and jumps to it. In protected mode you can not execute from a data segment, so a general protection fault occurs. The routine in MSCINT.C does the same thing, but it uses AllocDStoCSAlias() to create a code segment alias for the data segment. The int86x() function uses this alias to call the subroutine on the stack.

The same technique would work with a pure DPMI program (one that doesn't require the Windows API). The Windows GlobalFix() and GlobalUnfix() calls would change to DPMI functions 0x600 and 0x601, respectively. The AllocDStoCSAlias() function requires two

continued

> continued
>
> DPMI calls, function 0xA (Create Alias) to make a data segment alias, and function 9 (Set Descriptor Access Rights) to transform the new data segment into a code segment. Finally, the FreeSelector() call translates into DPMI function 1. ■

Figure 5-1. Run Program

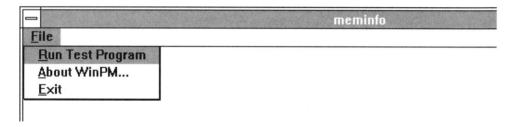

Listing 5-4. PMWIN.C

```c
/* Window test frame
   compile with
   Borland: BWINCOMP appname
   Microsoft: MWINCOMP appname
*/
#include <windows.h>
#include <stdlib.h>
#include <stdarg.h>
#include "pmwin.h"

#define MKSTR(x) #x
#define STR(x) MKSTR(x)

#ifndef TITLE
#define PMWIN_TITLE "Protected Mode Test Bed"
#else
#define PMWIN_TITLE STR(TITLE)
#endif
```

```
HANDLE hInst;
HWND topwindow;

/* user's function */
char *test(void);
/* stray prototype */
int vsprintf(char *s,char *fmt,...);



/* Main window function */
int PASCAL WinMain(HANDLE hInstance, HANDLE hPrevInstance,
                   LPSTR lpCmdLine, int nCmdShow)
    {
    MSG msg;
/* check for protected mode */
    if (!(GetWinFlags()&WF_PMODE))
        {
        MessageBox(NULL,"You must run " PMWIN_TITLE
                        " in standard or enhanced mode",
                        "Error",MB_OK|MB_ICONSTOP);

        }

    if (!hPrevInstance)
        {
        if (!InitApplication(hInstance))
/* Exit if unable to initialize */
            return FALSE;
        }
    else
        {
/* Only allow one copy to run since some interrupt routines
   that we will experiment with want to run alone */
        MessageBox(NULL,"You may only run one "
                        "copy of " PMWIN_TITLE " at a time",
                        "Error",MB_OK|MB_ICONSTOP);
        return FALSE;
        }
    /* Perform instance init */
    if (!InitInstance(hInstance, nCmdShow))
        return FALSE;
```

```
    /* Vanilla loop */
    while (GetMessage(&msg,NULL,NULL,NULL))
        {
        TranslateMessage(&msg);
        DispatchMessage(&msg);
        }
    return (msg.wParam);
    }




/* Create window class here */
BOOL InitApplication(HANDLE hInstance)
    {
    WNDCLASS  wc;
    wc.style=NULL;
    wc.lpfnWndProc=(void _far *)MainWndProc;
    wc.cbClsExtra=0;
    wc.cbWndExtra=0;
    wc.hInstance=hInstance;
    wc.hIcon=LoadIcon(NULL, IDI_APPLICATION);
    wc.hCursor=LoadCursor(NULL, IDC_ARROW);
    wc.hbrBackground=GetStockObject(WHITE_BRUSH);
    wc.lpszMenuName= "WinPMMenu";
    wc.lpszClassName="WPM_Class";
    return (RegisterClass(&wc));
    }




/* Create window here */
BOOL InitInstance(HANDLE hInstance, int nCmdShow)
    {
    HWND             hWnd;
    /* Save the instance handle in global variable */
    hInst=hInstance;

    /* Create a main window */
    topwindow=hWnd=CreateWindow(
        "WPM_Class",
        PMWIN_TITLE,
        WS_OVERLAPPEDWINDOW,
```

```
              CW_USEDEFAULT,
              CW_USEDEFAULT,
              CW_USEDEFAULT,
              CW_USEDEFAULT,
              NULL,
              NULL,
              hInstance,
              NULL
         );

    if (!hWnd)
         return FALSE;

/* Make the window visible, update its client area,
    and return "success" */
    ShowWindow(hWnd, nCmdShow);
    UpdateWindow(hWnd);
    return (TRUE);
    }


/* Window procedure */
long FAR PASCAL _export MainWndProc(HWND hWnd, WORD message,
                         WORD wParam, LONG lParam)
    {
/* pointer for "About" function */
    FARPROC lpProcAbout;

    switch (message)
        {
        case WM_COMMAND:
            if (wParam==IDM_ABOUT)
                {
                lpProcAbout=MakeProcInstance(About, hInst);
                DialogBox(hInst,"AboutBox",hWnd,lpProcAbout);
                FreeProcInstance(lpProcAbout);
                break;
                }
            else if (wParam==IDM_TEST)
                {
/* Run user's program */
                MessageBox(hWnd,test(),"Test result",MB_OK);
```

```
                break;
                }
        else if (wParam==IDM_STOP)
            {
            DestroyWindow(hWnd);
            }
        else
            return (DefWindowProc(hWnd, message,
                    wParam, lParam));

    case WM_DESTROY:
        PostQuitMessage(0);
        break;

    default:
        return (DefWindowProc(hWnd, message,
                wParam, lParam));
    }
    return NULL;
    }


/* Ordinary about box */
BOOL FAR PASCAL _export About(HWND hDlg, unsigned message,
                    WORD wParam, LONG lParam)
    {
    switch (message)
      {
      case WM_INITDIALOG:
            return (TRUE);

        case WM_COMMAND:
            if (wParam==IDOK|| wParam==IDCANCEL)
                {
                EndDialog(hDlg, TRUE);
                return (TRUE);
                }
            break;
      }
    return FALSE;
    }
```

```c
/* buffers for I/O dialogs */
static char print_buf[513];
static char in_buf[513];

/* Sort of a printf for user's program -- maximum output
   is 512 characters */
int win_printf(char *title,char *fmt,...)
  {
  int rc;
  va_list alist;
  va_start(alist,fmt);
  rc=vsprintf(print_buf,fmt,alist);
  if (rc!=-1)
    MessageBox(NULL,print_buf,title?title:"Output",MB_OK);
  return rc;
  }




/* Dialog callback for input function */
BOOL FAR PASCAL _export inp_dlg(HWND hDlg, unsigned message,
                      WORD wParam, LONG lParam)
    {
    switch (message)
      {
      case WM_INITDIALOG:
/* Set title */
          SendMessage(hDlg,WM_SETTEXT,0,lParam);
/* Set prompt */
          SetDlgItemText(hDlg,101,print_buf);
          return (TRUE);

        case WM_COMMAND:
            if (wParam==IDOK)
              {
/* read input */
              GetDlgItemText(hDlg,102,in_buf,sizeof(in_buf));
              EndDialog(hDlg, TRUE);
              return (TRUE);
              }
            break;
      }
```

```c
   return FALSE;
    }


/* line input for user's program
   title is the dialog title -- the
   remaining arguments are used as a prompt */
char *win_input(char *title,char *fmt,...)
  {
  FARPROC dlgfunc;
  int rc;
  va_list alist;
  va_start(alist,fmt);
/* print prompt to print_buf */
  rc=vsprintf(print_buf,fmt,alist);
  if (rc!=-1)
     {
     dlgfunc=MakeProcInstance(inp_dlg,hInst);
     if (!dlgfunc)
        win_printf("Error","MakeProcInstance failed");
     else
        {
/* call dialog */
        rc=DialogBoxParam(hInst,"InputBox",topwindow,
           dlgfunc,(long)title);
        FreeProcInstance(dlgfunc);
        }
     }
  return in_buf;
  }
```

Listing 5-5. PMWIN.H

```c
/* Header for WIndows test bed
   see PMWIN.C for compile instructions */

#ifndef _PMWIN_H
#define _PMWIN_H

#define IDM_ABOUT 100
#define IDM_STOP 101
```

```
#define IDM_TEST 102

int PASCAL WinMain(HANDLE, HANDLE, LPSTR, int);
BOOL InitApplication(HANDLE);
BOOL InitInstance(HANDLE, int);
long FAR PASCAL _export MainWndProc(HWND, WORD, WORD, LONG);
BOOL FAR PASCAL _export About(HWND, unsigned, WORD, LONG);

#endif
```

Listing 5-6. MSCINT.C

```
/* Windows int86 routines for use with Microsoft C
   in small model. Do not use with INT 0x25 or 0x26 */

#include <dos.h>
#include <windows.h>

/* register structure equates */
#define Res [si]
#define Rds [si+6]
#define Rax [si]
#define Rbx [si+2]
#define Rcx [si+4]
#define Rdx [si+6]
#define Rsi [si+8]
#define Rdi [si+10]
#define Rcfl [si+12]


int int86x(int intno,union REGS *rin,union REGS *rout,
           struct SREGS *s)
  {
  void (_far * pgm)(void);
  char ary[5];
  int rv;   /* return value */
  UINT sel,sel1;  /* general selector values */
  _asm
       {
       push ds
       mov byte ptr ary, 55H     /* push bp */
```

```
        mov byte ptr ary+1, OCDH  /* INT */
        mov ax, intno
        mov byte ptr ary+2, al
        mov word ptr ary+3, 5DH    /* pop bp */
        mov byte ptr ary+4, OCBH   /* ret */
        lea cx, ary
        mov word ptr pgm, cx
        mov sel,ss
        }
/* Fix SS segment. If Windows moves SS for memory management
   reasons, the CS alias we will create won't move with it.
    Fixing it will prevent Windows from moving it. */
  GlobalFix(sel);
  sel1=AllocDStoCSAlias(sel);  /* Get alias for ss */
   _asm
        {
        mov ax,sel1
        mov word ptr pgm+2, ax

        /* Set registers */

        mov si, s
        push Res
        push Rds
        mov si, rin
        mov ax, Rax
        mov bx, Rbx
        mov cx, Rcx
        mov dx, Rdx
        mov di, Rdi
        mov si, Rsi
        pop ds
        pop es
        }
/* Call interrupt */
        (* pgm)();
   _asm
        {
/* Set register structure  */
```

```
        pushf
        push si
        push ds
        push es
        mov ds, [bp-24]
        mov si, s
        pop Res
        pop Rds
        mov si, rout
        pop Rsi
        pop Rcfl
        and word ptr Rcfl, 1
        mov Rdi, di
        mov Rdx, dx
        mov Rcx, cx
        mov Rbx, bx
        mov Rax, ax
        push ax        /* save AX */
        }
/* free alias selector */
    FreeSelector(sel1);
/* unfix ss */
        GlobalUnfix(sel);
    _asm
        {
        pop ax        /* restore AX */
        pop ds
/* Just in case */
        mov rv,ax
        }
    return(rv);
    }


int int86(int intno,union REGS *rin,union REGS *rout)
    {
    struct SREGS s;
    segread(&s);
    return int86x(intno,rin,rout,&s);
    }
```

Listing 5-7. WINDOSX.H

```
/* Header for programs that use PMWIN.C */
int win_printf(char *title,char *fmt,...);
char *win_input(char *title,char *fmt,...);
```

Listing 5-8. PMWIN.DEF

```
Name            PMWIN
Description     'Protected mode test frame'
Exetype         WINDOWS
Code            PRELOAD MOVEABLE DISCARDABLE
Data            PRELOAD MOVEABLE SINGLE
Heapsize        4096
Stacksize       5120
Stub            'WINSTUB.EXE'
```

Listing 5-9. PMWIN.RC

```
/* Resources for Windows test bed
   see PMWIN.C for instructions */

#include "windows.h"
#include "pmwin.h"

WinPMMenu MENU
BEGIN
    POPUP       "&File"
    BEGIN
        MENUITEM "&Run Test Program",IDM_TEST
        MENUITEM "&About WinPM...",IDM_ABOUT
        MENUITEM "&Exit",IDM_STOP
    END
END

AboutBox DIALOG 22,17,144,75
STYLE DS_MODALFRAME | WS_CAPTION | WS_SYSMENU
CAPTION "About WinPM"
BEGIN
    CTEXT "WinPM"      -1,0,5,144,8
```

```
      CTEXT "By Al Williams" -1,0,14,144,8
      CTEXT "Version 1.0"              -1,0,34,144,8
      DEFPUSHBUTTON "OK"              IDOK,53,59,32,14,WS_GROUP
END


InputBox DIALOG 22,17,144,75
STYLE DS_MODALFRAME | WS_CAPTION | WS_SYSMENU
CAPTION "Input"
BEGIN
   LTEXT "Prompt" 101,0,5,144,32
   EDITTEXT 102,10,34,130,12,WS_TABSTOP | ES_AUTOHSCROLL
   DEFPUSHBUTTON "OK" IDOK,53,59,32,14,WS_GROUP
END
```

Listing 5-10. BWINCOMP.BAT

```
@echo off
REM Compile PMWIN applications with Borland
if .%1==. goto help
if NOT EXIST %1.c goto help
set LIBS=mathws import cws
bcc -WE -2 -v -w-par -c -DTITLE=%1 %1.c pmwin.c
if ERRORLEVEL 1 goto err
tlink -v -x -c -P- -Twe cOws %1 pmwin,%1,,%LIBS%,pmwin.def
if ERRORLEVEL 1 goto err
set LIBS=
rc -t pmwin.rc %1.exe
if ERRORLEVEL 1 goto err
goto end
:help
echo Usage: BWINCOMP fname
echo Do not include the extension for fname
goto end
:err
echo An error occured
:end
```

Listing 5-11. MWINCOMP.BAT

```
@echo off
REM Compile PMWIN applicaitons with Microsoft
if .%1==. goto help
if NOT EXIST %1.c goto help
```

CHAPTER ▪ 6

Stretching Your Data

Since 286 extenders use DOS or OS/2 1.x compilers, they support the same data types used with real-mode DOS. A 386 extender is another matter. There are three major differences between 32-bit data types and 16-bit data types: pointer size, integer size, and data alignment. Table 6-1 shows the standard data types and their characteristics under common 16-bit and 32-bit C compilers. Chapter 7 explores the pointer size difference in detail. This chapter looks at differences in integer size and data alignment.

Table 6-1. Data Types (cont.)

Type	32-bit Size (bytes)	16-bit Size (bytes)
char	1	1
short	2	2
int	4	2
long	4	4
float	4	4
double	8	8
flat pointer	4*	N/A

Table 6-1. Data Types (cont.)

Type	32-bit Size	16-bit Size
near pointer	4*	2
far pointer	6*	4
size_t	4	2

Where applicable

Big Integers, Little Integers

With a 386 compiler, both ints and longs are 32 bits wide—the same width as the general-purpose registers such as EAX (see Figure 4-2a). This gives signed integers a range of -2,147,483,648 to 2,147,483,647; unsigned integers can contain numbers from 0 to 4,294,967,296.

If you want to use a 16-bit integer to conserve space, use the short data type. However, short data types may not save as much space as you think, since in 32-bit code the compiler must generate extra code (16-bit over-rides) to manipulate them. You'll need the short data type when using structures or unions that MS-DOS or other programs define. For example, Figure 6-1 show the format of a DOS Memory Control Block (MCB), which we'll be using as an example later in this chapter. A 32-bit program must refer to the PID and SIZE fields with the short data type.

Conventional DOS compilers also support short and long integers. A DOS short integer is 16 bits long and a long integer contains 32 bits. If you want to simplify porting code between DOS and the 386 environment, use short and long instead of int whenever you want a specific integer size.

If you are porting code from Unix or a similar operating system, watch for code that assumes that pointers are the same size as integers—far pointers on the Intel architecture are never the same size as integers. If you use a 386 extender this isn't a problem. Near pointers are the same size as integers and you will normally not use far pointers when translating Unix code. This greatly simplifies life when moving code from Unix to a 32-bit extender, and in fact is a major reason to use a 32-bit extender in the first place.

Still, it is a good idea not to use pointers and integers interchangeably in new programs. Modern compilers check for proper types, and switching pointers and integers will cause them to complain. Not only is this annoying, but the many compiler warnings may make it harder to notice when the compiler flags legitimate type mismatches.

Figure 6-1. DOS Memory Control Block

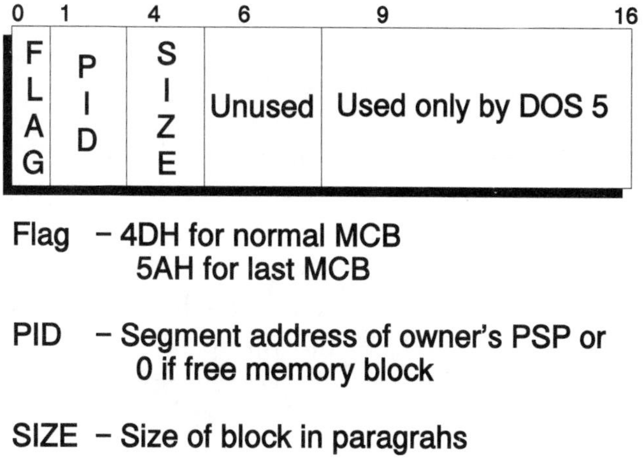
0 1 4 6 9 16
FLAG
PID
SIZE
Unused
Used only by DOS 5
Flag - 4DH for normal MCB
5AH for last MCB
PID - Segment address of owner's PSP or
0 if free memory block
SIZE - Size of block in paragrahs

Extending Size

The standard C library uses a special type, size_t, to represent memory object lengths. Functions like malloc(), fread(), and strlen() use size_t to refer to variables that contain lengths of memory blocks and strings. DOS compilers, both 16- and 32-bit, declare size_t like this:

```
typedef unsigned int size_t;
```

Since a 386 extender's compiler uses int to represent a 32-bit quantity, the 32-bit C library automatically uses 32-bit integers for lengths. This means code like:

```
p=malloc(2000000);
```

is perfectly legal in a 32-bit DOS extender—it may or may not succeed (depending on available memory), but it is legal.

While much is said about the DOS 640K (or 1M) limit, DOS has another limit: the 64K segment limit. A 32-bit extender breaks both of these limits. It allows you to access more memory and access it in arbitrarily sized blocks. We already saw some of this in DFIT386.C (Listing 1-5), which could read and write entire files, including files over 64K bytes long, in a single call.

Alignment

The 386 and 486 perform best when reading 32-bit words that are aligned on a 4-byte boundary. That is, it is quicker to read a word at offset 104H than a word at 102H. Many compilers take advantage of this by aligning structure members on 4-byte boundaries. (The 286 works best when data is aligned on word, or 2-byte, boundaries.) When the compiler aligns a structure, it ensures no data element will span the alignment boundary. The compiler treats array members as separate elements.

Consider the following declaration:

```
struct
    {
    short id;
    long type;
    char name[9];
    long info;
    char c1;
    } namelist[10000];
```

Each structure in the namelist array contains 20 bytes of data. Since a typical 32-bit compiler will align the items on double word boundaries (see Figure 6-2), each structure consumes 28 bytes. In the interest of time efficiency, the compiler wastes 8 bytes of space in each structure.

If you only use one of these structures, this waste is probably accept-able. However, the array of 10,000 items takes up 280,000 bytes, wasting 80,000 bytes. Packing the structure on a word boundary would cut the waste per item to 2 bytes, and packing to the byte would result in no waste.

In cases where the compiler is wasting too much space, you'll want to align the structure differently. How you do this depends on your compiler (see Table 6-2 for details).

Figure 6-2. Example Aligned Structure

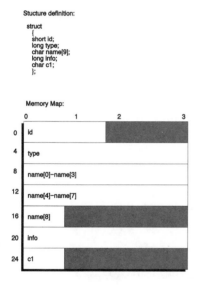

You also may need to change alignment when modeling data structures you don't control, or can't change. For example, Figure 6-1 shows the lay-out of a DOS MCB.

You might be tempted to create a C structure for this control block:

```
struct MCB
  {
  unsigned char flag;
  unsigned short owner;
  unsigned short size;
  char not_used[11];
  };
```

This will not work if the compiler word-aligns the structure. If you allow the compiler to align the structure on 2-byte boundaries, the structure will effectively look like this:

```
struct MCB
  {
  unsigned char flag;
  char __DUMMY1__;
  unsigned short owner;
  unsigned short size;
  char not_used[11];
  char __DUMMY2__;
  };
```

The compiler creates the __DUMMY1__ and __DUMMY2__ structure members; they are not directly accessible to your program. Of course, the DOS MCB doesn't have any holes in it. You must match the existing layout exactly. If you byte-align any externally-defined structures using one of the commands in Table 6-2, you shouldn't have any problems.

Table 6-2. Compiler Alignment Commands (cont.)

Borland

Default:	BYTE	
Switches:	-a	*(WORD)*
	-a-	*(BYTE)*
Pragmas:	#pragma option -a *(WORD)*	
	#pragma option -a- *(BYTE)*	
Keyword:	None	

Microsoft

Default:	WORD	
Switches:	-Zp1	*(BYTE)*
	-Zp2	*(WORD)*
	-Zp4	*(DWORD)*
Pragmas:	#pragma pack(*alignment*)	
Keyword:	None	

Intel

Default:	DWORD
Switches:	-zalign(*struct_name = alignment*)

WATCOM

Default:	BYTE	
Switches:	-Zp1	*(BYTE)*

Table 6-2. Compiler Alignment Commands (cont.)

Intel		WATCOM	
	-znoalign(*struct_name*) (BYTE)		-Zp2 *(WORD)*
			-Zp4 (DWORD)
Pragmas:	#pragma align(*struct_name = alignment*)	**Pragmas:**	#pragma pack(*alignment*)
Keyword:	None	**Keyword:**	None

MetaWare

Default:	DWORD	
Switches:	-Hon=Align_members	*(DWORD)*
	-Hoff=Align_members	(BYTE)
Pragmas:	#pragma On(Align_members)	*(DWORD)*
	#pragma Off(Align_members)	*(BYTE)*
Keyword:	_packed struct	*(BYTE)*
	_unpacked struct	*(DWORD)*

Maintaining Portability

Varying type sizes can hinder portability between real-mode DOS and extended programs. If you want to maintain portable source code, you should follow these guidelines:

- Don't assume the size of any variable; use the sizeof() operator instead. The sizeof operator will return the length, in bytes, of a variable or type. For example:

```
p=(LONG*)malloc(sizeof(long)*10) /* 10 longs */
p=(int *)malloc(sizeof(int)*100); /* 100 ints */
```

- Use the preprocessor or typedefs to define types in a portable way. The preprocessor can cover a multitude of portability problems. You can write:

```
#ifdef __HIGHC__
#define WORD short
#define INT32 int
#else
#define WORD int
#define INT32 long
#endif
```

You could use the typedef statement, instead:

```
#ifdef __HIGHC__
typedef short WORD;
       .
       .
       .
```

- Explicitly use short and long instead of int. As a rule, 16-bit PC compilers treat short and int types as the same size (16 bits), and the long type as 32 bits. A 32-bit PC compiler will use 16 bits for a short, and 32 bits for an int or a long. Since shorts are always 2 bytes wide and longs are always 4, use short or long rather than int where you want a variable with a specific size. Note that compilers on non-PC platforms may not conform to these definitions, but you will have to change your int declarations in those cases anyway.

- Don't rely on fixed-length bit masks to clear bits. Programs often use the & and | operators to set, clear, and test bits in an integer. For instance:

```
flags|=0x100;            /* set bit */
if (flags&0x100)  . . . ;  /* test bit */
flags&=0xFEFF;           /* clear bit */
```

The set and test operations will work on a 16- or 32-bit compiler. The code to clear the bit, however, assumes the flags variable is 16 bits wide. Problems will arise if you port this code to a 32-bit compiler and try to use the upper 16 bits of flags. Every time the original code clears a bit, it also will wipe out the top 16 bits. The correct way to rewrite the last example is:

```
flags&=0xFFFFFEFF;
```

This, however, won't work in the 16-bit code. A better solution is:

```
flags&=~0x100;
```

This has two advantages. First, the code now works correctly, regardless of the size of flags. Second, the constant (0x100) refers to the cleared bit, not a mask. Modern compilers will compute ~0x100 at compile time, so there isn't any performance penalty. You also can hide these operations with the preprocessor. For example:

```
#define SET_BIT(f,b) ((f)|=1<<(b))
#define CLR_BIT(f,b) ((f)&=~(1<<(b)))
#define TEST_BIT(f,b) ((f)&(1<<b)))
```

A better solution is to use bit fields in a structure. This hides the detail of bit manipulation, shifting the burden to the compiler. For example:

```
struct flag_struct
  {
  unsigned out_bit:1;
  unsigned in_bit:1;
  unsigned recovery:1;
  unsigned retry:4;
  } flag;
```

Here, out_bit, in_bit, and recovery each represent a single bit with no additional effort on your part. The retry field will hold a 4-bit integer that ranges from 0 to 15.

This approach still isn't perfect. The compiler may allocate a full 32-bit word for a flag_struct even if you only need a single character. Also, if flag maps to an external entity (like an operating system data structure), you can't be sure that a particular compiler will arrange the bits to match the predefined layout. Bit fields vary greatly from one compiler to the next.

Review

Although 16 and 32 bit compilers treat ints differently, this presents little problem for code portability. Use short and long where you must to insure the correct sizing of variables. While this is somewhat inconvenient when porting existing code from a 16-bit to a 32-bit environment, you will reap the benefits of longer ints—increased numeral capability, larger malloc() calls, and so on.

CHAPTER ■ 7

Segments: Take Them or Leave Them

Pure ANSI C compilers have no direct way to represent Intel's segmented architecture, but most real-mode DOS C compilers have extensions to deal with segmentation. While many compilers have their own special extensions to deal with segments, there is some commonality. This chapter focuses on those common segment extensions.

16-bit DOS C compilers typically support three types of pointers. Pointers can be *near*, *far*, or *huge*. A near pointer contains only an offset—it can reference 64K of memory via an implied segment. Far and huge pointers contain both a segment and offset value. Since near pointers only contain an offset, they require 16 bits of storage. In 16-bit code, far and huge pointers need 32 bits. Later in this chapter we will see the difference between far and huge pointers. For now, you can consider them equivalent.

Compilers create programs in various *models*. A model specifies how C deals with segmentation. Perhaps the simplest case is the *small model*. A small model program has a data segment and a code segment. With standard, real-mode DOS, segments can't exceed 64K in length. Therefore, a small model program can have a maximum of 64K of code, and another 64K of data.

When a small model program contains a normal pointer declaration, the compiler assumes it is near. If the pointer refers to data, the compiler forms the address using the pointer and the program's single data segment. Similarly, using the pointer in a code context (a call to a function pointer, for instance), will reference the program's code segment.

Large model is the exact opposite of small model. A large model program can have multiple code and multiple data segments. In this case, the compiler assumes all normal pointers are *far*. Any reference with a pointer will use its segment and offset values to form the address.

Near pointers are more efficient than far pointers, both from a the storage space and the execution time standpoint. Yet the 64K segment limit is too restrictive for many programs. Since many programs need large amounts of code or data but not both, C compilers also support composite models. (See Table 7-1 for a complete list of common models.) The *compact model*, for example, only allows one segment of code, but allows multiple data segments. In the compact model, code pointers are near, but data pointers (including void pointers) are far.

Table 7-1. Memory Models in 16-Bit Code in 16-Bit Code

Name	Code Pointers	Data Pointers	Notes
Tiny	Near	Near	(DS==CS)
Small	Near	Near	(DS!=CS)
Medium	Far	Near	
Compact	Near	Far	
Large	Far	Far	(No single item > 64K)
Huge	Far	Far	(Items may be > 64K)

Occasionally, you need only a few far (or near) pointers in your code. For example, suppose you need to write a short C program to copy a pattern (from an array) to text page 0 on a CGA (or compatible) video adapter. To do this, you must copy the array to memory location B800:0000.

The screen buffer is 4,000 bytes that represent what you see on the video display in text mode. Each even numbered byte is a character and each odd numbered byte is the previous character's attribute byte. The attribute byte sets the character's color and intensity. SHOARY uses the attribute byte 0x70 (black on white); 0x7 is a normal white on black character.

Clearly, this program will not need 64K of code or data. Yet, the screen buffer (at B800:0000) is outside the program's default data segment. If the program could create a single far pointer, you could easily use the small model. Luckily, you can explicitly override pointer attributes, although the syntax for doing so is not part of the ANSI C standard. Most PC compilers support the same method (but a few accept other methods too).

Listing 7-1 shows a short program (SHOARY.C) that will compile under Microsoft C or Borland (Turbo) C. Notice that the program creates two pointers: *aryptr*, which points to the array, and *scrptr*, which points to the screen. Only *scrptr* is a far pointer (assuming you compile in small model). There are several ways to set *scrptr* depending on which compiler you use. SHOARY uses the line

```
unsigned int far *scrptr=(char far *)0xB8000000;
```

to initialize *scrptr*. (Change this to 0xB0000000 if you have a monochrome video adapter.) Other popular methods include the *MK_FP()*, *FP_SEG()*, and *FP_OFF()* macros that some compilers support (see your compiler's DOS.H file or its documentation).

Listing 7-1. SHOARY.C

```
/* Example of mixed model programming -- use small model
   Borland:   BCC -ms SHOARY.C
   Microsoft: CL -AS SHOARY.C
*/
#include <stdio.h>
#include <conio.h>
#define SCREEN_SIZE (80*25)

unsigned short new_screen[SCREEN_SIZE];
void fill_screen(void);

main()
  {
  short i;
  for (i=0;i<SCREEN_SIZE;i++)
```

```
    new_screen[i]=0x7040;    /* Inverse @ sign */
  fill_screen();
/* wait for a key */
  if (!getch()) getch();
  return 0;
  }


void fill_screen(void)
  {
/* far pointer */
  unsigned short _far *scrptr=
          (unsigned short _far *)0xb8000000;
  unsigned short *aryptr;  /* near pointer */
  short i;
  aryptr=new_screen;
  for (i=0;i<SCREEN_SIZE;i++)
    *scrptr++=*aryptr++;
  }
```

DOS Huge Pointers

Far pointers are simply containers that hold a segment value and an offset. The two values are not connected in any way. This causes problems with some code. Consider this function:

```
void badcode(char far *badptr)
  {
  *badptr++='A';
  *badptr=0x70;
  }
```

The *badcode()* function intends to write to two consecutive bytes of memory. However, incrementing a far pointer only changes its offset portion. If the offset is less than 0xFFFF, *badcode()* will work fine. When the offset is 0xFFFF, the increment operation changes it to zero (overflow occurs), but the segment value remains unchanged. In effect, the pointer "wraps around" to the start of the 64K segment. A similar problem occurs when decrementing a pointer with a zero offset.

The solution to this dilemma is the huge pointer. The compiler properly handles offset overflow with huge pointers. When overflow occurs, the program simply adds the value __AHINCR (0x1000 in real-mode) to the segment value. Of course, this extra overhead increases program size and execution time.

In large model, the compiler won't allocate items (at compile or run time) that span a segment boundary, so huge pointers are often not necessary. When a single data item (such as an array or structure) must be larger than 64K, or if you are using a specific region of memory (like a network card buffer) that might span 64K, however, huge pointers are a necessity.

DOS Extender Models

For those who find models and pointers confusing, there is good news. Some 386 DOS extenders, such as Intel's Code Builder, dispense with segmentation altogether. With Code Builder, all address offsets are relative to one 4G segment. Programmers often call this scheme a *flat address space* or *flat model*. To convert a segmented address to a flat address, just shift the segment over 4 bits (1 HEX digit), and add the offset. Therefore, the screen buffer is at 0xB8000. Listing 7-2 (SHOARYCB.C) contains a Code Builder version of SHOARY.

You may have noticed that SHOARY.C declares *short* variables instead of *int*s. As you saw in Chapter 6, this simplifies porting the code to the 32-bit environment. Try changing the *scrptr*, *aryptr*, and *new_screen* variables to type *int*. With a 16-bit compiler, everything works as before. With a 32-bit compiler like Code Builder, every other character becomes blank. In 32-bit mode, the line

```
*scrptr++=*aryptr++;
```

stores four bytes to the screen—not two; and it advances the pointers by four, also. The compiler interprets the constant 0x7040 as 0x00007040, leaving a blank space on every other character.

Listing 7-2. SHOARYCB.C

```
/* SHOARY for CodeBuilder
   ICC SHOARYCB.C
```

```
*/
#include <stdio.h>
#include <conio.h>
#define SCREEN_SIZE (80*25)

unsigned short new_screen[SCREEN_SIZE];

main()
  {
  short i;
  for (i=0;i<SCREEN_SIZE;i++)
     new_screen[i]=0x7040;    /* Inverse @ sign */
  fill_screen();
/* wait for a key */
  if (!getch()) getch();
  return 0;
  }


fill_screen()
  {
  unsigned short *scrptr=(unsigned short *)0xb8000;
  unsigned short *aryptr;
  short i;
  aryptr=new_screen;
  for (i=0;i<SCREEN_SIZE;i++)
    *scrptr++=*aryptr++;
  return 0;
  }
```

It would be faster, in 32-bit code, to use 32-bit integers instead of shorts. You would have to replace the constant 0x7040 with 0x70407040 and adjust *SCREEN_SIZE* to 80*25/2. This would take advantage of the 386's 32-bit word size and cut the number of iterations in half. We will look at performance enhancement in more detail in Chapter 14.

Flat 386 extenders don't need far and near pointers for normal programs (this isn't true of 32-bit extenders in general—just flat extenders). They also don't need memory models—all pointers are 32 bits. For portability reasons, Code Builder can ignore any near, far, or huge modifiers in pointer declarations and casts (use the */znoansi* switch). The flat model is very simple to program. Also, porting code from nonsegmented systems (like Unix) is usually easiest in a flat environment.

A flat memory model is more convenient than a segmented architecture, but it can be risky. A program running in a flat address space can access every byte of its memory on any memory reference—the flat model subverts memory protection. Since many flat model extenders provide programs with direct access to physical memory (especially below 1M), a misbehaving program can easily wreak havoc in conventional and extended memory. Of course, this is not much worse than regular DOS programming. A conventional DOS program also can easily destroy conventional memory (an extended program can trash all memory). Consider the following program:

```
/* Pointer to 0 */
#ifdef _HIGHC_
char _far *p;
#else
char *p;
#endif
main()
  {
  int i;
  for (i=0;i<100;i++) *p++=i;
  }
```

Since *p* is a null pointer, the assignment, **p++=i;* should be illegal. Code Builder (and similar extenders), however, will blindly assign values over the real-mode interrupt vector table at address 0, just like a conventional DOS program. Eventually, the program will destroy an important memory location, and cause the machine to crash.

Other 386 DOS extenders (or compilers) support models and segmentation to some extent. For example, consider the Phar Lap 386|DOS extender and the MetaWare High C compiler. With segmentation, the above program will refuse to perform the improper assignment. Figure 7-1 contains an error message printed by the misbehaving program. When the loop body uses the null pointer (for reading or writing), the CPU causes a memory protection fault. The DOS extender has a built-in function to handle these faults (it prints the message in Figure 7-1). Later you will see how to replace a built-in handler with your own code that might take some more useful action.

Figure 7-1. Null Pointer Error Message

```
Abnormal program termination: Memory protection fault
CS:EIP = 000FH:00000006H
```

The extender defines special segment values to refer to a certain hardware address (like the video buffer). Table 7-2 lists the Phar Lap segment definitions. (Ergo's OS/386 uses a subset of the Phar Lap definitions).

Table 7-2. Phar Lap 386 Segment Definitions

Selector	Description
0x 0004-0x0007	Program's MS-DOS PSP
0x 000C-0x000F	Program's initial CS[*]
0x 0010-0x0017	Program's initial DS[*]
0x 001C-0x001F	Screen segment (see text)[*]
0x 0020-0x0027	Duplicate of 0007H (MS-DOS PSP)
0x 002C-0x002F	Environment block[*]
0x 0030-0x0037	First megabyte of physical memory[*]
0x 003C-0x003F	Weitek coprocessor (if present)
0x 0040-0x0047	Japanese graphics segment (same as 001F on PC)
0x 004C-0x004F	Cyrix coprocessor (if present)

[*] *Also present in Ergo OS/386.*
Note: Selectors shown with RPL=3

The Metaware High C compiler only uses one code and data segment. Therefore, it is a small model compiler. Of course, because this is the 386, the segments can be 4G long—here, small refers to the number of segments, not their size.

Phar Lap defines segment selector 0x1F (or 0x1C if RPL=0) as the video buffer address. This leads to a new version of SHOARY, SHOARYPL.C (Listing 7-3).

Listing 7-3. SHOARYPL.C

```
/* SHOARY for Phar Lap/MetaWare C
   HC386 SHOARYPL.C
*/
#include <conio.h>
#include "ptrset.h"

#define SCREEN_SIZE (80*25)

unsigned short new_screen[SCREEN_SIZE];


main()
  {
  short i;
  for (i=0;i<SCREEN_SIZE;i++)
    new_screen[i]=0x7040;    /* Inverse @ sign */
  fill_screen();
/* wait for a key */
  if (!getch()) getch();
  return 0;
  }

fill_screen()
  {
  unsigned short _far *scrptr;
  unsigned short *aryptr;  /* near pointer */
  short i;
  FP_SEG(scrptr)=0x1C;              /* Phar Lap video segment */
  FP_OFF(scrptr)=0;
  aryptr=new_screen;
  for (i=0;i<SCREEN_SIZE;i++)
    *scrptr++=*aryptr++;
  return 0;
  }
```

Since Metaware High C is a small model compiler, far pointers appear again. In 32-bit code, far pointers are 48 bits. However, You can't create 48-bit constants to initialize the pointer. The correct way to initialize a far pointer is:

```
char _far *ptr;
struct overlay { int off, short seg; };
((struct overlay *)&ptr)->seg=seg_value;
((struct overlay *)&ptr)->off=offset_value;
```

You can encapsulate this technique using a set of macros that resemble the ones found in Microsoft C (see PTRSET.H; Listing 7-4). When using these macros to initialize a 48-bit far pointer, the compiler may not understand that you have placed an initial value in the pointer since the pointer's name hasn't appeared on the left side of an assignment. If this is the case, it will issue a warning. You may safely ignore this warning. Your 32-bit compiler may already provide FP_SEG() and FP_OFF() macros (or a MK_FP() macro), in which case you don't need PTRSET.H.

Listing 7-4. PTRSET.H

```
/* Header for initializing 48-bit far pointers */
#ifndef PTRSET_H
#define PTRSET_H

struct PTRSET_OVERLAY
  {
  int off;
  short seg;
  };

#define FP_SEG(p) (((struct PTRSET_OVERLAY *)&p)->seg)
#define FP_OFF(p) (((struct PTRSET_OVERLAY *)&p)->off)
#endif
```

386 Huge Pointers

There are no 386 huge pointers since regular 32-bit pointers already correctly handle blocks larger than 64K. In 386 protected mode, each segment has a specified size. Any block of memory (up to 4G, of course) can always reside in a single segment.

286 Models

Since 286 segments must be 64K or less in length, 286 extended programs must rely on traditional memory models. They may also use huge pointers. From a programming standpoint, protected-mode huge pointers function the same as their real-mode counterparts. However, the compiler implements them in a very different way (see the sidebar, *286 Huge Pointers*).

286 HUGE POINTERS

Real-mode huge pointers are simple to implement. When an offset overflow occurs, the compiler adds 0x1000 (the distance to the next segment) to the pointer's segment value. In protected mode, segment selectors are arbitrary numbers—adding 0x1000 to a selector is unlikely to yield a useful address.

The DOS extender (or compiler) will supply a function to allocate a memory object and return a huge pointer to it. If the item is larger than 64K, the function must allocate more than one segment because of the limitations of the 286. Then, the allocation function selects segments separated by a fixed amount (perhaps even adjacent entries in the LDT or GDT). The compiler adds this fixed amount (the segment increment often called __AHINCR) to the huge pointer's selector when the offset overflows.

continued

continued

Recall that adjacent entries in a descriptor table are 8 bytes apart—that is, selectors 0x10, 0x18, and 0x1C are sequential. Then assume that the DOS extender reserves two descriptor table entries for each segment you allocate. This would make the segment increment equal to 16 (0x10). If a huge pointer calculation overflows, the compiler will add 0x10 to the segment selector. Similarly, a subtraction underflow will deduct 0x10 from the segment.

When using normal references to huge pointers in a C program these details make no difference. But if you manipulate pointers in assembly language, you need to know how your extender and compiler handle the segment increment. The Phar Lap 286 extender, for example, defines the **DosGetHugeShift()** function that returns the segment increment. DPMI servers also provide a function to return the segment increment value (see Chapter 5).

Ergo's OS/286 extender takes an unusual approach to segment management. OS/286 can allocate logical segments larger than 64K. However, you can't directly access memory using these logical segments. Instead, you define **tiles** (physical segments) that overlay the logical segment. OS/286 can't create tiles larger than 64K.

A segment may have any number of tiles, and the tiles may overlap. The distance from the start of one tile to the start of the next tile is the **stride**. If the stride is equal to the tile length, the tiles do not overlap. If the stride is less than the tile length, the tiles overlap. All tiles in a segment use consecutive selectors.

Huge pointers are simple to create with tiles. The compiler simply sets up a segment with 64K tiles and sets the stride to 64K. If the stride equals 16, the tiling mechanism can emulate real-mode segments, too. While the tiling system is flexible, it places a great demand for consecutive slots in the segment descriptor tables.

Of course, if you don't directly manipulate segment values in your programs (and you shouldn't), all is well. Assuming your compiler and extender agree how to form huge pointers, you don't have to know how they work. ■

Windows Models

Conventional Windows programs for standard and enhanced mode are very similar to 286 extended programs. Windows uses the same traditional models that ordinary DOS programs use. Since Windows is a protected-mode environment, however, the compiler must implement huge pointers differently than real-mode compilers do (see the Sidebar, *286 Huge Pointers*).

Windows programs have access to two pools of memory. The *local heap* is memory that is in the program's default data segment (therefore, there is never more than 64K of memory in the local heap). The *global heap* comprises the remaining memory available to the program. Each global memory allocation (via GlobalAlloc()) creates one or more segments in the local descriptor table (LDT, see Chapter 4). Although the 16-bit mode limits each segment to 64K or less, Windows can allocate multiple segments for use with huge pointers. Since the LDT can only contain 8,192 segments, you can easily exaust the LDT before you run out of memory.

Windows adds some complexity to segmentation. A Windows program must specify how it will use a segment. You may make a segment that contains code or data (you can't execute code from a data segment or write to code segments—this in enforced by the CPU). In addition, you can allow (or prevent) Windows from manipulating the segment during memory management. Segments may be movable, fixed, or movable and discardable.

In simple terms, Windows can relocate a movable block of memory to make space for future allocations. A movable and discardable block may be relocated or removed. This may seem strange, but consider a large font in memory. If Windows needs the space, it can remove the font. If it needs the font later, it can always reload it from disk—fonts do not change under normal circumstances.

Thanks to the sophisticated segmentation of 286, 386, and 486 processors, these segment types are not as important as they were in real mode Windows. In Windows enhanced mode, the 386 MMU makes them almost unimportant. If you would like to learn more about Windows memory management, refer to one of the Windows books in the bibliography.

Memory Access from Windows

Since Windows is a graphical operating system, the SHOARY example programs are not portable to Windows. Instead, Listing 7-5 (SHOCOM1.C) reads the address of the COM ports from the BIOS area under Windows. This is similar to SHOCOM.C (Listing 5-3), but instead it uses some built-in segment selectors provided by Windows.

Windows provides built-in selectors to commonly accessed physical memory locations, such as __0000H, __0040H, __B000H, and __B800H. These selectors point to the real-mode selectors you would expect (0000H, 0040H, 0B000H, and 0B800H, respectively). Don't make the mistake of assuming that these values are the same as the real-mode values. For instance __0000H might equal 0x170. Due to a fluke in Windows, __0040H actually equals 0x40, but don't count on that—other DPMI hosts are not obligated to make that equivalence true.

Because of the way Windows exports these selectors, you have to declare them as near and take their address to use them. SHOCOM1 uses:

```
FP_SEG(p)=(unsigned)&__0000H;
```

You will see other ways to create pointers to arbitrary addresses in Chapter 8.

Listing 7-5. SHOCOM1.C

```
/* SHOCOM1 - Show serial port addresses using Windows
   test bed.
   Alternate version: uses predefined selector _0040H

   Compile with:
   Borland: BWINCOMP SHOCOM1
   Microsoft: MWINCOMP SHOCOM1 */

#include "winpmode.h"
#include <dos.h>


/* Windows predefined selectors */
```

```
extern unsigned _near _0040H, _near _0000H;

char *test()
  {
  union REGS r;
  unsigned short _far *p,i;
/* create far pointer to BIOS data segment */
  FP_SEG(p)=(unsigned)&_0040H;
  FP_OFF(p)=0;

/* As an alternate, you could use:
 * FP_SEG(p)=(unsigned)&_0000H;
 * FP_OFF(p)=0x400; */

/* read COM port addresses from BIOS table */
  for (i=0;i<=3;i++)
    win_printf("COM Port I/O Address","COM%d: "
             "%04X",i+1,p[i]);
  return "Done";
  }
```

Performance

Because protected-mode segments are much more complex than real-mode segments, extended programs should avoid using far pointers if possible. Loading segment registers in protected mode is a time-consuming operation (relative to other instructions, at least). For example, consider a POP DS instruction (this loads the DS register from the stack). On a 386 in real mode, this instruction takes 7 clock cycles to execute. In protected mode it takes 21—triple the amount of time the real-mode instruction takes. This is enough time to perform 10 32-bit integer additions or an average 32-bit integer multiply. For 386 extenders, a flat or small model is usually acceptable, and will produce the fastest programs since there will be less use of segment registers. Many 386 compilers offer no choice of models, anyway.

For 286 extenders, you may have to abandon the small model. Since you are using a DOS extender, you presumably need plenty of memory for your program anyway. However, if you only need a few very large objects, you might consider using the small model and declaring a few huge or far data objects and pointers.

Maintaining Portability

Varying pointer sizes can cause incompatibilities between DOS and extended programs. Many of the portability rules concerning integers are also valid for pointer types. If you want to maintain portable source code for DOS and DOS extenders, follow these guidelines:

- Don't assume the size of any pointer. Use the *sizeof* operator instead. The *sizeof* operator will return the length, in bytes, of a variable or type. For example:

```
p=(char **)malloc(sizeof(char *)*10)
p=(int far**)malloc(sizeof(int far *)*10);
```

- Use the preprocessor to define pointer types in a portable way. The preprocessor can hide many portability problems. You might write:

```
#ifdef __HIGHC__
#define INTPTR short *
#else
#define INTPTR int *
#endif
```

You also could obtain this effect with the *typedef* statement:

```
#ifdef __HIGHC__
typedef short* INTPTR;
   .
   .
   .
```

- Where possible, don't manipulate segments. Often, you can use huge pointers, and let the compiler worry about segments. Of course, initializers for pointers to hardware addresses (like the video buffer) will require changes (see the listings in this chapter for examples).

CHAPTER ▪ 8

Looking Up an Old Address

The point to using a DOS extender is to get away from the 1M memory limit. Still, serious PC programming often requires direct access to memory below 1M. Video cards, network adapters, SCSI adapters, and even some coprocessors use memory to communicate with the CPU. There also are some programming techniques that manipulate the BIOS data segment at 0040:0000, undocumented DOS data structures, and other predefined memory regions. Since many extenders protect or rearrange memory, you'll frequently need special methods to use specific regions of memory.

Most DOS extenders that require segments provide simplified methods for common situations. For instance, the programs in Chapter 6 employed some simple built-in methods to utilize the text video buffer and the BIOS data area. Still, there are times you'll need to use memory not directly supported by all extenders. Windows, for example, only provides built-in selectors for real-mode segments 0x0000, 0x0040, and 0xA000 to 0xF000. To access other regions you must use one of the methods in this chapter.

Listings 8-1 and 8-2 show examples of each technique in the following sections. You may want to refer to the listings as you read each section.

Flat Model Extenders

Flat model extenders like Code Builder take the first megabyte of memory and map it into the first megabyte of your program's address space. This simplifies accessing I/O or BIOS memory. You can construct pointers to a physical real-mode address (less than 1M) using this formula:

```
pointer=segment*16+offset;
```

or:

```
pointer=segment<<4+offset;
```

In Chapter 7, SHOARYCB.C (Listing 7-2) uses this method to create a pointer to the text buffer at B800:0000. The resulting 32-bit near pointer is 0xB8000. This greatly simplifies access to memory, but strips protected mode of its chief benefit: protection. You can easily form pointers to access any region of memory—even by mistake.

Split Model Extenders

Some flat model extenders map the first megabyte and your program in separate noncontiguous regions of memory. If the first megabyte is mapped to the first megabyte of logical memory, the flat model formula applies. Rational's 4G/W extender, for instance, places the first megabyte of memory at location zero, and your program starts at 4M. Remember, these are logical addresses. Your program doesn't require 4M of memory for this scheme to work.

The GNU C++/386 package (see Chapter 3) contains a DOS extender (GO32) that uses a different form of split addressing. With GO32, your program begins at address zero. The first megabyte of memory starts at location 0xE0000000. In this case, you may compute a physical pointer using the above formula. Then, add 0xE0000000 to the result to obtain the correct value.

Segmented 386 Extenders

Segmented 386 extenders (like Phar Lap's, for instance), usually provide several data segments to simplify direct memory access. In Chapter 7, the SHOARYPL.C program (Listing 7-3) uses the predefined segment 0x1F or 0x1F to write to the video buffer at B800:0000. Another segment (0x37) points to the entire first megabyte of memory—using this selector is similar to working with the flat model. For example, you could address the video buffer with the following statements:

```
char _far *ptr;
FP_SEG(ptr)=0x37;
FP_OFF(ptr)=0xB8000;
*ptr='X';    /* Write X on screen */
```

Phar Lap supplies segments for the DOS PSP, the DOS environment, the screen, the Wietek and Cyrix coprocessors, and the first megabyte of memory (see Figure 7-2). Avoid using segment 0x37 if another predefined segment will work. If you use segment 0x37, a programming error involving far pointers to that segment can damage any address in the first megabyte of memory. If you use the other segments, only the specified portion of memory is at risk.

Of course, with any far pointers, you can't use standard library routines like memcpy() or memset(). They expect nonsegmented 32-Bit pointers and will fail if you pass a far pointer to them. Some compilers, like the Watcom, do offer 48-bit far versions of these functions (for example, _fmemcpy(), and _fmemset()). If your compiler doesn't offer them, you will have to write your own functions. For example:

```
void _far *_fmemset(void _far *target, int c, size_t bytes)
  {
  while (bytes--) *target++=c;
  }
```

You can define segments for specific address ranges of memory with the Phar Lap 386 extender in several ways. The most general method uses interrupt 0x21 function 0x250A. (*Note:* Phar Lap, unfortunately, chose interrupt 0x21 function 0x25 for its API calls—under 386|DOS-Extender, it is not the DOS function that sets interrupt vectors.)

To map a address range to a segment, you must first create an empty segment using interrupt 0x21 function 0x48 (the standard DOS memory allocation call). To make the segment empty, specify its length (in the EBX register) as zero. Once you have the segment selector, you can modify its base address and length using interrupt 0x21 function 0x250A. You place the address in EBX, and the length (in 4K pages) in ECX.

This method is very flexible. You can create segments that point to any physical address (even ones above 1M). Although there are other procedures you can use for this purpose, function 0x250A is the only one that will work consistently with DPMI.

Segments you create with function 0x250A are safe—the CPU will disallow accesses outside the segment. Of course, if you don't mind its lack of protection, you can always use segment 0x37 for addresses less than 1M.

Other extenders have similar functions to create selectors for arbitrary addresses. Ergo's OS/386, for example, uses interrupt 0x21 function 0xE803 to create a segment that points to a physical address region. Listing 8-1 later in this chapter illustrates the methods required by many DOS extenders.

286 Extenders

Unlike a 386 extender, a 286 extender can't encompass the entire 1M real address space in a single segment. You must create segments that map to real memory by using a special API call.

Ergo's OS/286 uses the same technique (using interrupt 0x21 function 0xE803) as OS/386 (see above). You can also create a window (a 64K or smaller segment) inside segment 0x37, the 1M real memory segment. (See Chapter 6 for more about Ergo's tiling mechanism.)

Other 286 extenders supply calls to create arbitrary segments. For instance, DosMapRealSeg() will do the job for 286|DOS Extender. You may also retrieve a selector for the BIOS data segment with DosGet-BIOSSeg(). Ergo's DMP16 extender supplies two functions: ParaToSel()

for addresses below 1M, and the more general CreatePhysicalWindow() function. Refer to Listing 8-1 for examples of using these functions.

DPMI

DPMI servers also provide functions to create segments that point to specific addresses. The simplest way to do this uses interrupt 0x31 functions 0, 7, and 8 (see Appendix B). The technique is similar to the Phar Lap 386 method. First, you allocate an empty segment using function 0. Next, you can change the segment's address and limit using functions 7 and 8, respectively. There are other DPMI functions that can achieve the same results, but this one is the most general.

Selectors are a limited resource. The LDT can contain 8,191 selectors, and many servers require allocate one or more hidden selectors for each selector you create. Therefore, you should always free selectors when you are done with them. DPMI function 1 will free a selector obtained via function 0.

You can also use DPMI function 2 to create a selector that corresponds to a real mode segment. However, you can never modify or free these selectors so you should only use this function for commonly used segments (e.g., the video buffers or the BIOS data segment). Don't use this function to access private data below 1M.

Access Under Windows

Windows programs can use DPMI to create selectors, but there is a better way. First, you may be able to use one of the predefined selectors that Windows creates using DPMI function 2 (see Chapter 7, Listing 7-5 for an example). The predefined segments are: __0000H, __0040H, __A000H, __B000H, __B800H, __C000H, __D000H, __E000H, and __F000H. (Note: the __0000H and __0040H selectors are undocumented by Microsoft, but can be found in *Undocumented Windows*, another volume in this series.)

If one of the predefined segments won't fit the bill, you must construct one yourself. Instead of directly calling DPMI, you can use the AllocSelector(), SetSelectorBase(), and SetSelectorLimit() calls. These calls are simple replacements for DPMI functions 0, 7, and 8 (although they do not call DPMI—Windows manipulates the LDT directly). Since selectors are a limited resource, be sure to call FreeSelector() when you no longer need the segment.

An Example: CGA Graphics

Many graphics programs directly access video memory to improve their performance. Listing 8-1 contains PMCGA.C, a program that directly manipulates the graphics buffer in CGA mode. It will work with a CGA, EGA, VGA, or compatible adapter. Although some extenders supply a predefined video segment, PMCGA creates its own segment, where required.

At the beginning of the program, you must select a #define statement to enable code for your extender. The program contains four major functions: setmode() uses a standard BIOS interrupt to set the video mode; setptr() initializes a pointer to the video buffer; plot() plots a point on the screen; and draw() performs the drawing. Note that the only extender-specific code is the pointer declaration (cgaptr) and the setptr() and freeptr() routine. The remaining code is the same, no matter which extender you use.

Details about CGA programming are beyond the scope of this book. If you look at the plot() routine, you'll notice that the video adapter places physically adjacent pixels in noncontiguous memory blocks (banks). If you want more information about graphics programming, refer to the bibliography.

A Windows Example

Listing 8-2 contains another version of an old friend, SHOCOM. This version, SHOCOM2.C, uses the AllocSelector() method to create its pointer to the BIOS data area (at segment 0040H). It is interesting to contrast the two versions of SHOCOM. SHOCOM1.C (Listing 7-5 in Chapter 7) uses a predefined selector. Instead of rolling its own.

Listing 8-1. PMCGA.C

```
/* Example of direct memory access
   This program works with Code Builder, DOS, Ergo OS/386,
   Ergo DPM16, GNU C++, Phar Lap 286, Phar Lap 386, or
   Rational. You must set one of the #define statements
   below for your extender.
   (Ergo and Rational assume Watcom C).

   For specific compiler directives, see the comment
   preceding each #define.
*/

/* icc /znoansi cga.c  */
#define CODEBUILDER 0

/*  bcc pmcga.c
or: cl pmcga.c */
#define DOS 0

/* generic DPMI (tested with DPM/16):
cl -AL -G2 pmcga.c ergo.def
(note: you can't test with Code Builder since it
doesn't support far pointers) */
#define DPMI 0

/* wcl386 -l=ergo pmcga.c */
#define ERGO 0

/* cl -AL -G2 pmcga.c ergo.def ergoapi.lib */
#define ERGODPMI 0

/* gcc -o cga cga.c
  == NOTE == You must press ENTER to continue if compiled
  with GNU */
#define GNU 0
```

```
/* cl -AL -G2 -Lp pmcga.c llibpe.lib (versions before 2.5 -- */
/* cl -AL -G2 -Lp pmcga.c (version 2.5 and later */
/* bcc286 pmcga.c */
#define PHARLAP286  1

/* HC386 pmcga.c */
#define PHARLAP386 0

/* wcl386 -l=dos4g pmcga.c */
#define RATIONAL4GW 0

#if RATIONAL4GW || ERGO
#define WATCOM 1
#endif

#if \
    CODEBUILDER+DOS+DPMI+ERGO+ERGODPMI+GNU+\
    PHARLAP386+PHARLAP286+RATIONAL4GW!=1
#error One and only one extender must be defined
#endif

#include <stdio.h>
#include <stdlib.h>
#include <dos.h>


/* Extender/Compiler specific things */
#if PHARLAP286
#include <phapi.h>
#endif

#if GNU
#define _far
#define wait4key() getchar();
#else
#include <conio.h>
#define wait4key()  { if (!getch()) getch(); }
#endif


#if WATCOM
#define int86 int386
```

```c
#define x w
#endif


/* prototype for setptr function
   int is deliberate here -- we want 64K for 16-bit
   and 4G for 32-bit */
char _far *setptr(long base,unsigned int limit);
/* free pointer when done, if required */
void freeptr(char _far *);
int setmode(int);
int draw(void);


/* pointer to cga buffer */
char _far *cgaptr;


main()
  {
/* change video mode */
  setmode(4);
/* draw a picture */
  draw();
/* wait for a key */
  wait4key();
/* return to 80X25 mode */
  setmode(3);
/* quit */
  freeptr(cgaptr);
  exit(0);
  }

/* Set the specified mode using INT 0x10 (BIOS call) */
int setmode(int mode)
  {
  union REGS r;
  r.x.ax=mode;
  int86(0x10,&r,&r);
  return 0;
  }
```

```
/* plot a point at (x,y) using color */
void plot(int x,int y,int color)
  {
  int offset,bitno,mask;
/* if 1st time, make pointer */
  if (!cgaptr) cgaptr=setptr(0xb8000L,0x7FFF);
  if (!cgaptr)
    {
    printf("Can't create pointer\n");
    exit(1);
    }
/* compute offset */
  offset=((y&1)<<13)+(80*(y>>1))+(x>>2);
/* compute bit position of pixel */
  bitno=(~x&3)<<1;
  mask=3<<bitno;
/* clear any bits in that position */
  cgaptr[offset]&=~mask;
/* set the right bits */
  cgaptr[offset]|=color<<bitno;
  }

/* draw a simple line */
int draw()
  {
  int x,y;
  y=120;
  for (x=0;x<150;x++) plot(x,y,1);
  return 0;
  }

/* The following routines compute the cgaptr variable
   for various extenders */

#if CODEBUILDER||RATIONAL4GW
/* limit ignored */
/* _far is only to match prototype -- no "far"
   in these compilers */
char _far *setptr(long add,unsigned limit)
  {
```

```
  char *val;
/* simple case -- use linear address */
  val=(char *)add;
  return val;
  }

/* No freeptr */
void freeptr(char *p)
  {
  }
#endif

#if GNU
/* limit ignored */
char *setptr(long add,unsigned limit)
  {
  char *val;
/* linear address + 0xE0000000 */
  val=(char *)add+0xE0000000;
  return val;
  }

/* No freeptr */
void freeptr(char *p)
  {
  }
#endif

#if PHARLAP386
char _far *setptr(long add,unsigned limit)
  {
  void _far *p;
  union REGS r;
  struct SREGS s;
/* init segment registers */
  segread(&s);
/* allocate 0 length segment */
  r.h.ah=0x48;
  r.w.ebx=0;

  int86(0x21,&r,&r);
```

```
/* check for error */
  if (r.x.cflag)  return NULL;
/* modify base/length of segment */
  s.es=r.x.ax;
  r.x.ax=0x250a;
/* new address */
  r.w.ebx=add;
/* map 4K pages */
  r.w.ecx=((limit+1)+4095)/4096;
  int86x(0x21,&r,&r,&s);
/* error check */
  if (r.x.cflag) return NULL;
/* Set pointer using macros in DOS.H */
/* Note these macros don't work as lvalues in WATCOM.C
   use p=MK_FP(s.es,r.w.eax); instead */
  FP_SEG(p)=s.es;
  FP_OFF(p)=r.w.eax;
  return p;
  }

void freeptr(char _far *p)
  {
  union REGS r;
  struct SREGS s;
  segread(&s);
  s.es=FP_SEG(p);
  r.h.ah=0x49;
  int86x(0x21,&r,&r,&s);
  }
#endif

#if PHARLAP286
char _far *setptr(long add,unsigned limit)
  {
  void _far *p;
  int seg,off,sel;
/* compute segment and offset of address */
  seg=add>>4;
  off=add-(seg<<4);

/* make segment */
  if (DosMapRealSeg(seg,limit+1,&sel)) return NULL;
```

```
/* make pointer if successful */
  FP_SEG(p)=sel;
  FP_OFF(p)=off;

  return p;
  }

/* No freeptr required for DosMapRealSeg() */
void freeptr(char _far *p)
  {
  }
#endif

#if ERGODPMI
/* limit ignored */
char _far *setptr(long add,unsigned limit)
  {
  void _far *p;
  int sel,seg;
/* compute segment */
  seg=add>>4;
/* make segment */
  ParaToSel(seg,&sel);
/* construct pointer */
  FP_SEG(p)=sel;
  FP_OFF(p)=add-(seg<<4);
  return p;
  }

/* Freeing selector from ParaToSel is unwise since they
   are a global resource */
void freeptr(char _far *p)
  {
  }

#endif


#if ERGO
/* Size must be <64K for this function */
char _far *setptr(long add,unsigned limit)
  {
```

```
  union REGS r;
  char _far *p;
/* use create real window function */
  r.x.ax=0xe803;
/* cx:dx is limit */
  r.x.cx=0;
  r.x.dx=limit;
/* si:bx is address */
  r.x.si=add>>16;
  r.x.bx=add&0xFFFF;
  int86(0x21,&r,&r);
/* construct pointer */
  p=MK_FP(r.x.ax,0);
  return p;
  }


void freeptr(char _far *p)
  {
  union REGS r;
  struct SREGS s;
  segread(&s);
  s.es=FP_SEG(p);
  r.h.ah=0x49;
  int86x(0x21,&r,&r,&s);
  }

#endif



#if DOS
/* limit ignored */
char _far *setptr(long add,unsigned limit)
  {
  void _far *p;

/* DOS is easy case, compute segment and offset */
  int seg=add>>4;
  FP_SEG(p)=seg;
  FP_OFF(p)=add-(seg<<4);
```

```
    return p;
    }


/* no free required, of course */
void freeptr(char _far *p)
    {
    }

#endif

#if DPMI
/* siz<64K for this function */
char _far *setptr(long add,unsigned limit)
    {
    void _far *p;
    union REGS r;
/* allocate 1 descriptor */
    r.x.ax=0;
    r.x.cx=1;
    int86(0x31,&r,&r);
    if (r.x.cflag) return NULL;
/* set base address */
    r.x.bx=r.x.ax;
    r.x.ax=7;
    r.x.cx=add>>16;
    r.x.dx=add&0xFFFF;
    int86(0x31,&r,&r);
    if (r.x.cflag) return NULL;
/* set limit   */
    r.x.ax=8;
    r.x.cx=0;
    r.x.dx=limit;
    int86(0x31,&r,&r);
    if (r.x.cflag) return NULL;
    FP_SEG(p)=r.x.bx;

    FP_OFF(p)=0;
    return p;
    }
```

```
void freeptr(char _far *p)
  {
  union REGS r;
 r.x.ax=1;
  r.x.bx=FP_SEG(p);
  int86(0x31,&r,&r);
  }

#endif
```

Listing 8-2. SHOCOM2.C

```
/* SHOCOM2 - Show serial port addresses using Windows
   test bed.
   Alternate version: uses AllocSelector()

   Compile with:
   Borland: BWINCOMP SHOCOM1
   Microsoft: MWINCOMP SHOCOM1 */

#include <windows.h>
#include "winpmode.h"
#include <dos.h>


char *test()
  {
  unsigned sel;
  unsigned short _far *p,i;
  struct SREGS s;
  segread(&s);
/* create far pointer to BIOS data segment
  Use data segment as model since we want
  a data segment anyway. */
  sel=AllocSelector(s.ds);
  if (!sel) return "Can't acquire selector";
  SetSelectorLimit(sel,7);
```

```
   SetSelectorBase(sel,0x400);
   FP_SEG(p)=sel;
   FP_OFF(p)=0;

/* read COM port addresses from BIOS table */
   for (i=0;i<=3;i++)
     win_printf("COM Port I/O Address","COM%d: "
               "%04X",i+1,p[i]);
   FreeSelector(sel);
   return "Done";
   }
```

CHAPTER ■ 9

Interrupts: A Function Call By Any Other Name

Interrupts play a vital role in PC operations. The PC uses interrupts to support I/O devices, and for system calls. In previous chapters, we have used int86() and related functions to call interrupts. In this chapter, we will write interrupt service routines (ISRs)—the functions that process interrupts when they occur. Interrupt handling techniques and capabilities vary widely among different DOS extenders and compilers. (To review real-mode PC interrupt handling, see the Sidebar, *Real-mode Interrupt Processing*.)

REAL-MODE INTERRUPT PROCESSING

Note: For more information on protected-mode interrupt processing, please refer to Chapter 4.

Interrupts may come from two different sources: internal software interrupts and external hardware devices. Each interrupt has a unique number from 0 to 255. When a real-mode interrupt occurs, the processor saves the current CS, IP, and FLAG registers on the

continued

continued

stack. Next, the CPU locates the ISR for the interrupt (the interrupt vector) and jumps to that address. When the ISR gains control, interrupts are disabled.

When the ISR completes, it executes an IRET instruction. This reloads the flags, CS, and IP from the stack. If the ISR preserves all of the registers it uses, the original program can continue as though nothing happened. Some software interrupts, however, deliberately modify registers to pass values back to the original program.

The processor maintains a table of ISR addresses (interrupt vectors). In real mode, the table usually begins at address 0000:0000 (on the 386 and 486, the IDTR register can change this address). Each entry takes four bytes, enough for a segment and offset. You can compute a vector's offset in the table by multiplying the interrupt number by 4. Therefore, interrupt 0's vector is at 0000:0000; interrupt 4's is at 0000:0010.

Real-mode C compilers offer several features for dealing with interrupts. The most common are:

- The int86() function to call an interrupt.
- The _dos_setvect() and _dos_getvect() functions for writing and reading vectors in the interrupt table.
- The _enable() and _disable() functions to control interrupt execution.
- The _chain_intr() function to chain ISRs.
- The _interrupt function modifier.

The _interrupt function modifier allows you to write ISRs completely in C. However, each compiler implements it in a slightly different fashion. Here is a simple example:

```
void _far _interrupt isr(short Ax, short Bx,....)
  {
  Ax=0;
```

continued

```
continued

  return;
  }
```

The order of the register arguments is compiler-dependent (see the listings in this chapter). They contain the interrupted program's registers. If you modify them, you'll change the register's value when you return. The above code fragment, for example, set the AX register to 0 before it returns. Hardware interrupts should never modify registers, however. Since they occur asynchronously, you can not know what part of your program would have its registers mysteriously changed. ■

Two Flavors

In Chapter 2, we saw that there are two very different methods DOS extenders use to handle system calls. Some extenders (switchers) switch to real mode to process events like DOS calls or hardware interrupts. Other extenders (V86 extenders) emulate real mode using V86 mode. Switchers must handle interrupts in a very different fashion than V86 extenders.

Switching extenders may receive interrupts in real or protected mode. The extender can process an interrupt without switching modes, or it may switch to the opposite mode to service it.

All V86 interrupts invoke protected-mode handlers. The protected-mode ISR may call a real-mode ISR (in V86 mode), or it may process the interrupt and return. It is not possible for a V86 extender to process interrupts in real (or V86) mode directly.

Switchers

Switching extenders maintain two distinct interrupt vectors: a real-mode vector and a protected-mode vector. In some cases, each may eventually call the same routine. For example, a hardware interrupt's protected-mode vector might simply switch to real mode and reissue (or reflect) the interrupt.

Other interrupt handlers are more complex. The system service interrupts require a more sophisticated protected-mode handler. The interrupt 0x21 ISR, for example, determines the function call type and performs argument translation before calling (chaining to) the real-mode ISR.

Before switching to the ISR, the extender translates addresses to real-mode format. To do this, it may have to copy buffers to addresses below 1M. Alternatively, the protected-mode ISR may handle some simple functions without switching to real mode.

You may set up some real-mode ISRs so that they switch to protected mode (a pass-up ISR). For example, if you need to process keyboard interrupts with a protected-mode ISR, you must also point the real-mode vector to your new ISR. Otherwise, you won't see any keyboard events that occur while the CPU is in real mode.

On many PCs, mode switching is a slow operation. Consequently, some applications use "split" ISRs. To set up split ISRs, you simply set the real-mode vector to a real-mode ISR and the protected-mode vector to a protected-mode ISR. Usually, these ISRs share one or more data structures, and perform the same function.

Programs that use serial communications often require split ISRs. The serial port generates an interrupt when it requires service. Since characters may be coming in at high speed, it is critical to service these interrupts quickly. If your program had to switch modes to service many interrupts, it might be unable to keep up and would lose data.

The split serial port ISRs could share a buffer (below 1M, of course). Your main program could read the buffer to obtain characters, regardless of their origin (real or protected mode).

If you are accustomed to manipulating real-mode interrupt vectors, you may find that protected-mode vectors present a few surprises. For example, a conventional DOS program may hook the video BIOS interrupt (interrupt 0x10) to change the color of all text output by the program using DOS or BIOS output calls. Hooking the interrupt 0x10 protected-mode vector, however, won't provide the same effect. A protected-mode interrupt 0x10 ISR will still intercept BIOS calls, but DOS output calls will switch to real mode—once the switch occurs, all further interrupt processing is in real mode. You may have to experiment a bit to find the correct vector (or combination of vectors) to replace existing DOS code.

Functions

As you might expect, these different cases require several DOS extender API calls. Table 9-1 summarizes the pertinent calls for several extenders. You can alter either interrupt vector individually, or set them both at once. You can often select one ISR for both protected- and real-mode interrupts. With some extenders, you can also call _dos_setvect() and _dos_getvect() (standard functions in many PC C libraries) to set or read a protected-mode vector.

Table 9-1.

	DPMI	Ergo DPM/16	Ergo OS/x86	Intel
Set Real ISR	Function 0x0201	SetRealInt()	Function 0x25 (Real Mode)	
Get Real ISR	Function 0x0200	GetRealInt()	Function 0x35 (Real Mode)	
Set Protected ISR	Function 0x0203	SetProtectedInt()	Function 0x25 or 0xE402	
Get Protected ISR	Function 0x202	GetProtectedINT()	-NONE-	U
Set Separate Split ISRs	-NONE-	-NONE-	-NONE-	S E S
Get Both ISR Vectors	-NONE-	-NONE-	-NONE-	
Set Protected Mode Split ISR	-NONE-	-NONE-	-NONE-	D P
Set Real Mode Split ISR	-NONE-	-NONE-	-NONE-	M I
Set Exception Handler	Functions 0x0212, 0x0213	SetExceptionVec()	-NONE-	
Get Exception Handler	Functions 0x0210, 0x0211	GetExceptionVec()	-NONE-	
Chain to Real ISR	-NONE-	-NONE-	Function 0xE400	
Chain to Protected ISR	-NONE-	-NONE-	-NONE-	

Table 9-1. (cont.)

	Phar Lap 286	Phar Lap 386	Rational DOS4GW	Windows
Set Real ISR	DosSetRealVec()	Function 0x2505		
Get Real ISR	DosGetRealVec()	Function 0x2503		
Set Protected ISR	DosSetProtVec()	Function 0x2504		
Get Protected ISR	DosGetProtVec()	Function 0x2502	U S E S	U S E S
Set Separate Split ISRs	DosSetRealProtVec()	Function 0x2507		
Get Both ISR Vectors	DosGetRealProtVec()	-NONE-		
Set Protected Mode Split ISR	DosSetPassToProtVec()	Function 0x2506	D P M I	D P M I
Set Real Mode Split ISR	DosSetPassToRealVec()	-NONE-		
Set Exception Handler	DosSetExceptionHandler()	Function 0x2533		
Get Exception Handler	DosGetExceptionHandler()	Function 0x2532		
Chain to Real ISR	DosChainToRealIntr()	-NONE-		
Chain to Protected ISR	DosChainToProtIntr()	-NONE-		

V86 Extenders

Since V86 extenders (like Windows, Code Builder, or my own PROT) always handle interrupts in protected mode, they maintain only one vector. During processing, you can decide to call the real-mode interrupt, or not.

Under Code Builder, interrupt functions may request a pointer to the stack frame by using the _get_stk_frame() function. This frame (an

_XSTACK structure) contains several important values including the contents of the processor's registers. It also contains the opts field. By default, Code Builder will issue a V86 interrupt after the protected-mode ISR completes its processing. If opts contains a special value (STK_NOINT), then no real-mode processing will take place.

For a complete example of the Code Builder interrupt mechanism, refer to the Copy Builder program in Chapter 18 (Listing 18-4). The ourint9() function is an ISR that intercepts the keyboard interrupt to prevent rebooting via the Ctrl-Alt-Del key sequence.

V86 extenders are usually slower than mode switching extenders since each interrupt takes more processing. However, switching modes brings multitasking to a halt. If you are interested in multitasking—as Windows Enhanced mode is—you must run interrupts in V86 mode. Of course, when an extender that usually switches runs under Windows it uses the Windows DPMI server to reflect interrupts. This means even extenders that normally switch modes will run in V86 mode with the right DPMI host. Conversely, an extender that normally runs in V86 mode—Code Builder, for example—might reflect interrupts to real mode if you run it with a DPMI host that switches modes.

Interrupt Chaining

Interrupt chaining is a common practice in PC programming. The idea is to partially replace one ISR with another. The new ISR does some processing when it detects an interrupt, and then calls the original ISR to do most of the work. Often the new ISR then regains control and does further processing before returning. If you are not familiar with interrupt chaining, refer to the sidebar on the following page.

Chaining between protected-mode handlers is straightforward—you simply call the next interrupt function or use the _chain_intr() function that most compilers supply. Chaining between real-mode handlers is also simple with most DOS extenders (you can use conventional techniques). Unfortunately, chaining from a real-mode ISR to a protected-mode ISR (or vice versa) is more complex with most extenders. In the next chapter we will examine the cross-mode calls that must occur for this type of chaining.

CHAINING INTERRUPTS

Interrupt chaining is a technique often used in PC programming. As an example, suppose you wanted to prevent users from erasing files with a .DBF extension. One way to do this would be to write an ISR to take over interrupt 0x21. The new ISR would examine each interrupt 0x21 call. If the call was not a file delete function, it would pass the interrupt (chain it) to the previous interrupt 0x21 ISR. If the call was a file delete call, it would only chain to the previous handler if the file name did not end in .DBF.

Before installing the new ISR, you must get the existing ISR's address (using _dos_getvect(), for example), and save it. Your ISR would examine each interrupt 0x21. If the function code (in the AH register) is not 0x13 or 0x41 (the file deletion calls), it simply transfers control to the previous ISR's address. If the code is a delete command, the ISR examines the file name. If it ends in .DBF, the ISR can return an error code. Otherwise, it passes control to the previous ISR.

Interrupt chaining is often easiest to accomplish using assembly language. However, most C compilers that support interrupt functions can do the job. Given a pointer to an ISR, you can call it using the _chain_intr() function (both Borland C++ 3.0 and higher and Microsoft C/C++ support this function, or by declaring it as an interrupt function pointer and calling it as a function pointer. For instance:

```
void _far _interrupt (*isr)();
```

You may have difficulties altering arguments to the ISR, depending upon your compiler.

Here is a short fragment of a C program that intercepts interrupt 0x10 and chains to the old ISR. The setup() function kicks off the processing, and the cleanup() routine restores the interrupt table.

```
void _far _interrupt (*isr)();

void _far _interrupt newisr()
  {
  /* new processing here */
```

continued

```
continued

  _chain_intr(isr);
  }

void setup()
  {
  isr=_dos_getvect(0x10);
  _dos_setvect(0x10,newisr);
  }

void cleanup()
  {
  _dos_setvect(0x10,isr);
  }
■
```

Phar Lap's 286 extender has a simple method for chaining to real-mode ISRs in some situations. The DosChainToRealIntr( ) function passes control from a protected-mode ISR to a real-mode ISR. However, as in all chaining calls, the protected-mode ISR never regains control. You must use the more complex methods in Chapter 10 if you need to resume processing after the real-mode ISR completes its task.

Controlling Interrupts

There are several circumstances in which you may need to disable interrupts:

- An ISR that is not reentrant should disable interrupts while it executes.
- A critical timing loop must disable interrupts to ensure accuracy.
- Routines that share data structures with an ISR can disable interrupts to prevent conflicts.

Most C compilers provide the _disable( ) and _enable( ) functions (or variants of them) that translate to CLI and STI instructions. These functions control interrupt handling. The _disable( ) call inhibits all external interrupts, except the special nonmaskable interrupt (NMI). Since NMI signals a catastrophic error, this is usually not a problem. PC motherboards allow you to disable NMI—if you must do this, you can refer to the technical manuals for the computer, or the pertinent books in the bibliography. In most cases, you'll have no reason to disable NMI.

Many protected-mode environments (including Windows) never allow you to actually disable interrupts. Instead, they support a virtual interrupt flag. There is one virtual flag for each task. If the flag is set, the task receives interrupts. When the flag is clear, the task does not receive interrupts. With a virtual interrupt flag, the system always services interrupts. This prevents a user task from taking over the system. DPMI provides functions to manipulate its virtual interrupt flag (functions 0x900, 0x901, and 0x902). Function 0x900 disables interrupts, 0x901 enables them, and 0x902 reads the current value of the interrupt flag. The C library's _disable() and _enable() functions control the virtual interrupt flag, if it exists. Be careful using these functions in time-critical code. The _disable() and _enable() functions may take much longer to execute than you would expect if they cause an exception and the DPMI host manipulates the virtual interrupt flag. The DPMI specification (see the bibliography) says that these simple instructions may take more than 300 clock cycles to execute under some hosts.

Processor Exceptions

The PC's hardware interrupts conflict with the internal processor exceptions (this reflects poor planning on IBM's part). For example, the PC's second serial port uses interrupt 0xB. Interrupt 0xB also occurs when a program attempts to access an absent segment. In real mode this is rarely important. These exceptions (like interrupt 0xB or 0xD), however, are critical to protected-mode operation.

To prevent problems, many DOS extenders alter the PC's interrupt controller to remap the offending interrupts. However, the extender usually translates the interrupt numbers internally so you can still use the customary numbers. If you need to handle a processor exception, you can use a special function instead of _dos_setvect(). For example, 286|DOS Extender provides the DosSetExceptionHandler() function for this purpose. DPMI servers use functions 0x210 to 0x213 (see the appendix) to control exception processing. Windows programs can use functions in the TOOLHELP.DLL (discussed later in this chapter) to handle exceptions without the trouble of directly dealing with DPMI.

An Example

There is no uniform method for manipulating interrupt vectors and functions. Each DOS extender is different, and the compiler may make a difference as well. Table 9-1 summarizes the available options.

Listing 9-1 contains INT286.C, an example of interrupt handling using Phar Lap's 286|DOS Extender. The main program hooks the protected-mode interrupt 0x10 vector, which handles output to the screen. The ISR shifts all BIOS output to uppercase.

INT286 uses the DosSetPassToProtVec() call to point both the real- and protected-mode vectors to the same ISR (new_int10). The DosSetRealProtVec() function, used here just before exiting, ordinarily sets split ISRs, but here it simply restores the two previous vectors.

Before new_int10() ends, it uses the DosChainToRealIntr() function to pass control to the original real-mode handler. Of course, that function never returns—the real-mode handler returns to the interrupted program.

Listing 9-1. INT286.C

```
* INT286.C - Replace interrupt 0x10 with Phar Lap 286DOSX
   Borland: bcc286 int286.c
   Microsoft: cl -AL -G2 -Lp int286.c */

#include <stdio.h>
#include <ctype.h>
#include <stdlib.h>
#include <phapi.h>

#ifdef __BORLANDC__
#define INT_REGS REGS_BINT
#else
#define INT_REGS REGS16
#endif
```

```
/* prototype for new ISR */
void _interrupt _far new_int10(INT_REGS r);

/* place to store old ISR addresses -- global so
   new_int10() can get at oldrint10 */
PIHANDLER oldpint10;
REALPTR   oldrint10;


void main()
  {
/* capture both real and protected vectors and pass them
   to new_int10() */
  DosSetPassToProtVec(0x10,
          (PIHANDLER)new_int10,&oldpint10,&oldrint10);
/* print from protected mode */
  printf("hello from protected mode\n");
/* run command.com in real mode to print */
  system("command /cecho hello from real mode");
/* restore previous vectors */
  DosSetRealProtVec(0x10,oldpint10,oldrint10,NULL,NULL);
  }

void _interrupt _far new_int10(INT_REGS r)
  {
  unsigned int ah=(r.ax&0xFF00)>>8;
/* If it is an output call shift character up */
  if (ah==9||ah==0xa||ah==0xe)
    r.ax=(r.ax&0xFF00)|toupper(r.ax&0xFF);
/* go to original handler */
  DosChainToRealIntr(oldrint10);
  }
```

Exception Handling In Windows

Windows programmers can use functions in the TOOLHELP.DLL library to intercept any faults that occur during program execution. Microsoft provides TOOLHELP.DLL with Windows 3.1, but it also works with Windows 3.0, and you can distribute it with your applications.

TOOLHELP provides many functions—it's a grab bag of programming gadgets. The two functions of special interest here are InterruptRegister() and InterruptUnRegister().

When a Windows program causes a processor exception, Windows 3.1 displays a warning and allows the user to terminate the program or attempt to ignore the error. While this is better than Windows 3.0's inscrutable unrecoverable application errors (UAEs), it is still inappropriate for many applications.

Windows exceptions are tricky. Windows often generates exceptions on purpose to force a privilege level transistion (see Chapter 4). Any method you use to capture exceptions must not interfere with these expected "errors." Luckily, the TOOLHELP library filters these expected exceptions.

First, you install a callback function using InterruptRegister(). Your callback routine will gain control when a true exception occurs (see Table 9-2 for the exceptions TOOLHELP supports). The callback can then do one of three things:

1. Terminate the program (using TOOLHELP's TerminateApp() function).
2. Pass control to the next exception handler (which may be the default Windows error handler).
3. Retry the operation (after fixing the problem).

Table 9-2. TOOLHELP Exceptions

INT_DIV0	0	Divide-error exception
INT_1	1	Debugger interrupt
INT_3	3	Breakpoint interrupt
INT_UDINSTR	6	Invalid-opcode exception
INT_STKFAULT	12 (0xC)	Stack exception
INT_GPFAULT	13 (0xD)	General protection violation
INT_BADPAGEFAULT	14 (0xD)	Unexpected Page fault
INT_CTLALTSYSRQ	256 (0x100)	CTRL+ALT+SysRq key*

This is not a real processor exception— it is artificially generated by TOOLHELP.

The InterruptRegister() function requires two parameters: a handle to the calling task and a far pointer to the callback function that you get from the MakeProcInstance() call. If the task handle is NULL, it indicates the current task (the usual case).

As you might expect, an InterruptRegister() callback is an unusual function. Like an interrupt function, the callback must preserve all registers. Unlike an interrupt function, it returns with a far return—not an interrupt return. Of course all callback functions must be exported.

The callback function receives register values on the stack (see Figure 9-1) and has no return value. The function must be reentrant—an error during processing can cause Windows to invoke the callback multiple times without an intervening return.

Figure 9-1. Interrupt Callback Stack Frame

faulting SS*	SP+0x12
faulting SP*	SP+0x10
faulting FLAGS	SP+0x0E
faulting CS	SP+0x0C
faulting IP	SP+0x0A
reserved	SP+0x08
exception number	SP+0x06
AX	SP+0x04
TOOLHELP CS	SP+0x02
TOOLHELP IP	SP+0x00

*Only present on low–stack faults

You must also page lock the callback routine using GlobalPageLock(). This ensures the callback is always present and prevents Windows from having to swap in the function when the system is in distress.

The interrupt callback doesn't have an ordinary return value, but it still can select several ways of dealing with exceptions. The choices are:

1. Return to Windows. This causes the next interrupt handler (usually Window's default handler) to gain control.

2. Correct the problem that caused the exception, remove the first 10 bytes from the stack frame (see Figure 9-1) and execute an IRET instruction to restart the application. Alternately, you can remove 14 bytes from the stack, push a new address on the stack, and then issue an IRET. This is difficult to do in C.

3. Call TerminateApp() to end the application. Some system resources may be lost when you do this.

More About the Callback

Since there are so many unusual requirements for the exception callback, it is often easiest to write it using assembly language. If you prefer, you can write it mostly in C and only use assembly where absolutely necessary.

Ordinary C functions do not preserve registers—you must use the _saveregs keyword with the callback function. You will also need the _loadds modifier since DS may contain any value when the callback gains control.

Since Windows passes arguments to the callback function on the stack, you can use the conventional C calling convention to access them. Putting it all together, the callback function looks like this:

```
void _far _loadds _saveregs _export int_callback(unsigned AX,
    unsigned exception_nr,unsigned reserved,
    unsigned IP,unsigned CS,unsigned FLAGS,
    unsigned SP, unsigned SS)
  {
  }
```

If you want to pass control to the next exception handler, a simple return will do. Calling TerminateApp() to end the program is also simple. Simply pass the task handle (NULL for the current task) and a flag (UAE_BOX or NO_UAE_BOX) to tell Windows if it should display a UAE box or not. For example:

```
TerminateApp(NULL,NO_UAE_BOX);
```

Restarting the program via an IRET is more difficult. You have to resort to assembly language to clean the stack and generate the IRET instruction. The InterruptRegister() example in this chapter (Listing 9-2) shows how it is done.

An Example

Listing 9-2 is a simple example program that uses InterruptRegister(). The exception function, on_gp(), will receive control when any exception occurs. If the intno parameter is not 0 (divide by zero) or 13 (general protection fault), on_gp() returns to Windows, which will then display its normal error box.

When exception 0 or 13 occurs, on_gp() displays a message box with 3 buttons: Abort, Retry, and Fail. The ignore button causes on_gp() to return to Windows and let the default handler take over. The abort button calls TerminateApp() to end the program. The retry button restarts the program at the point of failure. Since on_gp() doesn't attempt to repair the problem, this is sure to cause the error again.

The retry button logic uses the _asm keyword to incorporate assembly language into the function. The first assembly language instruction removes all local variables from the stack. The following POP instructions reverse the effect of the _savereg keyword (note that the code discards the saved stack pointer, SP). Following the POP instructions, on_gp() adds 10 to the stack pointer to remove the TOOLHELP information and then issues an IRET. This causes the program to restart where the error occurred.

The test() function deliberately causes a GP fault and a divide by zero error to test on_gp()'s operation. First, it must lock the segment containing on_gp( ) using the GlobalPageLock( ) function, and install the handler via InterruptRegister( ). Note that the pointer passed to InterruptRegister( ) is one that MakeProcInstance( ) returns—not the actual address of the function.

To run the entire program, press the ignore buttons that on_gp( ) and Windows present. Before the program terminates, it must unregister on_gp( ) (using InterruptUnRegister( )), free the pointer created with MakeProcInstance( ) with a call to FreeProcInstance( ), and unlock the on_gp( ) function (via GlobalPageUnlock( )).

Listing 9-2.FAULTS.C()

```
Catching faults with InterruptRegister()
   Compile:
   Borland: BWINCOMP faults
   Microsoft: MWINCOMP faults
*/
#include "winpmode.h"
#include <windows.h>
#include <toolhelp.h>
#include <dos.h>

#ifndef __BORLANDC__
#pragma check_stack(off)
#endif


/* Fault handler */
void _far _saveregs _loadds on_gp(
    WORD ax, WORD intno, WORD hand, WORD faultip,
    WORD faultcs, WORD flags,WORD sp, WORD ss)
    {
    int cmd;
    static char ad[25];
/* Set up box title */
    wsprintf(ad,"Fault - CS:IP=%04X:%04X",faultcs,faultip);
    if ((intno&0xFF)==0)
       cmd=MessageBox(NULL,"Divide by zero",ad,
           MB_ICONSTOP|MB_ABORTRETRYIGNORE|MB_TASKMODAL);
    else if ((intno&0xFF)==13)
       cmd=MessageBox(NULL, "GP Fault", ad,
           MB_ICONSTOP|MB_ABORTRETRYIGNORE|MB_TASKMODAL);
```

```c
/* Only look at GP and /0 faults */
    else return;
/* Act on command */
    switch (cmd)
        {
/* Abort -- terminate application */
        case IDABORT:
            MessageBox(NULL,
"Some system resources may not be freed",
            "Warning",MB_ICONSTOP|MB_OK|MB_TASKMODAL);
            TerminateApp(NULL,NO_UAE_BOX);

/* Retry -- since we don't try to correct things this will
   just cause the same fault again. */
        case IDRETRY:
/* Can't do this in C easily (if at all) */
            _asm {
/* blow C's stack */
                mov sp,bp
/* restore registers from _savereg */
                pop es
                pop ds
                pop di
                pop si
                pop bp
                pop bx    /* ignore pushed sp! */
                pop bx
                pop dx
                pop cx
                pop ax
/* remove toolhelp's stack */
                add sp,10
/* return to application */
                iret
                }

/* no action for ignore -- pass to default handler */
        }
    }

#ifndef __BORLANDC__
#pragma check_stack
```

```
#endif


char *test()
  {
  extern HANDLE hInst;
  char _far *p,x,y=0;
  FARPROC gphnd;
  GlobalPageLock(FP_SEG(on_gp));
  gphnd=MakeProcInstance((FARPROC)on_gp,hInst);
  InterruptRegister(NULL,gphnd);
/* create bad pointer */
  FP_SEG(p)=0;
/* access it */
  x=*p;
/* divide by zero */
  x=10/y;

/* Clean up */
  InterruptUnRegister(NULL);
  FreeProcInstance(gphnd);
  GlobalPageUnlock(FP_SEG(on_gp));
  return "Done";
  }
```

The TOOLHELP library's primary purpose is to support Windows debuggers. However, with a little effort, you can use the InterruptRegister() function to help bulletproof your program. By correcting errors, or returning to a known address to continue processing, you can have a truly robust application. At the very least, you can display more helpful error messages.

Of course, you can use the InterruptRegister() function for its intended purpose: debugging. You could easily write any important information to a debugging file before passing control back to Windows. This is how Microsoft's Dr. Watson program works. With InterruptRegister(), you can make your custom debugger an integral part of your application rather than a separate program like Dr. Watson.

CHAPTER ▪ 10

Return to Real Mode

As liberating as protected-mode programming can be, there are times when you will need to use real-mode code from inside an extended program:

- If you need to call interrupts that your extender does not directly support (undocumented DOS calls are especially important).

- If you need to call existing (possibly third-party) libraries that you can't easily convert to protected mode.

- You can sometimes increase performance by directly calling DOS and BIOS functions.

- With a real-mode handler, you can rapidly service interrupts that occur in real mode.

Real Code, Real Data

When your protected-mode program calls a DOS or BIOS interrupt supported by the DOS extender, the extender takes care of moving any arguments in memory above 1M to buffers below 1M. This allows real-mode functions to access the arguments. For example, when you pass a string to

175

DOS interrupt 0x21 function 9 (print string), the extender copies the string to the memory area, called a "transfer buffer" below 1M. It then passes a pointer to the copied string to DOS (which cannot access memory above 1M). Conversely, the extender converts any pointers to returned data to point to the transfer buffer. When the call completes, the extender copies the buffer to your protected-mode data area. Each interrupt requires special handling—the extender must know which function calls deal with in-memory arguments and what registers contain the pointers to them.

When you call real-mode code directly, the extender doesn't perform these translations; the programmer is responsible. DOS extenders provide calls to allocate memory that will reside below 1M (see Table 10-1). Don't use the I/O address mapping calls discussed in Chapter 8 for this purpose. Those calls don't properly reserve memory from DOS—they should only map hardware addresses, or predefined data buffers.

Table 10-1. Real Mode Memory Allocation Functions

	Allocate DOS Memory	Free DOS Memory	Resize DOS Memory
DPMI	Function 0x0100	Function 0x0101	Function 0x0102
Ergo DPM/16	AllocRealMem( )	FreeRealMem( )	ResizeRealMem( )
Ergo OSx86	Functions 0x48 or 0xE802	Function 0x49	Function 0x4A or 0xE905
Intel	Funtion 0x48	Funtion 0x49	Function 0x4A or 0xE905
Phar Lap 286	DosAllocRealSeg( )	DosFreeSeg( )	DosReallocSeg( )
Phar Lap 386	Function 0x25C0	Function 0x25C1	Function 0x25C2
Rational DOS4GW	USES DPMI		
Windows	GlobalDosAlloc( )	GlobalDosFree( )	N/A

Once you have a DOS buffer, you can place arguments to DOS functions in it directly, freeing the buffer when you are done. Often this is faster than copying data between protected mode and real-mode buffers. If efficiency is a concern, you might consider using these techniques even to call some interrupts that your extender *does* support to avoid the block copy overhead.

Classifying Real-Mode Code

Most DOS extenders can explicitly call two types of real-mode procedures: subroutines and interrupt service routines (ISRs). Some extenders can only call real-mode ISRs. Depending on your extender, you will need to supply the routine's address or interrupt number and any parameters it expects.

Table 10-2 outlines the functions required to call real-mode code in various DOS extenders. Since DPMI supplies functions to call subroutines and ISRs, some DPMI-only extenders don't duplicate them—you simply use the DPMI service directly.

Table 10-2. Real-Mode Procedure Call Functions

	Call Real Interrupt	Call Real Function	Call Real ISR
DPMI	Function	Function	Function
Ergo DPM/16	0x0300 DoRealInterrupt()	0x0301 CallRMwithFRET()	0x0302 CallRMwithIRET()
Ergo OS/x86	Function 0xE3	Function 0xE1	-NONE-
Intel	USES DPMI		
Phar Lap 286	DosRealIntr()	DosRealFarCall()	DosRealFarCall()* DosChainToRealIntr()
Phar Lap 386	Function 0x2511	Functions 0x250E or 0x2510	-NONE-
Rational DOS4GW	USES DPMI		
Windows	USED DPMI		

*See text

Calls

DOS extenders only support real-mode subroutines that use far calls. A subroutine is far if it expects, its return address to contain a segment and an offset. This is the default in huge large and medium model C programs;; in other memory models, you can use the far keyword.

Another subroutine concern is calling convention. Most subroutines expect arguments to appear on the stack, just before the return address. When a program calls a subroutine it must know a few things about it:

- What is the entry point address?
- How many arguments does it expect?
- What types are the arguments?
- In what order do the arguments appear?
- Who removes the arguments from the stack?

There are two common calling conventions: C and Pascal (see the sidebar). They differ in the order of the arguments and their removal from the stack. Invoking a function with the wrong calling convention is a guaranteed prescription for misery. At best, the subroutine will misbehave. In the worst cases, your program will crash or generate a fault.

CALLING CONVENTIONS

Since C supports functions with a variable number of arguments (like printf()), it places arguments on the stack from right to left. This way, the first argument is always on top of the stack. For example, the call:

```
fn(a,b,c);
```

generates the following psuedo-assembly language code:

```
PUSH c
PUSH b
PUSH a
CALL fn
```

Functions like printf() use the first argument to decide how many parameters the caller passed to it.

continued

continued

Pascal only allows functions that take a fixed number of parameters. It places its arguments on the stack in the order they appear in the source code. This results in the top of the stack containing the last argument:

```
PUSH a
PUSH b
PUSH c
CALL fn
```

Since a C function can have any number of arguments, it is customary for the caller to remove the arguments from the stack. This requires extra code for each call to a function. Pascal functions economize by cleaning up the stack before they return; the clean-up code appears once per **function** rather than once per function **call**.

Many C compilers allow a function modifier to select the Pascal calling convention. For example:

```
void _pascal odd_function(int a, int b);
```

prototypes a function that follows the Pascal convention. Since Pascal calls are slightly more efficient, some software (like Microsoft Windows) uses them when they don't need a variable number of arguments.

When a DOS extender calls a real-mode procedure, it needs to know if it should remove the arguments upon return or not. As an example, consider Phar Lap's 286|DOS Extender, which uses the DosRealFarCall() function to call real-mode code. The fourth parameter to DosRealFarCall() is the number of 16-bit words to pass on the stack. If this number is negative, the extender treats it as though it were positive, but it assumes the function will clean up the stack (pascal convention). If the number is positive, the extender clears the stack when the call is complete (convention). ■

When calling real-mode code, DOS extenders require that you organize the argument order yourself. You must arrange the arguments as a list of 16-bit integers, and you are responsible for converting any data types that are longer.

Interrupts

Calling real-mode interrupts is straightforward. Since interrupts generally pass arguments via registers, and not on the stack, parameter passing is simplified. Interrupts always clean up the stack, which contains the return address and a copy of the flags. (Note: The DOS direct disk access interrupts 0x25 and 0x26 are notable exceptions—don't call these interrupts unless your extender explicitly allows it.)

To call a real-mode interrupt routine, you simply tell the extender what register-based parameters you want (usually placing them in a structure), and make the call (using one of the functions in Table 10-2). The extender will copy the return registers into a structure for your program to inspect.

Calling a real-mode interrupt using these techniques is analogous to, but not the same as using the int86() function that your compiler may provide. In extended programs, the int86() function calls a protected-mode interrupt. When you write:

```
int86(0x21,&r,&r);
```

you actually invoke the DOS extender's interrupt 0x21 protected mode ISR. This ISR does any argument translation required, and calls the real-mode ISR. Upon return, the extender converts any return parameters for you.

Some extenders allow you to issue a real-mode interrupt by specifying its vector number (such as interrupt 0x60). This requires that the ISR actually be attached to an interrupt. Other extenders will accept the address of the ISR—this is useful if you want to chain to an ISR and then regain control.

Even if your extender doesn't explicitly allow an ISR call by address, you may be able to fake it. You can treat a real-mode ISR as a Pascal-type function with the following prototype:

```
void _far _pascal isr(short flags);
```

Why does this work? An interrupt places three words on the stack. First, it pushes the flags, then the current value of CS, then IP. When the interrupt executes an IRET, it removes all three words from the stack and returns to the calling program. A far call is very similar. The main difference is that a far call does not store the flags on the stack.

Since a function call pushes argument values on the stack, you can push two bytes as an "argument" to the ISR. This alleged argument is really the flags that a true interrupt would have pushed. When an ISR returns, the flags are no longer on the stack. This is exactly how a Pascal function with one argument would act. A C call function would incorrectly try to remove the argument upon return and crash the stack.

Given a pointer to the ISR, you can easily call it using the normal subroutine techniques. XCI.C (Listing 12-2 in Chapter 12) uses this technique to chain the keyboard interrupt (0x16) under Phar Lap's 286|DOS Extender. The usual DosChainRealIntr() won't work for this purpose. When your program calls DosChainRealIntr(), it gives up control—the real-mode ISR will return directly to the interrupted program.

A caveat: When calling real-mode code, set the flags parameter to a reasonable value. A stray one bit can cause unexpected results. If the single-step flag is set, for instance, a debug interrupt may occur upon return and crash your program. Several extenders allow you to set the flags to zero. Then they fill in a harmless value for the flags.

Round-Trip

With most extenders real-mode code can call, or at least signal, protected-mode code. This is important when a real-mode program needs to asynchronously communicate with your DOS extended program. A mouse driver, for example, calls an event function in your program to report mouse activity. If the driver couldn't call the protected-mode program, you would be forced to write a real-mode event function that shared memory with your extended program. Your main program would then poll the shared memory area, waiting for events. This defeats the purpose of using event functions.

The trick is to allocate a real-mode callback. Most extenders (and DPMI) allow this in some form. When you create a callback, you bind a protected-mode function to a real-mode address. When a program (like a mouse driver) calls that real-mode address it triggers the protected-mode function. In some systems callbacks may be a scarce resource—you should free them when you no longer need them. DPMI servers must support at least 16 callbacks.

Table 10-3 summarizes the callback-related functions present in several extenders (the Ergo OS/286 and OS/386 Real Procedure Signals are similar to callbacks). Note that you don't need to use callbacks to intercept real-mode interrupts—Chapter 9 covered better ways to do that.

Table 10-3. Real-Mode Callback Functions

	Allocate Callback	Free Callback	Locate Real Entry	Call Protected-Mode Function	Set Real Handler Signal
DPMI	Function 0x0303	Function 0x0304	N/A	N/A	N/A
Ergo DPM/16	AllocCallBack()	FreeCallBack	N/A	N/A	N/A
Ergo OS/x86	N/A	N/A	N/A	N/A	Function 0xE2
Intel			USES DPMI		
Phar Lap 286	N/A	N/A	N/A	DosProtFarCall()	N/A
Phar Lap 386	N/A	N/A	Function 0x250D	N/A	N/A
Rational DOS4GW			USES DPMI		
Windows			USES DPMI		

Adding Real Code

If you need to call a DOS or BIOS function, you don't need to worry about loading real-mode code—DOS and BIOS code is already present. But other real-mode code presents a problem: How can a protected-mode program contain real-mode functions?

There is no single method that all extenders use to include real-mode code with protected-mode programs. The most convenient method is to include a real-mode DLL. You can also load your real-mode subroutines as a terminate-and-stay-resident (TSR) program, and communicate with them via interrupts. Some extenders allow you to modify a portion of their own source code (a loader) to include real-mode functions. Others can load real-mode executables as an overlay.

DLLs

We will examine dynamic link libraries (DLLs) in detail in Chapter 12. In their simplest form, DLLs are similar to ordinary object code libraries (.LIB files, for example). The difference is that programs link with DLLs at execution time—not when you compile and link the program. DLLs reside in their own files, and many programs can share one DLL.

DOS extenders (with the notable exception of Windows; which does not support real-mode DLLs) that support DLLs allow you to create them for protected-mode or real-mode code. With DLLs, you can refer to real-mode functions by their symbolic names—you don't need to deal with hex addresses. These symbolic names may represent the protected-mode addresses of the real-mode functions. You must convert them to real mode before calling them. See Chapter 12 for more about using real-mode DLLs.

TSRs and Related Methods

You can also package your real-mode code as a TSR. TSRs are DOS programs that exit to DOS but remain in memory. The TSR then waits for an interrupt to activate it. A TSR can intercept a user interrupt (interrupts 0x60-0x66) or the multiplex interrupt (0x2F) and exit using interrupt 0x21 function 0x31. You must load the TSR before your protected-mode program runs. In addition, you must tell the protected-mode program which interrupt the TSR is using. For example, you could pass the interrupt number as an argument, in a configuration file, or in the DOS environment.

When your TSR receives the proper interrupt it can pass back the addresses of its functions. Armed with these addresses you can easily call the functions using the real-mode call techniques discussed earlier in this chapter. Alternatively, you can pass a function code (or message if you prefer) to the TSR to request an operation.

General-purpose TSRs like PRINT.COM or Borland's SideKick are difficult to write and debug. However, the TSRs you need for embodying real-mode code are much simpler. You don't have to deal with DOS multitasking (or lack thereof), hot keys, and other DOS trivia. If you want to try your hand at TSR writing, look up some of the references in the bibliography. In particular, *DOS 5: A Developer's Guide* has a toolkit for creating special TSRs called interceptors that are exactly what you need for storing real-mode code.

If you don't want to try TSRs, you can often achieve almost the same results with simple C programming. Listing 10-1 shows a real-mode C program that intercepts an interrupt, and then runs a 286|DOS Extender program (Listing 10-2) using the spawnlp( ) function.

The real-mode program passes the interrupt number as an argument to the protected-mode program. When the extended program terminates, the real-mode program removes its ISR, and exits. This is the same idea as a TSR but much simpler to implement, especially in C. Real-mode DLLs would be more elegant, but you'll have to wait for Chapter 12 to learn more about them. Besides, only a few extender support DLLs (presently, Ergo's DPM16 and Phar Lap's 286 product), whereas almost all extenders will work with the TSR method (or the quasi-TSR "spawn wrapper" method Listings 10-1 and 10-2 use). Although a true TSR would be more complex, it would also consume less memory than REALMODE.C.

Listing 10-1. REALMODE.C

```
/* Real mode program that interfaces with
   286|DOS Extender
   Borland: bcc realmode.c
   Microsoft: cl realmode.c
*/

#include <stdio.h>
#include <stdlib.h>
#include <process.h>
#include <dos.h>
```

```c
#define SET 1
#define RESET 0

int hookint(int);

main()
  {
  int intno,rc;
  char tempstr[16];
/* hook interrupt */
  if ((intno=hookint(SET))!=-1)
    {
/* if successful, call run286 and pass it interrupt number
   as command line argument */
    rc=spawnlp(P_WAIT,"run286.exe","run286.exe",
                      "protmode.exe",itoa(intno,tempstr,10),
                      NULL);
    if (rc==-1)
      printf("Can't find RUN286.EXE or PROTMODE.EXE\n");
/* unhook interrupt */
    hookint(RESET);
    }
  return rc;
  }


/* clear screen in real mode (for no good reason) */
void _far _interrupt isr()
  {
/* set constant to 0xb0000000 if using mono monitor */
  int i;
  int _far *video=(int _far *)0xb8000000;
  for (i=0;i<2000;i++) *video++=0x720;
  return;
  }

/* hook and unhook a user interrupt
   (from 0x60-0x67) */
int hookint(int action)
  {
/* interrupt number used */
  static int intno=-1;
```

```c
  void (_far _interrupt *oldvector)();
  int i;
  if (action==SET)
    {
    for (i=0x60;i<=0x67;i++)
      {
      oldvector=_dos_getvect(i);
      if (!oldvector)
        {
/* found unused interrupt */
        intno=i;
        _dos_setvect(i,isr);
        break;
        }
      }
    return intno;
    }
  else
    {
/* mark vector as unused */
    _dos_setvect(intno,NULL);
    intno=-1;
    return -1;
    }
  }
```

Listing 10-2. PROTMODE.C

```c
/* 286 protected mode program for use with realmode.c
   Borland: bcc286 -w-eff protmode.c
   Microsoft: cl -AL -G2 -Lp protmode.c

   Ignore Borland's "code has no effect" message */

#include <stdio.h>
#include <phapi.h>
#include <stdlib.h>

main(int argc,char *argv[])
  {
  int intno;
/* error check */
```

```
  if (argc!=2||(intno=atoi(argv[1]))<0x60||intno>0x67)
    {
    printf("Don't run this program directly. "
           "Use REALMODE.EXE.\n");
    exit(1);
    }

/* print a message */
  printf("This message comes to you from protected mode.\n");
  printf("Press <ENTER> to see the real mode ISR clear the "
         "screen.\n");
  printf("Then press <ENTER> again to exit.\n");
/* wait for enter key */
  getchar();
/* call real mode interrupt; if you wanted to pass
 * an integer, say 10, to the ISR, you'd use:
 *       DosRealIntr(intno,NULL,0,sizeof(int),10);
 * but in this case there are no arguments. */
  DosRealIntr(intno,NULL,0,0);
/* wait for enter key again */
  getchar();
  printf("Back in protected mode.\n");
  return 0;
  }
```

If you use an existing library of real-mode functions that for one reason or another can't be ported to protected-mode, you may have to write a special interrupt service routine to work with it. Your ISR would process a function code passed by the protected-mode program. Depending on the function code, the ISR would call the library routines supplying any parameters from the registers you passed, or from a block of real-mode memory you allocated for this purpose. Alternatively, your ISR could return an array of real-mode pointers to each function's entry point.

When using the quasi-TSR method, be careful about processing during the real-mode program's initialization. If you open files before loading the extended program, for example, those files won't be open to the protected-mode program or the real-mode ISR. Unless if it takes special measures to set the DOS PSP, the ISR executes in the same context (PSP, current directory, etc.) as the protected-mode program. Usually, you should limit the real-mode main() function to loading the extended program. If you must set up files or other things, make a special interrupt function code for initialization, which your protected-mode program can call right away to perform any initial tasks.

Likewise, you may need to assign a function code for the protected-mode program to call as it exits. Before the real-mode program regains control, DOS will close any files opened by the ISR function. The same holds true for DOS memory that the ISR allocates—it will be free by the time the real-mode main() function regains control.

TSRs and Windows

You can use the TSR technique to access real-mode code from Windows programs too. However, the TSR must load before Windows starts (or in WINSTART.BAT). If you load a TSR in an enhanced mode DOS box, it will live it its own virtual machine and will not communicate with other DOS boxes or Windows programs (unless if you want to get into Windows VxD programming). In standard mode, DOS programs can't run concurrently with Windows programs, so again the TSR loaded after Windows is inaccessible.

All Windows programs and DOS boxes can communicate with a program (a TSR or a loader, see below) that was present before Windows started. You can use this technique to communicate between DOS boxes, Windows programs, and real-mode TSRs and device drivers. In Chapter 19, you will see an example of this technique.

Loaders

A *loader*, or *stub program*, is a real-mode program that you bind with a protected-mode executable. When the user runs your protected-mode program the loader takes control and executes the DOS extender. The DOS extender then loads your program and executes it. If you have access to the loader source code (as you do with Ergo's OS/x86, or Rational's DOS4G/W extenders), you can modify them to include real-mode routines. The technique is similar to the one Listing 10-1 uses.

Real Mode Segments and Overlays

Some extenders (like Phar Lap's 386|DOS Extender) allow you to link real-mode code together with protected-mode code. While this is convenient you must take great care to ensure that the real-mode routines load below 1M. Unless you have a special reason for linking the code together, you should consider using the quasi-TSR method in Listing 10-1 instead.

The Ergo OS/286 and OS/386 extenders can load a real-mode .EXE file at run time and communicate with it. The executable must follow a special protocol that requires some assembly language functions to interface with the C routines. Usually, you can use the quasi-TSR method from Listing 10-1 with far less trouble.

Using Existing Real-Mode Code

By using real-mode calls, interrupts, and callbacks, you can use existing real-mode software with extended DOS or Windows programs. For example, if you use a commercial graphics or interface library you probably don't have the option to recompile it for protected mode.

MUSIC.COM is a real-mode TSR program you can find on the companion disk. It plays notes on the PC speaker while other programs are executing, and you *don't* have the source code for it. MUSIC uses interrupt 0x15 functions for its API (see Table 10-4). Alternatively, you can directly call the function (interrupt 0x2F function 0xF700 returns the entry point). When MUSIC completes a sequence of notes, it will call a far subroutine set by your program via interrupt 0x15 function 0xAA05.

Table 10-4. MUSIC API

Interrupt	AX	Other Registers	Function
0x2F	0xF700		Returns AL=0xFF if installed and BX:CX=entry point*
0x15	0xAA00		Stops tones
0x15	0xAA01		Starts tones

Table 10-4. MUSIC API

Interrupt	AX	Other Registers	Function
0x15	0xAA02		Reset buffer and stop tones
0x15	0xAA03	DX=note CL=duration	Store note
0x15	0xAA04	CL=delay	Set repeat delay (0=no repeat)
0x15	0xAA05	DX=segment AX=offset	Set callback address

*Calling this address is equivalent to using interrupt 15H to access the API.

The first time you run MUSIC it loads itself into memory where it remains until you run it again. You can program up to 200 notes into MUSIC's internal buffer.

MUSIC demonstrates a common problem—how can you make your Windows (or other protected-mode) program communicate with an "alien" real-mode TSR program?

The first step to using existing real-mode software is to load it. Since MUSIC is a TSR, this presents no problem. Simply load MUSIC prior to starting Windows or other DOS extended programs.

Listing 10-3 shows PLAYWIN.C, a Windows program that interfaces with MUSIC.COM. The real_int() function uses DPMI function 0x300 to handle calls to the MUSIC API. Since MUSIC needs to call the protected-mode program, PLAYWIN must allocate a real-mode callback. For variety, PLAYWIN also uses DPMI function 0x302 (in the real_icall() function) to call MUSIC's direct entry point. Note that you must use function 0x302 instead of function 0x301 since MUSIC's API expects an interrupt-style call. Function 0x301 handles subroutines that expect a far call (see Appendix B for details about DPMI).

The alloc_callbk() function creates a real-mode callback using DPMI function 0x303. Each callback has a function address and a structure address associated with it. When the real-mode program passes control to the callback address, the DPMI server stores the real-mode registers in the structure associated with the callback and calls the indicated function.

The extender calls the callback function as though it were an interrupt. Therefore, the callback function must have the _interrupt attribute. When the callback function gets control, the ES:DI (or ES:EDI in 32-bit code) registers point to the real-mode register structure. The callback function can read these registers or modify them to affect the return values.

The callback function's DS:SI (or DS:ESI) registers point to the real-mode stack. This allows the callback function to read arguments from the stack, and control how the extender returns to real mode. Some real-mode programs will execute the callback address as an interrupt, and push the flags register and the return address on the stack. Others will use a far call and only push the return address. In either event, the callback function is responsible for calculating the return address and placing it in the register structure's CS and IP fields. Your callback function must also adjust the real-mode stack pointer the same way that an IRET (interrupt) or RETF (far subroutine) instruction does.

PLAYWIN's callback() function creates two pointers, rmregs and stack, to point to the registers and the stack. The callback must emulate a RETF instruction to properly return control to MUSIC. A RETF pops 4 bytes off the stack: the return segment (2 bytes) and the return offset (2 bytes). To imitate a far return, PLAYWIN uses the following code:

```
rmregs->CS=stack[1];
rmregs->IP=stack[0];
rmregs->SP+=4;
```

This restores the CS and IP values from the stack and adjusts the stack pointer (SP) the same way a far return instructions would.

To simulate an IRET instruction (to return from an interrupt call), the code is similar, but must take the extra flag word on the stack into account:

```
rmregs->flags=stack[2];
rmregs->CS=stack[1];
rmregs->IP=stack[0];
rmregs->SP+=6;
```

Listing 10-3. PLAYWIN.C

```
/* Calling real mode TSR from Windows
   Compile:
   Borland: BWINCOMP PLAYWIN
```

```
    Microsoft: MWINCOMP PLAYWIN
*/
#include <dos.h>
#include <ctype.h>
#include <string.h>
#include <windows.h>
#include "winpmode.h"

int setnotes(void);

/* Multiplex interrupt used to communicate with TSRs */
#define MUXINT      0x2f

/* DPMI register structure */
struct RM_REGS
    {
    unsigned long EDI, ESI, EBP,
    reserved, EBX, EDX, ECX, EAX;
    unsigned short flags, ES, DS, FS,
    GS, IP, CS,SP, SS;
     };

/* DPMI real interrupt */
real_int(int intno,struct RM_REGS *r)
  {
  union REGS pr;
  struct SREGS s;
  void _far *fp=(void _far *)r;
  segread(&s);

/* DPMI real interrupt function */
  pr.x.ax=0x300;
  pr.x.bx=intno;
  pr.x.cx=0;
  s.es=FP_SEG(fp);
  pr.x.di=FP_OFF(fp);

/* ask for default stack */
  r->SS=0;
  r->SP=0;

/* set flags to something appropriate */
```

```
  r->flags=0;
  int86x(0x31,&pr,&pr,&s);
  return pr.x.cflag;
  }

/* DPMI real mode call (return w/IRET) */
real_icall(struct RM_REGS *r)
  {
  union REGS pr;
  struct SREGS s;
  void _far *fp=(void _far *)r;
  segread(&s);

/* DPMI real mode call function */
  pr.x.ax=0x302;
  pr.h.bh=0;
  pr.x.cx=0;
  s.es=FP_SEG(fp);
  pr.x.di=FP_OFF(fp);

/* ask for default stack */
  r->SS=0;
  r->SP=0;

/* set flags to harmless value */
  r->flags=0;
  int86x(0x31,&pr,&pr,&s);
  return pr.x.cflag;
  }

/* allocate a real mode callback */
alloc_callbk(void _far *f,struct RM_REGS _far *r,
             void _far **cb)
  {
  union REGS pr;
  struct SREGS s;
  void _far *p;
  segread(&s);

/* DPMI Allocate callback function */
  pr.x.ax=0x0303;
  pr.x.si=FP_OFF(f);
```

```
  s.ds=FP_SEG(f);
  s.es=FP_SEG(r);
  pr.x.di=FP_OFF(r);
  int86x(0x31,&pr,&pr,&s);
  if (!pr.x.cflag)
    {
    FP_SEG(p)=pr.x.cx;
    FP_OFF(p)=pr.x.dx;
    *cb=p;
    }
  return pr.x.cflag;
  }

/* Free real mode callback */
free_callbk(void _far *p)
  {
  union REGS r;

/* DPMI callback free function */
  r.x.ax=0x0304;
  r.x.cx=FP_SEG(p);
  r.x.dx=FP_OFF(p);
  int86(0x31,&r,&r);
  return r.x.cflag;
  }



/* Table of musical notes */
int notes[6][12]=
  {
    {18357,17292,16345,15297,14551,13715,12830,12175,
    11473,10847,10198,9701},
    {9108,8584,8117,7649,7231,6818,6450,6088,5736,5424,
    5121,4811},
    {4554,4308,4058,3837,3616,3419,3225,3044,2875,2712,
    2560,2415},
    {2281,2154,2033,1918,1811,1709,1612,1522,1436,1356,
    1280,1208},
    {1147,1082,1015,961,910,858,802,761,718,678,639,605},
    {570,538,508,479,452,427,403,380,359,339,320,302}
  };
```

```c
/* Musical notes */
char xlat[]="CDEFGAB";

/* MUSIC command */
#define M_STOP     0xaa00
#define M_PLAY     0xaa01
#define M_RESET    0xaa02
#define M_SETNOTE  0xaa03
#define M_DELAY    0xaa04
#define M_CALLBK   0xaa05
#define M_LOADED   0xF700


/* number of times tones have played
   (updated by callback) */
int ctr=0;

/* Define callback routine. The real mode TSR can
   call this function. DPMI treats this
   function like an interrupt, so you must use the
   _interrupt attribute. The register order differs
   between Borland C++ and Microsoft C */
#ifdef __BORLANDC__
void _far _interrupt callback(unsigned bp,unsigned di,
                              unsigned si, unsigned ds,
                              unsigned es)
#else
void _far _interrupt callback(unsigned es,unsigned ds,
                              unsigned di, unsigned si)

#endif
  {
  struct RM_REGS _far *rmregs; /* real mode registers */
  unsigned _far *stack;  /* pointer to real mode stack */
  FP_SEG(rmregs)=es;   /* calculate pointer to registers */
  FP_OFF(rmregs)=di;
  FP_SEG(stack)=ds; /* calculate pointer to real mode stack */
  FP_OFF(stack)=si;
  ctr++; /* increment counter */

/* simulate far return -- "pop" return address
```

```c
      from stack and adjust SP */
   rmregs->CS=stack[1];
   rmregs->IP=stack[0];
   rmregs->SP+=4;
   }


char *cmd;

char *test()
   {
/* Allocate two structures for real mode registers
   rmregs holds registers passed to the callback
   routine and r holds registers for real mode
   interrupts and calls */
   struct RM_REGS rmregs,r;
/* real mode pointer to callback address */
   void _far *cb;

/* alternate entry point for MUSIC TSR */
   int music_ip,music_cs;

/* see if MUSIC is loaded */
   r.EAX=0xF700;
   real_int(MUXINT,&r);
   if ((r.EAX&0xFF)!=0xFF)
     {
     win_printf("Error","Music TSR not found!\n");
     return "Done";
     }

/* save entry point */
   music_ip=r.ECX&0xFFFF;
   music_cs=r.EBX&0xFFFF;

/* Reset MUSIC */
   r.EAX=M_RESET;
   real_int(0x15,&r);

/* Set replay delay to 1 second */
   r.EAX=M_DELAY;
   r.ECX=18;
```

```
/* Call entry point instead of using
   INT 15H -- both are equivalent */
  r.IP=music_ip;
  r.CS=music_cs;
  real_icall(&r);

/* set callback address */
  alloc_callbk(callback,&rmregs,&cb);
  r.EDX=FP_SEG(cb);
  r.ECX=FP_OFF(cb);
  r.EAX=M_CALLBK
  real_int(0x15,&r);

  while (1)
    {
    int n=0;
/* read command */
    cmd=win_input("Main Menu","(%d) "
        "E=enter notes, P=play, S=stop, R=reset, Q=quit",ctr);
    while (isspace(cmd[n])) n++;
    if (!cmd[n]) continue;
    switch (toupper(*cmd))
      {
      case 'E':
        setnotes();
        break;

      case 'P':
/* play notes (use alternate entry point */
        r.EAX=M_PLAY;  /* Music play command */
        r.IP=music_ip;
        r.CS=music_cs;
        real_icall(&r);
        break;

      case 'S':
/* stop notes */
        r.EAX=M_STOP;  /* Music stop command */
      case 'R':
/* reset notes */
        r.EAX=M_RESET;  /* Music reset command */
```

```
          real_int(0x15,&r);
          r.EAX=M_DELAY;  /* Music set delay */
          r.ECX=18;
          real_int(0x15,&r);
          break;

      case 'Q':
/* quit (but release callback first) */
          r.EAX=M_CALLBK;
          r.EDX=r.ECX=0;
          real_int(0x15,&r);
          free_callbk(cb);
          return "Done";

      default:
          win_printf("Error","I don't understand!\n");
          break;
      }
    }
  }


/* Read notes and pass to MUSIC TSR */
setnotes()
  {
  struct RM_REGS r;
  int beat=8;
  int octave=3;
  win_printf("Instructions",
          "Enter notes using the following notation:\n"
          "1C - Whole note C\n"
          "2D - 1/2 note D\n"
          "4E - 1/4 note E\n"
          "E  - 1/4 note E\n"
          "8F - 1/8 note F\n"
          "G# - 1/4 G sharp\n"
           real_int(0x15,&r);
           break;

          "A- - 1/4 A flat\n"
          ".  - 1/4 rest\n"
          "@2 - Change octaves (1-6)\n"
```

```
                "Enter a blank line to return to the main menu\n");
        while (*(cmd=win_input("Enter Notes","Notes:")))
         {
         int i,n=strlen(cmd);
         for (i=0;i<n;i++)
            {
            int c;
            int noteindex;
            int newbeat;
            c=toupper(cmd[i]);
            if (c=='@')
              {
              c=cmd[++i]-'1';
              if (c>=0&&c<=6) octave=c;
              continue;
              }
            newbeat=beat/4;
            if (isdigit(cmd[i]))
              {
              newbeat=beat/(cmd[i++]-'0');
              c=cmd[i];
              }
/* rest? */
            if (c=='.')
              {
              noteindex=999;
              }
            else
              {
/* ignore non-notes */
              if (!strchr(xlat,c)) continue;
              noteindex=strchr(xlat,c)-xlat;
              noteindex*=2;
              if (noteindex>4) noteindex--;
              }
            if (cmd[i+1]=='#')
             {
             noteindex++;
             i++;
             }
            else if (cmd[i+1]=='-')
              {
```

```
        noteindex--;
        i++;
        }
/* send note to MUSIC */
     r.EAX=M_SETNOTE;
     r.EDX=noteindex<900?notes[octave][noteindex]:0;
     r.ECX=newbeat;
     real_int(0x15,&r);
     }
   }
  return 0;
  }
```

Conclusion

A robust DOS extender must allow you to call real-mode code because no extender could forsee every undocumented DOS interrupt, device driver, and program API that you may need to use. Also, many applications depend on existing libraries for graphics or device functions that you can't easily port to protected mode, especially if you don't have the source code for them. Although the MUSIC example works with Windows, the same principles apply to most DOS extenders—especially those that support DPMI.

Calling real-mode code from DOS extenders is easy—loading the real-mode code with your program is more complicated. With the TSR and quasi-TSR techniques in this chapter, you should have few problems integrating real-mode routines with your Windows and other DOS extended programs.

CHAPTER ■ 11

Extending Extenders—
Virtual Memory to the Rescue

Most 32-bit, and some 16-bit, extenders support virtual memory (VM). With VM, your programs can use more memory that the computer contains. All VM systems rely on the same principle: no matter how much memory a program needs, it can't use it all at one time. VM systems transparently move memory to and from secondary storage (e.g., DISK) as needed.

Of course, disk memory isn't as fast as main memory—programs that use VM may run more slowly than those that don't. Still, when a program accesses a memory address, it is likely that future accesses will be nearby. VM systems improve performance by retaining the most recently accessed areas of memory because there are most likely to be needed again in the rear future. Memory is only moved to disk when absolutely necessary. The memory regions that the system moves to disk are the ones that were least recently used. This is known as the least recently used (LRU) swapping algorithm.

Virtual memory systems try to only swap memory blocks (or pages) that have not been used within some period of time. The pages that have been used inside of that time period are the program's working set. The

VM systems tries to give each program enough physical memory pages to contain its working set at any given time. This helps prevent *thrashing*—the phenomena that occurs when the VM system must keep moving the same page back and forth betwen the disk and main memory.

Overview

When a VM system begins operation, it creates a pool of free memory blocks in physical memory. A simple 286 VM system uses the following logic to satisfy memory requests from this pool:

1. Search for a free block that will satisfy the request.

2. If the search is successful, mark the block as used, create a segment descriptor, and return the segment selector to the requesting program.

3. If the search is not successful, find a block that would satisfy the request that has not recently been used. Mark the segment as absent, and write its contents to the swap file on disk. Then mark the block as free, and start over at step 1.

These steps are simplified by the protected-mode segment structure (see Chapter 4). The processor allows segments to be present or absent, and sets a special flag when a program accesses a segment. If you access a segment that is not present, the processor raises an exception. An operating system can intercept this exception and load the segment from disk. Of course, it may have to move other segments to disk to make room. Since the operating system restarts your program at the point of the exception, this process is transparent to your program. Since disk speeds are slower than memory speeds, there will be some performance degradation. Without these features, VM would be difficult to implement.

286 Problems

The 286 marks segments as absent when they reside in the swap file. When a program uses an absent segment, the VM system must allocate enough space to hold the segment (using the above steps) and read the block in from the swap file. That space in the swap file may now be reused.

This scheme provides virtual memory, but it does have some drawbacks. A 64K segment will take longer to swap to disk than a smaller segment. On the other hand, many small segments are more likely to require swapping than one, larger segment. Another drawback is that the entire segment must be in memory, or on disk. Since the 286 has no MMU (see Chapter 4), there must be contiguous memory available for a segment.

386 Advantages

Thanks to the MMU (see Chapter 4), 386 processors can improve VM performance considerably. A 386 VM system uses uniform-sized 4K pages as units to swap, instead of segments. With the 386, you can mark a 4K page instead of a segment as absent. This allows the 386 to have large segments partially in memory, and partially on disk. It also prevents the VM manager from wasting time swapping small segments—each swap involves a 4K block.

Since the MMU can map 4K pages together, a segment doesn't need to reside in contiguous locations. The MMU allows a small number of pages to simulate the entire 4G address range.

The operating system moves pages from disk to memory on demand. Accessing a not-present page causes a page fault. This signals the virtual memory system to move the page, moving other pages to disk if necessary. Like segment-based VM, this processs (demand paged VM) is effectively transparent to your program.

Optimizations

Both 286 and 386 systems can benefit from some simple optimizations. If the system knows a segment is read-only, it never has to swap the segment (or a portion of it) out to disk. Instead, the segment can be read again from its original file. Common examples of read-only segments are fonts and program code. This is the idea behind discardable segments in Microsoft Windows.

The 386 MMU sets a flag (the "dirty" bit) when a program writes to a page. Most VM systems clear this flag when they load a page into real memory from the swap file. When it is time to write the page back to the swap file, the system examines this bit. If it is still clear, there is no need to write the page—the existing entry may be reused if it is still in the swap file.

When a program requests a segment on a 386, the VM system usually doesn't allocate any actual pages. Just allocates the not-present page-table entries. Instead, it creates the pages when the program uses them for the first time. This allows programs to create large segments (4G, for instance) with minimal overhead.

DOS Extender VM

Some extenders have VM support built into them. Others rely on an additional package to provide VM services. The Windows DPMI server (and possibly other DPMI servers) support VM internally. Extenders that use such a DPMI server (e.g., DOS-extended apps running under Windows Enhanced mode) will automatically use VM. In that case, any extender-specific VM system is superfluous and remains unused.

When a 286 extender that supports DPMI runs with a 386 DPMI server, it gains the improved 386 VM capabilities. Of course, a 286 extended program is still limited to 16M of address space.

Using VM

Ideally, VM is completely transparent to the programmer. From the programmer's point of view, VM supplies main memory that is indistinguishable from regular memory. Still, there are some cases where you may want to exercise some control over the system. After all, virtual memory may be distinguishable from regular memory in the way: *speech*. Typical VM systems allow you to configure virtual memory using option switches on the command line (or in an environment variable) or with function calls. Of course, if the extender is using a DPMI server's VM system, command line options are not likely to work. Some extenders may, however, translate some of their VM function calls to work with DPMI, if it is present. In Windows Enhanced mode, many VM options are settable in the SYSTEM.INI file. For more details, you should consult your extender's manual.

Many VM systems allow you to configure the name and location of the swap file, the size of the swap file, and other configuration details. From a programming point of view, the key VM operation is locking. When you lock a page (or segment), you prohibit the VM system from swapping that page to disk. You may want to do this in several cases:

- Time-critical subroutines, particularly ISRs, are often locked to improve performance or because VM can't run at interrept time.

- Exception handlers that process errors are usually locked so a system error won't initiate a swap.

- Programmers dealing with hardware devices that perform DMA access must lock memory prior to allowing DMA cycles.

Even if your extender doesn't ordinarily support VM, you many need to consider locking if it can run on top of a DPMI server that does. The DPMI interface provides a call to lock memory, and a call to unlock it (functions 0x0600 and 0x0601). Extenders that supply their own VM provide similar calls. Function 0x0600 increases a counter associated with the memory block. Function 0x0601 decrements this counter. This means for each lock (function 0x0600) there must be a corresponding unlock (function 0x0601). The block is locked when the counter is non-zero and unlocked when it is zero.

You can find an example of locking an ISR in the lockint9() function (see Chapter 18, Listing 18-4). Ordinary programs, however, should rarely need to lock memory.

Of course, when memory is locked, you may interfere with the VM system's ability to satisfy future memory requests. You should only lock blocks when absolutely necessary, and then unlock them as soon as possible.

Windows programs are subject to swapping in 386 enhanced mode, so the same considerations apply to them. The GlobalPageLock() and GlobalPageUnlock() functions allow you to lock a global memory block. You pass these functions the segment selector of the block you want to lock. The fault handling example in Chapter 9 uses GlobalPageLock() to protect the interrupt handler from being swapped out.

An Example

Listing 11-1 (VM.C) is a short program that will attempt to allocate the largest block it can from your system. The program uses a form of binary search to determine the largest single block of memory it can allocate. Figure 11-1 shows the output from VM.C compiled with Code Builder and executed on a 386 with 8M of physical memory and running Microsoft Windows 3.1.

VM.C clearly illustrates how transparent VM is to the programmer. There is no special code for VM in the program—a simple malloc() easily accesses virtual memory. The program is generic enough for most real- or protected-mode C compilers to handle.

Listing 11-1. VM.C

```
/* VM.C - Exercise malloc() with virtual memory
   (or without, for that matter)

   Compile with most any compiler -- some versions of
   High C won't work with very large mallocs --
   adjust the maximum number (ULONG_MAX, below) to
   a smaller number, if you get run time errors when
   using High C.

   Some early DPMI hosts will cause a page fault
   when you try to malloc near the upper limit
   of the swap file.

   Sixteen-bit compilers can only malloc <64K so
   this is pretty uninteresting with these compilers.

   Examples:
   Borland: bcc vm.c
   Microsoft: cl vm.c
   High C: hc386 vm.c
   Intel: icc vm.c
   Watcom: wcl386 /l=dos4gw vm.c

*/

#include <stdio.h>
#include <stdlib.h>
#include <limits.h>

void main()
  {
  size_t amt=0,lo=0,lo0,a1;
  void *p=NULL;

/* Figure out if we are on a 16 or 32 bit compiler */
```

```
#if sizeof(size_t)==sizeof(long)
      a1=amt=ULONG_MAX;
#else
      a1=amt=USHRT_MAX;
#endif

/* do forever */
  while (1)
    {
/* the unsigned long casts are required for 16 bit compile */
    printf("high=%08lX\ttry=%08lX\tlow=%08lX\t",
      (unsigned long)a1,(unsigned long)amt,
                        (unsigned long)lo);
    lo0=lo;
/* allocate memory */
    p=malloc(amt);

/* if successful */
    if (p)
      {
      printf("success\n");
/* free it, and establish new lo limit */
      free(p);
      lo=amt;
      }
    else
      {
/* otherwise establish new hi limit */
      printf("fail\n");
      a1=amt;
      }
/* when the hi and lo marks are 1 apart, we are done */
    if (amt-lo0<=1) break;

/* compute new attempt */
    if (p)
      amt+=(a1-lo)/2;
    else
      amt-=(a1-lo)/2;
    }

/* DONE! */
```

```
if (lo)
  {
  printf("Allocated %lu bytes\n",(unsigned long)lo);
  }
else
  {
  printf("Couldn't allocate any memory!\n");
  }
}
```

Figure 11-1. Output from VM.C

```
high=FFFFFFFF    try=FFFFFFFF    low=00000000    fail
high=FFFFFFFF    try=80000000    low=00000000    fail
high=80000000    try=40000000    low=00000000    fail
high=40000000    try=20000000    low=00000000    fail
high=20000000    try=10000000    low=00000000    fail
high=10000000    try=08000000    low=00000000    fail
high=08000000    try=04000000    low=00000000    fail
high=04000000    try=02000000    low=00000000    fail
high=02000000    try=01000000    low=00000000    fail
high=01000000    try=00800000    low=00000000    success
high=01000000    try=00C00000    low=00800000    success
high=01000000    try=00E00000    low=00C00000    fail
high=00E00000    try=00D00000    low=00C00000    success
high=00E00000    try=00D80000    low=00D00000    success
high=00E00000    try=00DC0000    low=00D80000    success
high=00E00000    try=00DE0000    low=00DC0000    success
high=00E00000    try=00DF0000    low=00DE0000    success
high=00E00000    try=00DF8000    low=00DF0000    success
high=00E00000    try=00DFC000    low=00DF8000    fail
high=00DFC000    try=00DFA000    low=00DF8000    fail
high=00DFA000    try=00DF9000    low=00DF8000    fail
high=00DF9000    try=00DF8800    low=00DF8000    success
high=00DF9000    try=00DF8C00    low=00DF8800    fail
high=00DF8C00    try=00DF8A00    low=00DF8800    fail
high=00DF8A00    try=00DF8900    low=00DF8800    success
```

Figure 11-1. Output from VM.C (cont.)

```
high=00DF8A00    try=00DF8980    low=00DF8900    fail
high=00DF8980    try=00DF8940    low=00DF8900    success
high=00DF8980    try=00DF8960    low=00DF8940    success
high=00DF8980    try=00DF8970    low=00DF8960    fail
high=00DF8970    try=00DF8968    low=00DF8960    success
high=00DF8970    try=00DF896C    low=00DF8968    fail
high=00DF896C    try=00DF896A    low=00DF8968    fail
high=00DF896A    try=00DF8969    low=00DF8968    fail
Allocated 14649704 bytes
```

CHAPTER ■ 12

Something Borrowed

Many DOS extenders imitate features found in other operating systems. Ergo's DPM extenders and Phar Lap's 286 extender both support Dynamic Link Libraries (DLLs), for example. These DLLs are very similar to DLLs in Windows or OS/2. Such similarities helpful when porting code to and from operating systems.

The New and Linear Executable Formats

OS/2 and Windows use several executable file formats including the new executable (NE) and the linear executable (LE). These formats are supersets of the DOS .EXE format. Although they still use the .EXE extension, the NE and LE files contain information specific to protected mode operating systems. NE and LE files can contain a protected-mode program and a related DOS program simultaneously. Some DOS extenders use one of these formats to store protected-mode executables.

.DEF Files

Linkers that create NE or LE files use a special definition (.DEF) file to control the link process. The .DEF file can contain information about the program's type, copyright information, and data about segments and external references.

Most DOS extended programs don't need much, if any, data in the .DEF file. However, you will see some important uses for .DEF files in the following sections.

Stubs

NE and LE files have an important characteristic that makes them useful for DOS extenders: they can contain a small regular DOS program in addition to their protected-mode code. If you run the .EXE file under regular DOS, the DOS program (known as the stub) executes.

Stub programs have three main purposes:

1. Many stubs simply print a message that informs the user that the program can't run under DOS.

2. You can bind a real-mode and protected-mode version of a program together. Microsoft C 6.0, for example, appears to run either as a DOS program or an OS/2 program. CL.EXE, the compiler, contains two programs: an OS/2-hosted compiler and a DOS-hosted compiler. Here the DOS-hosted compiler is the stub program. Each compiler can create (target) code for either OS/2 or DOS.

3. The stub can load a DOS extender (or be the DOS extender) which can then load the protected-mode portion of the .EXE file.

Several extenders use OS/2-style .EXE files for programs (Phar Lap's 286|DOS Extender, Ergo's DPM extenders, and Rational's 4G extender, for example). These extenders supply default stubs you can bind to your protected-mode programs.

When you run your protected-mode program, execution doesn't start at the main() function. Instead, the real-mode stub gets control. The stub executes the DOS extender, passing it all of the original program's arguments (including argv[0], the program's name). The extender then reopens the executable file, skips past the stub, and loads the protected-mode program. Now your compiler's start up code and your main() function get control.

Occasionally you will want to write your own stub program. A stub program is an ideal place to insert real-mode code in your program (see Chapter 10). You can pass an address (or interrupt number) to the protected-mode program as a command line parameter or in an environment variable.

Listing 12-1 (RSTUB.C) is a simple custom stub program for the Rational 4G/W extender. RSTUB inserts an extra argument, FROM_STUB, into the protected-mode program's command line (in practice, this could be an address or interrupt number). Listing 12-2 (RHELLO.C) is an elementary program that uses RSTUB.

The definition file RHELLO.DEF (Listing 12-3) uses the OPTION STUB command to bind RSTUB.EXE with the RHELLO.EXE file. For simple programs this is often the only command you'll need in the .DEF file. This .DEF file syntax is unique to WLINK, the WATCOM linker. If you use other Microsoft-compatible linkers, the stub command usually looks like this:

```
STUB='RSTUB.EXE'
```

Listing 12-1. RSTUB.C

```c
/* Replacement Stub for Rational 4GW -- adds additional
   argument to command line. This is a real mode program.

   Borland: bcc rstub.c
   Microsoft: cl rstub.c */

#include <stdio.h>
#include <process.h>
#include <string.h>
#include <stdlib.h>

main(int argc, char *argv[])
  {
  char *p,**newargv;
  int nextarg=3;
/* set up new argv */
  newargv=(char **)malloc((argc+3)*sizeof(char *));
/* and new program name */
  p=strdup(argv[0]);
```

```
  if (p&&newargv)
    {
/* name of extender (must be in current directory or
   on DOS path */
    newargv[0]="dos4gw.exe";
    newargv[1]=argv[0];
/* ADD NEW ARGUMENT */
    newargv[2]="FROM_STUB";
/* copy any other arguments */
    while (argc--)
      newargv[nextarg++]=*++argv;
    newargv[nextarg]=NULL;
/* Execute extender */
    execvp(newargv[0],newargv);
    }
/* If we ever get here, something is wrong! */
  printf("Fatal error loading RHELLO.EXT\n");
  exit(1);
  }
```

Listing 12-2. RHELLO.C

```
/* Simple program to test RSTUB.C
   Watcom: wcl386 rhello.c @rhello.def
*/

#include <stdio.h>

main(int argc, char *argv[])
  {
  printf("Hello!\n");
/* echo arguments */
  while (--argc) printf("%s\n",*++argv);
  }
```

Listing 12-3. RHELLO.DEF

```
option stub=rstub.exe
```

Dynamic Link Libraries

Dynamic Link Libraries (DLLs) are another feature that several extenders borrow from OS/2 and Windows. DLLs are similar to regular object libraries with one major difference: DLLs link with your program at load time or run time—not when you compile and link your program. Each DLL resides in its own file and when your program loads, the extender loads the DLL file providing access to the functions and/or data in the DLL.

DOS extender DLLs are somewhat similar to overlays in a conventional program. Unlike overlays, however, DLLs need not be present when you build the .EXE file. You can use DLLs to provide pseudo-drivers for your program. For example, one DLL can handle printing to a laser printer, while another prints to a dot matrix printer. Your program only loads the appropriate DLLs at run time. Windows uses this approach itself; Windows device drivers are simply DLLs.

You also can use DLLs to customize your software. For example, later in the chapter, you will see a program that uses DLLs to implement user-installable commands. This allows for simple customization: sophisticated users can add commands to your program by writing a new DLL.

The most important use of extender DLLs is to incorporate real-mode routines into protected-mode programs. A single DLL may contain either real- or protected-mode code, but not both.

Creating DLLs

DLLs use the same NE (or LE) format that executable programs do, but their .DEF file must contain a LIBRARY statement. This statement identifies the DLL, and usually (though not always) matches the file name. In addition, real-mode DLLs must contain the line: EXETYPE DOS4 (regardless of the DOS version in use). The linker uses the .DEF file to produce the correct type of executable file.

You should consult your extender's manuals for the exact compiler options you need to use when creating DLLs. Usually you have to suppress stack checking (functions in a DLL use the caller's stack), and instruct the compiler to generate special function entry code for DLLs.

You may not be able to use all C library functions within DLLs. Some library routines assume that a program's stack and its default data segment are the same (the infamous SS==DS assumption). With DLLs, this is not true—a DLL's data segment is definitely not in the same segment as the calling program's stack. Again, consult your compiler and extender documentation for more details.

The DLL must export any functions it will supply to other programs. To export a function, you can include its name in the EXPORTS section of the .DEF file. Alternatively, many compilers support the _export and _loadds keywords. These allow you to write functions like:

```
void _far _export _loadds f(void)
  {
  .
  .
  .
```

Of course, exported functions must be far. The calling program, in another module, will certainly be in a different segment. The _loadds keyword forces the function to use its own default data segment. The DLL needs to use its own default data segment—rather than the data segment of the calling program.

Listing 12-4 shows a typical DLL definition file that uses an EXPORTS section. You can alter a function's external name by using a special syntax. For example:

```
EXPORTS
  _dll_foo=_foo
```

creates a reference to function dll_foo(). When a program calls this function, it will invoke the function named foo() in the DLL. Remember, the compiler normally prepends an underscore to C-style function names, and doesn't add underscores to functions that use the Pascal calling convention.

Listing 12-4. Typical DLL .DEF File

```
Library EXDLL
EXPORTS
  _dll_foo=_foo
  _dll2
```

DLLs have a CS:IP entry point just as executable programs do. You need a simple assembly language END declaration to create this entry point. If you want to start with the C routine dll_init(), you could assemble and link the following code with your DLL:

```
extrn _dllstart:proc
end _dllstart
```

Be sure your assembler preserves the case of external symbols (the /Ml option for MASM and TASM, for example).

Using DLLs

There are three ways to use functions from DLLs in your program. You can define an IMPORTS section in the program's .DEF file, use an import library, or dynamically link in DLLs by using special DOS extender calls.

If you use the IMPORTS method, you will need to modify your .DEF file. Under the IMPORTS keyword, you need a line for each imported function. The line consists of the DLL name and the function name separated by commas. For example:

```
IMPORTS
    GROUCHO._dll_function
imports dll_function() from GROUCHO.DLL.
```

A more convenient method to include DLL functions relies on an import library. You can process your DLL with an import librarian (IMPLIB.EXE) to create a library (.LIB) file. You can then link your program with this library as though it were a conventional .LIB file. The import library doesn't contain the actual code. Instead, it contains import-definition (IMPDEF) records that have the same effect as the IMPORTS statements in a .DEF file. These special records cause the program to automatically link to the DLL's functions when the program loads.

DOS extenders that support DLLs also supply functions to load and manipulate the DLLs directly at run time. This is occasionally useful for selecting one of several libraries at run time. The example later in this chapter uses this technique to dynamically add user-installable commands to its user interface.

Real-Mode Considerations

Under Phar Lap's 286|DOS Extender, real-mode DLLs are nearly indistinguishable from protected-mode DLLs, which can create a problem. Exported functions from a real-mode DLL generate protected-mode addresses—not the required real-mode addresses. Before using a real-mode function from a DLL, you must convert the address with the DosProtToReal() function. Once you convert the address, you can use functions like DosRealFarCall() to execute the exported subroutine (see Chapter 10). On the other hand, if your protected-mode program needs to access exported data from a real-mode DLL, you can use the protected-mode address directly.

Ergo's DPM extenders automatically treat real-mode DLL exports as real-mode addresses. Of course, that means you must not try to use the addresses in protected mode. Instead, you must use them as arguments to functions like CallRMwithFRET() (see Chapter 10).

A DLL Example

DLLs can provide an interface for end users to link their code with your program. You supply a header file with any required definitions (data types, functions, etc.), and an import library that references any routines in your code the users might need. A sophisticated end-user or third-party developer can then write a DLL that your program can interact with at run time.

Many products allow users to add custom code to do specialized processing (Lotus 1-2-3 and AutoCad, for example, both support custom add-ins). DLLs allow users to do this in a very straightforward manner. You also can export functions from your code that users can call from their DLLs.

Programs that accept command lines can take advantage of this technique. Users can add additional commands via one or more DLLs. You can even use DLLs for built-in commands to simplify customization.

Listings 12-5 and 12-6 contain an extensible command interpreter (XCI.H and XCI.C) for the Phar Lap 286|DOS Extender. This interpreter is generic—any program can use it. XCI only supplies four basic commands: DO, HELP, LINK, and QUIT. The HELP and QUIT commands are self-explanatory. DO executes commands from a file. LINK loads additional commands from a DLL. Your program must add additional commands.

An application that uses XCI (a client) can also enable a fifth command, GOTO. Listing 12-7 shows a simple program (XCITEST.C) that uses XCI. The associated DLL (XCITST.C in Listing 12-8) provides a few simple commands to print text strings. You also need DLLSTART.ASM (found in Listing 12-9). Listing 12-10 is the MAKE file that compiles both XCITEST and XCITST. If you are using the Borland compiler, you'll also need the file in Listing 12-11 (XCITST.DEF) to build the programs.

Listing 12-5. XCI.H

```
/* XCI.H  Header for XCI command interpreter
 See MAKEFILE.XCI for compile instructions
*/

#ifndef XCI_HEADER
#define XCI_HEADER

/* type for command functions */
#define XCICMD void far

/* Pointer to command function */
typedef void (far * XCICMDP)(int cmd,char far *line,void
*udata);

/* Various hooks */
extern char *xci_prompt;   /* string to prompt with */
extern FILE *xci_infile;   /* input file */
extern int xci_exitflag;   /* set to exit XCI */
extern int xci_defaultbrk; /* default break handling */
/* function to prompt with */
extern void (*xcif_prompt)();
```

```
/* function to call before help */
extern void (*xcif_prehelp)();
/* function to call after help */
extern void (*xcif_posthelp)();
/* function to get input */
extern char *(*xcif_input)();

/* main function prototype */
int command(char *dll,char *startfile,int caseflag,
            void far *ustruc,XCICMDP userfunc);

/* add command (not from DLL) */
int addcmd(char *cmdnam,XCICMDP fn);
#define addcmd(a,b) addcmd(a,(XCICMDP)b)

#endif
```

Listing 12-6. XCI.C

```
/* XCI.C      An extensible command interpreter for the
   Phar Lap 286|DOS Extender
   See MAKEFILE for compile information
*/

#include <stdio.h>
#include <stdlib.h>
#include <string.h>
#include <malloc.h>
#include <dos.h>
#include <phapi.h>
#include <setjmp.h>
#include <conio.h>
#include "xci.h"

/* Mask for Zero flag (used by keyboard routines) */
#define Z_FLAG 0x40

static int adddll(char *);
static int findcmd(char *);

/* Table of commands (dynamically allocated) */
static struct cmdtbl
```

```c
  {
  char far *cmd;
  XCICMDP f;
  } *cmds=NULL;

/* Number of commands in table */
static unsigned int nrcmds=0;

/* Case sensitive? */
static int truecase=0;

/* secret dummy definition for udata */
struct udata
  {
  int unknown;
  };

/* default hook function prototypes */
void xci_prompter();     /* func to prompt */
char *xci_input();       /* func to get input */
void xci_preposthelp();  /* pre & post help command */

/* default prompt string -- can be changed by client */
char *xci_prompt="? ";

/* default routines -- can be changed by client */
void (*xcif_prompt)()=xci_prompter;
void (*xcif_prehelp)()=xci_preposthelp;
void (*xcif_posthelp)()=xci_preposthelp;
char *(*xcif_input)()=xci_input;

/* flag set when break detected */
static int broke;

/* Jump to top level command loop */
jmp_buf cmdloop;


/* default command function prototypes */
XCICMD dofunc(int cmd,char *s,struct udata *data);
XCICMD linkfunc(int cmd,char *s,struct udata *data);
XCICMD quitfunc(int cmd,char *s,struct udata *data);
```

```
XCICMD helpfunc(int cmd,char *s,struct udata *data);

/* default commands
   although GOTO is a built-in command, the client program
   must explicitly enable it if it wants to use it */
static char *defcmd[]= { "quit", "help", "link", "do" };

/* addresses of default commands */
static XCICMDP deffunc[]={
                          (XCICMDP)quitfunc,
                          (XCICMDP)helpfunc,
                          (XCICMDP)linkfunc,
                          (XCICMDP)dofunc
                         };

/* non-zero if running a script via DO */
static int interactive=0;

/* stack of file positions for nested DO commands */
/* Files are closed and reopened to avoid DOS file limit */
static struct fstack
      {
      char *fp;              /* file name */
      long pos;              /* position in file */
      struct fstack * next;  /* next fstack record */
      } *instack;


/* default stdin handle */
static FILE *baseio;

/* Current input file */
FILE *xci_infile;

/* Set to 1 when someone wants to exit */
int xci_exitflag=0;

/* Default break action */
int xci_defaultbrk=1;

/* Break vectors */
PIHANDLER oldbreak;  /* PIHANDLER=Prot. Int. Handler */
```

```
REALPTR oldbreal; /* REALPTR=Pointer to real mode address */
PIHANDLER old1b;
REALPTR old1breal;

/* Bios segment (you can't call DosGetBIOSseg from ISR) */
USHORT biosseg;

/* ^Break handlers */
void _interrupt _far xci_int1b(REGS16 r)
  {
  union REGS rr;
  unsigned int *keyhead,*keytail;
/* If xci_defaultbrk is clear, then we are in DOS shell
   and don't want to take any action */
  if (!xci_defaultbrk)
    {
/* Chain to old break handler (never returns) */
    DosChainToRealIntr(old1breal);
    }
  keyhead=MAKEP(biosseg,0x1A);
  keytail=MAKEP(biosseg,0x1C);
  broke=1;
/* purge keyboard buffer */
  *keyhead=*keytail;
/* push ^C at head of keyboard buffer */
  rr.h.ah=5;
  rr.x.cx=3;
  int86(0x16,&rr,&rr);
  }


void _interrupt _far xci_int16(REGS16 r)
  {
  REGS16 r1;
  unsigned ah=r.ax>>8;
  _enable();
  if (xci_defaultbrk&&(ah==0||ah==0x10||ah==1||ah==0x11))
    {
    do
      {
      r1.ax=0x100;
      r1.flags=0;
/* Simulate interrupt to old INT 16H handler */
```

```
      DosRealFarCall(oldbreal,&r1,0,-1,r1.flags);
      if ((r1.flags&Z_FLAG)&&(ah==1||ah==0x11))
        {
        r.flags=r1.flags;
        return;
        }
/* Wait for key press */
      } while (r1.flags&Z_FLAG);
/* If break character -- replace it with a carriage return */
      if ((r1.ax&0xff)==3||r1.ax==0x300)
        {
        unsigned int *keyhead;
        keyhead=MAKEP(biosseg,0x1A);
        keyhead=MAKEP(biosseg,*keyhead);
        *keyhead='\r';
        broke=1;
        }
    }
  DosChainToRealIntr(oldbreal);
  }


/* XCI Clean up */
/* Note: DosExitList requires this to be a pascal function */
void pascal far xci_clean(unsigned int reason)
  {
/* restore interrupt vectors */
  DosSetRealProtVec(0x16,oldbreak,oldbreal,NULL,NULL);
  DosSetRealProtVec(0x1b,old1b,old1breal,NULL,NULL);
/* Exit handler must call DosExitList with EXLST_EXIT
   to proceed with the termination */
  DosExitList(EXLST_EXIT,NULL);
  }


/* default functions */
void xci_prompter(char *s)
  {
  printf("%s",s);
  }
```

```
char *xci_input(char *inbuf,unsigned int siz,FILE *input)
   {
   return fgets(inbuf,siz,input);
   }

/* No pre or post help action by default */
void xci_preposthelp()
   {
   }



/* Main command routine */
/* dll is initial DLL to load
   startfile is initial file to DO
   cases is 1 if case sensitivity is required
   userfunc is pointer to user function called at
            start and end */
int command(char *dll, char *startfile, int cases,
            void far *user,XCICMDP userfunc)
  {
  int i;
  char inbuf[129],*p;
  if (!cmds)
    {
/* first time  (not done for recursive calls) */
   DosGetBIOSSeg(&biosseg);
/* Due to a 286 DOS extender bug in versions prior to 1.4,
   you must set the INT 16H ProtVec before
   using PassToProtVec... */
   DosSetProtVec(0x16,(PIHANDLER)xci_int16,&oldbreak);
   DosSetPassToProtVec(0x16,(PIHANDLER)xci_int16,NULL,
                    &oldbreal);
   DosSetPassToProtVec(0x1b,(PIHANDLER)xci_int1b,
                    &old1b,&old1breal);
/* set up exit handler */
   DosExitList(EXLST_ADD,(PFNEXITLIST)xci_clean);
   truecase=cases;
   xci_infile=stdin;

/* install default commands */
   cmds=(struct cmdtbl *)malloc(4*sizeof(struct cmdtbl));
   if (!cmds) return 1;
```

```
    nrcmds=4;
    for (i=0;i<nrcmds;i++)
      {
      cmds[i].cmd=defcmd[i];
      cmds[i].f=deffunc[i];
      }
/* load default DLL (if specified) */
    if (dll&&*dll)
      if (adddll(dll))
        printf(
          "Warning: unable to load default command DLL\n");

/* call user function */
    if (userfunc) userfunc(0,NULL,user);

/* execute default DO file */
    if (startfile&&*startfile) dofunc(0,startfile,user);

/* set jump buffer for future longjmp's --
   when longjmp() executes, control returns here */
    setjmp(cmdloop);
    }

/* initialization done -- begin main processing */
  while (1)
    {
    char *token,*tail;
/* if someone wants to quit then quit */
    if (xci_exitflag)
      {
/* call user function */
      if (userfunc) userfunc(1,NULL,user);
/* reset some things in case we are called again */
/* restore interrupt vectors */
      DosSetRealProtVec(0x16,oldbreak,oldbreal,NULL,NULL);
      DosSetRealProtVec(0x1b,old1b,old1breal,NULL,NULL);
      DosExitList(EXLST_REMOVE,(PFNEXITLIST)xci_clean);
      xci_infile=stdin;
      interactive=0;
      instack=NULL;
      free((void *)cmds);
```

```
      cmds=NULL;
      return 0;
      }

/* If interactive==0 (not script) then prompt */
   if (!interactive) (*xcif_prompt)(xci_prompt);

/* get input from user or file */
   *inbuf='\0';
/* Call input function -- can be set to different
   functions depending on client's needs */
   (*xcif_input)(inbuf,sizeof(inbuf),xci_infile);

/* If break detected then go to top level */
   if (broke)
     {
     struct fstack *f;
     broke=0;
     /* free fstack entries */
     for (f=instack;f;f=f->next) free(f->fp);
     instack=NULL;
     interactive=0;
     xci_infile=stdin;
/* Jump to setjmp() at top of command loop */
     longjmp(cmdloop,1);
     }

/* If end of do file, return. If end of console, ignore */
   if (!*inbuf&&feof(xci_infile))
     {
     if (interactive)
       {
       return 0;
       }
     clearerr(xci_infile);
     continue;
     }

/* got some input -- lets look at it */
   i=strspn(inbuf," \t");

/* skip blank lines and comments */
```

```c
    if (inbuf[i]=='\n') continue;
    if (inbuf[i]=='#') continue;

/* eat off \n from line */
    p=strchr(inbuf+i,'\n');
    if (p) *p='\0';

/* get a token */
    token=strtok(inbuf+i," \t");
    if (!token) continue;  /* this should never happen */

/* do we recognize the command? (internal or from dll) */
    i=findcmd(token);
/* NO: error */
    if (i==-1)
      {
      printf("Unknown command %s\n",token);
      continue;
      }

/* YES: compute command's tail (arguments) */
    tail=token+strlen(token)+1;
    tail+=strspn(tail," \t");
/* execute command */
    cmds[i].f(0,tail,user);
    }
  }


/* Find a command -- search backwards so new commands
   replace old ones */
static int findcmd(char *s)
  {
  int i,stat;
  for (i=nrcmds-1;i>=0;i--)
    {
    if (!(truecase?
          strcmp(s,cmds[i].cmd)
          :
          stricmp(s,cmds[i].cmd)))
      return i;
    }
```

```
    return -1;
    }


/* Add a DLL to the command input table
   returns 0 if successful  */
static adddll(char *dll)
  {
  char cmdnam[33],*p;
  HMODULE h=0;
  unsigned ord=0;
  p=strrchr(dll,'\\');

/* check to see if module is already loaded */
  if (!DosGetModHandle(p?p+1:dll,&h))
    {
    printf("%s already loaded\n",p?p+1:dll);
    return 1;
    }

/* Load module if possible */
  if (DosLoadModule(0,0,dll,&h))
       return 1;

/* find all exported functions in module */
  while (!DosEnumProc(h,cmdnam,(PUSHORT)&ord))
     {
     PFN fn;
/* Get function's address */
     DosGetProcAddr(h,cmdnam,&fn);
/* add command -- skipt 1st character (it is a _) */
     if (addcmd(cmdnam+1,(XCICMDP) fn)) return 1;
     }
  return 0;
  }

/* add a command -- returns 0 for success */
#ifdef addcmd
#undef addcmd
#endif

addcmd(char *cmdnam,XCICMDP fn)
```

```
  {
  struct cmdtbl *ct;
/* make more room in table  */
  ct=(struct cmdtbl *)
      realloc(cmds,(nrcmds+1)*sizeof(struct cmdtbl));
  if (!ct) return 1;
  cmds=ct;
/* add name and function */
  cmds[nrcmds].cmd=strdup(cmdnam);
  if (!cmds[nrcmds].cmd) return 1;
  cmds[nrcmds++].f=(XCICMDP) fn;
  return 0;
  }


/* currently executing file name */
static char curfile[67];

/* Command to transfer execution from one file to another
   Only works from inside a file, and is not enabled by
   default. If your program wants to use GOTO it must enable
   the command by calling: addcmd("GOTO",gotocmd); */
XCICMD gotofunc(int cmd,char *s,struct udata *data)
  {
  FILE *f;
  if (cmd==2)
    {
    printf("Execute commands from an ASCII file\n");
    return;
    }
  if (cmd==1||!s||!*s)
    {
    printf("goto executes commands from an ASCII file\n"
           "Usage: goto FILENAME\n");
    return;
    }
/* open file */
  f=fopen(s,"r");
  if (!f)
    {
    printf("Can't open %s\n",s);
    perror(s);
    return;
```

```
      }
  if (!interactive)
    {
    printf("Use goto only from command files\n"
           "Use do to execute a file\n");
    return;
    }
/* register as current file */
  strcpy(curfile,s);
  fclose(xci_infile);
  xci_infile=f;
  }


/* Do a command file (sort of like a batch file) */
XCICMD dofunc(int cmd,char *s,struct udata *data)
  {
  FILE *ifile;
  struct fstack recall;
  if (cmd==2)
    {
    printf("Do commands from an ASCII file\n");
    return;
    }
  if (cmd==1||!s||!*s)
    {
    printf("Do executes commands from an ASCII file\n"
           "Usage: do FILENAME\n");
    return;
    }


/* open file */
  ifile=fopen(s,"r");
  if (!ifile)
    {
    printf("Can't open %s\n",s);
    perror(s);
    return;
    }
  if (interactive)
    {
/* store current file name so we can resume later */
    if (!(recall.fp=strdup(curfile)))
```

```
        {
        printf("Out of memory\n");
        fclose(ifile);
        return;
        }
/* store position in current file and close it */
      recall.pos=ftell(xci_infile);
      fclose(xci_infile);
      }
  else
      {
/* no current file, so remember this handle but don't close it
*/
      baseio=xci_infile;
      recall.fp=NULL;
      }
/* add recall to linked list of nested files */
  recall.next=instack;

/* make new file current */
  strcpy(curfile,s);
  xci_infile=ifile;

/* mark nesting level */
  interactive++;

/* make recall the head of the fstack linked list */
  instack=&recall;

/* call command recursively */
  command(NULL,NULL,0,data,NULL);

/* close useless file */
  fclose(xci_infile);
/* restore old file */
  if (instack->fp!=NULL)  /* is it a file? */
      {
/* open it */
      xci_infile=fopen(instack->fp,"r");
      if (!xci_infile)
          {
/* serious error! file vanished! reset to top level */
```

```
        printf("Error opening %s\n",instack->fp);
        xci_infile=baseio;
        interactive=0;  /* bad error if nested */
        }
     else
        {
/* reposition old file */
        fseek(xci_infile,instack->pos,SEEK_SET);
/* make it current */
        strcpy(curfile,instack->fp);
        }
/* release memory used for file name */
     free(instack->fp);
     }
  else
     {
/* reset to console */
     xci_infile=baseio;
     }
/* fix up linked list */
  instack=instack->next;
  interactive--;
  }

/* Link a dll */
XCICMD linkfunc(int cmd,char *s,struct udata *data)
  {
  if (cmd==2)
    {
    printf("Add user-defined commands\n");
    return;
    }
  if (cmd==1||!s||!*s)
    {
    printf("Add user-defined commands via a DLL\n"
      "Usage: link DLLNAME\n");
    return;
    }
  if (adddll(s))
    {
    printf("Unable to load dll: %s\n",s);
    }
```

```
  }

/* Quit */
XCICMD quitfunc(int cmd,char *s,struct udata *data)
  {
  if (cmd==0) { xci_exitflag=1; return; }
/* long and short help message */
  printf("Exits to DOS\n");
  }


/* provide general help (scan from end to 0 call with cmd==2)
   or specific help find command and call with cmd==1 */
XCICMD helpfunc(int cmd,char *s,struct udata *data)
  {
  int i,j=0;
  if (cmd==2) printf("Get help\n");
  if (cmd==1) printf(
  "Use the help command to learn about the available"
  " commands\nUse HELP for a list of help topics"
  " or \"HELP topic\""
  " for help on a specific topic.\n");
  if (cmd) return;
/* call user's prehelp */
  (*xcif_prehelp)();
/* if specific command... */
  if (s&&*s)
    {
/* find it and ask it about itself (command==1)
   This allows user DLL commands to provide help
   for themselves */
    i=findcmd(s);
    if (i==-1) printf("No such command: %s\n",s);
    else cmds[i].f(1,NULL,NULL);
    }
  else
/* No specific command -- do help for them all (command==2)
   Again, this allows user DLL commands to provide their own
   help */
    for (i=nrcmds-1;i>=0;i--)
      {
      char buf[22];
/* might be a lot of commands -- pause on screenfulls */
```

```
      if (!(++j%25))
        {
        printf("--More--");
        j=0;
        if (!getch()) getch();
        putchar('\n');
        }
/* print header */
      strncpy(buf,cmds[i].cmd,20);
      strcat(buf,":");
      printf("%-21.21s",buf);
/* ask command for short help */
      cmds[i].f(2,NULL,NULL);
      }
/* call user's post help */
  (*xcif_posthelp)();
  }
```

Listing 12-7. XCITEST.C

```
/* XCITEST.C -- example using XCI interpreter
   see MAKEFILE for compile instructions
*/
#include <stdio.h>
#include <phapi.h>
#include "xci.h"

/* XCI client's application data */
struct udata
  {
  int dummy;
  } appdata;

/* built-in print command */
XCICMD print_cmd(int cmd, char far *cmds, struct udata *data)
  {
  if (cmd)
    {
    printf("PRINT [string]\n");
    if (cmd==1)
      {
      printf("The PRINT command displays the string\n");
      printf("on the screen.\n");
```

```
        }
      }
    else
      printf("%s\n",cmds);
    }

/* XCI startup command */
XCICMD startup(int cmd, char far *dummy)
    {
    if (cmd) return;
    addcmd("print",print_cmd);
    return;
    }



/* MAIN PROGRAM */
main()
    {
/* Print banner */
    printf("XCITEST by Al Williams\n"
           "Type HELP for help\n");

    command("XCITST.DLL",NULL,0,
            &appdata,(XCICMDP)startup);
    }
```

Listing 12-8. XCITST.C

```
/* Example XCI DLL
   See MAKEFILE for compile instructions */
#include <stdio.h>
#include <string.h>
#include <malloc.h>
#include "xci.h"

/* Dummy definition */
struct udata
    {
    int dummy;
    };


#define EXPORT _far _loadds _export
```

```c
/* uppercase print */
XCICMD EXPORT uprint(int cmd, char far *cmds,
                     struct udata *data)
  {
  if (cmd)
    {
    printf("UPRINT [string]\n");
    if (cmd==1)
      {
      printf("The UPRINT command displays the string\n");
      printf("on the screen in upper case.\n");
      }
    }
  else
    printf("%s\n",strupr(cmds));
  }

/* lower case print */
XCICMD EXPORT lprint(int cmd, char far *cmds,
                     struct udata *data)
  {
  if (cmd)
    {
    printf("LPRINT [string]\n");
    if (cmd==1)
      {
      printf("The LPRINT command displays the string\n");
      printf("on the screen in lower case.\n");
      }
     }
    else
     printf("%s\n",strlwr(cmds));
  }


/* Init DLL so we can use C library (MICROSOFT ONLY) */
unsigned far pascal _loadds dllstart()
  {
#ifndef __BORLANDC__
  extern void far pascal C_INIT(void);
```

```
/* Init Microsoft C library */
  C_INIT();
#endif
  return 1;
  }
```

Listing 12-9. DLLSTART.ASM

```
;* DLLSTART.ASM  - Required startup code for DLL Initilization
extrn DLLSTART:far
        end DLLSTART
```

Listing 12-10. MAKEFILE.XCI

```
# Makefile for XCITEST.EXE and XCITST.DLL
# Use Microsoft NMAKE
# or Borland MAKE to compile
# !!! Be sure to set the right variable below
# depending on your compiler

# Note: Since 286|DOS Extender 2.5 doesn't fully support
# DLLs with MSC 7.0, this example will not work if you
# use this combination. Use Borland C or MSC 6.0. Future
# releases of 286|DOS Extender will probably offer full
# DLL support, but may require different compiler
# directives

BORLAND=1
MICROSOFT=0
# Set to 0 if Using 286 extender version 2.5 or later
CL7=1

!if $(BORLAND)
CC=bcc286
COPT=-c -w-rvl -w-par -w-pro
DLLOPT=-dll -w-rvl -w-par -Dprintf=pl_printf xcitst.def
```

```
LD=bcc286
LOPT=
AS=tasm
AOPT=-ml
!endif


!if $(MICROSOFT)
CC=cl
COPT=-AL -Ox -G2 -c
DLLOPT=-ML -Gs -Lp -Ox -G2
LD=cl
AS=masm
AOPT=-ml
!if $(CL7)
XLIB=
!else
XLIB=LLIBPE.LIB
!endif
LOPT=-AL -Lp $(XLIB)
!endif

all : xcitest.exe xcitst.dll

xcitest.exe : xcitest.obj xci.obj
        $(LD) $(LOPT) xcitest.obj xci.obj

xcitst.dll : xcitst.c dllstart.obj xci.h
        $(CC) $(DLLOPT) xcitst.c dllstart.obj

xcitest.obj : xcitest.c xci.h
        $(CC) $(COPT) xcitest.c

xci.obj : xci.c xci.h
        $(CC) $(COPT) xci.c

dllstart.obj : dllstart.asm
        $(AS) $(AOPT) dllstart.asm;
```

Listing 12-11. XCITST.DEF

```
IMPORTS _pl_printf=PHAPI._wilprintf
```

Inside XCI

A program (like XCITEST.C in Figure 12-7) can directly add commands to XCI's command table via the addcmd( ) function in Listing 12-6. In addition, the client or the user can add commands dynamically from a DLL to XCI. Figure 12-1 shows the format of an XCI command function. The XCI.H file (Listing 12-5) defines the type XCICMD, for these functions.

Figure 12-1. Prototype for XCI command functions

```
XCICMD function(int cmd, char *string, void *data)
```

where:
- cmd is one of the following:
- 0 - execute function;
- 1 - provide detailed help;
- 2 - provide one-line help. The cmd parameter has special significance for startup functions (see Figure 12-2).
- string is the command line (not including the command's name).
- data is a pointer to a user-defined structure. This structure must contain any data the application's commands need.

XCI passes an integer command to an XCICMD function. If the command is 0, the function will perform its duty. If it is 1, the function will print detailed help information. When the command is 2, the function will print a one-line help message. If you wish, the long and short message can be the same.

XCI handles Control-C input properly. Don't worry about the code that does that yet (xci_int16(), and xci_int1b()). In Chapter 13 you will learn about handling Control-C, and other user exceptions.

XCI Initialization

A program can register a function that XCI will call before the program starts and as it is ending. This function can install commands and do other specific client processing. XCITEST in Listing 12-7 uses its startup() function for this purpose. XCI calls the function with the cmd argument equal to 0 when the program starts, and equal to 1 when it ends.

Clients specify several parameters when they call command(), XCI's main function (see Listing 12-6). These parameters allow the client to link a DLL, execute a file of start-up commands, and control XCI's behavior. Figure 12-2 shows a prototype for command(). You can also control XCI via several global variables (see Figure 12-3). These variables have defaults—you may not need to set them.

Figure 12-2. Prototype for XCI's command() Function

```
int command(char *dll, char *startfile, int cases,
     void far *user,XCICMD(*userfunc)());
```

where:
- dll is the name of a DLL to load.
- startfile is the name of a file to execute first with the DO command (similar to COMMAND.COM's AUTOEXEC.BAT file).
- cases is 0 if upper- and lower-case commands are the same, nonzero if case is important.
- user is a pointer to a user-defined structure.
- userfunc is a pointer to a command function that will execute when XCI begins and ends. The cmd argument to this function (see Figure 12-1) will be 0 when XCI starts and nonzero when it ends.

Figure 12-3. XCI Global Variables

```
char *xci_prompt;
```

- XCI uses this string to prompt the user for input (default: "?").

Figure 12-3. XCI Global Variables (cont.)

```
void (*xcif_prompt)();
```

- Pointer to a function to print the prompt string; XCI passes the function the prompt string as an argument (normally xci_prompter(), which calls printf()).

```
void (*xcif_prehelp)();
```

- Pointer to a function to call before handling a help command; by default, this function does nothing.

```
void (*xcif_posthelp)();
```

- Pointer to a function to call after a help command; the default function does nothing.

```
void (*xcif_input)();
```

- Pointer to the input function (normally fgets()).

The two key data structures in XCI are the cmds array and the instack pointer. XCI dynamically allocates the cmds array. It contains a list of commands and function pointers for each command. When XCI executes a file (via the DO command) it maintains a linked list of files via the instack pointer. During the processing for a DO command (the dofunc() function in Listing 12-6), XCI makes an entry in the linked list that contains the file name, and an fseek() offset in the file. It then closes the file before opening the new one. In this way, XCI avoids exceeding the DOS open file limit. At the end of a file, XCI unravels the linked list to reopen the previous file for processing.

The adddll() function (in Listing 12-6) links in a DLL. This function uses the DOS extender (and OS/2) function DosGetModHandle() to decide if the DLL is already present. It then loads the DLL using DosLoadModule(). Finally, XCI calls DosEnumProc() to find the names of the functions that the DLL exports. XCI expects these names to be C functions (not Pascal functions), and therefore strips off the first character of the function name before entering it in the cmds array. This is necessary because the compiler prefixes C function names with an underscore.

Windows has similar functions for dealing with DLLs. You can use LoadLibrary() to load a DLL and GetModuleHandle() to get its handle (a magic number you need to access the DLL—sort of like a file handle). You can then use GetProcAddress() to find a specific routine's address. Unfortunately, Windows doesn't provide an equivalent to DosEnumProc().

The XCITST DLL

XCITST.C (Listing 12-8) provides two commands (UPRINT and LPRINT) for XCITEST. The commands are just trivial examples, but there are a few interesting twists to set up the DLL. Depending on the compiler, there may be some C library calls you cannot make from a DLL. This happens when the library makes the SS==DS assumption (see the discussion earlier in this chapter).

With Borland C, one of the forbidden functions is printf(). Since this is a serious omission, Phar Lap provides a function, _wilprintf(), that you can call from a DLL (insiders at Phar Lap say that the name has something to do with a talking horse from TV and his owner). You must import the function from PHAPI if you use it. In XCITST, a .DEF file contains the line:

```
IMPORTS _pl_printf=PHAPI._wilprintf
```

This allows the DLL to use pl_printf() instead of printf(). To further improve things, the make file contains the compiler option "-Dprintf=-pl_printf" if you select the Borland compiler. This has the same effect as:

```
#define printf pl_printf
```

Therefore, when you use printf() in XCITST.DLL you are actually using the special Phar Lap version.

Most of the Microsoft 6.0 library is usable from inside a DLL if you call the C_INIT() function first (Phar Lap doesn't fully support DLLs with Microsoft C 7.0). The dllstart() function does this when the system first loads the DLL. Every DLL has an entry point, just like an ordinary program. The trick is to get your entry point into the DLL file. Listing 12-9 contains a short assembly program, DLLSTART.ASM. This file contains no actual code, just directives to tell the linker to start at the dllstart() function. Listing 12-8 (XCITST.C) contains the actual dllstart() routine.

XCITEST is a very simple XCI client. A more interesting example of XCI's use appears in Chapter 17.

Comparing Extender DLLs to Windows DLLs

DLLs under DOS extenders are slightly different from their OS/2 or Windows counterparts. The primary difference is that ordinary DOS extenders doesn't multitask. With OS/2 or Windows, a DLL may have to serve several clients simultaneously. This requires the DLL to allocate private data for each client, and worry about concurrency problems. With the DOS extender, you don't have these concerns. The DLL is more like an overlay that doesn't actually overlay—the extender loads it for your program's exclusive use at load-time or run-time.

The Phar Lap extender will only call the DLL's entry point when it loads the DLL. Windows DLLs can do this, or you can set up the DLL so that the entry routine runs for each client that links to it.

Another difference stems from the way many extenders (including the Phar Lap 286|DOS-Extender) loads DLLs. With OS/2 or Windows, you may specify that a DLL only loads when your program calls it. The DOS extender loads any DLLs that you link with your program immediately. The only way to achieve true dynamic loading is to manage the process manually as XCI does for its LINK command.

Borrowed Features in Review

The features that this chapter describes are not special protected-mode features. However, many extenders support them to simplify common programming problems. None of them are strictly essential, but many tasks (incorporating real-mode code, starting your program from DOS, and supporting user-written add-ins, for example) are much simpler with these features.

CHAPTER ▪ 13

Handling User Exceptions—
Expect the Unexpected

Most practical applications require careful attention to user exceptions and errors. User exceptions arise when the user presses the Control-C, Control-Break, or Control-2 keys (the break keys). User errors (or critical error exceptions) are device related. Table 13-1 shows the possible DOS critical errors.

Windows programs, being event driven, don't need to worry about user exceptions, as they don't deal with break exceptions. Everything the user does generates a message which is similar to an exception—they aren't special cases. Critical errors under Windows usually return an error code to the calling program. The remainder of this chapter will cover protected-mode DOS programs exclusively.

By default, break exceptions print "^C" on the screen and terminate the program. Critical errors produce the infamous "Abort, Retry, Fail?" message. For many programs, you may need to close files or reset interrupt vectors before termination. If your program is screen oriented, you probably don't want these error messages to corrupt your display. For some programs, you may just want to ignore user exceptions.

Like many PC features, user exceptions rely on interrupts. The PC BIOS generates interrupt 0x1B when it detects the Control-Break key (but not the Control-C or Control-2 keys). When DOS detects a Control-C, a Control-2, or the flag set by the BIOS interrupt 0x1B handler, it issues interrupt 0x23. It is the default interrupt 0x23 handler that terminates the program. Critical errors cause interrupt 0x24. This default handler generates the "Abort, Retry, Fail?" message.

Table 13-1. Critical Errors

Value	Meaning
0x00	Write protected disk
0x01	Unknown unit
0x02	Drive not ready
0x03	Unknown command
0x04	CRC data error
0x05	Bad request length
0x06	Seek error
0x07	Unknown media type
0x08	Sector not found
0x09	Out of paper
0x0A	Write fault
0x0B	Read fault
0x0C	General failure
0x0F	Invalid disk change

Simple Methods

Most C libraries provide some means of dealing with user exceptions which are adequate for many programs. In addition, some extenders provide functions that can sometimes replace the need for more complicated user-exception handling.

The signal() Function

The ANSI standard signal() function can invoke a C function when a break event occurs. The SIGINT signal corresponds to a break. Here is a simple example:

```
#include <signal.h>
void onbreak(int sig)
   {
   /* reset signal handler */
   signal(SIGINT,onbreak);
   printf("\n--Break--\n");
   }

main()
   {
   signal(SIGINT,onbreak);
   .
   .
```

When a break event occurs, the onbreak( ) function executes. However, before onbreak( ) takes control, the library disables further SIGINT signals. If you want to continue to intercept these signals, you must reissue the signal( ) call as the first instruction of the handler.

You can use two special pseudo-functions with signal( ): SIG_IGN, and SIG_DFL. SIG_IGN ignores the given signal; SIG_DFL restores the signal's default action. For break events, the default action terminates the program.

There is one major limitation to the signal method. Although you can capture or ignore break events, you can't prevent the "^C" display by using signal( ). Often this renders signal( ) useless. In Chapter 19, you will see a screen-oriented program (CB386) that manages to use signal( ). It completely redraws the screen after a break occurs. Later in this chapter, we will look at ways to catch control-C events and avoid the "^C" display.

_harderr()

Most Microsoft-compatible libraries support three functions that simplify critical error handling: _harderr( ), _hardresume( ), and _hardretn( ). The _harderr( ) function is analogous to the signal( ) function—it specifies a C function that will handle critical errors. There are several differences between the two handlers, however:

- The error handler cannot call some library functions.
- The error handler must use _hardresume( ) or _hardretn( ) to return.

- The error function does not have to call _harderr() again—the handler remains in force without additional action.

Critical error handlers must avoid certain library calls, particularly those that do DOS I/O. Consult your compiler documentation to learn exactly which calls are invalid. You will be able to use any function that calls interrupt 0x21 functions 0x01-0x0C, 0x30, or 0x59. Other DOS calls are off limits. Since BIOS calls are usually safe, you will often need to resort to BIOS-based functions (e.g., _bios_keybrd()) for input and output.

The C library passes your handler three arguments. The first two arguments contain the values of the AX and DI registers at the time of the critical error. DOS supplies error information in these registers (see Figure 13-1). The third argument is a far pointer to a device driver header. The header belongs to the faulting driver. Very few handlers will need this information.

Figure 13-1. Critical Error Information

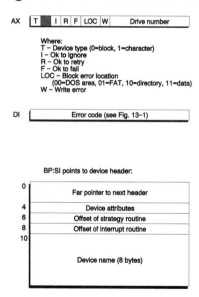

The handler must use the _hardresume() or _hardretn() functions to return. The _hardresume() function expects a single argument that tells DOS what to do. You may use _HARDERR_ABORT, _HARDERR_FAIL,

_HARDERR_IGNORE, or _HARDERR_RETRY. Note that DOS doesn't allow certain actions with some errors (see Figure 13-2).

Listing 13-1 shows a simple Phar Lap 286|DOS Extender program that dumps files to the screen (CAT286.C). The main() routine calls x_init() to set up break and critical error handlers. Listing 13-2 (COMMON.H) and Listing 13-3 (CAT286B1.C) provides an x_init() function that uses the signal() and _harderr() functions. When a break occurs, the onbreak() function prompts for confirmation. The new critical error routine, criterr(), is similar to the default DOS handler, but it provides more helpful messages.

Listing 13-1. CAT286.C

```
/* Demonstrate user exception handling.
   For Phar Lap 286 extender

   Compile with cat286b1.c or cat286b2.c In example
   compile commands, X=1 or 2

   Borland: bcc286 -w-par cat286.c cat286bX.c
   Microsoft :
   286|DOS Extender version 2.5 and later:
   cl -AL -Lp -G2 cat286.c cat286bX.c
   286|DOS Extender versions prior to 2.5
   cl -AL -Lp -G2 cat286.c cat286bX.c llibpe.lib
*/
#include <stdio.h>
#include <conio.h>
#include <string.h>
#include <ctype.h>
#include <stdlib.h>
#include <io.h>

/* flag set on break */
extern int broke;
/* set up exception handlers */
extern void x_init(void);

/* work space */
char tbuf[1024];

main()
  {
/* set up exception handlers */
  x_init();
```

```
   printf("Press ^C or ^Break to exit\n");
   while (1)
      {
      int c;
      while (!broke)
        {
        char *p;
        FILE *f;
        printf("File name:");
        if (!fgets(tbuf,sizeof(tbuf),stdin)) break;
        if (broke) break;
        p=strchr(tbuf,'\n');
/* ignore blank line */
        if (p==tbuf) continue;
        if (p) *p='\0';
        if (!access(tbuf,0))
          f=fopen(tbuf,"r");
        else
          f=NULL;
        if (f)
          {
          int c;
/* type file until EOF or break key -- we explicitly check
   for broke flag in this example, but the break interrupt
   (signal) handler could easily do a longjmp() to transfer
   control to some other point in the program. */
          while (broke==0&&(c=getc(f))!=EOF) putchar(c);
          putchar('\n');
          fclose(f);
          }
        else
          printf("Error opening file.\n");
        }
/* if you got here, broke==1 */
      printf("\nQuit? (Y/N) ");
      do
        {
        c=getch();
        if (!c)
          {
          getch();
          continue;
```

```
        }
      c=toupper(c);
      } while (c!='N'&&c!='Y');
      printf("%c\n",c);
      if (c=='Y')
        exit(0);
/* reset broke flag */
      broke=0;
      }
    }
```

Listing 13-2. COMMON.H

```
/* Common stuff for CAT286B1 and CAT286B2 -- only include once
*/
#ifndef CAT_COMMON
#define CAT_COMMON
/* strings... */
static char *cerr_msg="Critical Error: ";
static char *cerr_prompt="\n\r<R>etry, <F>ail, <I>gnore? ";
static char *err_tbl[]=
  {
  "Write protect",
  "Invalid drive",
  "Drive not ready",
  "Bad command",
  "CRC error",
  "Bad request",
  "Seek error",
  "Unknown format",
  "Sector not found",
  "Paper out",
  "Write error",
  "Read error",
  "General error",
  "??? - error",    /* unused error codes */
  "??? - error",
  "Invalid disk change"
  };

#define FAIL_OK 0x800
#define RETRY_OK 0x1000
#define IGNORE_OK 0x2000
```

```
/* Zero flag */
#define ZFLAG 64

/* output character via bios -- avoid using DOS call inside
   critical error handler */
void bios_out(char *p)
  {
/* Don't take up too much room on the stack! */
  static union REGS r1;
  while (*p)
    {
    r1.x.ax=0xE00|*p++;
    r1.x.bx=0;
    int86(0x10,&r1,&r1);
    }
  }

int bios_in(void)
  {
/* Don't take up too much room on the stack! */
  static union REGS r1;
  r1.x.ax=0;
  int86(0x16,&r1,&r1);
  return r1.h.al;
  }

int critical(unsigned int rax,unsigned int rdi)
  {
  int c;
  char key[4],beep[2];
  key[1]='\r';
  key[2]='\n';
  beep[1]=key[3]='\0';
  beep[0]='\a';
/* use BIOS function to print message */
  bios_out(cerr_msg);
  bios_out(err_tbl[rdi&0xF]);
  bios_out(cerr_prompt);
/* get character from BIOS */
  while (1)
    {
    c=toupper(bios_in());
    key[0]=c;
```

```
    bios_out(key);
    if (c=='F'&&(rax&FAIL_OK))
      return 3;
    if (c=='R'&&(rax&RETRY_OK))
      return 1;
    if (c=='I'&&(rax&IGNORE_OK))
      return 0;
/* No abort option implemented in this example */
    bios_out(beep);
    }
  }

#endif
```

Listing 13-3. CAT286B1.C

```
/* Example break handler for cat286.c. Uses
   signal and _harderr(). See cat286.c for instructions */

#include <stdio.h>
#include <signal.h>
#include <dos.h>
#include <ctype.h>

/* break flag  */
int broke;

/* Common things for break handlers */
#include "common.h"

/* this function happens on a ^C/^Break
   (This is "event driven" code -- not too different
   from Windows. An event (^C) triggers this function */
void on_break(void)
  {
/* reset signal handling */
  signal(SIGINT,on_break);
/* set flag */
  broke=1;
  }

/* this function happens on a critical error */
void on_crit(unsigned int rax,unsigned int rdi,
            unsigned *hdr)
```

```
  {
  int status;
  status=critical(rax,rdi);   /* see common.h */
  switch (status)
    {
    case 0:
      _hardresume(_HARDERR_IGNORE);
      break;

    case 1:
      _hardresume(_HARDERR_RETRY);
      break;

    case 3:
      _hardresume(_HARDERR_FAIL);
      break;
    }
  }


/* set up */
void x_init(void)
  {
  signal(SIGINT,on_break);
  _harderr(on_crit);
  }
```

Alternate Methods

Many programs trap user exceptions so they can perform some final processing. For example, a program might need to restore interrupt vectors
and close files before it exits. Some extenders provide services designed to
simplify these tasks.

Phar Lap's 286|DOS Extender, for example, supports the DosExitList()
function (borrowed from OS/2). With DosExitList(), you can instruct the
extender to call a C function before it terminates. This is similar to the
ANSI atexit() function. However, when you use atexit(), the exit function
only executes when the program terminates normally (from an exit() call,
or when main() returns). The extender always calls DosExitList() functions
before returning to DOS. The Ergo DPM extenders support exit threads
which provide a similar capability.

XCI.C (Listing 12-8 in Chapter 12) uses DosExitList() to restore the system's original interrupt vectors before it exits. First, XCI uses the call:

```
DosExitList(EXLST_ADD,(PFN)xci_clean);
```

to register the xci_clean() function. The xci_clean() routine must be declared as a _pascal function. For example:

```
void _pascal far xci_clean(unsigned int reason);
```

The exit function must call DosExitList() again to confirm the termination. For example:

```
DosExitList(EXLST_EXIT,NULL);
```

Interrupt Methods

The most versatile way to deal with user exceptions is to manipulate the interrupt 0x1B, 0x23 and 0x24 vectors. You can also capture break events with the keyboard interrupt (0x16). Although the C language signal() and _harderr() functions are simpler, sometimes you need to take direct control. For instance, you can catch break events with signal(), but you can't prevent the "^C" display. By using custom interrupt handlers, you can catch the event and prevent the "^C" display.

The Control-Break Interrupts

When the BIOS detects the Control-Break key, it generates an interrupt 0x1B. This interrupt simply sets a flag in the BIOS data area. During some interrupt 0x21 functions, DOS examines this flag, and the top of the keyboard buffer. If the flag is set, or the next keyboard character is a Control-C, DOS prints "^C" and calls interrupt 0x23. Since DOS generates the interrupt 0x23, the interrupt occurs in real mode under extenders that switch modes.

If the "^C" display doesn't bother you, you can detect break events by replacing the real-mode interrupt 0x23 handler. Then, when you return using an IRET instruction, as you would from a C interrupt function, the program will resume. To terminate the program, set the carry flag and return with a FAR RETURN instruction—this usually requires assembly language. Of course, the signal( ) function can provide the same effect without assembly language—you'll probably use signal( ) instead of this method.

Removing ^C

If the "^C" display interferes with your screen, you have several options. First, redrawing the screen after the break event occurs is a simple alternative (assuming you have the information to do so). Second, if you write directly to the screen and don't use DOS or BIOS services for output, you can move the cursor off the screen. DOS will still print the break message, but it will be off the screen. Be careful to handle critical errors as they will also be invisible.

A third way to suppress the "^C" display is more complicated. You must replace two interrupt vectors, 0x1B and 0x16 (the keyboard interrupts). The 0x1B interrupt can invoke your break handler directly. The 0x16 handler should examine the keyboard buffer during function 0, 1, 0x10 and 0x11. If the next character is a Control-C, the handler removes it and calls the break handler. XCI (see Chapter 12) uses this method; see Listing 12-8 if you want an example of how its done.

The Critical Error Interrupt

You can detect critical errors by intercepting interrupt 0x24. When the interrupt occurs, the AH and DI registers contain information about the error (see Figure 13-1). The BP:SI pair holds a pointer to the device header for the driver that signaled the error.

A critical error handler must return with an IRET instruction. In C, using the _interrupt function modifier will insure this. Before it returns, the function must place a code in the AL register to tell DOS how to proceed. The possible codes are:

```
0x00        Ignore
0x00        Retry
0x02        Abort
0x03        Fail
```

Critical error handlers can't call many DOS functions. It is safe to call interrupt 0x21 functions 1 through 0x0C, 0x30 and 0x59. You may also call any BIOS functions. Most C compilers list the functions that you can (or can't) call from inside a critical error handler (see the discussion under _harderr() on page 3).

Listing 13-4 shows alternate user exception handlers for CAT286.C (CAT286B2.C). These handlers have better control than those in CAT286B1.C since they intercept interrupts instead of using signal() and _harderr().

Listing 13-4. CAT286B2.C

```
/* Example break handler for cat286.c. Uses
    interrupts. See cat286.c for instructions */

#pragma check_stack(off)
#include <stdio.h>
#include <phapi.h>
#include <dos.h>
#include <conio.h>
#include <ctype.h>

/* Break vectors */
static PIHANDLER oldbreak;
static REALPTR oldbreal;
static PIHANDLER old1b;
static REALPTR old1breal;
static PIHANDLER old24;
static REALPTR old24real;

/* break flag -- declared volatile since
an interrupt routine might change it. The volatile
keyword tells the compiler that the value could
change at any time. */
int volatile broke=0;

/* Bios segment (you can't call DosGetBIOSseg from ISR) */
static USHORT biosseg;

#include "common.h"
```

```c
/* The following define hides the fact that Borland and
   Microsoft push the registers in a different order for
   interrupt functions */
#ifdef __BORLANDC__
#define REGS_16 REGS_BINT
#else
#define REGS_16 REGS16
#endif



/* ^Break handlers */
void _interrupt _far new_int1b(REGS_16 r)
  {
  union REGS rr;
  unsigned int *keyhead,*keytail;
/* get pointers to keyboard buffer */
  keyhead=MAKEP(biosseg,0x1A);
  keytail=MAKEP(biosseg,0x1C);
/* set break flag */
  broke=1;
/* purge keyboard buffer */
  *keyhead=*keytail;
/* push ^C at head */
  rr.h.ah=5;
  rr.x.cx=3;
  int86(0x16,&rr,&rr);
  }

/* new keyboard int */
void _interrupt _far new_int16(REGS_16 r)
  {
  REGS16 r1;
  unsigned ah=r.ax>>8;
  _enable();
  if (ah==0||ah==0x10||ah==1||ah==0x11)
    {
    do
      {
      r1.ax=0x100;
      r1.flags=0;
```

```
/* Simulate interrupt to old INT 16H handler */
     DosRealFarCall(oldbreal,&r1,0,-1,r1.flags);
/* if char not ready... */
     if ((r1.flags&ZFLAG)&&(ah==1||ah==0x11))
       {
       r.flags=r1.flags;
       return;
       }
     } while (r1.flags&ZFLAG); /* while char not ready */
/* If break character -- replace it with a carriage return
   3==^C  0x300==^2 -- ^2 (control-2) generates a break...
   its true! Try it from the DOS prompt. */
     if ((r1.ax&0xff)==3||r1.ax==0x300)
       {
       unsigned int *keyhead;
/* Find 1st byte of keyboard typeahead buffer */
       keyhead=MAKEP(biosseg,0x1A);
       keyhead=MAKEP(biosseg,*keyhead);
       *keyhead='\r';
/* set break flag */
       broke=1;
       }
   }
/* continue with old INT 16 handler */
  DosChainToRealIntr(oldbreal);
  }


void _interrupt _far new_int24(REGS_16 r)
  {
  int status;
/* status == 0 for ignore, 1 for retry, 3 for fail */
  status=critical(r.ax,r.di);   /* see common.h */
  r.ax|=status;
  return;
  }


/* function to clean up -- installed with DosExitList */
void pascal x_clean(USHORT arg)
  {
  DosSetRealProtVec(0x16,oldbreak,oldbreal,NULL,NULL);
```

```
   DosSetRealProtVec(0x1b,old1b,old1breal,NULL,NULL);
   DosSetRealProtVec(0x24,old24,old24real,NULL,NULL);
   DosExitList(EXLST_EXIT,NULL);
   }


/* setup */
void x_init(void)
  {
  DosGetBIOSSeg(&biosseg);
/* Due to a bug in versions prior to 1.4, you must set
   the INT 16H ProtVec before using PassToProtVec... */
  DosSetProtVec(0x16,(PIHANDLER)new_int16,&oldbreak);
  DosSetPassToProtVec(0x16,(PIHANDLER)new_int16,NULL,
                   &oldbreal);
  DosSetPassToProtVec(0x1b,(PIHANDLER)new_int1b,
                   &old1b,&old1breal);
  DosSetPassToProtVec(0x24,(PIHANDLER)new_int24,
                   &old24,&old24real);
  DosExitList(EXLST_ADD,x_clean);
  }
```

You will find another example of this technique (for break handling only) in the XCI program (Listing 12-8 in Chapter 12). The xci_int1b() and xci_int16() functions intercept interrupts 0x1B and 0x16, respectively. When XCI terminates, the xci_clean() function executes since the main program registered it using DosExitList().

Take a Break

As we've seen, you can handle break events and critical errors using the C library functions, signal() and _harderr(). While this is simple, these routines might not offer enough control for all applications. If you find that these functions are not adequate for your program, you will have to directly handle the break and critical error interrupts. Where possible, you should try to use the standard functions—they are more portible and require less work.

CHAPTER ▪ 14

Windows (and DOS) Times 32

Microsoft Windows 3.0 and 3.1 are 16-bit DOS extenders—even in 386 enhanced mode. Application programs (and most of the system software) are 16-bit. Some Windows system software and virtual device drivers (VxDs) run in 32-bit mode, but they also run at privilege level 0—great for writing powerful system software, but undesirable for applications.

Programmers familiar with 32-bit protected mode often wonder if there is a way to capitalize on 386/486 power in Windows programs. Some DOS extender vendors addressed the 16-bit limitation by providing Windows extenders. These programs essentially duplicate the Windows API with 32-bit parameters. The extender handles some of the 32-bit API calls directly. For other calls, it translates parameters to a 16-bit form and passes them to the Windows kernel.

Windows extenders have been largely replaced by Microsoft's Win32 API. Win32 is the 32-bit Windows API developed for Windows NT—Microsoft's advanced 32-bit operating system. While you normally develop Win32 applications for the Windows NT operating system, you can also create Win32 programs that will run under Windows 3.1.

The ability to target Win32 code for multiple operating systems is very important. Although Windows NT may be the dominant operating system one day, it will take some time for it to catch up to Windows 3.1 and DOS. By using techniques to retarget Win32 code, you can write code for DOS and Windows 3.1 users today and still be ready for Windows NT.

Win32

You can think of the Win32 API as a superset of the conventional Windows API (the Win16 API). Most parameters in Win32 are 32 bits wide. For example, the wParam and lParam parameters in a Window function are the same size—32 bits.

Win32 is more than just a wide Win16 interface, however. Windows NT is a complete operating system and it also runs on machines other than the PC (such as, MIPS or the DEC Alpha machines). Therefore, Win32 must provide functions that are absent from 16-bit Windows. Win32 supports character I/O to virtual consoles, for example.

Win32S

Since Win32 is similar to Win16, it is possible to support a subset of the Win32 API under Windows 3.1. The Win32S libraries (both DLLs and VxDs) supply all Win32 functions, however, some of the functions simply return an error. Your program must take appropriate action when it detects an unsupported call. There is no such thing as a Win32S executable. Win32S is a set of DLLs and drivers that allow Windows 3.1 to execute some Win32 programs. The Windows 3.1 loader recognizes NT's executable format (the portable executable or PE file format) and allows the special Win32S drivers to control the program's execution.

Some Win32 functions, such as memory management calls, are handled directly by the Win32S system. Many other calls are "thunked": the Win32S system translates these 32-bit calls to 16-bit calls and passes them to the Windows kernel. This process is similar to the operation of the early Windows extenders (although the pieces are more closely integrated with Windows).

Like conventional DOS extenders, Win32S penalizes a program for switching back and forth between 16- and 32-bit modes. Programs that largely call functions that are thunked will run more slowly under Win32S than an equivalent conventional Windows 3.1 program. Programs that can remain in 32-bit mode will run faster than a similar Windows program. A 16-bit API call that requires large amounts of processing (BitBlt(), for example) won't suffer much from thunking since the thunk time represents a small percentage of the total processing time. Of course a program written for Win32S will execute under Windows NT with no performance penalty.

Passing control through a thunk is much like switching modes in a regular DOS extender. You should try to structure your Win32S programs to do as much work as possible per API call. For example, use the PolyLine() call over Win16-type MoveTo() and LineTo() functions; read and write as much data to a file as possible per call.

Differences Between Windows NT and Win32S

Although Win32 programs make the same calls under Win32S and Windows NT, there are some differences in the run-time environment. For example, Win32S programs all run in a single address space (the same space used by conventional Windows programs). Like regular Windows programs, they share processor time in a cooperative fashion. Other programs can only get control of the CPU when the current program makes certain calls (notably, GetMessage()). Under Windows NT, Win32 programs run preemptively in separate address spaces. The bottom line: if you expect a Win32 program to run under different platforms, you must test them on each one.

Be sure to test the return value for every Win32 call that you make. If you make a call that the current environment doesn't support, you will get an error return and will have to take some appropriate action.

Currently, Win32S supports most Win32 calls that can directly map to Win16 API calls. Win32S also supports structured exception handling, sparse memory, and memory-mapped files (although some limits apply). (See the *Win32 API Reference* for more details about the Win32 API.)

Examples of Win32 calls that the current version of Win32S does not support are console I/O, bezier curves, threads, and asynchronous file I/O. Since Win32S is simply a collection of DLLs and a VxD, it is possible that Microsoft or some other vendor will add functions to Win32S that are not present today. Some of these functions (console I/O, for example) may one day reside in a future version of DOS itself.

Win32 and DOS

The Win32 API isn't just a Windows interface—it is a 32-bit standard. Just as DOS extender manufacturers use Windows and OS/2 1.X compilers and tools to create 16-bit protected-mode programs, they can use Win32 compilers and tools to create 32-bit programs.

One such product is Phar Lap's TNT 32-bit DOS extender (the only one available at this writing). The TNT extender provides a subset of the Win32 API—the console I/O functions required to run the Windows NT C compiler and most of its associated tools under DOS. You then use the NT tools to create 32-bit programs that also run under the TNT extender.

The TNT extender supports the non-graphical console I/O portion of Win32—it isn't a replacement for the Windows GUI. It can't run the NT debugger. Phar Lap supplies a simple debugger that runs under DOS.

TNT binds the NT programs you create with a special real-mode stub (see Chapter 12 for more about stubs). This stub causes the TNT extender to load and execute your program from DOS.

With a little care, you can write one program that will work under Windows NT (on a PC, MIPS, DEC Alpha, and so on), Windows 3.1 (via Win32S), and DOS (using an extender like TNT). Of course, this portability has a price: it multiplies many times over the amount of testing you will need to do before you release your software.

Developing for Win32

You can develop Win32 programs in a variety of environments. You can develop under Windows NT Win32S environments available from Borland and Microsoft, or run the NT tools under DOS with Phar Lap's TNT extender. If you don't need to create protected-mode DOS executables, you can get the QuickStart disk free of charge from Phar Lap. QuickStart allows you to run the NT tools under DOS to produce NT executables. It doesn't allow you to create DOS executables.

Regardless of your choice of development environment, it is important to test your program on all the target platforms. There are slight differences between the Windows NT, Win32S, and TNT environments.

The 32-Bit World

As Windows (both 3.1 and NT) become increasingly important, Win32 becomes harder and harder to ignore. You can expect future versions of Win32S to support more of the full Win32 interface and third-party dynamic libraries to further fill in the gaps.

In the same way that OS/2 and Windows 3.0 legitimized 16-bit protected-mode development, Windows NT will legitimize 32-bit development. The 32-bit world will see two major benefits from NT: portability across many platforms, and the increased availability of high-quality tools from a variety of vendors.

CHAPTER ■ 15

Protected Performance

Once your protected-mode program is running, you will probably want to spend some time fine-tuning it for better performance. If you have done this for DOS programs, you'll have to forget much of what you know. Many fast techniques in real mode are slow under protected mode (loading segment registers, for example). Also, many things that are not generally available in real mode can supercharge your protected-mode code.

A little experience goes a long way when optimizing protected-mode programs. A good profiler goes even further (see the sidebar, *Profiling for Performance*). There are several good profilers available for Windows and for many of thepopular protected-mode C compilers.

Many optimization techniques are not readily available to C programmers. Often you are at the mercy of your compiler. While many modern compilers employ sophisticated optimization strategies and produce surprisingly good code, there are still some cases where manual optimization of C code will be worthwhile. In other cases, it might pay off to rewrite some portions of your code in assembly language.

This chapter covers some important protected-mode optimizations. However, a complete treatment of program optimization could (and does) fill another book. If you want to know more, check out the bibliography.

PROFILING FOR PERFORMANCE

It is often difficult to guess which routines in a large program are consuming the most processor time. Luckily, many compiler vendors offer profilers to help analyze your programs.

Profilers are similar to debuggers. When you run your program with the profiler, it reports the amount of time spent executing each routine.

Most profilers allow you to select which routines are timed. Often you won't want to time calls that read the keyboard, as these routines often take a long time since they wait for input. In some cases you might not want to see the times for operating system calls, or you might want to examine just one module.

Many profilers operate by sampling. They speed up the PC timer interrupt and install a timer interrupt handler. On each timer tick, the profiler notes the interrupt's return address. When the program ends, the profiler can correlate these addresses with the program's symbols and produce a table or histogram of the results.

When a profiler samples, you'll need to provide enough data for it to get a good average of your program. Also, you may have difficulties profiling functions that run with interrupts disabled.

Other profilers work by placing psuedo-breakpoints at each function's entry and exit points. Again, the profiler gathers statistics at each breakpoint and displays the results after the program terminates. ■

C and Assembly Language Improvements

There are several general optimizations available to C programmers. Some of these simply apply common sense rules while others are more subtle and require careful application. Assembly programs can use any optimization technique that a C program can.

Segment Registers

Conventional DOS programs play fast and loose with segment registers. After all, in real mode, a segment register is just another 16-bit number. In protected mode, however, each segment register is an index into one of the segment descriptor tables. As noted in Chapter 4, each table entry is eight bytes long. The processor would quickly bog down if it had to read these eight bytes every time it used a segment register. Instead, it caches the entry in hidden registers onboard the CPU.

While this onboard cache speeds segment register *access*, it stands to reason that loading these registers is more time consuming than *loading* a real mode segment register. Intel's 80386 documentations shows that an LDS instruction (which loads a far pointer) takes 7 clock cycles in real mode, and 22 in protected mode. Other segment register manipulations (such as the popular LES BX) incur similar penalties. The moral is: in protected mode, avoid changing segment register values whenever possible. In C you have limited control over segment register usage. You still may be able to improve performance by limiting your use of far pointers. Near calls are much more efficient than far calls in protected-mode.

Alignment

Code and data misalignment can also hobble your real- or protected-mode programs. The 386 and 486 always read 32-bit words from addresses that are evenly divisible by four. The 286 always reads 16-bit words from addresses that are evenly divisible by two. Therefore if you access a word on an odd address, the processor must load two words and paste them together to form the word you want. As a rule this doubles the time the processor requires to read the word. The same holds true for writing words—any memory access is faster when you align it on a word boundary.

Some C compilers automatically try to align stacks, function entry points, and structures. Others will do so if you set the right options (see Chapter 6). If your compiler won't align code and stacks, you can't do much about it. You can manually ensure alignment of some data items, however.

Manually aligned structures are the simplest case. You can insert dummy members to pad each element to a two- or four-byte boundary. Just make sure the results are what you expect—a compiler that already aligns structures will align your data *and* your dummy fields. You might do something like this:

```
struct _critical
 {
 short foo;
```

```
#ifdef MANUAL_ALIGN32
 short dummy0;
#endif
 char c;
#ifdef MANUAL_ALIGN32
 char dummy1[3];
#endif
  }
```

Of course, if the structure is externally defined (say a disk record or a DOS data structure), you can't align it (see Chapter 6 for more about this).

Arrays are somewhat more complex. The idea is to declare (or malloc()) the array a few bytes larger than you need. Then, at run time you assign the address to a pointer. Your program can examine the address and adjust it until it is aligned. For two-byte alignment, an extra byte will do; for four-byte alignent, you need three extra bytes. Here is an example for two-byte alignment:

```
#include <stdio.h>
#include <stdlib.h>
#define ALIGN16 1
#define ARY_SIZE 30000
/* ary1 is static, ary2 is dynamic */
char xary1[ARY_SIZE*sizeof(int)+1];
int *ary1,*ary2,*oary2;
main()
 {
 int i,j;
 ary1=(int *)xary1;
/* adjust ary1 to alignment */
 if (((int)ary1&1)==ALIGN16) (char *)ary1+=1;
/* oary2 holds the original address for free() */
 oary2=ary2=malloc(ARY_SIZE*sizeof(int)+1);
 if (!ary2)
   {
   printf("Out of memory\n");
   exit(1);
   }
 if (((int)ary2&1)==ALIGN16) (char *)ary2+=1;
 for (j=0;j<100;j++)
```

```
   {
   for (i=0;i<ARY_SIZE;i++)
    ary1[i]=i;
   for (i=0;i<ARY_SIZE;i++)
    ary2[i]=i;
   for (i=0;i<ARY_SIZE;i++)
    if (ary1[i]!=i) printf("Error in ary1\n");
   for (i=0;i<ARY_SIZE;i++)
    if (ary1[i]!=i) printf("Error in ary2\n");
   }
/* Be sure to free original pointer! */
 free(oldary2);
 exit(0);
 }
```

This program deliberately wastes time accessing the arrays in order to exaggerate the timing difference. For demonstration purposes, when ALIGN16 is 0, the program deliberately misaligns the arrays. Try compiling the program (under nearly any compiler—Borland or Microsoft C will do) with ALIGN16 set to 1 and 0 and notice the difference in execution speed. On a 25Mhz 386 the aligned version was nearly 7% faster than the unaligned version.

Register Use

Placing frequently used variables in registers is an old trick for boosting performance. So old, that the C language has a built-in cue to suggest to the compiler which variables to store in registers. For example, the following code might be faster than usual because of the register keyword:

```
void numlist()
  {
  register int i;
  for (i=0;i<100;i++) printf("%d\n",i);
  }
```

In practice, the above code may not be any faster for a couple of reasons. First, the register keyword is only a suggestion—the compiler may elect to ignore the register keyword on any or all variable declarations. Second, many modern compilers would automatically place i in a register without being explicitly told to do so. In fact, sometimes using the register ketword can actually slow down your code. This usually happens when the compiler would have made better register choices than you did. Since there are usually just a few registers available for each function, you will prevent the compiler from automatically allocating registers when you use the register keyword. When in doubt, try it several ways including without any register variables.

If you write some or all of your code in assembler, make sure you don't neglect the additional registers available to you on 386 and 486 CPUs. You can use two new segment registers (FS and GS), by using a segment override (similar to the way you use the ES register). Better still, you can use most general purpose registers in most instructions.On the 286, only the BX, BP, SI, and DI registers can serve as an offset. On the 386 and 486, any register will work. For example, you could write:

```
mov eax,0B8000H
mov byte ptr [eax],41H
```

Avoid Change

The CPU, like many people, abhors change. Avoid switching modes and privledge levels when possible. When you must switch modes, try to do as much as possible before returning. For example, use BIOS interrupt 0x10 function 0x13 to write a string instead of writing each character with interrupt 0x10 function 0x0E. This way you only incur two mode switches: one to make the call and another to return. Better still, write directly to the screen and stay in protected mode (see Chapter 7 for an example).

Any time you pass pointers to or from DOS, the extender must move the data between your buffer and a special buffer below 1M (see Chapter 4). This can be time consuming so again, do as much work in protected mode as possible. Then switch to real-mode (e.g., call DOS or the BIOS) and do as much work as you can before returning to protected mode. Don't read 2 or 4 bytes at a time from a file; read and write data to files in the largest-possible size.

A few extenders may allow you to avoid using a special translation buffer below 1M for file I/O calls. You can allocate your own buffer below 1M and use setvbuf() to associate it with a stream setvbvf() is a standard C function; you would pass it a protected-mode pointer to the conventional-memory transfer buffer. This buffer must not be more than 64K in length. This allows the extender to simply pass a real mode version of the buffer's address to DOS an BIOS routines. The extender won't have to copy the data to a special buffer—a potentially time-consuming operation.

The DOS transfer buffer can be a real bottleneck. Sometimes you can speed up your programs by increasing the size of this buffer (if your extender allows it). If the buffer is too small, the extender may have to make extra switches in and out of protected mode to satisfy your DOS requests. Of course, the larger the translation buffer the less real memory will be available for other purposes (direct real-mode calls, spawning DOS programs, and so on).

Word Size Optimizations

You can speed up many operations by increasing the amount of data you handle at one time. This is especially true when working with 32-bit programs. Suppose you want to clear the screen by writing 0x0720 to each 16-bit word in video memory. The obvious way to do this is:

```
int _far *scrptr=get_video_address();
for (i=0;i<2000;i++) *scrptr=0x0720;
```

For 32-bit programs, here is a quicker way to do it:

```
long _far *scrptr=get_video_address();
for (i=0;i<1000;i++) *scrptr=0x07200720;
```

By making full use of a 32-bit word, you can cut the number of iterations in half.

For 32-bit programs, try to use the int data type in preference to short. The processor is much more efficient when it deals with 32-bit quantities. Although you may think about using short to save data space, there is extra code needed to handle 16-bit data that will quickly outweigh your savings. The only time you need the short data type is when you have data from an external source (MS-DOS or a disk file) that is 16-bits wide.

Make Use of the Library

A good C library often uses assembly for many functions. Some assembler instructions often allow these functions to be much faster than even the tightest C code. A good example is strcpy(). On Intel processors, a well-written strcpy() will use the special 8086 string instructions (a good 386 library will use the 32-bit version of the same instruction) to boost performance. Therefore:

```
while (*dest++=*src++);
```

may never be as fast as:

```
strcpy(dest,src);
```

Assembly Improvements

What's good for C programmers is even better for assembly programmers. Assembly programs can exercise greater control over segmentation and register use. There are also many optimizations that you can only achieve with assembly.

On the 386 and 486, conditional jumps can be short (1-byte displacement) or long (4-byte displacement). When you jump to a forward reference, your assembler will reserve space for a 4-byte jump. To avoid this, override the label's type with the SHORT modifier. For example:

```
JZ AHEAD      ; 4-byte
JC SHORT AHEAD ; 1-byte
  .
  .
  .
AHEAD:
```

A conditional jump instruction will always take longer to execute if it succeeds. If possible, arrange your jumps so that they fail more often than succeed. For example, in the following code, if AX is usually zero, then change:

```
   OR AX,AX
   JZ SHORT AZ
ANZ:
    .
    .
    .
AZ:
```

to:

```
   OR AX,AX
   JNZ SHORT ANZ
AZ:
    .
    .
    .
ANZ:
```

Mixing in Assembly Language

No matter how well you (and your compiler) optimize C code, there will be some instances when you need to turn to assembly language. Luckily, you can easily mix C and assembly subroutines. Many compilers will even allow you to insert assembly statements in the middle of C functions. The MSCINT.C program in Chapter 5 uses inline assembler.

When to Use Assembly Language

If you despair at the thought of rewriting your entire program in assembly, don't worry. Most programs spend most of their time in only a few key routines. If you can identify these routines and rewrite them in assembly, the rest of the program can remain in C.

Don't waste time writing assembly language to perform functions that occur once or twice. Instead, optimize the computations that happen over and over again. Always ask: "What would happen if I could completely remove this subroutine?".

Say you have a program that takes five minutes to complete. If function setup() runs in 10 seconds, and function calc1() takes two minutes, the choice is clear. Even if you could remove setup(), it wouldn't make much difference. The calc1() routine, however, is a good candidate for optimization. It represents 40% of the total processing time.

As noted earlier in this chapter, a profiler is the best way to select nominees for optimization. However, if you don't have a profiler, you can still gauge the performance of your code using other techniques. Often, you can use the standard library clock() function (or something similar) to store time marks during your program. At the end of the program you can print these out to see which functions took the most time.

An Assembly Language Example

Floating-point calculations can significantly slow down programs. While a coprocessor can speed up floating-point operations, it still may be slower than integer arithmetic. Worse, many programs may run on computers that lack a coprocessor. Since many PCs and embedded systems don't have a coprocessor, C compilers often supply emulation libraries. These libraries emulate a coprocessor if the target system lacks one.

Emulation libraries are notoriously slow and many programs don't need the precision these libraries provide. There is a faster way to do floating point math by taking advantage of the 80386's 32-bit instructions. The remainder of this chapter presents a library called FPM32. These techniques can be applied to other 32-bit processors. You can even adapt the routines to run on 16-bit processors, although you will see some loss of performance.

Interestingly, FPM32 will work with regular DOS programs or 16-bit extended programs (including Windows programs). You can also use FPM32 with many 386 DOS extenders.

You'll need MASM or TASM to assemble the main source file of the FPM32 package. You can use FPM32 from assembly, C, or C++ programs. Since FPM32 takes advantage of several 386 instructions, you'll also need a 386- or 486-based computer. One caveat: FPM32 is not as accurate as a coprocessor (or an emulation library) that uses an 80-bit word. Still, it is accurate enough for many programs.

How FPM32 Works

When you do arithmetic by hand, you don't work directly with floating-point numbers. Instead, you calculate an integer answer, and decide where to put the decimal point. When you add, for example, you align the number's decimal points, and add them. The answer's decimal point remains in the same position. When multiplying by hand, you treat the numbers as integers, and place the answer's decimal point by counting the number of digits to the right of the decimal point in the two multiplicands. FPM32 uses similar procedures on binary numbers.

Using 32-bit integer arithmetic, the 386 can easily perform real number math with reasonable accuracy. Since FPM32 uses binary numbers, there isn't a decimal point. To avoid confusion, this chapter refers to the point in a FPM32 number as the radix point.

Figure 15-1 shows how FPM32 stores floating-point numbers. The val field contains a 32-bit binary number. The scale field determines the location of the assumed radix point. The sign field is zero for positive numbers, or 0xFF for negative numbers.

FPM32 uses two routines to adjust numbers. RADJ shifts numbers right until bit 0 is a 1, and LADJ shifts them left until the leftmost bit is a 1. These routines update the scale field by the amount of the shift so that the number's value doesn't change—just its representation.

Figures 15-2a through 15-2d show the psuedo code for FPM operations. Before adding two numbers, FPM32 must line up their radix points using the algorithm in Figure 15-2a. FPM32 uses RADJ on both numbers to allow for as many significant digits as possible (see Figure 15-3). If the scales are then equal, the addition proceeds. If they are not, FPM32 adjusts the number with the smaller scale to the left until the scales are equal, or until a left shift would cause a 1 bit to fall off the end of the word. If the scales still are not equal, FPM32 will right shift the number with the larger scale. While some bits on the right may be lost, these bits have less significance than the bits on the left.

Figure 15-1. FPM Storage Format

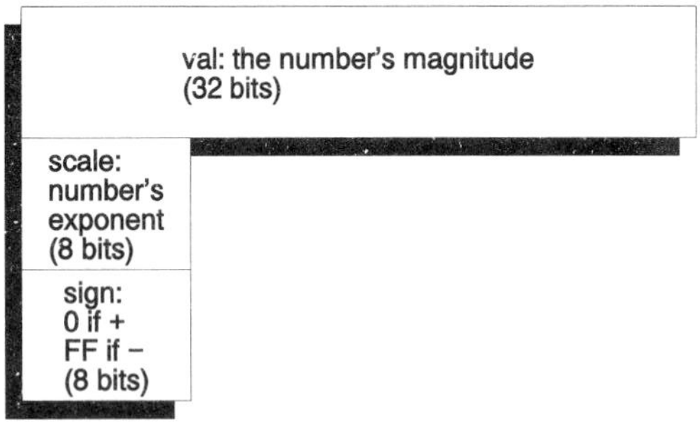

```
                    val: the number's magnitude
                    (32 bits)

scale:
number's
exponent
(8 bits)

sign:
0 if +
FF if −
(8 bits)
```

Examples:

If:
val=10101 (binary)
scale=1
sign=0
Then:
number=1010.1 (binary) or 10.5 (decimal)

If:
val=11 (binary)
scale=−1
sign=0
Then:
number=110 (binary) or 6 (decimal)

Figure 15-2a. Psuedocode for FPM Operations

Addition

```
if (x.value==0) return y
if (y.value==0) return x
right_adjust(y)
right_adjust(x)
if x.scale!=y.scale then
   A=number with larger scale
   B=number with smaller scale
   sdiff=A.scale-B.scale
   idx=left_bit_index(B) /* find index of leftmost '1' bit */
   if 31-idx>=sdiff then
     B.value=B.value<<sdiff
     B.scale+=sdiff
   else
     B.value=B.value<<31-idx
     B.scale+=31-idx
```

```
      A.value=A.value>>sdiff-(31-idx)
      A.scale-=sdiff-(31-idx)
   endif
endif
if bit 31 of A.value or B.value is set then
   A.value=A.value>>1
   B.value=B.value>>1
   A.scale--
   B.scale--
endif
if A.sign==0xff A.value=-A.value
if B.sign==0xff B.value=-B.value
result.value=A.value+B.value
if result.value<0 then
   result.value=-result.value
   result.sign=0xff
endif
result.scale=A.scale
```

Figure 15-2b. Psuedocode for FPM Operations

Subtraction

```
if y.value!=0 y=-y
jump to add routine
```

Figure 15-2c. Psuedocode for FPM Operations

Multiplication

```
right_adjust(x)
right_adjust(y)
if x.value==0||y.value==0 return 0
product=x.value*y.value /* product is 64 bit */
shift product left until top 32 bits are all zero
x.scale=x.scale-amount_shifted
if bit 31 of product set then
   product=product>>1
   x.scale--
endif
result.value=product
result.scale=x.scale+y.scale
result.sign=x.sign^y.sign /* exclusive-or */
```

Figure 15.2d. Psuedocode for FPM Operations

Division

```
left_adjust(x)
right_adjust(y)
if x.value==0 return 0
if y.value!=1 then
    idx=left_bit_index(y) /* find index of leftmost '1' bit */
    divx=x.value       /* divx is 64 bit */
    divx=divx<<idx
    x.scale+=idx
    result.value=divx/y.value
else
    result.value=x
endif
result.scale=x.scale-y.scale
result.sign=x.sign^y.sign  /* exclusive-or */
```

Figure 15-3. Addition with and Without Right Adjustment

Problem: add 10110.100 and 10010.000 (binary) using 8 bits

With no adjustments:
```
  10110.100
 +10010.000
1010000.100
```
↑
└───── **Overflow**

With right adjustments:
```
 0010110.1
+0010010.0
 01010000.1
```

Subtraction is simple (see Figure 15-2b). FPM32 inverts the sign of the second argument, calls the addition routine, and restores the second argument's original sign.

The 386's multiply instruction can directly act on the two numbers in the val fields. The scale of the result is the sum of the two original scales. Figure 15-2c outlines the multiplication algorithm. The MUL instruction places a 64-bit result in the EDX:EAX register pair. FPM32 shifts any significant bits out of EDX to the EAX register (and adjusts the answer's scale).

The DIV instruction divides a 64-bit number (in EDX:EAX) by a 32-bit number. To maximize precision, FPM32 shifts the divisor to the right until its bit 0 is a 1 (adjusting the scale, of course). If the divisor is equal to 1, the division is complete. Otherwise, FPM32 shifts the 64-bit dividend left by the number of significant bits in the divisor. This assures a 32-bit result with the maximum number of significant digits.

Next, the DIV instruction divides the two numbers. FPM32 then subtracts the divisor's scale from the dividend's scale to locate the result's radix point. Figure 15-2d illustrates this process.

Implementation

Listing 15-1 contains FPM32.ASM, the core functions for FPM32. FPM32.H and FPMC.C (Listings 15-2 and 15-3) simplify using FPM32 from C programs.

The faddxy(), fsubxy(), fmulxy(), and fdivxy() functions provide the basic mathematical operations. To round out the library, two routines (fixtofloat() and floattofix()) perform conversions between FPM32 numbers and standard C floats.

Listing 15-4 (FPMTIME.C) shows a Windows program that pits FPM32 against the standard floating-point library. FPMTIME uses our standard Windows test program (see Chapter 5). However, you can't use the simple batch files BWINCOMP.BAT (or MWINCOMP.BAT) to compile FPMTIME. Instead, use MAKE (Borland) or NMAKE (Microsoft) to compile via the MAKEFILE (Listing 15-5). Be sure to change MAKEFILE to reflect which compiler you are using.

In informal tests on several machines, FPM32 outperformed the standard emulation library by a factor of at least 2.5. A real coprocessor is still about five times faster than FPM32 (and over 12 times faster than the average emulation libraries).

Optimizations

FPM32 takes full advantage of the 386 instruction set. Of course the 32-bit register width is a significant advantage, but other 386 instructions help, too.

FPM32 often shifts words until their rightmost (or leftmost) bit is a 1 (see LADJ and RADJ in Listing 15-1). A conventional DOS program might use this code to right adjust EAX:

```
SLOOP:  TEST EAX,1
        JZ  DONE
        SHR EAX,1
        JMP SLOOP
DONE:
```

The 386 bit scan instructions, BSF and BSR, can considerably speed up this operation. BSF starts at bit 0 and returns the index of the first 1 bit that it finds. BSR starts with bit 31 (for a 32-bit operand). If there are no 1 bits in the word, the bit scan instructions set the zero flag. The above code fragment can be rewritten:

```
BSF ECX,EAX  ; scan EAX - store bit index in ECX
SHR EAX,ECX  ; if bit 0 set this is a NOP
```

This avoids the expensive looping and jumping that the first method requires.

FPM32 provides a C language interface to the bit scan instructions (bitscan() in Listing 15-1). The prototype is:

```
int bitscan(int dir,unsigned long lword);
```

If the dir flag is zero, bitscan() uses the BSF instruction. Otherwise, it uses BSR. The lword parameter is a 32-bit integer to scan. Unlike BSF and

BSR, bitscan() numbers the bits from 1 (rightmost) to 32 (leftmost). If no bits are set in lword, bitscan() returns zero.

FPM32 uses other 386 instructions, such as the SHLD instruction, in several places. SHLD shifts an operand left, filling the rightmost bits from its other operand. For example:

```
MOV EAX,10H
MOV EBX,0FA000000H
SHLD EAX,EBX,8
```

would leave 10FAH in EAX.

Listing 15-1. FPM32.ASM

```
;############################################################
;#                                                          #
;# File: FPM.ASM                                            #
;#                                                          #
;# 386 Floating point package by Al Williams                #
;#                                                          #
;############################################################
.MODEL          SMALL,C


; enable 386 instructions
.386


.DATA


; Number format
FPM_NUM         STRUC
SIGN            DB      ?       ; 0 for + FF for -
SCALE           DB      ?       ; position of decimal point
NUM             DD      ?       ; unsigned magnitude
FPM_NUM         ENDS

IF MICROSOFT
FPM_RET         FPM_NUM   <>        ; static return value
ANSOFF          DW      OFFSET FPM_RET
ANSSEG          DW      @data
ENDIF
```

```
.CODE
; C  routines
PUBLIC          faddxy,fsubxy,fmulxy,fdivxy,bitscan


;***********************************************
; Helper for C routines bitscan(dir,lword)
; if dir==0 do BSF on num
; if dir!=0 do BSR on num
; Returns index 1-32 or 0 if word was zero
bitscan         PROC
                ARG     DIR:WORD, LWORD:DWORD
                MOV     AX,DIR
                OR      AX,AX
MOV     EAX,LWORD
                JZ      SHORT SCANFWD
                BSR     EAX,EAX
                JMP     SHORT BITSC0
SCANFWD:        BSF     EAX,EAX
BITSC0:         JNZ     SHORT BITSC1
                XOR     AX,AX
                RET
BITSC1:         INC     AX
                RET
bitscan         ENDP



;***********************************************
; Adjust temp register @BX so that rightmost bit is 1
RADJ            PROC
; Find last set bit
                BSF     ECX,[BX].NUM
; If all zeros, jump to ZOUT
                JZ      SHORT ZOUT
; Shift right and adjust scale
                SHR     [BX].NUM,CL
                SUB     [BX].SCALE,CL
                RET
ZOUT:
                MOV     [BX].SCALE,0
                RET
RADJ            ENDP
```

```
;************************************************
; Adjust temp register @BX so leftmost bit is 1
LADJ            PROC
; Find first bit set
                BSR     ECX,[BX].NUM
; If all zero's goto zout (above in proc RADJ)
                JZ      ZOUT
; 31-Bit_index -> # places to shift
                MOV     CH,31
                SUB     CH,CL
                MOV     CL,CH
; Shift number and adjust scale
                SHL     [BX].NUM,CL
                ADD     [BX].SCALE,CL
                RET
LADJ            ENDP


;************************************************
; Add x+y
; FIXED faddxy(FIXED xarg,FIXED yarg)
; Note: Borland functions that return structure have
; "hidden" 1st argument that points to return
; value


faddxy          PROC    USES SI
IF MICROSOFT
                ARG     XARG:FPM_NUM,YARG:FPM_NUM
ELSE
                ARG     ANSOFF:WORD,ANSSEG:WORD,XARG:FPM_NUM,\
                        YARG:FPM_NUM
ENDIF
; Check for zero addition (x=0)
                MOV     EAX,XARG.NUM
                OR      EAX,EAX
                JNZ     SHORT YZA
                MOV     EAX,YARG.NUM
                MOV     CH,YARG.SIGN
                MOV     CL,YARG.SCALE
                JMP     DOADD3
```

```
; Check for y=0
YZA:            MOV     EAX,YARG.NUM
                OR      EAX,EAX
                JNZ     SHORT NZA
                MOV     EAX,XARG.NUM
                MOV     CH,XARG.SIGN
                MOV     CL,XARG.SCALE
                JMP     DOADD3
NZA:
                LEA     BX,YARG
CALL    RADJ
                LEA     BX,XARG
                CALL    RADJ
; if eq then ok
                MOV     CL,XARG.SCALE
                MOV     CH,YARG.SCALE
                CMP     CL,CH
                JE      SHORT DOADD
; if xscale>yscale ...
                LEA     SI,YARG
                JG      SHORT PLUSADJY
                XCHG    CH,CL
                XCHG    BX,SI
PLUSADJY:
;     amt=xscale-yscale
                SUB     CL,CH
;     find top bit in y
                BSR     EAX,[SI].NUM
                MOV     CH,31
                SUB     CH,AL
                CMP     CH,CL
;     if 31-topbit>=amt shift y left by amt; yscale+=amt
                JL      SHORT PLUSELSE
                SHL     [SI].NUM,CL
                ADD     [SI].SCALE,CL
                JMP     SHORT DOADD
PLUSELSE:
;     else ...
;        shift y left by 31-topbit; yscale+=31-topbit
                XCHG    CH,CL
                SHL     [SI].NUM,CL
                ADD     [SI].SCALE,CL
```

```
                XCHG    CH,CL
                SUB     CL,CH
;       shift x right by amt-(31-topbit)
;       xscale-amt-(31-topbit)
                SHR     [BX].NUM,CL
                SUB     [BX].SCALE,CL
DOADD:
; Make certain bit 31 of each number is off and
; keep scales equal
                MOV     EAX,XARG.NUM
                MOV     EBX,YARG.NUM
                MOV     CL,XARG.SCALE

                MOV     EDX,EAX
                OR      EDX,EBX
                JNS     SHORT SETSIGN
                SHR     EAX,1
                SHR     EBX,1
                DEC     CL
SETSIGN:

                XOR     DH,DH           ; Set positive flag
                MOV     DL,XARG.SIGN
                OR      DL,DL
                JZ      SHORT DOADD1
                NEG     EAX
                INC     DH
DOADD1:         MOV     DL,YARG.SIGN
                OR      DL,DL
                JZ      SHORT DOADD2
                NEG     EBX
                INC     DH
DOADD2:
                                        ; Assume positive sign in CH
                XOR     CH,CH
                ADD     EAX,EBX
                JNS     SHORT DOADD3
                OR      DH,DH
                JZ      SHORT DOADD3 ; Large positive number
                NEG     EAX
                NOT     CH
DOADD3:
```

```
                    PUSH    DS
                    LDS     BX,DWORD PTR ANSOFF
; Store sign, scale, and value
                    MOV     [BX].SIGN,CH
                    MOV     [BX].SCALE,CL
                    MOV     [BX].NUM,EAX
                    POP     DX
IF MICROSOFT
                    MOV     AX,OFFSET FPM_RET
                    MOV     DX,@data
ENDIF
                    RET
faddxy              ENDP

;************************************************
; FIXED fsubxy(FIXED x,FIXED y)
fsubxy              PROC
                    PUSH    BP
                    MOV     BP,SP
; If X-0 then compute X+0
IF @CodeSize
IF MICROSOFT
XX                  EQU 10
ELSE
XX                  EQU 16
ENDIF
ELSE
IF MICROSOFT
XX                  EQU 12
ELSE
XX                  EQU 14
ENDIF
ENDIF
                    MOV     EAX,[BP+XX].NUM
                    OR      EAX,EAX
                    JZ      SHORT SUBBY0
; else compute X+-1*Y
                    NOT     [BP+XX].SIGN
SUBBY0:
                    POP     BP
; Let + do the work
                    JMP     faddxy
```

```
fsubxy          ENDP


;************************************************
; FIXED fmulxy(FIXED xarg,FIXED yarg)
; Note: Borland functions that return structure have
; "hidden" 1st argument that points to return
; value
fmulxy          PROC
IF MICROSOFT
                ARG     XARG:FPM_NUM,YARG:FPM_NUM
ELSE
                ARG     ANSOFF:WORD,ANSSEG:WORD,XARG:FPM_NUM,\
                        YARG:FPM_NUM
ENDIF
; Right adjust X
                LEA     BX,XARG
                CALL    RADJ
; Right adjust Y
                LEA     BX,YARG
                CALL    RADJ
; Check for X*0 or 0*Y
                MOV     EAX,XARG.NUM
                OR      EAX,EAX
                JZ      SHORT RETZM
                MOV     EBX,YARG.NUM
                OR      EBX,EBX
                JZ      SHORT RETZM
; Do it
                MUL     EBX
TSTZLP:
; Find bits in EDX (overflow of 32 bits)
                BSR     ECX,EDX
; If none, goto DXZ
                JZ      SHORT DXZ
; Shift bits to EAX and adjust scale
                INC     CL
                SHRD    EAX,EDX,CL
                SUB     XARG.SCALE,CL
DXZ:

                OR      EAX,EAX
```

```
                 JNS      SHORT NOOF
; keep answer positive
                 SHR      EAX,1
                 DEC      XARG.SCALE
NOOF:
; store answer
                 PUSH     ES
                 LES      BX,DWORD PTR ANSOFF
                 MOV      ES:[BX].NUM,EAX
; compute new scale
                 MOV      AL,YARG.SCALE
                 ADD      AL,XARG.SCALE
                 MOV      ES:[BX].SCALE,AL
; compute new sign
                 MOV      AL,YARG.SIGN
                 XOR      AL,XARG.SIGN
                 MOV      ES:[BX].SIGN,AL
                 POP      ES
IF MICROSOFT
                 MOV      AX,OFFSET FPM_RET
                 MOV      DX,@data
ENDIF
                 RET
; Jump here to return a zero
; shared by MUL & DIV
RETZM:           PUSH     ES
                 LES      BX,DWORD PTR ANSOFF
                 XOR      EAX,EAX
                 MOV      ES:[BX].NUM,EAX
                 MOV      ES:[BX].SCALE,AL
                 MOV      ES:[BX].SIGN,AL
                 POP      ES
IF MICROSOFT
                 MOV      AX,OFFSET FPM_RET
                 MOV      DX,@data
ENDIF
                 RET
fmulxy           ENDP


;*************************************************
; FIXED fdivxy(FIXED,FIXED)
```

```
; Note: Borland functions that return struct have a
; "hidden" 1st argument that points to return
; value
fdivxy          PROC
IF MICROSOFT
                ARG     XARG:FPM_NUM,YARG:FPM_NUM
ELSE
                ARG     ANSOFF:WORD,ANSSEG:WORD,XARG:FPM_NUM,\
                        YARG:FPM_NUM
ENDIF
; left adjust X
                LEA     BX,XARG
                CALL    LADJ
; right adjust Y
                LEA     BX,YARG
                CALL    RADJ
; check for divide by zero
                MOV     EAX,XARG.NUM
                OR      EAX,EAX
                JZ      RETZM
; check for divide by 1
                MOV     EBX,YARG.NUM
                CMP     EBX,1
; Don't divide by 1 -- besides if we rotated EDX:EAX left,
; / by 1 would result in overflow
                JZ      SHORT DODIV
; Shift X bits into EDX based on size of Y
                XOR     EDX,EDX
                BSR     ECX,EBX
                SHLD    EDX,EAX,CL
                SHL     EAX,CL
; Adjust scale
                ADD     XARG.SCALE,CL
                DIV     EBX
DODIV:
                PUSH    ES
                LES     BX,DWORD PTR ANSOFF
                MOV     ES:[BX].NUM,EAX
; Computer answer's scale
                MOV     AL,XARG.SCALE
                SUB     AL,YARG.SCALE
                MOV     ES:[BX].SCALE,AL
```

```
; Find answer's sign
                MOV     AL,YARG.SIGN
XOR     AL,XARG.SIGN
                MOV     ES:[BX].SIGN,AL
                POP     ES
IF MICROSOFT
                MOV     AX,OFFSET FPM_RET
                MOV     DX,@data
ENDIF
                RET
fdivxy          ENDP

                END
```

Listing 15-2. FPM32.H

```c
/**************************************************
 *                                                *
 * FPM32.H - C language header for FPM32          *
 *                                                *
 **************************************************/
#ifndef FPMHEADER
/* fixed point type */
typedef struct
 {
 char sign;
 char scale;
 unsigned long num;
 } FIXED;


/* Scale factor
   use - 1000.0 for 3 places, 100.0 for 2 places etc. */
#define SFACTOR (10000.0)

#define CVTTYPE float

#ifdef __cplusplus
extern "C"
{
#endif
```

```c
/* Assembly core functions (from FPM32.ASM) */
#ifdef __BORLANDC__
extern FIXED faddxy(FIXED,FIXED),fsubxy(FIXED,FIXED),
       fmulxy(FIXED,FIXED),fdivxy(FIXED,FIXED);
#else
/* Microsoft handles functions that return struct
   different than Borland! */
FIXED fpmmsc_rv;  /* Global return value */

extern void faddxy(FIXED _far *,FIXED,FIXED),
            fsubxy(FIXED _far *,FIXED,FIXED),
            fmulxy(FIXED _far *,FIXED,FIXED),
            fdivxy(FIXED _far *,FIXED,FIXED);

#define faddxy(a,b) (faddxy(&fpmmsc_rv,a,b),fpmmsc_rv)
#define fsubxy(a,b) (fsubxy(&fpmmsc_rv,a,b),fpmmsc_rv)
#define fmulxy(a,b) (fmulxy(&fpmmsc_rv,a,b),fpmmsc_rv)
#define fdivxy(a,b) (fdivxy(&fpmmsc_rv,a,b),fpmmsc_rv)
#endif

extern int bitscan(int dir,unsigned long lword);

/* C helpers (from FPMC.C) */
FIXED floattofix(CVTTYPE f);
CVTTYPE fixtofloat(FIXED f);
int fixtoint(FIXED f);

#ifdef __cplusplus
}
#endif

#endif
```

Listing 15-3. FPMC.C

```c
/***************************************************
 *                                                 *
 * FPMC.C - C language routines for FPM32          *
 *                                                 *
 ***************************************************/
#include <stdio.h>
#include <stdlib.h>
#include <string.h>
```

```
#include <math.h>
#include "fpm32.h"

/* convert fpm to float */
FIXED floattofix(CVTTYPE f)
  {
  FIXED ans;
  unsigned long i,whole,frac=0L;
  CVTTYPE fp=.5;
  ans.sign=0;
/* special case */
  if (f==0.0)
    {
    ans.scale=0;
    ans.num=0L;
    return ans;
    }
  if (f<0.0)
    {
    ans.sign=0xff;
    f=-f;
    }
  whole=(unsigned long)f;
  f-=whole;
/* scale is number bits in whole */
  ans.scale=32-bitscan(1,(unsigned long)whole);
  ans.num=(unsigned long)whole<<ans.scale;
  if (ans.scale)
/* compute fractional part */
    for (i=1L<<(ans.scale-1);i!=0&&f!=0.0;fp/=2)
      {
      if (f>=fp)
        {
        f-=fp;
        frac|=i;
        }
      if (!frac&&!whole)
```

```
      ans.scale++;
    else
      i>>=1;
    }
  ans.num|=frac;
  return ans;
  }



/* convert FPM32 number to float */
/* Uses SFACTOR for rounding (see FPM.H) */
CVTTYPE fixtofloat(FIXED f)
  {
  unsigned long i;
  CVTTYPE fp=0.5,res,sg=1.0;
  if (f.sign)
    {
    sg=-1.0;
    }
  if (f.scale<0)
    res=(CVTTYPE)(f.num<<-f.scale);
  else
    {
    res=(CVTTYPE)(f.num>>f.scale);
    while (f.scale>>5)
      {
      f.scale--;
      fp/=2.0;
      }
    for (i=1L<<f.scale-1;i!=0;i>>=1,fp/=2)
      if (f.num&i) res+=fp;

    }
  return floor(sg*res*SFACTOR+.5)/SFACTOR;
  }

/* convert FPM32 number to int (truncate fraction) */
int fixtoint(FIXED f)
  {
```

```
   int r;
   if (f.scale>=0) r=f.num>>f.scale; else r=0;
   if (f.sign) r=-r;
   return r;
   }
```

Listing 15-4. FPMTIME.C

```
/* FPMTIME.C - Timing example for FPM32
   Compile:
   Borland: MAKE
   Microsoft: NMAKE */
#include <stdio.h>
#include <stdlib.h>
#include <string.h>
#include <time.h>
#include "fpm32.h"
#include "winpmode.h"


void test1(int i,FIXED a,FIXED b);
void test2(int i,float a,float b);

char retstr[64];  /* return string */
char *test()
   {
   FIXED a,b;
   float a1,b1;
   int i=10000,op;
   clock_t s,e,t1;
   a1=100.25;
   b1=33.17;
   a=floattofix(a1);
   b=floattofix(b1);
   s=clock();
   test1(i,a,b);
   e=clock();
   win_printf("FPM32 Time (in ticks)","%lu",t1=e-s);
   i=10000;
   s=clock();
   test2(i,a1,b1);
   e=clock();
```

```
    win_printf("FLOAT Time (in ticks)","%lu",e-s);
    sprintf(retstr,"Time difference: %ld (%3.1f:1)",
                                  (e-s)-t1,
                                  (e-s)/(float)t1);
    return retstr;
    }


void test1(int i,FIXED a,FIXED b)
  {
  while (i--)
    {
    faddxy(a,b);
    fmulxy(a,b);
    fdivxy(a,b);
    fsubxy(a,b);
    }
    }

/* Declare c1 volatile -- this tells compiler it might
   change unexpectedly and prevents the compiler from
   optimizing it away since we really don't use it */
volatile int c1;

void test2(int i,float a1,float b1)
  {
  while (i--)
    {
    c1=a1+b1;
    c1=a1*b1;
    c1=a1/b1;
    c1=a1-b1;
    }
  }
```

Listing 15-5. MAKEFILE for FPMTIME

```
# Makefile for FPMTIME
# Use Microsoft NMAKE
# or Borland MAKE
# !!! Be sure to set the right variable below
# depending on your compiler
```

```
# Some versions of MSC 7.0 can't properly compile
# floating point constants and will
# erroneously report a C2177 error on any program
# that contains floating point constants when you
# compile in a Windows DOS box -- if this happens
# try compiling the program without Windows running

BORLAND=1
MICROSOFT=0

!if $(BORLAND)
CC=bcc
COPT=-WE -2 -v -w-par -w-aus -c -DTITLE=FPMTIME
LD=tlink
LOPT=-v -x -c -P- -Twe
AS=tasm
AOPT=-ml
!endif

!if $(MICROSOFT)
CC=cl
COPT=-Zi -c -GA -Zp -G2
LD=link
LOPT=/CO
AS=masm
AOPT=-ml
!endif


!if $(MICROSOFT)
fpmtime.exe : fpmtime.obj fpmc.obj fpm32.obj pmwin.obj\
  mscint.obj
        $(LD) $(LOPT) fpmtime.obj fpmc.obj fpm32.obj\
        pmwin.obj mscint.obj,,,slibcew libw,pmwin.def
        rc -t pmwin.rc fpmtime.exe
mscint.obj : mscint.c
    $(CC) $(COPT) mscint.c

!else
fpmtime.exe : fpmtime.obj fpmc.obj fpm32.obj pmwin.obj
        $(LD) $(LOPT) cOws fpmtime.obj fpmc.obj fpm32.obj\
        pmwin.obj,fpmtime,,mathws import cws,pmwin.def
```

```
        rc -t pmwin.rc fpmtime.exe
!endif

fpmtime.obj : fpmtime.c fpm32.h
        $(CC) $(COPT) fpmtime.c

fpmc.obj : fpmc.c fpm32.h
        $(CC) $(COPT) fpmc.c

pmwin.obj : pmwin.c pmwin.h
        $(CC) $(COPT) pmwin.c

fpm32.obj : fpm32.asm
        $(AS) $(AOPT) fpm32.asm;
```

Conclusion

If you program in C++, you have probably already thought about writing a class wrapper for FPM32. By using C++'s operator overloading, you can make FPM32 calls with conventional C operators. In fact, a FPM32 class is simple to construct. Unfortunately, the overhead of C++ constructors reduce FPM32's performance. Several experimental class wrappers for FPM32 ran more slowly than the normal C float type. If FPM32 isn't faster than the math library, there is little point in using it.

FPM32 can provide your programs a fast alternative for real number arithmetic. The fundamental techniques FPM uses—utilization of 386 instructions and 32-bit integers—will help you optimize your own protected-mode software.

Part III:
Big Problems, Big Solutions

CHAPTER ▪ 16

Welcome to the Real (Protected) World

Creating your own protected-mode programs is not too different from writing real-mode applications. You will probably even start with existing code and convert it.

Although the examples in the previous chapters will help you grasp protected-mode concepts, most of them are not complete application programs. The examples in the remainder of the book, however, are robust real-world protected-mode applications. By examining these examples, you can get a feel for writing large protected-mode programs.

Porting Existing Code

If you are planning to move existing DOS code to a protected-mode environment (including Windows), you should watch for a few pitfalls. Standard C code will often compile and run on the first try. The problems arise with some PC-specific code and assembly language modules.

Segment Usage

In real mode, segment registers directly map to physical addresses. In protected mode, they select an entry from one of the descriptor tables. This has several important ramifications:

- Don't use segment registers as scratch registers—most values will cause a general protection fault.

- Any segment arithmetic that you do in real-mode code will require changes (see Chapter 7 for more about protected-mode segment arithmetic). Be especially careful of code that normalizes (minimizes the offset portion) of far pointers.

- Segments that you initialize to a particular value will usually require change (see Chapter 8).

Of course with 32-bit code, you may try to (or have to, depending on the compiler) avoid segmentation completely. Often, you can simply use a 32-bit near pointer, and dispense with segments and far pointers. This is simpler and is more efficient.

Use of Code and Data Segments

In protected mode, you can't write to a code segment, and you can't execute code in a data (or stack) segment. In some cases, you might not be able to read from a code segment either, though most extenders make code segments readable. If you write code on the fly, you should look for another solution. If you can't, your extender probably provides calls to alias code and data segments (see MSCINT.C in Chapter 5 for one way to do this). DPMI function 000AH, for instance, will return a data segment alias for any segment (including a code segment).

Segment Overrun

In real mode, each segment has a limit of 64K—the maximum possible byte offset. In protected mode, segment limits vary. You must not allow address offsets to stray over the segment's limit value. For ordinary code and data segments, the byte offset must always be less than or equal to the limit. For stack segments the offset must always be greater than or equal to the limit. It is not unusual for real-mode code to harmlessly overrun an array or structure and never cause a problem. The same code will hopefully (if you're lucky) fault in protected mode.

Interrupt Usage

You should closely scrutinize any interrupt that you call directly in your existing code. Depending on your DOS extender, you may have to slightly modify the interrupt parameters. If your extender doesn't directly support the call, you will need to use the appropriate real-mode interrupt call (see Chapter 10).

Some interrupts change meaning in protected mode. For example, a Windows program can call interrupt 0x21 function 0x25 to set an interrupt vector. However, this function sets the protected-mode interrupt, not the real-mode vector that the standard DOS call modifies. Sometimes this will suit you, but there may be times when you want to use DPMI function 0x0201 to set the real-mode vector instead.

Calling Real-Mode Code

If you have a large amount of real-mode code that won't be easy to convert, you may want to consider leaving it as real-mode code. You may have to write some interface code to marry the real-mode code to your protected program. Chapter 10 shows several examples of this technique.

Steps for Conversion

You should try to identify and correct as many major problems in existing code before you convert it. For example, if your program uses segment arithmetic, try and remove it in the real-mode program first. Identify one place that you use segment arithmetic and replace it with a technique that will work in real or protected mode. When that works, move to the next part of the code that uses segment arithmetic. Some changes will have to wait until you move the program to protected mode.

If your real-mode compiler has multiple warning levels, set it on the strictest setting. Examine the warnings—will they affect your protected-mode code? (Alternatively, you can use a lint program to generate the same type of warnings.) Again, fix as much as possible in real mode while the program still works.

Once the program is working and you have it as clean as possible, you are ready to take the big plunge. If you have a successful compile you can start attacking code that you need to change for protected mode. Unless you are using the same compiler for real and protected mode, you should carefully examine any #pragma statements and predefined preprocessor constants (such as __BORLANDC__).

No Holds Barred Programs

The next three chapters contain case studies of practical protected-mode programs. Careful study of these programs will help you write your own protected-mode applications.

Each of the three example programs use a different protected-mode environment (Phar Lap 286|DOS Extender, Intel Code Builder, and Windows). You may find it useful to note the differences between these environments.

TURTLE

TURTLE (Chapter 17) implements a simple graphics command language similar to Logo. You use simple commands to guide a "turtle" around the screen, optionally leaving a trail behind it. TURTLE can generate many interesting shapes and patterns.

TURTLE only works with the VGA's 320x200x256 mode. Each screen requires 64K of memory—challenge for a conventional DOS program. But TURTLE takes advantage of Phar Lap's 286|DOS Extender to provide 11 graphics buffers (a total of 704K just for data). Multiple buffers allow TURTLE to produce interesting animation.

Copy Builder 386

The CB386 program (Chapter 18) is a disk duplication system that uses Intel's 386 Code Builder. It can read a floppy disk and write multiple copies of it. It can also save floppy disk images on the hard disk for later duplication.

CB386 keeps the current floppy disk image in memory. This could be as much as 2.88M with modern floppy drives. Even a 720K floppy would overtax a conventional DOS program. (You may want to contrast CB386 with the DFIT programs in Chapter 1.)

To manage the screen, CB386 uses a simple subroutine library originally developed for Microsoft C. Don't ignore existing libraries when writing your programs—most real-mode C code will easily port to the protected-mode environment.

A Windows Example

In Chapter 19, you will see a set of programs that allow DOS programs to access Windows services and vice versa. The WINX program starts Windows and acts as a server program that can accept requests from DOS programs. The server is partially a real-mode DOS program and partially a protected-mode Windows program.

The WINRUN program uses the WINX server to execute Windows programs from a DOS box (even from a batch file). You can also run DOS programs (like MAKE or FORMAT) in a separate DOS box. However, the techniques that the WINX server uses allow you to create Windows and DOS programs that can easily communicate for any purpose.

CHAPTER ■ 17

A DOS Extended Mutant Turtle

Most people enjoy watching computer graphics programs, but only a few people enjoy *writing* computer graphics programs. However, there is a computer language, called LOGO, that simplifies many types of graphics programming. School children routinely use LOGO (developed at MIT) to draw fractals, recursive patterns, and other sophisticated drawings by controlling a graphics "turtle".

In this chapter, you will see an extensible graphics language that is loosely based on LOGO. The program uses the Phar Lap 286|DOS extender since it uses over 700K of graphics buffers for animation. You'll need Borland or Microsoft C, the DOS extender, a 286 (or better) PC, and a VGA graphics card.

TURTLE (the graphics program) is simple. It uses the general purpose extensible command interpreter found in Chapter 12. TURTLE maintains a text screen for entering commands and a graphics display screen. You can also enter commands at the top of the graphics screen, but any error messages will destroy part of the display. Figure 17-1 shows a summary of TURTLE's operation.

TURTLE works in the VGA's 320 x 200 x 256 mode. The top left corner of the screen is at (0,0) and the bottom right corner is (319,199). The differs from the Cartesian coordinates normally used in turtle graphics.

TURTLE allows coordinates to range from -999 to 999. Any points that fall outside the screen do not appear. Arguments to TURTLE commands can usually be absolute or relative. For example:

```
SETXY 100 100
```

moves the current position (or turtle) to (100,100). However:

```
SETXY -10 +0
```

moves the turtle ten units to the left (the X-axis), and doesn't move it at all on the Y-axis.

TURTLE provides 26 global integer variables (A-Z). Any numeric argument can be an algebraic expression (see Figure 17-1). Expressions must not contain spaces—a space marks the start of a new argument. (The expression analyzer is very simple.)

Drawing simple graphics with TURTLE is a snap. To draw a box, for example:

```
MOVE 100
TURN +90
MOVE 100
TURN +90
MOVE 100
TURN 90
MOVE 100
```

will draw a square. More complicated drawings are possible too (see Figure 17-2).

To support animation, TURTLE supplies 10 screen storage locations in memory. Each storage buffer requires 64,000 (320 x 200) bytes. In addition, one storage location contains the current screen when TURTLE is in text mode. These data buffers alone require 704,000 bytes—more memory than is available with unaugmented MS-DOS.

A DOS extender isn't the only option available for buffers of this size. EMS, extended memory, XMS, or disk paging would have worked too. However, these would add considerable complexity to the application.

Figure 17-1. Turtle Command Summary

Command	Function
setx *x*	Set x-coordinate
sety *y*	Set y-coordinate
setxy *x y*	Set both coordinates
forward *dist* ⎫ move *dist* ⎭	Move turtle specified distance
home	Move turtle to location (0,0)
turn *heading*	Turn turtle to new heading
show	Show graphics screen and wait for a key
show *ON*	Turn graphics screen on
show *OFF*	Turn graphics screen off
pencolor *color*	Set color
background *color*	Set background color
penup	Make turtle move without drawing
pendown	Make turtle draw as it moves
clear	Clear screen and home turtle
fill	Fill region
sto *buffer*	Store screen to buffer (1-10)
rcl *buffer*	Recall buffer to screen
prompt *string*	Write string as prompt
text *string*	Write string on graphics screen
textcolor *color*	Set text color
set *var value*	Set variable (A-Z) to value
do *file*	Execute file—resume current file when it ends
goto *file*	Transfer control to file
repeat *n file*	Execute file *n* times
if *expr* THEN EXIT	Exit current program file if expression is non-zero
if *expr* DO *file*	Execute file if expression is non-zero
if *expr* GOTO *file*	Transfer to file if expression is non-zero
help *[command]*	Get help
push *expr*	Push expression on stack

Figure 17-1. Turtle Command Summary (cont.)

Command	Function
pop *var*	Pop top of stack to var
delay *time*	Delay time/10 seconds
dos *[command]*	Run DOS command or COMMAND.COM if command is absent
edit *[file]*	Edit file with EDIT (DOS 5) or program named in TURTLEEDIT environment variable
dir *[arguments]*	Run DOS DIR command
cd *directory*	Change directory
quit	Exit TURTLE

Note: Arguments are in italics. Items in brackets ([ ]) are optional.

Operators:
Highest Precedence
*	Multiply
/	Divide (integer)
%	Modulus (integer remainder)

+	Addition
-	Subtract

&	Logical and (like && in C)
|	Logical or (like || in C)

=	Equality
#	Inequality
<	Less than
>	Greater than
<=	Less than or equal to
>=	Greater than or equal to

Figure 17-1. Turtle Command Summary (cont.)

Lowest Precedence

Constants

Constants are hexadecimal if you use the "0x" prefix (e.g., 0xFF). All other constants are decimal. TURTLE uses short integers for all numeric values.

Variables

The variables A-Z can hold any 16-bit integer values. You may use a variable any place you can use a constant.

Special variables

%c	Current color
%h	Current heading
%i	Numeric input from user (no checking is done—illegal input is returned as zero)
%r	Random integer from 0-32,767
%x	Current x-coordinate
%y	Current y-coordinate

Expression rules:

Expressions must not contain spaces.

Parentheses can be used freely and override precedence.

Most expressions can be relative. For instance:

```
SETXY -10 +0
```

will move the cursor 10 places to the left. This is not the same as:

```
SETXY 10 0
```

which moves the cursor to location (10,0).

Figure 17-2 Output of POLYTSH.T

The TURTLE Program

The TURTLE program depends heavily on the XCI command interpreter (see Chapter 12). TURTLE.C (Listing 17-2) simply sets up XCI and turns control over to it. XCI then calls various functions within TURTLE in response to certain commands and events.

Most of the commands reside in TCMDS.C (Listing 17-3). TEXPR.C (Listing 17-4) parses algebraic expressions in command arguments. Many source files include TURTLE.H (Listing 17-1) for global definitions.

The SAVE and LOAD commands reside in a DLL (TSAVE.C, Listing 17- 5). An end-user of TURTLE could rewrite this DLL to load and save other graphics formats by replacing this DLL. The end-user would not need the source or object code for TURTLE (see Chapter 12 for more about DLLs).

Accessing the Video Display

TURTLE uses the Microsoft C graphics functions for simplicity. If you use the Borland compiler you will need BGRAPH.C (included on the companion disk) to supply the graphics functions that TURTLE uses. The portable graphics header (PGRAPH.H, Listing 17-7) provides the correct definitions for either compiler. To simplify BGRAPH.C, the Borland version of TURTLE does not support the FILL command.

TURTLE also uses direct access to the screen buffer to save and restore screens. In a normal DOS application, this is simple. The text buffer is at segment 0xB800, and the graphics buffer is at 0xA000.

With the DOS extender, this isn't so simple. The setptr() function in Listing 17-3 (TCMDS.C) uses the DOS extender function DosMapRealSeg() to address the video buffers. It creates a protected mode segment at the specified address and of a specified length (you can find a similar function that works for many extenders in the PMCGA program in Chapter 6). Using this function, your programs can directly access any real-mode address. Once setptr() initializes the pointers to the screen buffers, TURTLE can't tell that they are special pointers. It uses them just like any other pointer in a normal C program.

Unsupported Calls

While the DOS extender supports most DOS and BIOS calls transparently, there are a few functions that it does not directly support. TURTLE uses interrupt 0x15 function 0x86 (the BIOS delay function) in its DELAY command. The DOS extender doesn't support any interrupt 0x15 functions directly. However this isn't a problem since it does allow you to set up the call yourself.

Phar Lap provides a DosRealIntr() function that can call almost any real mode interrupt. The delaycmd() function in TCMDS.C (Listing 17-3) uses this call. There are similar functions for making far calls to real-mode code (see Chapter 10).

Handling Control-Break

TURTLE uses XCI's Control-Break handling mechanism. The break handler interrupts are similar to the examples in Chapter 13. An interrupt

0x1B handler catches the BIOS break interrupt and an interrupt 0x16 routine (xci_int16()) prevents DOS from receiving Control-C characters.

You can't install xci_int16() as a normal protected-mode interrupt handler—DOS will call interrupt 0x16 from real mode. You can, however, install a protected-mode handler that receives interrupts from real and protected mode. XCI does this with the DosSetPassToProtVec() call.

The DOS extender uses separate vectors for real- and protected-mode interrupts. Calling DosSetPassToProtVec() changes both of them to point to the same protected-mode service routine. Before the program exits, XCI must restore both interrupt vectors using DosSetRealToProtVec(). XCI registers its shut-down code (xci_cleanup()) using the DosExitList() function. This is similar to using atexit() or onexit() with one important exception. A function set up with DosExitList() will execute when the program terminates for any reason. Exit functions using the C library's atexit() or onexit() only run when the program terminates normally. See Chapter 13 for more about DosExitList().

Versions of 286|DOS-Extender earlier than 1.4 had a problem using DosSetPassToProtVec() with interrupt 0x16. In these early versions, a DOS call triggers an interrupt 0x16 after the extender has set the real-mode interrupt, but before it has set the protected mode vector. This causes an endless loop of mode switches. The latest versions don't have this problem, but TURTLE uses a work-around in any case. It sets the protected-mode vector for interrupt 0x16 before calling DosSetPassToProtVec(). Instead of:

```
DosSetPassProtVec(0x16,xci_int16,&oldbreak,&oldreal);
```

XCI uses:

```
DosSetProtVec(0x16,xci_int16,&oldbreak);
DosSetPassProtVec(0x16,xci_int16,NULL,&oldreal);
```

The xci_int16() function needs to call the old interrupt 0x16 handler to check for control-C characters. The DOS extender provides the DosChain-ToRealIntr() function, but it does not return control to your program when the real-mode interrupt completes. Luckily, DosRealFarCall() can call an interrupt handler with a little subterfuge. XCI uses the line:

```
DosRealFarCall(oldbreal,&r1,0,-1,r1.flags);
```

to call the old interrupt handler (whose address is in oldbreal). The pointer to r1 contains the registers to pass to the interrupt handler. Be careful to set the flags in r1 to a legitimate value (zero is fine). If the single-step flag is set, for example, your program will crash. You should usually make sure the interrupt enable flag is clear, too. The first zero is a reserved parameter—it must be zero. The next argument (-1) informs DosRealFarCall() that it should push one word on the stack before calling the real-mode routine. Since the number of words is negative, the DOS extender expects the real-mode code to clean up the stack before returning (like a Pascal function does). The last zero in the call is the one word to push on the stack.

Why does this work? When an interrupt occurs, the CPU will push the flags and the far return address on the stack. The IRET instruction at the end of the interrupt service routine will restore the flags, and return to the calling routine. If DosRealFarCall() pushes a word on the stack, the IRET will restore that value to the flags, and return to the proper address.

286 Pointers

Writing programs for a 286 DOS extender doesn't provide you with the same luxuries as a 386 extender. In particular, in 16-bit mode segments cannot exceed 64K in length. You still have to resort to huge pointers to handle data larger than 64K in length. Of course, for the TURTLE program, this isn't an issue—the large graphics buffers are 64,000 bytes long.

Compiling

Compilation of the program is similar to compiling a real-mode program. Since the extender uses the standard NE format, the linker "thinks" it is creating a Windows (or OS/2 1.X) program and DLL.

The MAKEFILE (included on the companion disk) builds TUR-TLE.EXE and TSAVE.DLL, the two main portions of the program. It also creates TURTLE.LIB. This file is an import library for TURTLE DLLs. By linking with the import library, a DLL can reference routines that reside in TURTLE.EXE. The DOS extender will provide the correct address at run-time. If you were distributing TURTLE to end-users, they could write their own DLLs by using TURTLE.LIB and a header file to declare the appropriate functions and types.

The Microsoft makefile compiles the TSAVE DLL with the -ML option. The -Gs option is also necessary—the DLL's data segment will differ from TURTLE.EXE's stack segment. The Borland makefile uses the -dll switch with Phar Lap's BCC286 compiler driver to create the DLL. DLLSTART.ASM (Listing 17-6), provides an entry point for DLL initialization.

Once you create TURTLE.EXE you can run it by using the RUN286 program supplied with the DOS extender. You also can use the BIND286 utility to patch TURTLE.EXE to load RUN286 automatically when you execute it from the DOS prompt. If you own the distribution kit, you also can bind in a complete copy of the DOS extender making TURTLE.EXE a complete stand-alone program.

Analysis

Overall, the 286 DOS extender was a good choice for the TURTLE program. It provided enough memory to store screens, and the DLL system makes TURTLE easily extensible. Try the example program (Listings 17-8, 17-9, 17-10, and 17-11)—you will see that performance suffers little, if any, compared to real-mode programs using the Microsoft graphics library.

Accessing the video RAM directly wasn't much more trouble with the DOS extender than with a normal program. The most troublesome aspect was the interrupt handling.

Unless you change the options to RUN286, most of TURTLE runs in extended memory. This leaves plenty of conventional memory free to run an external editor in real mode (for the EDIT command). Calling a real-mode program from TURTLE was as simple as it would be in a regular DOS program.

Listing 17-1. TURTLE.H

```
/* TURTLE.H
   See TURTLE.C for instructions */

#include "pgraph.h"
typedef  unsigned long ulong;
typedef  unsigned int uint;

/* Size of text screen */
#define TEXT_SIZE 4000

/* graphics buffer */
#define SCREEN_SIZE 64000   /* 320 X 200 */
extern char far _gbuf[SCREEN_SIZE];

/* Application data (passed to XCI commands) */
struct  udata
  {
  char *gbuf;               /* pointer to graphics buffer */
  char tbuf[4000];          /* text buffer */
  char *gptr;               /* pointer to graphics screen */
  char *tptr;               /* pointer to text screen */
  struct xycoord graphxy;   /* x,y of graphic screen */
  struct rccoord textxy;    /* x,y of text screen */
  int color;                /* color */
  long backcolor;           /* background color */
/* store[10] & store[11] are for internal use */
  char *store[12];          /* screen storage */
  unsigned int pendown:1;   /* draw or move */
/* if 1, don't exit graphic mode */
  unsigned int textgraph:1;
  int heading;              /* turtle heading */

/* X and Y are stored as reals too to combat
   rounding errors */
  double realx;
  double realy;
/* 26 variables A-Z */
```

```
    long vars[26];
/* text color */
    int tcolor;
    };

/* Application data structure */
extern struct udata appdata;

int evalexpr(char *);
void turtleprompt(char *);
int _far _loadds _export getval(char *,int,
                                int,int,int *);
```

Listing 17-2. TURTLE.C

```
/* TURTLE.C       Main program for TURTLE.C

   TURTLE assumes large model -- see MAKEFILE

   Compile:
   Borland: MAKE
   Microsoft: NMAKE

*/

#include <stdio.h>
#define _MAIN_
#include "pgraph.h"
#include <dos.h>
#include <phapi.h>
#include <stdlib.h>
#include "turtle.h"
#include "xci.h"

/* XCI client's application data (see TURTLE.H) */
struct udata appdata;
int installcmds(void);

/* XCI startup command -- install commands */
XCICMD startup(int cmd, char far *dummy)
```

```
  {
  if (cmd) return;
  if (installcmds())
    {
    printf("Out of memory\n");
    exit(1);
    }
  }

/* Reset things before normal exit */
void preexit(void)
  {
  _setvideomode(_DEFAULTMODE);
  }


/* MAIN PROGRAM */
main()
  {
  void turtleprompt();
/* register exit routine */
  atexit(preexit);
  _setvideomode(_TEXTC80);
  _setactivepage(0);
  _setvisualpage(0);
  appdata.tcolor=appdata.color=15;
  appdata.pendown=1;
  appdata.backcolor=0x003f0000L;    /* blue background */
/* clear screen */
  clearcmd(0,"",&appdata);
/* Print banner */
  printf("TURTLE VGA by Al Williams\n"
         "Type HELP for help\n");

/* Take over XCI prompt function */
  xcif_prompt=turtleprompt;
  command("TSAVE.DLL","TURTLE.CMD",0,
          &appdata,(XCICMDP) startup);
  }
```

```c
/* XCI prompt -- if in graphics mode keep
   input on top line */
void turtleprompt(char *s)
  {
  union REGS r;
  if (appdata.textgraph)
    {
/* don't do newline in graphic mode */
    if (*s=='\n')
      {

      printf(" ");
      return;
      }
/* but do clear the line */
    r.h.ah=2;
    r.h.bh=0;
    r.x.dx=0;
    int86(0x10,&r,&r);
    r.x.ax=0x0a00|' ';
    r.x.bx=appdata.tcolor;
    r.x.cx=40;
    int86(0x10,&r,&r);          /* clear to end of line */
    }
  printf("%s",s);
  }
```

Listing 17-3. TCMDS.C

```c
/* TCMDS.C      XCI commands for TURTLE.EXE
   See MAKEFILE for instructions

*/

#include <stdio.h>
#include <stdlib.h>
#include <malloc.h>
#include <dos.h>
#include <conio.h>
```

```c
#include <string.h>
#include "pgraph.h"
#include <ctype.h>
#include <direct.h>
#define INCL_DOSPROCESS
/* 286 DOS Extender header */
#include <phapi.h>
#include <math.h>
#include <float.h>

#include "turtle.h"
#include "xci.h"

extern XCICMD gotofunc();

/* tokens for commands */
char *tokens[10];

#define NOARG if (parse(cmds)!=0) synerr;
#define synerr { _synerr(); return; }

/* syntax error */
void _synerr(void)
  {
  printf("Syntax error\n");
  }

/* parse a command line into the tokens array
   return the number of tokens */
int parse(char *cmd)
  {
  int i;
  char *t;
  t=tokens[i=0]=strtok(cmd," \t\n");
  while (t&&i<9)
    {
    t=strtok(NULL," \t\n");
    if (t)
      {
      if (i==9) return -1;
      tokens[++i]=t;
      }
```

```
    }
  return tokens[0]?i+1:0;
  }



/* Get a number from token. It must be between lo and hi
   (unless lo==hi) if it is preceeded by a + or a -, it
   is added to rel the final value is stored in *val)
   returns 1 if out of range, 0 if OK */
int _far _loadds _export getval(char *token,int rel,
                                int lo, int hi,int *val)
  {
  int flag=0;    /* add value to rel? */
  if (*token=='+') flag=1;
  if (*token=='-') flag=-1;
  if (flag) token++;

/* evaluate expression */
  *val=evalexpr(token);

/* adjust value relative */
  if (flag==-1) *val=-*val;
  if (flag) *val+=rel;

/* check range */
  if (lo!=hi&&(*val<lo||*val>hi))
    {
    printf("Bad value: %d. Use %d to %d\n",*val,lo,hi);
    return 1;
    }
  return 0;
  }

/* Get xcoordinate */
#define getxco(token,val) \
   getval(token,appdata.graphxy.xcoord,-999,999,val)

/* Get y coordinate */
#define getyco(token,val) \
   getval(token,appdata.graphxy.ycoord,-999,999,val)
```

```c
/* get heading */
#define gethead(token,val) \
    (getval(token,appdata.heading,0,0,val)%360)
/* get color value */
#define getcolor(token,val) \
    getval(token,appdata.color,0,255,val)

/* run a DOS command without XCI interfering with ^C */
static void rundos(char *line)
    {
    int brkstatus=xci_defaultbrk;
    xci_defaultbrk=0;
    if (system(line)==-1)
        {
        printf("Can't execute: %s\n",line);
        }
    xci_defaultbrk=brkstatus;
    }


/* EDIT file */
XCICMD editcmd(int cmd, char far *cmds,struct udata *data)
  {
  char cmdline[129];
  char *cmdst;
  unsigned long stat;
  if (cmd)
    {
    printf("Edit a file\n");
    return;
    }
/* Get editor name from $TURTLEEDIT */
  cmdst=getenv("TURTLEEDIT");
/* If not specified, use DOS 5 EDIT command */
  if (!cmdst) cmdst="EDIT";
/* build command line */
  strcpy(cmdline,cmdst);
  strcat(cmdline," ");
  strcat(cmdline,cmds);
  rundos(cmdline);
  }


/* DOS directory */
```

```
XCICMD dircmd(int cmd, char far *cmds,struct udata *data)
  {
  char cmdline[129];
  unsigned long stat;
  if (cmd)
    {
    printf("DOS directory\n");
    return;
    }
  strcpy(cmdline,"DIR ");
  strcat(cmdline,cmds);
  rundos(cmdline);
  }

/* DOS command */
XCICMD doscmd(int cmd, char far *cmds,struct udata *data)
  {
  char cmdline[129];
  char *cmdst;
  int rc;
  unsigned long stat;
  if (cmd)
    {
    printf("Run DOS or a DOS command\n");
    return;
    }
  rundos(*cmds?cmds:"COMMAND");  /* quick, yet dirty */
  }
/* change directory */
XCICMD cdcmd(int cmd, char far *cmds,struct udata *data)
  {
  int buf;
  if (cmd)
    {
    printf("Change the current working directory\n");
    return;
    }
  if (chdir(cmds))
     printf("Error changing directory\n");
  }

/* Get text xy coordinate */
```

```
struct rccoord getxy(void)
  {
  struct rccoord rc;
  union REGS r;
  r.h.ah=3;
  r.h.bh=0;
  int86(0x10,&r,&r);
  rc.row=r.h.dh;
  rc.col=r.h.dl;
  return rc;
  }
/* move text cursor to x,y */
goto_xy(short x,short y)
  {
  union REGS r;
  r.h.ah=2;
  r.h.bh=0;
  r.h.dh=y;
  r.h.dl=x;
  int86(0x10,&r,&r);
  }


/* Initilize pointers */
setptr(struct udata *data)
  {
  unsigned int rseg;
/* buffer 10 stores pointer to graphics buffer */
  data->store[10]=data->gbuf=_gbuf;
/* Get PM pointer to VGA screen */
  DosMapRealSeg(0xa000,(unsigned long)SCREEN_SIZE,(PSEL)&rseg);
/* buffer 11 points to screen */
  data->store[11]=data->gptr=MAKEP(rseg,0);
/* Get PM pointer to text screen */
  DosMapRealSeg(0xb800,TEXT_SIZE,(PSEL)&rseg);
  data->tptr=MAKEP(rseg,0);
  }


/* switch mode to graphics */
void gograph(struct udata *data)
  {
/* Init if required */
  if (!data->gptr) setptr(data);
```

```
/* if already in graphics, quit */
  if (data->textgraph) return;
/* save text screen */
  memcpy(data->tbuf,data->tptr,TEXT_SIZE);
/* save cursor position */
  data->textxy=getxy();
/* switch modes */
  _setvideomode(_MRES256COLOR);
/* set colors */
  _setcolor(data->color);
  _setbkcolor(data->backcolor);
/* restore graphics position */
  _moveto(data->graphxy.xcoord,data->graphxy.ycoord);
/* restore contents of buffer */
  memcpy(data->gptr,data->gbuf,(unsigned)SCREEN_SIZE);
  }


/* Switch to text mode */
void gotext(struct udata *data)
  {
/* INIT if required */
  if (!data->gptr) setptr(data);
/* If already in text mode quit */
  if (data->textgraph) return;
/* store graphics screen */
  memcpy(data->gbuf,data->gptr,(unsigned)SCREEN_SIZE);
/* save position */
  data->graphxy=_getcurrentposition();
/* switch to text mode */
  _setvideomode(_TEXTC80);
/* restore text screen */
  memcpy(data->tptr,data->tbuf,TEXT_SIZE);
/* restore text cursor */
  goto_xy(data->textxy.col,data->textxy.row);
  }


/* move turtle to x,y */
turmove(int x,int y)
  {
/* Since this function is built in, its OK to use appdata
   directly. A DLL command would need the pointer passed
   to it by XCI */
```

```
/* Draw or move based on mode */
  if (appdata.pendown)
    _lineto(x,y);
  else
    _moveto(x,y);
  }
/* Show graphics screen */
XCICMD showcmd(int cmd, char far *cmds,struct udata *data)
  {
  int n;
  if (cmd)
    {
    printf("Show graphics screen\n");
    return;
    }
  n=parse(cmds);
  if (n>1)
    synerr;
  if (!n)
    {
    gograph(data);
    if (!getch()) getch();
    gotext(data);
    return;
    }
  if (!stricmp(tokens[0],"ON"))
      {
      if (!data->textgraph)
        {
        gograph(data);
        data->textgraph=1;
        }
      return;
      }
  if (!stricmp(tokens[0],"OFF"))
      {
      if (data->textgraph)
        {
        data->textgraph=0;
        gotext(data);
        }
      return;
```

```
    }
  synerr;
}

/* SETX */
XCICMD setxcmd(int cmd, char far *cmds,struct udata *data)
  {
  int newx;
  if (cmd)
    {
    printf("Set X coordinate\n");
    return;
    }
  if (parse(cmds)!=1) synerr;
  if (getxco(tokens[0],&newx)) return;
  gograph(data);
  turmove(data->graphxy.xcoord=newx,data->graphxy.ycoord);
  data->realx=(double)newx;
  gotext(data);
  }
/* SETY */
XCICMD setycmd(int cmd, char far *cmds,struct udata *data)
  {
  int newy;
  if (cmd)
    {
    printf("Set Y coordinate\n");
    return;
    }
  if (parse(cmds)!=1) synerr;
  if (getyco(tokens[0],&newy)) return;
  gograph(data);
  data->realy=(double)newy;
  turmove(data->graphxy.xcoord,data->graphxy.ycoord=newy);
  gotext(data);
  }

/* SET both X and Y */
XCICMD setxycmd(int cmd, char far *cmds,struct udata *data)
  {
  int newx,newy;
  if (cmd)
```

```
    {
    printf("Set X & Y coordinates\n");
    return;
    }
  if (parse(cmds)!=2) synerr;
  if (getxco(tokens[0],&newx) || getyco(tokens[1],&newy))
    return;
  gograph(data);
  data->realx=(double)newx;
  data->realy=(double)newy;
  turmove(data->graphxy.xcoord=newx,
          data->graphxy.ycoord=newy);
  gotext(data);
  }

/* Set color */
XCICMD colorcmd(int cmd, char far *cmds,struct udata *data)
  {
  int col;
  if (cmd)
    {
    printf("Set color\n");
    return;
    }
  if (parse(cmds)!=1) synerr;
  if (getcolor(tokens[0],&col)) return;
  gograph(data);
  data->color=col;
  _setcolor(col);
  gotext(data);
  }

/* Clear screen */
XCICMD clearcmd(int cmd, char far *cmds,struct udata *data)
  {
  if (cmd)
    {
    printf("Clear the screen\n");
    return;
    }
    NOARG;
  gograph(data);
```

```
  _moveto(0,0);
  _clearscreen(_GCLEARSCREEN);
  data->heading=0;
  data->graphxy.xcoord=data->graphxy.ycoord=0;
  data->realx=data->realy=0.0;
  gotext(data);
  }
/* pen up (change mode) */
XCICMD penupcmd(int cmd, char far *cmds,struct udata *data)
  {
  if (cmd)
    {
    printf("Cause the turtle not to draw\n");
    return;
    }
  NOARG;
  data->pendown=0;
  }
/* pen down (change mode) */
XCICMD pendowncmd(int cmd, char far *cmds,
                  struct udata *data)
  {
  if (cmd)
    {
    printf("Cause the turtle to draw\n");
    return;
    }
  NOARG;
  data->pendown=1;
  }
/* change background color */
XCICMD backgcmd(int cmd, char far *cmds,struct udata *data)
  {
  long col;
  int index;
  if (cmd)
    {
    printf("Set the background color\n");
    return;
    }
  if (parse(cmds)!=1) synerr;
  getcolor(tokens[0],&index);
```

```
  gograph(data);
  col=_remappalette(index,OL);
  _remappalette(index,col);
  data->backcolor=col;
  _setbkcolor(col);
  gotext(data);
  }

/* Set cursor to 0,0 */
XCICMD homecmd(int cmd, char far *cmds,struct udata *data)
  {
  char cmdline[10];
  if (cmd)
    {
    printf("Move the turtle to the top left corner\n");
    return;
    }
  NOARG;
  strcpy(cmdline,"0 0\n");
  data->heading=0;
/* simulate XCI command */
/* NOTE: you shouldn't use a string constant (e.g.:
   setxycmd(0,"0 0\n",data))
   the parse algorithm will chop up the string constant
   the first time you call it which will cause a syntax
   error on subsequent calls. */
  setxycmd(0,cmdline,data);
  }
/* Turn heading */
XCICMD turncmd(int cmd, char far *cmds,struct udata *data)
  {
  int turn;
  if (cmd)
    {
    printf("Turn the turtle\n");
    return;
    }
  if (parse(cmds)!=1) synerr;
  if (gethead(tokens[0],&turn)) return;
  data->heading=turn;
  }
#define PI ((double)3.1415926536)
```

```
/* convert degrees to radians */
#define deg2rad(deg) (((double) deg)*(PI/180.0))
/* quick signum function */
#define SGN(a) ((a)<0?-1:(a)>0?1:0)
/* move turtle ahead */
XCICMD movecmd(int cmd, char far *cmds,struct udata *data)
  {
  int amt,x1,y1;
  double rads,tempreal;
  if (cmd)
    {
    printf("Move the turtle\n");
    return;
    }
  if (parse(cmds)!=1) synerr;
  getval(tokens[0],0,0,0,&amt);
  if (!amt) return;
/* Get heading in radians */
  rads=deg2rad(data->heading);
/* calculate new X & Y
    (cos=x/r     sin=y/r) */
  data->realx+=amt*cos(rads);
  x1=(int)(data->realx+.5*SGN(data->realx));
  data->realy+=amt*sin(rads);
  y1=(int)(data->realy+.5*SGN(data->realy));
  gograph(data);
  turmove(data->graphxy.xcoord=x1,data->graphxy.ycoord=y1);
  gotext(data);
  }

/* repeat a command file */
XCICMD rptcmd(int cmd, char far *cmds,struct udata *data)
  {
  int count;
  char fn[67];
  if (cmd)
    {
    printf("Repeat a command file\n");
    return;
    }
  if (parse(cmds)!=2) synerr;
  getval(tokens[0],0,0,0,&count);
```

```
  if (count<=0)
    {
    printf("Error: count must be >=0\n");
    return;
    }
  strcpy(fn,tokens[1]);
  while (count--) dofunc(0,fn,data);
  }

/* delay a specified number of .1 seconds */
XCICMD delaycmd(int cmd, char far *cmds,struct udata *data)
  {
  int amt;
  unsigned long t;
  REGS16 r;
  if (cmd)
    {
    printf("Delay for a time (in .1 second increments)\n");
    return;
    }
  if (parse(cmds)!=1) synerr;
  getval(tokens[0],0,0,0,&amt);
  if (amt<0)
    {
    amt=0;
    printf("Error: delay time must be >0\n");
    }
  if (!amt) return;
  t=amt*100000L;
  r.ax=0x8600;
  r.cx=(t&0xFFFF0000)>>16;
  r.dx=t&0xffff;
/* Use INT 15H Function 86H to delay -- DOS extender doesn't
   support this directly. We must use DosRealIntr() */
  DosRealIntr(0x15,&r,0L,0);
  }

/* If command */
/* Use XCI do and goto commands to perform do and goto */
XCICMD ifcmd(int cmd, char far *cmds,struct udata *data)
  {
  int bool;
```

```
    char fn[67];
    if (cmd)
      {
      printf("Conditionally execute a commmand file\n");
      return;
      }
    if (parse(cmds)!=3) synerr;
    if (getval(tokens[0],0,0,0,&bool)) return;
    if (bool)
      {
      if (!stricmp(tokens[1],"THEN")&&
          !stricmp(tokens[2],"EXIT"))
        {
/* goto EOF of current file -- XCI thinks it is done */
        fseek(xci_infile,0L,SEEK_END);
        return;
        }
      if (!stricmp(tokens[1],"DO"))
        {
        strcpy(fn,tokens[2]);
        dofunc(0,fn,data);
        return;
        }
      if (!stricmp(tokens[1],"GOTO"))
        {
        gotofunc(0,tokens[2],data);
        return;
        }
      synerr;
      }
  }

/* Set a variable */
XCICMD setcmd(int cmd, char far *cmds,struct udata *data)
  {
  int val;
  if (cmd)
    {
    printf("Set a variable\n");
    return;
    }
  if (parse(cmds)!=2) synerr;
```

```
   if (strlen(tokens[0])!=1||!isalpha(*tokens[0]))
     {
     printf("Variables must be A-Z\n");
     return;
     }
   getval(tokens[1],0,0,0,&val);
   data->vars[toupper(*tokens[0])-'A']=val;
   }
/* Stack for PUSH/POP commands */
static int intstack[512];
static int intstackp=0;
XCICMD pushcmd(int cmd, char far *cmds,struct udata *data)
   {
   int val;
   if (cmd)
     {
     printf("Push a value on the stack\n");
     return;
     }
   if (parse(cmds)!=1) synerr;
   getval(tokens[0],0,0,0,&val);
   if (intstackp==sizeof(intstack)/sizeof(int))
     printf("Stack overflow\n");
   else
     intstack[intstackp++]=val;
   }

XCICMD popcmd(int cmd, char far *cmds,struct udata *data)
   {
   int val;
   if (cmd)
     {
     printf("Pop the top of the stack to a variable\n");
     return;
     }
   if (parse(cmds)!=1) synerr;
   if (strlen(tokens[0])!=1||!isalpha(*tokens[0]))
     {
     printf("Variables must be A-Z\n");
     return;
     }
   if (!intstackp)
```

```
      printf("Nothing to pop\n");
    else
      data->vars[toupper(*tokens[0])-'A']=
                     intstack[--intstackp];
  }


/* Store the graphics screen to a buffer */
XCICMD stocmd(int cmd, char far *cmds,struct udata *data)
  {
  int buf;
  if (cmd)
    {
    printf("Store the screen to memory\n");
    return;
    }
  if (parse(cmds)!=1) synerr;
  if (getval(tokens[0],0,1,10,&buf)) return;
  if (!data->store[--buf])
      {
/* allocate storage if needed */
      data->store[buf]=malloc((unsigned)SCREEN_SIZE);
      if (!data->store[buf])
        {
        printf("Out of memory\n");
        return;
        }
      }
/* copy to the screen if in graphics mode, or to graphics
   buffer if not */
  memcpy(data->store[buf],data->store[10+data->textgraph],
        (unsigned)SCREEN_SIZE);
  }


/* Restore a buffer to the screen */
XCICMD rclcmd(int cmd, char far *cmds,struct udata *data)
  {
  int buf;
  if (cmd)
    {
    printf("Recall a screen from memory\n");
    return;
    }
```

```
  if (parse(cmds)!=1) synerr;
  if (getval(tokens[0],0,1,10,&buf)) return;
  if (!data->store[--buf])
    {
    printf("Buffer %d empty\n",buf+1);
    return;
    }
  memcpy(data->store[10+data->textgraph],data->store[buf],
       (unsigned)SCREEN_SIZE);
  }

/* Fill a region */
XCICMD fillcmd(int cmd, char far *cmds,struct udata *data)
  {
  int buf;
#ifdef __BORLANDC__
  printf("fill is only supported with the Microsoft "
       "graphics library\n");
  return;
#else
  if (cmd)
    {
    printf("Fill a region\n");
    return;
    }
  NOARG;
  gograph(data);
  _floodfill(data->graphxy.xcoord,data->graphxy.ycoord,
           data->color);
  gotext(data);
#endif
  }

/* Write text */
XCICMD textcmd(int cmd, char far *cmds,struct udata *data)
  {
  int buf;
  if (cmd)
    {
    printf("Print text\n");
    return;
    }
```

```
  gograph(data);
  _settextcolor(data->tcolor);
/* calculate text cursor based on graphics cursor */
  _settextposition(data->graphxy.xcoord/8,
                   data->graphxy.ycoord/8);
  _outtext(cmds);
  gotext(data);
  }
/* prompt user with string */
/* if string starts with ~ then don't add a new line */
XCICMD promptcmd(int cmd, char far *cmds,struct udata *data)
  {
  int buf;
  if (cmd||!*cmds)
    {
    printf("Prompt user\n");
    return;
    }
  turtleprompt(cmds+(*cmds=='~'));
  if (*cmds!='~') turtleprompt("\n");
  }


/* Set text color */
XCICMD textccmd(int cmd, char far *cmds,struct udata *data)
  {
  int col;
  if (cmd)
    {
    printf("Set text color\n");
    return;
    }
  if (parse(cmds)!=1) synerr;
  if (getval(tokens[0],data->tcolor,0,15,&col)) return;
  data->tcolor=col;
  }


/* Install commands. This is called by the XCI startup
   function in TURTLE.C. It is in this file so TURTLE.C
   doesn't need prototypes for each command function */
int installcmds()
  {
/* enable XCI's internal goto command */
```

```
    if (addcmd("goto",gotofunc)) return 1;
    if (addcmd("cd",cdcmd)) return 1;
    if (addcmd("dir",dircmd)) return 1;
    if (addcmd("dos",doscmd)) return 1;
    if (addcmd("edit",editcmd)) return 1;
    if (addcmd("repeat",rptcmd)) return 1;
    if (addcmd("if",ifcmd)) return 1;
    if (addcmd("set",setcmd)) return 1;
    if (addcmd("sto",stocmd)) return 1;
    if (addcmd("rcl",rclcmd)) return 1;
    if (addcmd("push",pushcmd)) return 1;
    if (addcmd("pop",popcmd)) return 1;
    if (addcmd("delay",delaycmd)) return 1;
    if (addcmd("prompt",promptcmd)) return 1;
    if (addcmd("show",showcmd)) return 1;
    if (addcmd("fill",fillcmd)) return 1;
    if (addcmd("textcolor",textccmd)) return 1;
    if (addcmd("text",textcmd)) return 1;
    if (addcmd("setx",setxcmd)) return 1;
    if (addcmd("sety",setycmd)) return 1;
    if (addcmd("setxy",setxycmd)) return 1;
    if (addcmd("background",backgcmd)) return 1;
    if (addcmd("pencolor",colorcmd)) return 1;
    if (addcmd("clear",clearcmd)) return 1;
    if (addcmd("home",homecmd)) return 1;
    if (addcmd("penup",penupcmd)) return 1;
    if (addcmd("pendown",pendowncmd)) return 1;
    if (addcmd("turn",turncmd)) return 1;
    if (addcmd("move",movecmd)) return 1;
    if (addcmd("forward",movecmd)) return 1;
    return 0;
    }
```

Listing 17-4. TEXPR.C

```
/* TEXPR.C   Expression evaluator for TURTLE.EXE
   See MAKEFILE for compile instructions

*/


#include <stdio.h>
```

```
#include <stdlib.h>
#include <string.h>
#include <ctype.h>
#include <dos.h>
#include "turtle.h"

int _getnum(int);
int specialvar(void);
int prec(int);
void perform(int);
int e_expr(void);

static char *s;


/* get a numeric value */
int getnum(char *token)
  {
  s=token;
  return _getnum(1);
  }


/* Internal get numeric value -- set allowneg to 1
   if negative numbers are OK */
int _getnum(int allowneg)
  {
  char *span;
  int n,val;
/* process negative number */
  if (allowneg&&*s=='-')
    {
    s++;
    return -getnum(0);
    }

/* is it an internal variable ? */
  if (*s=='%')
    {
    s++;
    return specialvar();
    }
```

```
/* Is it a user variable (A-Z)? */
  if (isalpha(*s))
    {
    val=(int)appdata.vars[toupper(*s)-'A'];
    s++;
    return val;
    }

/* Is it a hex number (0x...)? */
  if (*s=='0'&&(*(s+1)=='x'||*(s+1)=='X'))
    {
    span="0123456789ABCDEFabcdef";
    sscanf(s+=2,"%x",&val);
    }
  else
    {
/* normal number */
    val=atoi(s);
    span="0123456789";
    }
/* skip over decimal or hex digits */
  s+=strspn(s,span);
  return val;
  }


/* process special internal variables */
int specialvar(void)
  {
  static seeded=0;    /* has random number been seeded? */
  int op=*s++;
  op=toupper(op);

/* %i numeric input */
  if (op=='I')
    {
    char inbuf[81];
    fgets(inbuf,sizeof(inbuf),stdin);
    return atoi(inbuf);
    }
```

```
/* %r random number */
   if (op=='R')
     {
     if (!seeded)
       {
       struct dostime_t dostime;
       seeded=1;
       _dos_gettime(&dostime);
       srand(dostime.hsecond);
       }
     return rand();
     }

/* %x X coordinate */
   if (op=='X')
      return appdata.graphxy.xcoord;

/* %y Y coordinate */
   if (op=='Y')
      return appdata.graphxy.ycoord;

/* %c Color */
   if (op=='C')
      return appdata.color;

/* %h Heading */
   if (op=='H')
      return appdata.heading;

   return 0;
   }



#define LE 256
#define GE 257



/* expression error */
int eerror(void)
   {
```

```c
    printf("Expression error\n");
    return 0;
    }


/* stack size for expression parse */
#define STKSIZE 100

/* stack for values */
int valstack[STKSIZE];
/* top of valstack */
int valstackp=0;

/* stack for operators */
int opstack[STKSIZE];
/* top of opstack */
int opstackp=0;

/* Push, pop, and get top of stack */
/* The ## operator does "pasting" so:
   push(opstack,10);
   expands to:
   (opstackp<(STKSIZE-1)?opstack[opstackp++]=val:stkerr());
*/

#define push(stk,val) (stk##p<(STKSIZE-1)?stk[stk##p++]=\
                       val:stkerr())
#define pop(stk)      (stk[--stk##p])
#define tos(stk)      (stk[stk##p-1])

/* tell user about stack overflow */
int stkerr(void)
  {
  printf("Expression too complex\n");
  return 0;
  }


/* external interface to evaluate expression in str_in */
int evalexpr(char *str_in)
{
        int val;
```

```
        s=str_in;
        val=e_expr();
/* if parser didn't read all of string -- error */
        if (*(s-1)) eerror();
        return val;
}


/* Expression/subexpression parser */
int e_expr(void)
  {
  int op='+';
  int value;
  int topstack=opstackp;
/* Initilize stack */
  push(opstack,'+');
  push(valstack,0);

/* end at end of string or close paren */
  while (op&&op!=')')
    {
/* If open paren do a recursive call to get value */
    if (*s=='(')
      {
      s++;
      value=e_expr();
      if (*(s-1)!=')') ;  /* error if paren not matched */
      }
    else
/* get a number or variable */
      value=_getnum(1);
/* push it on */
    push(valstack,value);
/* read an operator */
    op=*s++;
/* see if two character (>= or <=) */
    if (op=='>'&&*s=='=') { op=GE; s++; }
    if (op=='<'&&*s=='=') { op=LE; s++; }

/* do calculations allowed by precedence */
    while ((opstackp!=topstack)&&prec(tos(opstack))
           >=prec(op))
```

```
        perform(pop(opstack));

/* push new operator on stack */
    push(opstack,op);
    }
/* not strictly required */
    pop(opstack);
    return pop(valstack);
    }

/* find precedence for given operator */
prec(int op)
  {
  switch (op)
    {
    case 0:
    case ')': return 0;
    case '<':
    case '>':
    case LE:
    case GE:
    case '=':
    case '#': return 1;

    case '&':
    case '|': return 2;

    case '-':
    case '+': return 3;

    case '/':
    case '%':
    case '*': return 4;
    }
  }

/* carry out operator on two top stack elements */
void perform(int op)
  {
  int value,v1,v2;
  v1=pop(valstack);
  v2=pop(valstack);
```

```
switch (op)
  {
  case '+':
            value=v2+v1;
            break;
  case '-': value=v2-v1;
            break;
  case '*': value=v2*v1;
            break;
  case '/': value=v2/v1;
            break;
  case '%': value=v2%v1;
            break;
  case '=': value=v2==v1;

            break;
  case '#': value=v2!=v1;
            break;
  case '<': value=v2<v1;
            break;
  case '>': value=v2>v1;
            break;
  case LE:  value=v2<=v1;
            break;
  case GE:  value=v2>=v1;
            break;
  case '&': value=v2&&v1;
            break;
  case '|': value=v2||v1;
            break;
  }
push(valstack,value);
}
```

Listing 17-5. TSAVE.C

```
/* TSAVE.C   Save DLL for TURTLE.EXE
   These functions link with DLLSTART.ASM to form TSAVE.DLL.
   See MAKEFILE for complete compile instructions.
```

```c
*/

#include <stdio.h>
#include <string.h>
#include <malloc.h>
#include "xci.h"
#include "turtle.h"

#define EXPORT _far _loadds _export

/* locate which buffer number is indicated. 0-9 is user
   buffer.
   buffer 10 is the screen. fn gets the file name from the
   command line */
getbuf(char *line,char **fn)
  {
  char *fnn,*buf;
  int bufno;
  bufno=11;          /* default to screen (11-1=10) */
/* read file name */
  fnn=strtok(line," \t");
  if (!fnn) { printf("Syntax error\n"); return -1; }
/* get buffer # (maybe) */
  buf=strtok(NULL," \t");
/* Call getval() in TCMDS.C (imported) to read number */
  if (buf) if (getval(buf,0,1,10,&bufno)) return -1;
  *fn=fnn;
  return --bufno;
  }


/* save buffer to file */
XCICMD EXPORT save(int cmd, char far *cmds,
                   struct udata *data)
  {
  FILE *f;
  char *fn;
  int bufno,i;
  if (cmd)
    {
    printf("Save the screen (or buffer) to disk\n");
    if (cmd==1)
```

```
        printf("Usage: save filename [buffer]\n");
      return;
      }
/* get arguments */
  bufno=getbuf(cmds,&fn);
  if (bufno==-1) return;
/* if in text mode, get screen from buffer
    if in graphics mode, get screen directly from screen */
  if (bufno==10) bufno+=data->textgraph;
/* insure buffer not empty */
  if (!data->store[bufno])
    {
    printf("Buffer %d is empty\n",bufno+1);
    return;
    }
/* open file for writing -- same as DOS program */
  f=fopen(fn,"wb");
/* write in one chunk */
  if (fwrite(data->store[bufno],(unsigned)SCREEN_SIZE,1,f)!=1)
    {
    printf("Error writing to file\n");
    }
  if (fclose(f)) printf("Can't close file\n");
  }


/* load command in */
XCICMD EXPORT load(int cmd, char far *cmds,
                   struct udata *data)
  {
  int bufno;
  FILE *f;
  char *fn;
  if (cmd)
    {
    printf("Load the screen (or buffer) from disk\n");
    if (cmd==1)
      printf("Usage: load filename [buffer]\n");
    return;
    }
/* call getbuf to interpret arguments */
  bufno=getbuf(cmds,&fn);
  if (bufno==-1) return;
```

```
/* if in text mode, get screen from buffer
   if in graphics mode, get screen directly from screen */
  if (bufno==10) bufno+=data->textgraph;
/* if buffer empty allocate space for it */
  if (!data->store[bufno])
    {
    if (!(data->store[bufno]=malloc((unsigned)SCREEN_SIZE)))
      {
      printf("Out of memory",bufno+1);
      return;
      }
    }
/* read buffer in one big chunk */
  f=fopen(fn,"rb");
  if (fread(data->store[bufno],(unsigned)SCREEN_SIZE,1,f)!=1)
    {
    printf("Error reading file\n");
    }
  fclose(f);
  }



/* Init DLL so we can use C library  -- Microsoft only */
unsigned far pascal _loadds dllstart()
  {
#ifndef __BORLANDC__
  extern void far pascal C_INIT(void);
  C_INIT();
#endif
  return 1;
  }
```

Listing 17-6. DLLSTART.ASM

```
; DLLSTART.ASM  - Required startup code for
;                 DLL Initilization
        extrn DLLSTART:far
        end DLLSTART
```

Listing 17-7. PGRAPH.H

```
/* PGRAPH.H  -- Portable graphics header for TURTLE.EXE
   See MAKEFILE for instructions

*/

#ifndef PGRAPH_H
#define PGRAPH_H 1

#ifndef __BORLANDC__
/* Microsoft -- easy case use native graphics */
#include <graph.h>
#else

/* Emulation of useful stuff from graph.h */
#define _DEFAULTMODE    3
#define _TEXTC80        3
#define _MRES256COLOR 19
#define _GCLEARSCREEN 0
/* We don't really use pages */
#define _setactivepage(x)
#define _setvisualpage(x)

struct xycoord
  {
  short xcoord;
  short ycoord;
  };

struct rccoord
  {
  short row;
  short col;
  };


void _setvideomode(int);
void _clearscreen(int);
void _setcolor(int);
unsigned long _remappalette(int,unsigned long);
void _setbkcolor(unsigned long);
void _moveto(int,int);
```

```
void _settextcolor(int);
void _settextposition(int,int);
void _outtext(char *);
void _plot(int ,int);
void _lineto(int,int);
struct xycoord _getcurrentposition(void);
/* unimplemented */
void _floodfill(int,int,int);

#endif /* Borland definitions */

#endif /* Header */
```

Listing 17-8. POLYTSH

```
# Shell for calling turnpoly -- Run with TURTLE
# DO POLYTSH.T
# Other fun values: 100,200,0,60
#                   100,124,45,60
#                   50,90,0,45
#                   50,90,0,20
show off
prompt Welcome to the TURNPOLY demonstration
prompt I will need a size, angle, direction, and delta to
create
prompt the drawing. If you don't know what to enter, try the
prompt values I suggest. (You must enter them -- don't just
prompt press Enter.) To return to the turtle prompt, press
prompt Control-Break
prompt Size? (100)
set s %i
prompt Angle? (124)
set a %i
prompt Direction? (0)
set d %i
prompt Delta? (60)
set c %i
do turnpoly.t
goto polytsh.t
```

Listing 17-9. TURNPOLY

```
# Draw rotated polygon -- see POLYTSH.T
# Set S to size, A to angle, D to direction, C to change
clear
pencolor 14
show on
do turnpoly.t01
show
show off
```

Listing 17-10. TURNPOLY.001

```
# File used by TURNPOLY.T -- see POLYTSH.T
penup
setxy 160 100
turn 0
pendown
if d>359 then exit
turn +d
push s
do inpoly.t
pop s
set d d+c
goto turnpoly.t01
```

Listing 17-11. INPOLY

```
# File used by TURNPOLY.T01 -- See POLYTSH.T
if s<5 then exit
move s
turn +a
set s s-2
goto inpoly.t
```

CHAPTER ■ 18

A 386 Disk Duplicator

In this chapter, you will see a disk duplication system built with Intel's 386/486 Code Builder. The program has an appealing pleasing user interface, and is a practical, useful application. It stores images of floppy disks entirely in memory—simple for a DOS extended program but difficult for normal DOS programs unless they resort to difficult techniques like EMS or XMS (see DFITEMS.C in Chapter 1). You will see how Code Builder, a 32-bit extender and C compiler, performs on these important issues:

- Microsoft C compatibility
- Interrupt handling
- Physical memory addressing
- Calling DOS/BIOS calls
- The speed penalty for calling DOS/BIOS

The Project

Copy Builder 386 (the disk duplication system) requires a lot of memory. It also accesses the screen directly, makes many DOS and BIOS calls, handles interrupts, and uses a display library originally developed under Microsoft C.

The program operates on a disk image in memory. The image can be read from a diskette or a previously-saved disk file. Copy Builder can write the image to another diskette or to a disk file that you can store on your hard disk for future use. The disk files include a title and a checksum to help insure the data's integrity.

Copy Builder normally displays the screen seen in Figure 18-1. From here, you may select from the choices at the top of the screen. If you press the F1 key Copy Builder displays a brief help screen (see Figure 18-2).

Figure 18-1 - Copy Builder 386 Main Screen

Read   Write   Load   Save   Options   Dos   Exit   **F1=Help**

386 Copy Builder

Current status:

Title: <EMPTY>

Size: 0   Copies: 0   Source: N/A

Checksums: Stored=0000 Computed=0000

When Copy Builder prompts you for a file name, you can enter it directly. If you enter a name that ends in a colon or a backslash, or enter a file name that contains wildcards, Copy Builder presents a menu of matching files. You can select the file from this menu. The default file is always "*.*". The menu will never contain more than 120 files—if the directory has too many files, you can narrow the search by using wildcards.

The source code for Copy Builder resides in several modules. CB386.C (Listing 18-1) contains the main code. FILEIO.C (Listing 18-2) and DISKIO.C (Listing 18-3) handle file and disk I/O, respectively. For the main menu, and other related code, see DISP.C (Listing 18-4). REBOOT.C (Listing 18-5) provides code to disable Control-Alt-Del to prevent accidental data loss. DISPLAY.C, HISTO.C, and DIRPICK.C (Listings 18-6, 18-7, and 18-8) make up a simple display library developed for Microsoft C. CB386.H and DISPLAY.H (Listings 18-9 and 18-10) contain declarations for CB386 and the display library, respectively. A MAKEFILE (Listing 18-11) controls the compilation via the MAKE utility.

Figure 18-2. Copy Builder 386 Main Help Screen

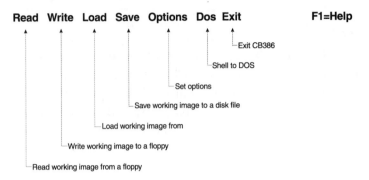

Read Write Load Save Options Dos Exit   F1=Help

               Exit CB386

             Shell to DOS

          Set options

       Save working image to a disk file

     Load working image from

   Write working image to a floppy

 Read working image from a floppy

CopyBuilder 386 by Al Williams

Press any key to continue

How it Works

Only two routines allocate memory using malloc(). the read_disk() function (in DISKIO.C, Listing 18-3), and loadit() (in FILEIO.C, Listing 18-2). Both routines read in new images.

Because sector_read() and sector_write() in DISKIO.C (listing 18-3) use BIOS interrupt 0x13 for disk I/O, they must allocate a special memory buffer below the 1M line (dosbuf).

Code Builder automatically copies extended memory data to a special buffer below 1M for many DOS calls. However, for the BIOS disk services, it does not. You are responsible for placing data buffers where the BIOS can access them. When writing, you must first copy the data to the special buffer. When reading, you must copy the data out of the special buffer when the BIOS call completes.

Code Builder allows programs to allocate this type of buffer using the standard DOS allocation call (interrupt 0x21 function 0x48). Unlike the normal DOS call, Code Builder expects the number of bytes (not paragraphs) in the 32-bit EBX register. If EAX=0x00004800, Code Builder allocates memory below 1M. If EAX=0x80004800, Code Builder allocates extended memory.

Structure Alignment

The Code Builder compiler normally aligns structure members on a four-byte boundary to improve performance (see Chapter 6). This is a good idea, unless the structure maps to an external entity. The _bpb structure in CB386.H (Listing 18-9), for instance, contains a disk's BIOS parameter block (BPB). This structure must exactly match the BPB on disk. CB386 uses the pragma:

```
#pragma align(_bpb=1)
```

to force Code Builder to place each structure member on the next available byte.

Larger Than Life DOS Calls

Notice in FILEIO.C (Listing 18-2) that CB386 calls fread() and fwrite() with 32-bit integer values for the size argument. For instance, when reading a 1.44M floppy disk, fread() must read 1.44M of data. Of course, Code Builder internally breaks the request into multiple DOS calls, each handling smaller pieces of data. This process is completly transparent to your program.

The buffer that Code Builder uses for DOS I/O is set by the /xiobuf option. The default, /xiobuf=40K, reserves 40K of memory for DOS communications. A larger DOS I/O buffer will increase performance, but will reduce the amount of conventional memory available for other purposes (running a DOS shell, for example).

Accessing Video RAM

DISPLAY.C (Listing 18-6)mainly uses video BIOS calls to manipulate the screen. Two functions, vidsave() and vidrestore(), do access the screen memory directly. This is very simple, since Code Builder uses a flat addressing scheme. For a color display, the buffer is at location B800:0000 (the vidmode() function ensures page 0 is active). Code Builder identity maps memory below 1M so that you can convert this address to a linear address. Simply shift the segment value left four places and add the offset. For example:

```
char *vptr=(char *)0xB8000;   /* (0xB800<<4)+0 */
```

will point vptr to the beginning of screen memory. (PMCGA in Chapter 8 shows how to directly address the screen from many extenders.)

CB386 uses the standard signal() and _harderr() functions to trap break interrupts and critical errors. The signal() method is usually unsatisfactory for programs like CB386 because it allows ^C to appear on the screen when a break occurs. However, the CB386 break handler (breakfunc() in DISP.C; Listing 18-4) does a longjmp() to reinitialize the main menu. This has the handy side-effect of redrawing the screen—the ^C doesn't last long enough to be a concern.

Interrupts

The interrupt 9 service routine (ourint9() in REBOOT.C; Listing 18-5) contains code to prevent the user from rebooting the machine with Control-Alt-Delete. It does this by hooking the keyboard interrupt (INT 9). If it detects the Delete key, it looks at the BIOS keyboard status word. If the Control and Alt keys are down, the interrupt handler consumes the Delete key—the BIOS never sees it. In all other cases, the BIOS receives the keystroke unaltered. This does not, however, interfere with Windows 3.1 local reboot since Windows acts on the keystrokes before CB386 even sees them. If you run CB386 under Windows 3.1 the Control-Alt-Delete keys will still bring up the standard reboot screen for Windows. Windows then discards the keys without sending them to CB386.

Handling interrupts in a DOS extender is usually very different from handling them under regular DOS. Still, Code Builder is extremely different, even for a DOS extender. Programs declare interrupt functions via a pragma. In REBOOT.C you can see the line:

```
#pragma interrupt(ourint9)
```

Further down in the code, the actual definition of ourint9() appears. Notice that the registers are not pushed on the stack, as in Microsoft C. You must call the special Code Builder function, _get_stk_frame() to get a pointer to an _XSTACK structure. The Code Builder header file STK.H declares the _XSTACK structure, which is poorly documented. It contains the interrupt registers, and other related fields. Chapter 9 covers interrupt handling in more detail.

Normally, Code Builder processes interrupts in protected mode, and then reissues them in V86 mode for DOS. The opts field in _XSTACK can alter this behavior. (Some Code Builder documentation incorrectly calls this field stk_opts.) By placing different values in this field, a program can prevent the V86 interrupt or abort the program. In ourint9( ), for example:

```
frame->opts=_STK_NOINT;
```

causes Code Builder not to reissue the keyboard interrupt. This prevents the BIOS from gaining control when CB386 detects the Control-Alt-Delete keys.

Virtual memory can cause special problems for interrupt service routines (ISRs). If an ISR is swapped out when its interrupt occurs, it must be swapped back in before the interrupt can proceed. At best, this delays the interrupt, holding up the entire system. As a worst case, imagine that the ISR controls the disk interrupt. When the ISR must be swapped in, Code Builder tries to read it from disk. Code Builder reissues the disk interrupt, which triggers another request to swap in the ISR. This is a deadlock situation and must be prevented.

The lockint9( ) function in REBOOT.C uses DPMI functions to lock the interrupt 9 handler in memory. The _dpmi_lockregion( ) function (identical to DPMI function 0x600) insures a block of memory will remain in RAM. Code Builder may swap unlocked blocks to disk. Locks always occur on 4K pages, so Copy Builder assumes ourint9( ) won't be larger than 4K and sidesteps the issue of computing the length of the function. (Windows programs use GlobalPageLock( ) to perform locking.)

The same problem arises when ISRs use global or static data—you should lock the data in memory to prevent swapping during an interrupt. Intel suggests examining the maps generated by the linker to find the address ranges to lock. Of course, when you recompile, you must reexamine the maps, alter the code, and compile again—a big waste of time. Since lockint9( ) doesn't use global or static data, this problem doesn't appear.

Environment Problems

One final note about CB386. The DOS menu command uses the standard putenv( ) function to change the DOS shell's prompt. With early versions of Code Builder, putenv( ) did not modify the environment so that child processes got the new values. Intel's latest versions handle this code correctly. If you have the older version, there is no harm but the prompt will remain unchanged.

Analysis

The Code Builder compiler is somewhat similar to the Microsoft C compiler. It accepts most Microsoft-style keywords (near, far, etc.) even if it doesn't act on some of them (there are no far pointers, for example). Certain features (ASM, interrupt handling, etc.) are missing or very different, so don't expect to port complex code effortlessly. Intel and Microsoft also implement a completely different set of pragmas. The graphics functions in Code Builder only support EGA and VGA monitors, and the presentation graphics library from Microsoft C 6.0 is not present.

It appears Intel chose to make the compiler as simple to use as possible. Code Builder is a 32-bit C compiler, with a simple DOS extender built in to support it. This simplicity means that you can learn Code Builder in short order, but it prevents you from taking advantage of many 386 features that other extenders allow you to use.

Since Code Builder maps DOS memory at its physical address, accessing the screen, or other physical memory, couldn't be easier. Flat 32-bit pointers also simplify programming. Of course, with any non-segmented extender, you lose many benefits of memory protection—you can't expect the DOS extender to catch null pointer references, for example.

Calling DOS and BIOS calls with Code Builder was straightforward. While it would be better if Code Builder did not require CB386 to manage a DOS buffer for its BIOS calls, Code Builder does lift this restriction on most other calls.

Listing 18-1. CB386.C

```c
/* CB386.C - main file for CopyBuilder 386
   See makefile for compile directives
*/
#include <stdio.h>
#include <dos.h>
#include <ctype.h>
#include "cb386.h"
#include "display.h"

/* current drive number */
int driveno;

/* current bios parameter block */
struct _bpb bpb;

/* size of disk */
unsigned disksize;

/* information about buffer */
struct _bufinfo bufinfo;


/* number of sectors */
unsigned sectorct;

/* storage for disk image */
unsigned char *diskbuf;

/* set when a critical error occurs */
int critical_err;

/* DOS buffer for disk BIOS reads and writes */
char *dosbuf;
unsigned dosbufsiz;

/* text of format command */
char fmtcmd[129];

/* set when a critical error occurs */
int critical_err;
```

```
/* critical error messages */
static char *cmsgs[]=
  {
  "Write protect",
  "Unknown unit",
  "Drive not ready",
  "Unknown command",
  "CRC error",
  "Bad Request",
  "Seek error",
  "Unknown media",
  "Sector not found",
  "Out of paper",
  "Write error",
  "Read error",
  "General failure",
  "Unknown",
  "Unknown",
  "Invalid change"
  };


/* Critical error handler */
void cerror(int dev,int code)
  {
  char msg[81];
  int choice;
  critical_err=code&=0xFF;
  sprintf(msg,"Critical error: %s (Retry, Fail, Ignore)",
          cmsgs[code]);
  choice=prompt(msg,"RIF",ERRCOLOR);
  if (choice==0) choice=_HARDERR_RETRY;
  else if (choice==1) choice=_HARDERR_IGNORE;
  else choice=_HARDERR_FAIL;  /* F or ESC */
  _hardresume(choice);
  }



/* main program */
main(int argc,char *argv[])
  {
```

```
/* set up critical error handler */
  _harderr(cerror);
/* Turn break on */
  if (argc>2||argv[1][0]=='?'||argv[1][1]=='?')
    error("CopyBuilder 386 by Al Williams\n"
          "A diskette duplication system\n"
          "Usage: CB386 [drive]\n");
/* save current drive/directory */
  cdsave();
/* set up video mode and detect monitor type */
  vidmode();
/* if mono monitor, set up neutral colors */
  if (mono)
    {
    TEXTCOLOR=7;
    SOCOLOR=0x70;
    ERRCOLOR=1;
    HELPCOLOR=7;
    }
/* reset title, etc. */
  strcpy(bufinfo.title,"<EMPTY>");
  strcpy(bufinfo.source,"N/A");
  strcpy(fmtcmd,"format");
  noreboot();
/* if user asked for a disk on the command line, read it */
  if (argc==2)
    {
/* show a display */
    disp();
/* read the disk */
    read_disk(*argv[1]);
    }
/* goto main menu */
  menu();
  }



/* Non-interactive error routine */
error(char *s)
  {
  printf("\n%s\n",s);
```

```
  cdrestore();
  exit(1);
  }


/* compute checksum
   add sixteen bit words and wrap carry around */
checksum()
  {
  unsigned char *bufp=diskbuf;
  int i=bufinfo.size;
  unsigned short cksum=0;
  unsigned cksum1;
  while (i--)
    {
    cksum1=cksum;
    cksum1+=*bufp++;
    cksum=cksum1&0xFFFF;
    if (cksum1&0xFFFF0000)
      cksum++;
    }
  bufinfo.ccsum=cksum;
  return cksum;
  }


/* Format a disk in the indicated drive */
format(int driveno)
  {
  char fcmd[80];
  int stat;
/* build command line */
  sprintf(fcmd,"%s %c:",fmtcmd,driveno+'A');
/* save video */
  vidsave();
  cls();
/* execute command */
  stat=system(fcmd);
  vidrestore();
  if (stat==-1) advise("Unable to execute format program");
  }
```

```
/* turn the blinking -wait- on at bottom of screen */
wait_on()
  {
  int ocolor=color;
  color=SOCOLOR|0x80;    /* make it blink */
  goxy(0,24);
  clreol();
  goxy(37,24);
  printfc("-WAIT-");
  curshide();
  color=ocolor;
  }

/* turn the blinking -wait- off at bottom of screen */
wait_off()
  {
  goxy(0,24);
  clreol();
  }
```

Listing 18-2. FILEIO.C

```
/* FILEIO.C File oriented I/O routines for CB386
*/
#include <stdio.h>
#include <malloc.h>
#include <errno.h>
#include "cb386.h"
#include "display.h"

void (*slbreak)();    /* place to hook break handler */

/* ^C handler when saving -- used in DISKIO.C too */
void save_break()
  {
  advise("\aOperation aborted");
  }

/* ^C handler when loading -- used in DISKIO.C too */
void load_break()
  {
```

```
  cleanup();
  }

/* Clean up an aborted load */
cleanup()
  {
  if (diskbuf) free(diskbuf);
  diskbuf=NULL;
  memset(&bufinfo,0,sizeof(bufinfo));
  strcpy(bufinfo.title,"<EMPTY>");
  strcpy(bufinfo.source,"N/A");
  }

/* save disk image to a file */
m_save()
  {
  slbreak=when_break;
  when_break=save_break;
  saveit();
  when_break=slbreak;
  slbreak=NULL;
  }

/* load disk image to a file */
m_load()
  {
  slbreak=when_break;
  when_break=load_break;
  loadit();
  when_break=slbreak;
  slbreak=NULL;
  }

/* actual routine to save data */
saveit()
  {
  char fn[66];
  FILE *f=NULL;
  int cnt1;
/* if no data to save, forget it */
  if (!diskbuf)
    {
```

```
      advise("No disk image in memory");
      return;
      }
/* get a file name */
   if (!getfilen(fn,65)) return;
   critical_err=0;
/* check if the file already exists */
   if (!access(fn,0))
      {
      if (prompt("\aFile exists. Overwrite? (Y/N)"
                 ,"NY",TEXTCOLOR)<=0)
        return;
      }
/* if checking for the file caused a critical error,
   don't even try to open the file */
   if (!critical_err) f=fopen(fn,"wb");

/* if the file can't be opened (or wasn't because of
   a critical error, forget it */
   if (!f)
      {
      advise("Can't open file for writing");
      return;
      }

/* Get a title */
   if (ask("Title: ",NULL,TEXTCOLOR,64,fn,NULL)==-1) return;
/* only change title if new one was entered */
   if (*fn) strcpy(bufinfo.title,fn);
/* Turn the wait indicator on */
   wait_on();
   /* set dirty bit in image.
      copies/source/csum are meaningless */
   bufinfo.dirty=1;
/* write signature */
   putw('C386',f);
/* write size of bufinfo */
   putw(sizeof(struct _bufinfo),f);
/* write bufinfo */
   fwrite(&bufinfo,1,sizeof(struct _bufinfo),f);
```

```
/***********************************
 * write entire buffer in one swoop    *
 * This is a BIG advantage of a 32-bit *
 * extender!                           *
 ***********************************/
  cnt1=fwrite(diskbuf,1,bufinfo.size,f);
/* one | is deliberate here -- we always want to fclose */
  if (ferror(f)|fclose(f)|(cnt1!=bufinfo.size))
    advise("\aError writing to file");
  else
    bufinfo.dirty=0;
  wait_off();
  }


/* routine to actually load file to disk image */
loadit()
  {
  char fn[66];
  FILE *f;
  int cnt,cnt1;
/* if buffer is full, confirm */
  if (!dirtyquery()) return;
/* get file name */
  if (!getfilen(fn,65)) return;
/* open it */
  f=fopen(fn,"rb");
/* can't open it, forget it */
  if (!f)
    {
    advise("Can't open file");
    return;
    }
/* Turn wait indicator on */
  wait_on();
/* check file type */
  cnt=getw(f);
  if (cnt!='C386')
    {
    advise("Not a C386 image file");
```

```
      return;
      }
/* get size of bufinfo structure */
  cnt=getw(f);
/* new versions of C386 can't make bufinfo smaller, only
   larger at the end */
  fread(&bufinfo,1,cnt,f);
/* kill old image */
  if (diskbuf) free(diskbuf);
/* allocate new image based on size */
  diskbuf=malloc(bufinfo.size);
  if (!diskbuf)
    {
    advise("Insufficient memory");
    cleanup();
    fclose(f);
    return;
    }


/***************************************
 * read entire buffer in one swoop     *
 * This is a BIG advantage of a 32-bit *
 * extender!                           *
 ***************************************/
  cnt1=fread(diskbuf,1,bufinfo.size,f);
/* one | is deliberate here also (see saveit(), above */
  if (ferror(f)|fclose(f)|(cnt1!=bufinfo.size))
    {
    advise("Error reading file");
    cleanup();
    return;
    }
  checksum();
  strcpy(bufinfo.source,fn);
  bufinfo.copies=0;
  wait_off();
  }
```

Listing 18-3. DISKIO.C

```c
/* DISKIO.C Whole disk I/O routines for CB386 */

#include <stdio.h>
#include <malloc.h>
#include <string.h>
#include <dos.h>
#include "cb386.h"
#include "display.h"

/* Simple call to make a harmless DOS function run so DOS
   can check for ^Break. Since the routines in this module
   don't call DOS, this is important -- without it break
   goes undetected. If BREAK=OFF this wouldn't work, so
   CB386.C sets BREAK ON and restores it before the
   program exits. */

check_break()
   {
   union REGS r;
   r.x.ax=0x3500;  /* Read int vector -- quick call  */
   int86(0x21,&r,&r);
   }

try13(int try,int cmd,int count,int head,int drive,int track,
      int sector,unsigned dosbuf)
  {
  union REGS r;
/* do operation up to try times */
  while (try--)
    {
    r.h.ah=cmd;
    r.h.al=count;
    r.h.dh=head;
    r.h.dl=drive;
    r.h.ch=track;
    r.h.cl=sector;
    r.x.bx=(unsigned)dosbuf;
    int86(0x13,&r,&r);
/* if error... */
    if (r.x.cflag)
      {
```

```
/* if not last try */
      if (try)
        {
/* reset drive and try again */
        r.x.ax=0;
        r.h.dl=drive;
        int86(0x13,&r,&r);
        }
/* continue on all errors */
      continue;
        }
   /* no error */
   break;
   }
  return r.x.cflag;
  }




/* The BIOS read/write routines use a DOS buffer since
   codebuilder does not transparently move data for these
   BIOS interrupts */

/* read count number of sectors via the BIOS
   returns 0 for success */
sector_read(int head,int track, int sector, int drive,
            unsigned char *buf,unsigned count)
   {
   union REGS r;
/* if no dos buffer then allocate one large enough for
   one track */
   check_break();
   if (!dosbuf)
     {
     r.h.ah=0x48;
     dosbufsiz=r.x.bx=bpb.bytespersec*bpb.secpertrack;
     int86(0x21,&r,&r);
     if (r.x.cflag)
       {
       advise("Not enough DOS memory");
       return 1;
       }
```

```
      dosbuf=(char *)r.x.ax;
      }

   if (try13(NRTRIES,2,count,head,drive,track,sector,
       (unsigned)dosbuf)) return 1;
    memcpy(buf,dosbuf,bpb.bytespersec*count);
    return 0;
   }

/* Read BIOS parameter block */
read_bpb(int driveno)
  {
  /* read BPB from specified drive */
  bpb.bytespersec=512;  /* default */
  bpb.secpertrack=1;
  if (sector_read(0,0,1,driveno,(unsigned char *)&bpb,1))
    return 0;
  return 1;
  }



/* read entire disk */
read_disk(int drive)
  {
  unsigned i,trk=0,head=0;
  unsigned char *diskp;
/* erase existing image, if any */
  if (diskbuf) free(diskbuf);
/* set up buffer info */
  strcpy(bufinfo.title,"<NONE>");
  bufinfo.source[0]=toupper(drive);
  driveno=bufinfo.source[0]-'A';
  bufinfo.source[1]=':';
  bufinfo.source[2]='\0';
  dosbuf_free();
/* turn on wait indicator on screen */
  wait_on();
  if (!read_bpb(driveno))
    {
    advise("Can't read bpb");
    return 0;
    }
```

```
if (dosbuf) dosbuf_free();
head=0;
/* determine size of disk */
bufinfo.size=disksize=
    (sectorct=bpb.nrsectors?bpb.nrsectors:
      bpb.hugesectors)
      *bpb.bytespersec;
/* allocate space */
diskbuf=(unsigned char *)malloc(disksize);
if (!diskbuf)
  {
  advise("Not enough free memory");
  return 0;
  }
/* read entire disk */
diskp=diskbuf;
goxy(0,12);
histogram(-1,60);
curshide();
for (i=0;i<sectorct;i+=bpb.secpertrack)
  {
  histogram(i,sectorct);
  if (sector_read(head,trk,1,driveno,diskp,
                  bpb.secpertrack))
      {
      char errbuf[80];
      sprintf(errbuf,"\aWarning: bad sector at %u:%u\n",
              head,trk);
      if (advise(errbuf)==-1)
        {
        cleanup();  /* kill incomplete buffer */
        return 0;
        }
      }
  diskp+=bpb.bytespersec*bpb.secpertrack;
  if (++head>=bpb.nrheads)
      {
      head=0;
      trk++;
      }
  }
bufinfo.dirty=1;
```

```
    histogram(i,i);
    bufinfo.csum=checksum();
    wait_off();
    return 1;
    }

/* free dos buffer */
dosbuf_free()
    {
    union REGS r;
    if (!dosbuf) return;
    r.h.ah=0x49;
    r.x.dx=(unsigned int)dosbuf;
    int86(0x21,&r,&r);
    if (r.x.cflag)
      advise("Memory allocation error");
    dosbuf=NULL;
    }


/* write count sectors via BIOS */
sector_write(int head,int track, int sector, int drive,
             unsigned char *buf,unsigned count)
    {
    union REGS r;
    check_break();
/* If no dos buffer, allocate one */
    if (dosbufsiz<bpb.bytespersec*bpb.secpertrack)
      dosbuf_free();
    if (!dosbuf)
      {
      r.h.ah=0x48;
      dosbufsiz=r.x.bx=bpb.bytespersec*bpb.secpertrack;
      int86(0x21,&r,&r);
      if (r.x.cflag)
        {
        advise("Not enough DOS memory");
        return;
        }
      dosbuf=(char *)r.x.ax;
      }
/* copy data to dosbuffer */
```

```
    memcpy(dosbuf,buf,bpb.bytespersec*count);
/* retry up to try times */
    return try13(NRTRIES,3,count,head,drive,track,sector,
        (unsigned)dosbuf);
    }


/* write entire disk */
write_disk(int drive)
  {
  int fmt=0;
  unsigned i,trk=0,head=0;
  unsigned char *diskp;
  drive=toupper(drive)-'A';
/* turn on wait indicator */
  wait_on();
  goxy(0,12);
  histogram(-1,60);
  curshide();
  head=0;
  diskp=diskbuf;
  if (!read_bpb(drive))
    {
    format(drive);
    if (!read_bpb(drive))
      {
      advise("Can't read BPB");
      return 0;
      }
    }
  sectorct=bpb.nrsectors?bpb.nrsectors:
      bpb.hugesectors;
  if (bufinfo.size!=sectorct*bpb.bytespersec)
    {
    advise("Incorrect disk size");
    return 0;
    }
/* write entire disk a track at a time */
  for (i=0;i<sectorct;i+=bpb.secpertrack)
    {
    histogram(i,sectorct);
    if (sector_write(head,trk,1,drive,diskp,
                  bpb.secpertrack))
```

```
        {
        advise("Write error");
        return 0;
        }
    diskp+=bpb.bytespersec*bpb.secpertrack;
    if (++head>=bpb.nrheads)
        {
        head=0;
        trk++;
        }
    }
  histogram(i,i);
  bufinfo.dirty=0;
  wait_off();
  return 1;
  }
```

Listing 18-4. DISP.C

```
/* DISP.C - menus, etc. for CopyBuilder 386
*/
#include <stdio.h>
#include <dos.h>
#include <string.h>
#include <ctype.h>
#include <direct.h>
#include <setjmp.h>
#include <signal.h>
#include "cb386.h"
#include "display.h"


/* display information screen */
disp()
  {
  color=TEXTCOLOR;
  cls();
  color=SOCOLOR;
  clreol();
  writes(" Read  Write  Load  Save  Options  Dos  Exit");
  goxy(73,0);
  writes("F1=Help");
```

```
  color=TEXTCOLOR;
  goxy(33,1);
  writes("386 CopyBuilder");
  goxy(1,3);
  writes("Current status:\n\n\r");
  printfc(" Title: %s\n\n\r",bufinfo.title);
  printfc(" Size: %-8d  Copies: %-6d  Source: %s\n\n\r",
      bufinfo.size,bufinfo.copies,bufinfo.source);
  printfc(" Checksums: Stored=%04X  Computed=%04X\n\n\r",
      bufinfo.csum,bufinfo.ccsum);
  writecc(0xc4,80);
  curshide();
  }


/* Jump buffer for break handling */
jmp_buf onbreak;
/* pointer to extra break function */
void (*when_break)()=NULL;

/* primary break function */
void breakfunc(int sig)
  {
/* recapture break key */
  signal(SIGINT,breakfunc);
/* do extra break function if present */
  if (when_break) when_break();
  when_break=slbreak=NULL;
/* go back to top of menu loop */
  longjmp(onbreak,1);
  }


static int oldbreakflag;

/* Set break flag -- returns old value */
int set_breakflag(int val)
  {
  int old;
  union REGS r;
  r.x.ax=0x3300;
  int86(0x21,&r,&r);
  old=r.h.dl;
  r.h.dl=val;
```

```
  r.x.a0x3301;
  int86(0x21,&r,&r);
  return old;
  }

#define reset_breakflag() set_breakflag(oldbreakflag)

/* main menu */
menu()
  {
  int c;
  char tfmtcmd[129];
/* Turn break on */
  oldbreakflag=set_breakflag(1);
/* catch ^C -- signal is OK since we redraw the whole
   screen first thing. */
  signal(SIGINT,breakfunc);
/* return here when ^C pressed */
  setjmp(onbreak);
/* display screen */
  disp();
/* main loop */
  while (1)
    {
/* get command */
    curshide();
    c=getch();
    if (!c) c=-getch();
/* process commands (extended keys are negative) */
    switch (c>0?(int)toupper(c):c)
      {
      char fn[66];
/* For each command the letter and ALT-letter are OK */
case -0x12:  /* ALT-E */
case 'E':
     m_exit();
     break;

case -0x20:    /* ALT-D */
case 'D':
     m_dos();
     disp();
```

```
            break;

case -0x13:    /* ALT-R */
case 'R':
        m_read();
        disp();
        break;

case -0x11:    /* ALT-W */
case 'W':
        m_write();
        disp();
        break;

case -0x1f:    /* ALT-S */
case 'S':
        m_save();
        disp();
        break;

case -0x26:    /* ALT-L */
case 'L':
        m_load();
        disp();
        break;

case -0x18:     /* ALT-O */
case 'O':
        goxy(0,23);
        printfc("Current: %-64.64s",fmtcmd);
        ask("Format command:",NULL,TEXTCOLOR,
            sizeof(tfmtcmd)-1,
            tfmtcmd,
            "Enter the format command string. CB386 appends"
            " the drive letter.");
        if (*tfmtcmd) strcpy(fmtcmd,tfmtcmd);
        goxy(0,23);
        clreol();
        break;

case -0x23:     /* ALT-H */
case 'H':
```

```
case -59:
      help();
      break;


default:
/* ring bell for unknown command */
      writec('\a');
      }
    }
  }


/* exit */
m_exit()
  {
/* confirm if buffer is full and hasn't been written */
  if (dirtyquery())
    {
    vidmode();
    cdrestore();
    okreboot();
    reset_breakflag();
    exit(0);
    }
  }

/* read a disk */
m_read()
  {
  int disk;
  if (!dirtyquery()) return;
  disk=prompt("Source drive: ",NULL,TEXTCOLOR);
  if (disk==-1) return;
  if (prompt(
    "\aInsert disk. Press <SPACE> to continue or"
    " <ESC> to exit.",
    " \r",TEXTCOLOR)==-1) return;
/* hook ^C handler to do load_break (in FILEIO.C) if ^C) */
  slbreak=when_break;
  when_break=load_break;
  read_disk(disk);
```

```
  when_break=slbreak;
  slbreak=NULL;
  }

/* write to disk */
m_write()
  {
  int disk;
  int copies=1;
  char buf[4];
  if (!diskbuf)
    {
    advise("No disk image in memory");
    return;
    }
  disk=prompt("Destination drive: ",NULL,TEXTCOLOR);
  if (disk==-1) return;
  /* prompt for copies */
  if (ask("Number of copies (default=1): "
          ,"0123456789",TEXTCOLOR,3,buf,
          " Enter the number of copies you want.")==-1)
      return;
  copies=atoi(buf);
  if (!copies) copies=1;
  while (copies--)
    {
    if (prompt(
    "\a\aInsert disk. Press <SPACE> to continue or"
    " <ESC> to exit.",
    " \r",TEXTCOLOR)==-1) return;
/* hook ^C handler to save_break (in FILEIO.C) */
    slbreak=when_break;
    when_break=save_break;
    if (write_disk(disk)) bufinfo.copies++;
    when_break=slbreak;
    slbreak=NULL;
    disp();
    }
  }


/* prompt user if buffer is "dirty" */
```

```
dirtyquery()
  {
  int stat=1;
  if (bufinfo.dirty)
    {
    stat=prompt("\aBuffer not saved. Discard (Y/N)",
              "NY",ERRCOLOR);
    if (stat==-1) stat=0;
    }
  return stat;
  }


/* Run DOS -- some old versions of Codebuilder won't set the
   prompt correctly (bug fixed in later versions) */
m_dos()
  {
/* clear screen and reset color */
  vidmode();
  putenv("PROMPT=Enter \"Exit\" to return to 386 "
         "CopyBuilder\r\n$p$g");
  if (system("command")<0)
    advise("Could not execute COMMAND.COM");
/* reset screen mode just in case */
  vidmode();
  curshide();
  }



/* main menu help screen */
help()
  {
  vidsave();
  color=TEXTCOLOR;
  cls();
  color=SOCOLOR;
  clreol();
  writes(" Read  Write  Load  Save  Options  Dos  Exit");
  goxy(73,0);
  writes("F1=Help");
  color=TEXTCOLOR;
  goxy(0,1);
```

```
  writes("    ↑       ↑       ↑       ↑         ↑         ↑     ↑\n\r");
  writes("    |       |       |       |         |         |     | \n\r");
  writes("    |       |       |       |         |         |     |__ "
  " Exit CB386\n\r");
  writes("    |       |       |       |         |         |\n\r");
  writes("    |       |       |       |         |         |__"
  "Shell to DOS\n\r");
  writes("    |       |       |       |         |\n\r");
  writes("    |       |       |       |         |__Set
options\n\r");
  writes("    |       |       |       |\n\r");
  writes("    |       |       |       |__"
  "Save working image to a disk file\n\r");
  writes("    |       |       |\n\r");
  writes("    |       |       |__"
  "Load working image from a disk file\n\r");
  writes("    |       |\n\r");
  writes("    |       |__Write working image to a
floppy\n\r");
  writes("    |\n\r");
  writes("    |__Read working image from a floppy\n\n\n\r");
  goxy(25,23);
  writes("CopyBuilder 386 by Al Williams");
  prompt("Press any key to continue","",SOCOLOR);
  vidrestore();
  }
```

Listing 18-5. REBOOT.C

```
/* REBOOT.C - Disable ^ALT-DEL for CodeBuilder programs
   See CB386.C
*/
#include <stdio.h>
#include <i32.h>
#include <stk.h>
#include <dos.h>
#include <conio.h>

/* Scan code for Delete */
```

```
#define DEL_SCANCODE 0x53
/* Shift status for Ctrl-Alt */
#define CTRL_ALT 0xC
/* Keyboard controller */
#define KBDATA 0x60
#define KBPORT 0x61
/* Where to send EOI command */
#define EOIPORT 0x20
/* Non-specific End of interrupt command */
#define NSEOI   0x20


/* When running DOS we replace the keyboard interrupt
   (INT 9) */

/* old INT 9 handler */
static void (*oldint9)();

#pragma interrupt(ourint9)

/* replacement interrupt handler */
static void ourint9()
  {
  int code,temp;
/* pointer to CodeBuilder stack frames */
  _XSTACK *frame=_get_stk_frame();
/* pointer to BIOS shift status byte */
  unsigned char *shift_status=(unsigned char *)0x417;
/* read keyboard */
  code=inp(KBDATA);

/* DEL is scan code 0x53 --
   if *shift_status&0xc==0xc then control and Alt are down */
  if (code!=DEL_SCANCODE||(*shift_status&CTRL_ALT)!=CTRL_ALT)
    _chain_intr(oldint9);
/* will not allow ^ALT-DEL */
/* consume key from keyboard -- these inp and outp
   statements are just like the ones you would use
   in a regular DOS program */
/* read control byte */
  temp=inp(KBPORT);
/* set bit 7 (acknowledge) and write */
```

```
  outp(KBPORT,temp|0x80);
/* write with bit 7 clear */
  outp(KBPORT,temp);
  outp(EOIPORT,NSEOI);
/* Tell CodeBuilder not to reissue interrupt */
  frame->opts=_STK_NOINT;
  return;
  }


/* This function locks the page ourint9 is on so it can't be
   swapped out. 4K is the minimum size, and surely ourint9
   isn't that big.... */
static lockint9(int flag)
  {
  static lock=0;
  if (flag!=lock)
    {
    lock=flag;
    if (flag)
      _dpmi_lockregion(ourint9,4096);
    else
      _dpmi_unlockregion(ourint9,4096);
    }
  }


/*********************** External interfaces ***************/

/* Disable ^ALT-DEL */
void noreboot()
  {
  lockint9(1);
  oldint9=_dos_getvect(9);
  _dos_setvect(9,ourint9);
  }


/* Enable ^ALT-DEL */
void okreboot()
  {
  lockint9(0);
  _dos_setvect(9,oldint9);
  }
```

Listing 18-6. DISPLAY.C

```
/* DISPLAY.C general purpose C text display library
   Originally written for Microsoft C and ported to
   Code Builder
   For CB386.C
   See also DISPLAY.H DIRPICK.C, and HISTO.C

*/
#include <stdio.h>
#include <dos.h>
#include <string.h>
#include <stdarg.h>
#include "display.h"

/* global variable sets color of output */
int color=7;

/* primary colors for color monitor (see display.h) */
int colors[4]={ 0x1e, 0x70, 0x1c, 0x7e };

/* 1=mono monitor, 0=color, -1=unknown */
int mono=-1;

/* set video mode and detect mono monitor
   this should always be called first */
void vidmode()
  {
  union REGS r;
  if (mono<0)
    {
    r.h.ah=0xf;
    int86(0x10,&r,&r);
    mono=r.h.al==7;
    }
  r.x.ax=mono?7:3;
  int86(0x10,&r,&r);
  r.x.ax=0x500;
  int86(0x10,&r,&r);
  }
```

```
/* goto point x,y (from 0-79 and 0-24) */
void goxy(int x,int y)
  {
  union REGS r;
  r.h.ah=2;
  r.h.dh=y;
  r.h.dl=x;
  r.h.bh=0;
  int86(0x10,&r,&r);
  }


/* clear screen region */
void clears(int x0, int y0,int x1,int y1)
  {
  union REGS r;
  r.x.ax=0x600;
  r.h.bh=color;
  r.h.ch=y0;
  r.h.cl=x0;
  r.h.dh=y1;
  r.h.dl=x1;
  int86(0x10,&r,&r);
  goxy(0,0);
  }

/* get x,y position */
void getxy(int *x,int *y)
  {
  union REGS r;
  r.h.ah=3;
  r.h.bh=0;
  int86(0x10,&r,&r);
  *x=r.h.dl;
  *y=r.h.dh;
  }

/* write count characters
   -- handle \r, \n, backspace, and \a
   updates the cursor if count==1 (w/o line wrap)
```

```
                otherwise, the cursor doesn't move */
void writecc(int c,int count)
  {
  union REGS r;
/* PS/2 BIOS will try to print 0 characters and hang! */
  if (count<=0) return;
/* if bell character... */
  if (c=='\a')
    {
/* use function 0eH to do count bells */
    while (count--)
      {
      r.x.ax=0xe00|'\a';
      r.x.bx=0;
      int86(0x10,&r,&r);
      }
    return;
    }
/* if regular character (not \n or \r or bs) */
  if (c!='\n'&&c!='\r'&&c!=8)
    {
/* print regular character */
    r.h.ah=9;
    r.h.al=c;
    r.h.bh=0;
    r.h.bl=color;
    r.x.cx=count;
    int86(0x10,&r,&r);
/* if count isn't 1 return else do cursor update
   NOTE: \n \r always update cursor */
    if (count!=1) return;
    }
/* get cursor position */
  r.h.ah=3;
  r.h.bh=0;
  int86(0x10,&r,&r);
/* if \r, zero x coordinate
   Note that 100 \r's is the same as 1 */
  if (c=='\r')
    r.h.dl=0;
/* if \n, increment y coordinate by count */
```

```
    else if (c=='\n')
      r.h.dh+=count;
/* if backspace back up by count or to start of line */
    else if (c==8)
      r.h.dl-=r.h.dl>count?count:r.h.dl;
    else
/* bump x coordinate. Assume it won't wrap over */
      r.h.dl++;
    r.h.ah=2;
    int86(0x10,&r,&r);
    }


/* write a string using writec, a writecc macro
   (see display.h) */
void writes(char *s)
  {
  while (*s) writec(*s++);
  }

/* printf using writecc max length 99 */
int printfc(char *fmt,...)
  {
  int rc;
  char outbuf[100];
  va_list aptr;
  va_start(aptr,fmt);
  rc=vsprintf(outbuf,fmt,aptr);
  writes(outbuf);
  return rc;
  }



/* prompt for single key @ coordinates x,y
   use str as prompt, resp is valid keys, pcolor
   is the color to use (0 for same color). Alpha characters
   in resp should be upper case. If resp is "" then all
   characters are valid. If resp is NULL then any alpha
   character is valid.

   returns:
   -1 if ESC pressed
   index of character if resp is valid
```

```
    character if resp is NULL or ""
    */
int prompt_at(int x, int y, char *str,char *resp,int pcolor)
  {
  int ocolor,c;
  char *index;
  goxy(x,y);
  ocolor=color;
  if (pcolor) color=pcolor;
/* clear to end of line */
  clreol();
  writes(str);
  while (1)
    {
/* get key */
    c=getch();
    if (!c)
      {
/* ignore extended keys */
      getch();
      continue;
      }
/* if esc quit */
    if (c==27) break;
/* shift upper */
    c=toupper(c);
/* if resp in not null, check it */
    if (resp&&(index=strchr(resp,c))) break;
/* if resp is null, check for alpha */
    if (resp==NULL&&isalpha(c)) break;
/* if resp=="" then anything is OK */
    if (resp&&!*resp) break;
    }
  color=ocolor;
  goxy(x,y);
  clreol();
  curshide();
  return c==27?-1:resp&&*resp?index-resp:c;
  }
```

```
/* prompt for input @x,y. Prompt with promptstr
   valid is a string of valid input characters
   (if NULL, all characters are OK., clr is the color
   (0 for same), len is the input length, buf is the
   buffer (should be at least len+1 long, and help is an
   optional help string (use NULL for the default help)

   returns: -1 if ESC
            # of characters input otherwise

   You can use the backspace key to edit entries */

int ask_at(int x, int y, char *promptstr,char *valid,
       int clr,int len,char *buf,char *help)
  {
  int count=0,c,ocolor=color;
  char *bp=buf;
/* clear buffer */
  memset(buf,0,len+1);
/* set color, goto input line, and clear it */
  if (clr) color=clr;
  goxy(x,y);
  clreol();
/* write prompt */
  writes(promptstr);

/* main loop */
  while (1)
    {
/* get a character. Extended keys are <0 */
    c=getch();
    if (!c) c=-getch();
/* handle backspace */
    if (c==8)
      {
      if (bp!=buf)
        {
        bp--;
        writec(8);
        writec(' ');
```

```
            writec(8);
            *bp='\0';
            count--;
            }
        continue;
        }
/* Escape or enter ends input */
    if (c=='\r'||c==27)
        {
/* restore color */
        color=ocolor;
/* clear line */
        goxy(x,y);
        clreol();
        curshide();
/* return */
        return c==27?-1:count;
        }
/* If F1 give help */
    if (c==-59)
        {
        vidsave();
        prompt(help?help:
        " Use <ENTER> to accept, <ESC> to quit, <Backspace>"
           " to correct.","",SOCOLOR);
        vidrestore();
        continue;
        }
/* ignore other extended keys (c<0) or regular keys if
   at input limit (count==len) */
    if (count==len||c<0) continue;
/* if not valid character, ignore */
    if (valid&&!strchr(valid,c)) continue;
/* echo input character */
/* update count */
    count++;
    }
  }


/**********************************************
 routines to save and restore the video context
```

```
Note: This was the big change for this module
from Microsoft C to Code Builder. The addresses
of the video buffers are different...
 */

/* places to save things */
static char vbuf[4096];
static int save_xy,save_color;

/* save video */
void vidsave()
  {
  union REGS r;
  save_color=color;
  r.h.ah=3;
  r.h.bh=0;
  int86(0x10,&r,&r);
  save_xy=r.x.dx;
/* For Microsoft, you need a far pointer B000:0000 and
   B800:0000 here... */
  memcpy((void *)vbuf,(void *)(mono?0xb0000:0xb8000),4096);
  }

/* restore video */
void vidrestore()
  {
  union REGS r;
/* For Microsoft, you need a far pointer B000:0000 and
   B800:0000 here... */
    writec(c);
/* store in buffer */
    *bp++=c;
  memcpy((void *)(mono?0xb0000:0xb8000),(void *)vbuf,4096);
  color=save_color;
  r.h.ah=2;
  r.h.bh=0;
  r.x.dx=save_xy;
  int86(0x10,&r,&r);
  }
```

Listing 18-7. HISTO.C

```c
/* HISTO.C display histograms for CB386
   Uses DISPLAY.C functions
*/
#include <stdio.h>
#include "display.h"

/* main function

First time: call histogram(-1,maximum_screen_columns);
Next time: call histogram(value,maximum_value);

Draws starting at cursor position in effect when first call
is made */

void histogram(int n,int maxm)
  {
  static nrcols;
  static int x0,y0;
  int x,y;
  int i,t;
  if (n==-1)  /* first time */
    {
    /* in this case, maxm=# of columns */
    nrcols=maxm;
    writes("Percent complete:\n\r");
    getxy(&x0,&y0);
    writecc((unsigned char)'\260',maxm);  /* empty bar */
    goxy(x0+maxm+1,y0);
    writes("100%");
    return;
    }
/* subsequent calls... save x,y */
  getxy(&x,&y);
/* restore our x,y */
  goxy(x0,y0);
/* draw bar */
  writecc((unsigned char)'\333',(n*nrcols)/maxm);
/* restore user's x,y */
  goxy(x,y);
  return;
  }
```

Listing 18-8. DIRPICK.C

```c
/* DIRPICK.C - directory pick routine
   Originally for Microsoft C -- easy port to Code Builder
   See CB386.C
*/
#include <stdio.h>
#include <dos.h>
#include <string.h>
#include <ctype.h>
#include "display.h"


/* structure to hold directory entries */
struct _dirnames
  {
  char name[13];
  unsigned short attr;
  } dirnames[5][24];

/* pointer to null string */
static char *nulls="";

/* function to print file names for dirpick */
static void pfname(int cursorx,int cursory)
    {
    writes(dirnames[cursorx][cursory].name);
    if (dirnames[cursorx][cursory].name[0]!='.'
        &&
        dirnames[cursorx][cursory].attr
            !=(unsigned short) 0xFFFF
        &&
        dirnames[cursorx][cursory].attr&_A_SUBDIR)
      writes("\\");
    }



/* Set drive safely -- returns 0 for success, 1 for error */
safe_setdrive(unsigned drive)
  {
  unsigned olddrive,maxdrive,newdrive;
  struct DOSERROR err;
```

```
/* get old drive in case */
  _dos_getdrive(&olddrive);
/* set new drive */
  _dos_setdrive(drive,&maxdrive);
/* did it take? */
  _dos_getdrive(&newdrive);
/* NO: return 1 */
  if (newdrive!=drive) return 1;
/* If, by some chance, there is a file X on the drive
   return success */
  if (!access("X",0)) return 0;
/* If not, see why not */
  dosexterr(&err);
/* If critical error... */
  if (err.exterror==83)
    {
/* reset old drive and fail */
    _dos_setdrive(olddrive,&maxdrive);
    return 1;
    }
/* No critical error -- there just isn't a file
   named X. return success */
  return 0;
  }


/* MAIN function  -- do a directory on the file spec and
   offer a menu of choices including directories and drives
   maximum of 120 files displayed at once */
char *dirpick(char *spec)
  {
/* set when recursing */
  static int recurse=0;
  int stat=0;
  unsigned nd,nrdrives;
  int x0,y0;
  char *cp,*dirpfx=spec;
  struct find_t info;
  short cursorx=0, cursory=0, x=0, y=0;
/* clear out directory structure */
  memset((void *)dirnames,0,5*24*sizeof(struct _dirnames));
/* check for drive specified */
```

```
   if (spec[1]==':')
     {
     unsigned int junk;
/* change to specified drive */
/*     _dos_setdrive(toupper(spec[0])-'A'+1,&junk);
     _dos_getdrive(&junk);
     stat=junk!=toupper(spec[0])-'A'+1; */
     stat=safe_setdrive(toupper(spec[0])-'A'+1);
     dirpfx+=2;
     }
/* see if directory specified */
  if (stat==0 && (cp=strrchr(spec,'\\')))
     {
/* make dirpfx equal to directory. If cp==dirpfx then
   change to root directory */
     *cp='\0';
     stat=chdir(cp==dirpfx?"\\":dirpfx);
     }
/* if stat is non-zero then drive or cd didn't work */
  if (stat) return NULL;
/* chop drive/directory off spec */
  spec=cp?cp+1:dirpfx;

/* find first file */
  if (stat=_dos_findfirst(*spec?spec:"*.*",
                _A_NORMAL|_A_SUBDIR,&info))
     return NULL;
/* save video if not recursive */
  if (!recurse) vidsave();
  color=TEXTCOLOR;
/* clear screen */
  cls();
/* setup psuedo-drives here */
  _dos_getdrive(&nd);
  _dos_setdrive(nd,&nrdrives);
  while (nrdrives--)
     {
     dirnames[cursorx][cursory].name[0]='[';
     dirnames[cursorx][cursory].name[1]=
            cursory*5+cursorx+'A';
     dirnames[cursorx][cursory].name[2]=']';
     dirnames[cursorx][cursory].name[3]='\0';
```

```
/* attribute =0xffff means this is a drive */
    dirnames[cursorx][cursory].attr=0xFFFF;
    goxy(x,y);
    writes(dirnames[cursorx][cursory].name);
    x+=16;
    if (++cursorx==5)
      {
      x=cursorx=0;
      cursory++;
      y++;
      }
    }
  x0=cursorx;
  y0=cursory;
/* while file names are found and screen isn't full */
  while (!stat&&cursory!=24)
    {
/* save name and attribute */
    strcpy(dirnames[cursorx][cursory].name,info.name);
    dirnames[cursorx][cursory].attr=info.attrib;
    goxy(x,y);
    x+=16;
    pfname(cursorx,cursory);
    if (++cursorx==5)
      {
      x=cursorx=0;
      cursory++;
      y++;
      }
    stat=_dos_findnext(&info);
    }
/* found all files... print help line */
  goxy(0,24);
  color=SOCOLOR;
  clreol();
  writes("Use arrows to select. Press <ENTER> to accept"
  " or <ESC> to cancel.");
  color=TEXTCOLOR;

/* place cursor on first real file (not drive) */
  cursorx=x0;
  cursory=y0;
```

```
    x=cursorx*16;
    y=cursory;

/* main loop */
    while (1)
      {
/* write file name under cursor */
      color=SOCOLOR;
      goxy(x,y);
      pfname(cursorx,cursory);
      color=TEXTCOLOR;
/* get character */
      stat=getch();
      if (stat=='\r'&&
          (dirnames[cursorx][cursory].attr&_A_SUBDIR))
        {
/* pressed enter on subdirectory  or drive */
        char *rc;
/* if drive ... */
        if (dirnames[cursorx][cursory].attr==
                  (unsigned short)0xFFFF)
          stat=safe_setdrive((unsigned)cursory*5+cursorx+1);
        else
          stat=chdir(dirnames[cursorx][cursory].name);
/* if dir/drive change was not successful */
        if (stat)
          {
          advise("\aCan't change to that directory");
          continue;
          }
/* recurse */
        recurse++;
        rc=dirpick(spec);
/* restore video */
        if (!recurse) vidrestore();
        recurse--;
/* return file picked */
        return rc;
        }
/* If escape or enter on a file */
      if (stat==27||stat=='\r')
        {
```

```
/* restore video
        if (!recurse) vidrestore();
/* return null string (ESC) or file name (ENTER) */
        return stat==27?nulls:dirnames[cursorx][cursory].name;
        }
/* if other normal key, keep going */
     if (stat) continue;
/* get extended scan code */
     stat=getch();
/* reset cursor */
     goxy(x,y);
     pfname(cursorx,cursory);
     switch (stat)
        {
/* up arrow */
case 0x48:
        if (cursory)
           {
           cursory--;
           y--;
           }
        break;

/* down arrow */
case 0x50:
        if (cursory!=23&&*dirnames[cursorx][cursory+1].name)
           {
           cursory++;
           y++;
           }
        break;

/* left */
case 0x4b:
        if (cursorx)
           {
           cursorx--;
           x-=16;
           }
        break;

/* right */
```

```
case 0x4d:
    if (cursorx!=4&&*dirnames[cursorx+1][cursory].name)
      {
      cursorx++;
      x+=16;
      }
    break;
    }
  }
}

/**********************************************************
 routines to save and restore the current working drive and
 directory
 **********************************************************/

/* saved information */
static unsigned save_drive;
static char save_cd[66];

/* save working drive/directory */
void cdsave()
  {
  _dos_getdrive(&save_drive);
  getcwd(save_cd,sizeof(save_cd));
  }

/* restore drive/directory */
void cdrestore()
  {
  unsigned junk;
  _dos_setdrive(save_drive,&junk);
  chdir(save_cd);
  }

/**********************************************************
 prompt for file name -- if file name ends with \ or : or
 contains ? or *, dirpick is called. returns 1 on success
 0 on failure.

 If user types in full name, that is passed to the program.
 If he picks name from dirpick, the current drive/directory
```

changes as the user picks them. Only the base name of the
file returns to the caller
*/
```c
int getfilen_at(int x, int y,char *fn,int len)
  {
    if (ask_at(x,y,"File: ",NULL,TEXTCOLOR,len,fn,
               " Enter a file name. Wildcards (?*) are OK."
               " Default=*.*")==-1) return 0;

/* if file contains wildcards do dirpick */
    if (*fn=='\0'||strchr(fn,'*')||strchr(fn,'?')||
        fn[strlen(fn)-1]=='\\'||fn[strlen(fn)-1]==':')
      {
      char *pick;
      pick=dirpick(fn);
      if (!pick)
        {
        advise_at(x,y,"No matching files");
        return 0;
        }
/* Escape or bad file */
      if (!*pick) return 0;
/* Fail if file name len exceeds buffer space */
      if (strlen(pick)+1>len) return 0;
      strcpy(fn,pick);
      }
    return 1;
    }
```

Listing 18-9. CB386.H
```c
/* CB386.H - include file for CopyBuilder 386
   See makefile for compile directives
*/
/* number of times to retry disk ops */
#define NRTRIES 3

/* force codebuilder to not align */
#pragma align(_bpb=1)

/* structre of disk BPB */
extern struct _bpb
```

```
  {
  unsigned char jump[3];
  char oemname[8];
  unsigned short bytespersec;
  unsigned char secperclust;
  unsigned short ressectors;
  unsigned char nrfats;
  unsigned short rootsize;
  unsigned short nrsectors;
  char media;
  unsigned short fatsectors;
  unsigned short secpertrack;
  unsigned short nrheads;
  unsigned int hiddensecs;
  unsigned int hugesectors;
  unsigned char physdrive;
  char notused;
  unsigned char signature;         /* should be 0x29 */
  unsigned int serno;
  char label[11];
  char type[8];
  char pad[512-60];                /* rest of 512 byte sector */
  } bpb;

/* various globals */
extern int driveno;
extern unsigned disksize;
extern unsigned sectorct;

/* disk image buffer */
extern unsigned char *diskbuf;
/* DOS buffer used to communicate with BIOS */
extern char *dosbuf;
extern unsigned int dosbufsiz;
/* set by critical errors */
extern int critical_err;

/* information on buffer */
extern struct _bufinfo
  {
  char title[65];
  unsigned size;
```

```
      unsigned short copies;
      char source[13];
/* checksums (stored and computed) */
      unsigned short csum, ccsum;
      short dirty;
      } bufinfo;

extern void (*slbreak)(); /* place to hook break handler */

/* holds disk format command */
extern char fmtcmd[];

/* additional break handler */
extern void (*when_break)();

/* prototypes for break handlers */
void load_break();
void save_break();

/* general prototypes */
int sector_read(int head, int track, int sector, int drive,
          unsigned char *buf,unsigned count);

int sector_write(int head, int track, int sector, int drive,
          unsigned char *buf,unsigned count);

/* disable reboot */
void noreboot(void);
void okreboot(void);
```

Listing 18-10. DISPLAY.H

```
/* DISPLAY.H header for DISPLAY.C, a text display library
   See also DISPLAY.C DIRPICK.C, and HISTO.C
*/

#ifndef DISPLAY_HEADER
#define DISPLAY_HEADER 1

/* global variables */
extern int colors[];  /* color set */
extern int color;     /* current color */
```

```
extern int mono;        /* mono monitor detected */

/* defines for color values */
#define TEXTCOLOR colors[0]    /* normal */
#define SOCOLOR colors[1]      /* stand out */
#define ERRCOLOR colors[2]     /* error color */
#define HELPCOLOR colors[3]    /* help color */

/* shortcut defines */
/* write 1 character */
#define writec(a) writecc(a,1)
/* clear entire screen */
#define cls() clears(0,0,79,24)
/* clear to end of line */
#define clreol() writecc(' ',80)
/* hide cursor */
#define curshide() goxy(255,255)
/* advisiory (error message) */
#define advise_at(x,y,msg) prompt_at(x,y,msg,"",ERRCOLOR)
/* ask_at bottom line */
#define ask(p,v,c,l,b,h) ask_at(0,24,p,v,c,l,b,h)
/* prompt_at bottom line */
#define prompt(p,r,c) prompt_at(0,24,p,r,c)
/* advisory (error) message at bottom line */
#define advise(m) advise_at(0,24,m)
/* get a file name on bottom line */
#define getfilen(f,l) getfilen_at(0,24,f,l)


/* prototypes */
/* set video mode (do this 1st) */
void vidmode(void);
/* printf using writec */
int printfc(char *fmt,...);
```

```c
/* clear screen region */
void clears(int x0, int y0,int x1,int y1);
/* goto xy */
void goxy(int x,int y);
/* get xy */
void getxy(int *x,int *y);
/* write mutliple characters (handles \a\n\r, backspace */
void writecc(int c,int count);
/* write string */
void writes(char *s);
/* prompt for a key */
int prompt_at(int x, int y, char *str,
              char *resp,int pcolor);
/* ask for input */
int ask_at(int x, int y, char *promptstr,char *valid,
      int clr,int len,char *buf,char *help);
/* save video */
void vidsave(void);
/* restore video */
void vidrestore(void);
/* get a file name w/menu pick */
int getfilen_at(int x, int y,char *fn,int len);
/* menu pick directory */
char *dirpick(char *spec);
/* save current drive/directory */
void cdsave(void);
/* restore current drive/directory */
void cdrestore(void);
/* draw histograms */
void histogram(int n,int maxm);
#endif
```

Listing 18-11. MAKEFILE for CB386

```
# Makefile for CopyBuilder 386
# If you have trouble with Intel's MAKE running other
# programs in some DPMI environments, try another make
# or do this:
#
# MAKE -n >script.bat
# Then edit script.bat to remark out the copyright info and
# execute the script batch file

CC=icc
CCOPTS=/c /g
LD=icc
LDOPTS=/g

cb386.exe : cb386.obj disp.obj histo.obj fileio.obj
display.obj\
        dirpick.obj diskio.obj reboot.obj
     $(LD) $(LDOPTS) cb386.obj disp.obj histo.obj
fileio.obj\
        display.obj dirpick.obj diskio.obj reboot.obj

cb386.obj : cb386.c cb386.h display.h
     $(CC) $(CCOPTS) cb386.c

disp.obj : disp.c cb386.h display.h
     $(CC) $(CCOPTS) disp.c

histo.obj : histo.c cb386.h display.h
     $(CC) $(CCOPTS) histo.c

fileio.obj : fileio.c cb386.h display.h
     $(CC) $(CCOPTS) fileio.c
```

```
diskio.obj : diskio.c cb386.h display.h
        $(CC) $(CCOPTS) diskio.c

display.obj : display.c display.h
        $(CC) $(CCOPTS) display.c

dirpick.obj : dirpick.c display.h
        $(CC) $(CCOPTS) dirpick.c
reboot.obj : reboot.c
        $(CC) $(CCOPTS) reboot.c
```

CHAPTER ■ 19

Windows, DOS, and You

While Windows lets you run DOS programs ("old apps," in Microsoft parlance), it allows very little interaction with them. DOS programs can use the clipboard (either programatically or via the print screen key), but little else. Each DOS box is a world unto itself.

Windows users often wish that DOS boxes were less isolated. For example, it would be helpful to run Windows programs directly from the DOS prompt. Constructing batch files that can tailor your Windows' environment is also an enticing prospect. Even launching other DOS programs (like MAKE or FORMAT) in another DOS box is not normally possible from a DOS box.

As a software developer, you may need to communicate with real-mode programs from Windows. You also may want DOS to have access to Windows programs or API calls. The Windows SDK documentation gives no clue about how this might be possible.

If you review the DPMI specification, you will notice that Windows programs can use DPMI to capture and generate real-mode interrupts. Obviously, DPMI is the key to communications between Windows and DOS programs. Actually, it is one key—you could use virtual device drivers (VxDs) to do the same thing. However, DPMI is more accessible to most Windows programmers.

A First Try

Since DPMI allows Windows programs to intercept real-mode interrupts, a common-sense (but incorrect) solution presents itself. Simply intercept an interrupt vector and provide an API for DOS programs to call your Windows code.

This simple approach will not work. Enhanced-mode Windows uses a preemptive task switcher. All Windows programs run in a single task (virtual machine). Each DOS box runs in a separate task. Figure 19-1 shows the conceptual layout. Each task can access the DOS context (drivers, TSRs, DOS services, etc.) in force when Windows started. Any change a program makes to the Windows context is only in effect for its private task.

Figure 19-1. Windows Execution Context

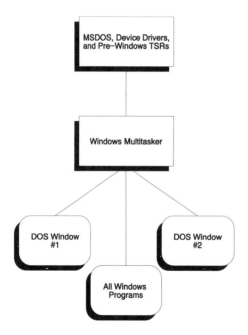

The Windows task switcher isolates each task from the other, but all tasks share most of the common pre-Windows DOS context. This is a key to inter-task communications.

The Right Stuff

To communicate between tasks, you need a program with multiple personalities—one portion runs before Windows (in the original DOS context), and the others run in individual Windows virtual machines. This is similar to the client/server architecture found in modern network systems where a server provides services for one or more clients. In a typical client/server system, each client and the server reside on different physical machines. For inter-task communications, the clients and their server reside in different tasks (or virtual machines).

You can create a server that will provide a variety of communication services between Windows virtual machines. In this chapter, you will see a DOS/Windows server that provides services for DOS tasks. Part of the server runs before Windows. When Windows starts, the remaining portion of the server executes. The server provides an API that allows DOS programs to call WinExec() to start new programs. Table 19-1 shows the commands the system accepts.

Although two separate programs comprise the server, they are logically one entity. It would be convenient to package both halves of the server in one executable. Thanks to the format of Windows .EXE file (the NE format) this is relatively simple to do.

The WINX Server

The WINX server is just such a split-personality server. WINX.EXE contains both a Windows program (WINX.C, Listing 19-1) and a separate DOS program (WINXDOS.C, listing 19-2). The WINXDOS portion is the stub program (see Chapter 12). The default stub program just prints, "This program requires Microsoft Windows" when you attempt to run a Windows program from DOS. However, WINX replaces this stub with the DOS communications server (via the STUB command in WINX.DEF, Listing 19-3). When you run WINX.EXE from DOS the server starts and executes Windows. From inside Windows, the WINX Windows server runs.

The DOS server installs an interrupt 0x2F ISR and starts Windows. The ISR manages a buffer in DOS memory and services both the Windows server and the DOS client programs.

The ISR responds to several commands (see Table 19-1). The Windows server first calls function 1 (using DPMI function 0x0300) to learn the address of the DOS server's buffer. Each time the Windows server receives a WM_TIMER message (roughly twice a second), it checks the DOS server's buffer for a command (a number from 2 to 0xFF in the first byte of the buffer). When it finds a command, the Windows server acts on it and leaves a 1 in the buffer's first byte. Bytes 2 through 5 of the buffer's data field will contain a return code from the command. When the DOS portion has a command pending, it waits for a 1 in the command field. When it detects the 1, it reads the return value from the buffer and resets the command to zero.

When a client calls the interrupt 0x2F API, it is possible that the buffer will be busy processing another task's request. Then the DOS portion of the server returns 0xFFFF in the AX register. This signals the client that it should try again later. If the server returns 0, it accepted the command—the return value is in the BX and CX registers.

Table 19-1. WINX Server Commands

Interrupt 0x2F Function 0xF2 Commands

Command	Function
0	Install check (AL=0xFF if installed)
1	Return address of server buffer in BX:CX
2	Set server's working directory (pointer to string in BX:CX)
3	Execute command (pointer to string in BX:CX)

Command Buffer Commands

Command	Function
0	Buffer available
1	Buffer contains result
2	Change directory
3	Execute program
0xFF	Terminate Windows portion of server

Using the Server

The Windows server only recognizes three commands, but you can easily add more. With some work, you can even interpret arbitrary API calls using

GetProcAddress(). Of course, you will need to parse arguments and push them on the stack correctly, too.

WINX is mildly inconvenient since you must start Windows with the WINX command (instead of WIN). However, you could easily convert the DOS portion of WINX to a TSR program (see the bibliography for more details on TSRs). Then the TSR would load once, probably in the AUTOEXEC.BAT file.

You also must make sure Windows loads WINX. You can easily add WINX to the LOAD= line of WIN.INI. If you use Windows 3.1 or Norton Desktop for Windows, you can add WINX to the startup group instead of modifying WIN.INI.

Using WINRUN and RUNSTUB

Once the server is running, any program can call the interrupt 0x2F API. Listing 19-4 contains WINRUN.C, a real-mode DOS program that uses the WINX API. You can use this file to create both WINRUN.EXE and RUNSTUB.EXE. WINRUN.EXE will start a Windows program (or a DOS program in its own DOS box) from a DOS box command line. Like WinExec(), WINRUN assumes the program is a .EXE file. If you need to run a different type of program (.COM, .PIF, etc.) you must explicitly supply the extension.

When using WINRUN, remember that the WinExec() call is running in the server's task, not the DOS box. Each task has its own context that includes the current directory and the environment. To help prevent confusion, WINRUN automatically forces the server to change directories before it calls WinExec(). However, changes you make in the environment (most notably, the PATH variable) will not affect the server. The server searches for files on the path in its environment, not the client's. Of course, you could add a command to set the server's PATH variable very easily.

RUNSTUB.EXE is a replacement for the default Windows stub program. By inserting this stub in your Windows programs, you can run them from Windows or a Windows DOS box when the WINX server is active. Just change the STUB line in your program's .DEF file to:

```
STUB 'RUNSTUB.EXE'
```

When you run a program that uses RUNSTUB from a DOS box it won't print "This program requires Microsoft Windows." Instead, providing the WINX server is active, it will execute.

The MAKEFILE (Listing 19-5) creates all of the WINX software. Be sure to select the correct constants for your compiler.

You can create aliases with Microsoft's DOSKEY program (for MSDOS 5.0) or JP Software's 4DOS that simplify executing Windows programs from the command line: For example (DOSKEY):

```
doskey sol=winrun sol
```

or (4DOS):

```
alias sol=winrun sol
```

You also can use aliases to make sure you use WINX instead of WIN to start Windows. For example:

```
doskey win=winx
```

WINRUN works from within batch files. You can create batch files that start up your favorite Windows and DOS programs together. If you directly use WINRUN from a full screen DOS window, you may notice that the DOS screen becomes corrupt when you switch back in to it. This is harmless—if it bothers you, start WINRUN from a DOS Window instead of a full screen. Borland's Turbo Debugger for Windows (TDW), which uses an unusual method of managing the screen, may become confused (or lock up Windows) when you start it from a full screen Window. TDW works with WINRUN if you don't use a full screen DOS Windows.

Other Options

The technique WINX uses to communicate between tasks isn't the only possible method. Since Windows allows DOS boxes to use the clipboard, you can use clipboard text to accomplish the same feat. (See the bibliography for an article that explains how to do this.) You can also use VxDs to create shared buffers similar to WINX's (Microsoft C 7.0 includes the WX server which uses this approach).

Conclusion

As you can see by examining WINX, there is more to the Windows programming interface than the standard API. DPMI is one of the buried Windows interfaces that you need to create many Windows programs.

Although WINX only launches programs, you could easily modify it to provide other services. For example, you could add a command that would allow a DOS program to learn the size of its window. A more ambitious addition would allow DOS programs to access Dynamic Data Exchange (DDE) servers. This would allow your DOS programs to read data directly from applications like Word and Excel.

Many programmers associate protected-mode programming with large amounts of memory. However, protected-mode techniques, like the ones WINX uses, are often the key to interacting with today's modern operating systems and environments.

Listing 19-1. WINX.C

```
/* Windows portion of WINX server
   See Makefile for compile instructions
*/

#include <windows.h>
#include <dos.h>
#include <ctype.h>
#include <string.h>
#ifdef __BORLANDC__
#include <dir.h>
#else
#include <direct.h>
#endif

/* MUX interrupt signature + command */
```

```
#define SIG(n) (0xF200|(n))

/* pointer to DOS buffer */
unsigned char _far *buffer;
/* local buffer */
char nbuffer[512];


/* DPMI register structure */
struct realregs
        {
        unsigned long EDI,ESI,EBP,reserved,
                EBX,EDX,ECX,EAX;
        unsigned short flags,ES,DS,FS,GS,
                IP,CS,SP,SS;
        };
/* DPMI real interrupt */
realint86(int intno,struct realregs *r)
  {
  union REGS pr;
  struct SREGS s;
  void _far *rp=(void _far *)r;
  segread(&s);
/* DPMI real interrupt function */
  pr.x.ax=0x300;
  pr.x.bx=intno;
  pr.x.cx=0;
  s.es=FP_SEG(rp);
  pr.x.di=FP_OFF(rp);
/* ask for default stack */
  r->SS=0;
  r->SP=0;
/* set flags to something appropriate */
  r->flags=0;
  int86x(0x31,&pr,&pr,&s);
  return pr.x.cflag;
  }


void _far *map_linear(unsigned long base,unsigned long limit)
  {
```

```
   union REGS r1;
   void _far *rv;
/* Get a descriptor (function 0) */
  r1.x.ax=0;
  r1.x.cx=1;
  int86(0x31,&r1,&r1);
  if (r1.x.cflag) ;
/* Set base address (function 7) */
  r1.x.bx=r1.x.ax;
  r1.x.ax=7;
  r1.x.cx=(base&0xF0000)>>16;
  r1.x.dx=base&0xFFFF;
  int86(0x31,&r1,&r1);
/* Set limit (function 8) */
  r1.x.ax=8;
  r1.x.cx=(limit&0xFFFF0000L)>>16;
  r1.x.dx=limit&0xFFFF;
  int86(0x31,&r1,&r1);
/* construct pointer */
  FP_SEG(rv)=r1.x.bx;
  FP_OFF(rv)=0;
  return rv;
  }


int  PASCAL WinMain(HANDLE Inst,HANDLE Prev,
                    LPSTR cmdline,int show)
  {
  char *cmd;
  struct realregs r;
  unsigned long base;
  WORD timer;
  MSG msg;
/* Only one server at a time, please */
  if (Prev)
    {
    MessageBox(NULL,"WINX Server already running!",
             "Error",MB_OK|MB_ICONSTOP);
    return 0;
    }
/* check for WINX */
  r.EAX=SIG(0);
```

```
   realint86(0x2f,&r);
   if ((r.EAX&0xFF)!=0xFF)
     {
     MessageBox(NULL,"WINX not loaded!",
            "Error",MB_OK|MB_ICONSTOP);
     return 0;
     }
/* Get buffer address */
   r.EAX=SIG(1);
   realint86(0x2f,&r);
   base=((r.EBX&0xFFFF)<<4)+(r.ECX&0xFFFF);
/* Convert buffer to PM pointer */
   buffer=map_linear(base,512);
   *buffer='\0';      /* buffer is ready */
/* Wait around in 1/4 second intervals */
   timer=SetTimer(NULL,1,250,NULL);
/* if *buffer==0xFF then time to go */

/* This program has no visible window. It has a
   normal message loop (here). Instead of dispatching
   messages to a window, it just processes timer
   and termination messages directly */
   while (*buffer!=0xFF&&GetMessage(&msg,NULL,0,0))
     {
     char _far *s;
     char *d;
     unsigned long rv;
/* only respond to timer messages */
     if (msg.message!=WM_TIMER) continue;
/* No activity in buffer .... */
     if (!*buffer) continue;
/* Something is there! */
     d=nbuffer;
     s=buffer+1;
/* copy to local buffer */
     while (*d++=*s++);
/* Is it command 2 (set working directory)? */
     if (*buffer==2)
       {
       unsigned int dummy;
/* Set drive too if specified */
       if (nbuffer[1]==':')
```

```
        _dos_setdrive(toupper(nbuffer[0])-'A'+1,&dummy);
      rv=chdir(nbuffer);
      }
/* Command 3 is WinExec */
    if (*buffer==3) rv=WinExec(nbuffer,1);
/* Command FF is abort server */
    if (*buffer==0xFF) rv=0;
/* store return value */
    *(unsigned long _far *)(buffer+1)=rv;
/* signal other side that task is complete */
    *buffer='\001';
    }

/* When command==0xFF come here to clean up */
  KillTimer(NULL,timer);
  return 0;
  }
```

Listing 19-2. WINXDOS.C

```
/* DOS portion of WINX server
   see MAKEFILE for details */
#include <stdio.h>
#include <stdlib.h>
#include <dos.h>
#include <process.h>

/* MUX interrupt signal */
#define SIG 0xF200

#define RT unsigned short
#ifdef __BORLANDC__
#define INTREGS RT Rbp, RT Rdi, RT Rsi, RT Rds, \
                RT Res, RT Rdx, RT Rcx, RT Rbx, \
                RT Rax, RT Rip, RT Rcs, RT Rfl

unsigned _stklen=1024;
unsigned _heaplen=1024;
#else
#define INTREGS RT Res,RT Rds,RT Rdi,RT Rsi, \
                RT Rbp,RT Rsp,RT Rbx,RT Rdx, \
```

```
                    RT Rcx,RT Rax,RT Rip,RT Rcs,RT Rfl
#endif

void (_interrupt _far *old2f)();
char buffer[512];

/* MUX interrupt handler */
void _far _interrupt new2f(INTREGS)
  {
/* If not SIG then this isn't for us */
  if ((Rax&0xFF00)!=SIG) _chain_intr(old2f);
/* process command */
  switch (Rax&0xFF)
    {
/* Install check */
    case 0:
      Rax=0xFF;
      return;

/* Get address */
    case 1:
      {
      char _far *b=(char _far *)buffer;
      Rbx=FP_SEG(b);
      Rcx=FP_OFF(b);
      return;
      }

/* Send string to Windows portion */
    case 2:    /* Change drive/directory */
    case 3:    /* Call WINEXEC */
    if (!*buffer)
      {
      char _far *s;
      char _far *d=buffer+1;
      unsigned timeout=0x8000;
      FP_SEG(s)=Rbx;
      FP_OFF(s)=Rcx;
      while (*d++=*s++);
      *buffer=Rax&0xFF;
      _enable();
      while (*buffer!=1&&timeout--)
```

```
            {
/* tell Windows we are idle -- calling INT 2F with AX=1680
   gives Windows a chance to do something else before returning
   to us. */
        union REGS r;
        r.x.ax=0x1680;
        int86(0x2F,&r,&r);
        }
/* Mark success */
        Rax=(*buffer==1)?0:0xFFFF;
        Rbx=*(unsigned short *)(buffer+1);
        Rcx=*(unsigned short *)(buffer+3);
        *buffer=0;
        return;
        }
    else
      Rax=0xFFFF;
    return;

    default:
    Rfl|=1;
    return;
    }
  }


void main(int argc,char *argv[])
  {
  union REGS r;
  int stat;
  r.x.ax=SIG;
  int86(0x2f,&r,&r);
  if (r.h.al==0xFF)
    {
    puts(
    "WINX already active or multiplex interrupt in use.\n");
    exit(1);
    }
/* Check for Windows 3.0 in real or std mode */
  r.x.ax=0x4680;
  int86(0x2f,&r,&r);
```

```
  stat=r.x.ax;
/* Check for enhanced mode (al!=0 and al!=0x80 if true) */
  r.x.ax=0x1600;
  int86(0x2f,&r,&r);
  if (r.h.al!=0&&r.h.al!=0x80&&stat!=0)
    {
    puts("Can't start WINX from a Windows DOS box.\n");
    exit(1);
    }
  old2f=_dos_getvect(0x2f);
  _dos_setvect(0x2f,new2f);
/* Set environment to contain WINX=YES */
  putenv("WINX=YES");
  if (spawnlp(P_WAIT,"win","win",NULL)==-1)
    puts("Couldn't execute Microsoft Windows\n");
  _dos_setvect(0x2f,old2f);
  exit(0);
  }
```

Listing 19-3. WINX.DEF

```
Name          WINX
Description   'DOS/WINDOWS COMMUNICATIONS SHELL'
Exetype       WINDOWS
Code          PRELOAD MOVEABLE DISCARDABLE
Data          PRELOAD MOVEABLE SINGLE
Heapsize      256
Stacksize     5120
Stub          'WINXDOS.EXE'
```

Listing 19-4. WINRUN.C

```
#include <stdio.h>
#include <string.h>
#include <dos.h>
#include <ctype.h>
#ifdef __BORLANDC__
#include <dir.h>
#else
#include <direct.h>
```

```
#include <stdlib.h>   /* Microsoft _psp */
#endif
#include <process.h>

#define SIG(x) (0xF200|(x))

/* To make this a stub program define WINRUN_STUB */

char cmd[129];

void help(void);
void timedout(void);


void main(int argc,char *argv[])
  {
  union REGS r;
  char _far *p=cmd;
  unsigned timeout=0xFFFF;
/* Check for WINX server */
  r.x.ax=SIG(0);
  int86(0x2f,&r,&r);
  if (r.h.al==0)
    {
    printf("Error: WINX or Windows not loaded\n");
    exit(2);
    }
/* Set current directory */
  getcwd(cmd,sizeof(cmd));
  while (timeout--)
    {
/* Send to server */
    r.x.ax=SIG(2);
    r.x.bx=FP_SEG(p);
    r.x.cx=FP_OFF(p);
    int86(0x2f,&r,&r);
    if (r.x.ax!=0xFFFF) break;
    }
  if (r.x.ax==0xFFFF)
    timedout();

  timeout=0xFFFF;
```

```
#ifdef WINRUN_STUB
  strcpy(cmd,argv[0]);
  strcat(cmd," ");
#else
  if (argc==1) help();
#endif
  if (argc!=1)
    {
    int count;
    unsigned char _far *cmdline;
#ifdef WINRUN_STUB
    unsigned char *d=cmd+strlen(cmd);
#else
    unsigned char *d=cmd;
#endif
/* get program name and command line */
    FP_SEG(cmdline)=_psp;
    FP_OFF(cmdline)=0x80;
    count=*cmdline++;
    while (isspace(*cmdline))
      {
      cmdline++;
      if (!count) break;
      }
    while (--count) *d++=*cmdline++;
    *d='\0';
    }
/* Send to server */
  while (timeout--)
    {
    r.x.ax=SIG(3);
    r.x.bx=FP_SEG(p);
    r.x.cx=FP_OFF(p);
    int86(0x2f,&r,&r);
    if (r.x.ax!=0xFFFF) break;
    }
  if (r.x.ax==0xFFFF) timedout();
  if (r.x.bx<32)
    {
    printf("Can't execute (error %d).\n",r.x.bx);
    r.x.bx++;
    }
```

```
  else r.x.bx=0;
  exit(r.x.bx);
  }

void timedout()
  {
  printf("WINX server is busy");
  exit(3);
  }


#ifndef WINRUN_STUB
void help()
  {
  printf("Usage: WINRUN program [arguments...]\n");
  exit(1);
  }
#endif
```

Listing 19-5. Makefile for WINX

```
# Makefile for WINX and WINRUN
# Use Borland MAKE or MICROSOFT NMAKE
# !!! Be sure to set the right variable below
# depending on your compiler


BORLAND=0
MICROSOFT=1

!if $(BORLAND)
CC=bcc
CCOPT=-2 -c -w-par -w-pia
WCCOPT=-2 -W -v -c -w-par -w-pia
LD=bcc
LDOPT=
WLDOPT=-W -v
OBJOPT=-o
!endif

!if $(MICROSOFT)
CC=cl
CCOPT=-G2 -c
```

```
WCCOPT=-G2 -GA -Zp -c
LD=cl
LDOPT=-G2 -F 0800
WLDOPT=-G2 -GA -Zp
OBJOPT=-Fo
!endif


all : winrun.exe runstub.exe winxdos.exe winx.exe


winrun.exe : winrun.obj
          $(LD) $(LDOPT) winrun.obj

runstub.exe : runstub.obj
          $(LD) $(LDOPT) runstub.obj

!if $(MICROSOFT)
# Makefile for WINX and WINRUN
# Use Borland MAKE or MICROSOFT NMAKE
# !!! Be sure to set the right variable below
# depending on your compiler


BORLAND=0
MICROSOFT=1

!if $(BORLAND)
CC=bcc
CCOPT=-2 -c -w-par -w-pia
WCCOPT=-2 -W -v -c -w-par -w-pia
LD=bcc
LDOPT=
WLDOPT=-W -v
OBJOPT=-o
!endif

!if $(MICROSOFT)
CC=cl
CCOPT=-G2 -c
WCCOPT=-G2 -GA -Zp -c
LD=cl
```

```
LDOPT=-G2 -F 0800
WLDOPT=-G2 -GA -Zp
OBJOPT=-Fo
!endif


all : winrun.exe runstub.exe winxdos.exe winx.exe


winrun.exe : winrun.obj
        $(LD) $(LDOPT) winrun.obj

runstub.exe : runstub.obj
         $(LD) $(LDOPT) runstub.obj

!if $(MICROSOFT)
mscint.obj : mscint.c
        $(CC) $(WCCOPT) mscint.c

winx.exe : winx.obj mscint.obj winxdos.exe
         $(LD) $(WLDOPT) winx.obj mscint.obj winx.def
!else
winx.exe : winx.obj winxdos.exe
         $(LD) $(WLDOPT) winx.obj
!endif

winxdos.exe : winxdos.obj
        $(LD) $(LDOPT) winxdos.obj

winxdos.obj : winxdos.c
        $(CC) $(CCOPT) winxdos.c

winx.obj : winx.c
         $(CC) $(WCCOPT) winx.c

winrun.obj : winrun.c
        $(CC) $(CCOPT) winrun.c

runstub.obj : winrun.c
      $(CC) $(CCOPT) $(OBJOPT)runstub.obj \
      -DWINRUN_STUB winrun.c
```

A P P E N D I X ▪ A

Glossary

386 Enhanced Mode An operating mode for Microsoft Windows. In this mode, Windows requires a 386 or 486 CPU and takes advantage of Extended Memory and other 386/486 protected-mode features. Unlike Standard Mode, 386 enhanced mode provides Virtual Memory, multiple Virtual Machines for DOS programs, and other sophisticated features. *See also*, Standard Mode.

A20 The twentieth address line on a 286, 386, or 486 PC. This address line controls access to memory above the 1 megabyte line. For compatibilty, Motherboards can disable this line to emulate the way the 8088 computes addresses above 1 megabyte.

ANSI American National Standards Institute.

API Applications Programming Interface. When a program, like Microsoft Windows, defines calls that other programs can use, the calls are known as the API (e.g., Windows API).

Binding The process of storing data in the same file as a program. For example, you bind Microsoft Windows resources to the executable program that uses them.

BIOS Basic Input Output System. All PCs have a ROM BIOS that controls basic I/O operations (keyboard, video, disk, etc.). The BIOS provides an API that DOS and other programs can use.

Callback An address a real-mode program can call to effect a transfer to a protected-mode subroutine.

CGA Color Graphics Adapter.

CMOS RAM   The non-volatile RAM that most PCs use to store important configuration information.

COM Port   A serial communications I/O port (usually, but not always, an RS232 port).

Conventional Memory   Memory accessible to real-mode DOS programs. That is, the memory up to 640K.

Coprocessor   An auxiliary CPU that cooperates with the main CPU to perform specialized processing. The most common coprocessors perform floating point calculations, for example.

CPL   Current Privilege level. The privilege level (from 0 to 3) associated with a protected-mode program. When a program accesses a segment, the processor uses CPL or the selector's RPL (whichever is larger) as the effective privlilege level (EPL). The EPL must be less than or equal to the segment's DPL for the access to succeed.

CPU   Central Processing Unit.

Critical Error   A DOS error that occurs when a hardware problem occurs. For example, attempting to read a file from an empty disk drive (or from a defective disk) will cause a critical error. Other critical errors occur when the printer is out of paper, or a device fails to respond within a reasonable time.

Descriptor   The definition of a protected mode segment. The definition includes the segment's base address, the limit, and other important attributes. There are three descriptor tables: the GDT, the LDT, and the IDT. Segment registers contain selectors that serve as an index into one of these tables.

Descriptor Table   An array of descriptors. There are three descriptor tables: the GDT, the LDT, and the IDT. Segment registers contain selectors that serve as an index into one of these tables.

DLL   *See* Dynamic Link Library.

DMA   Direct memory access. This is a method for high-speed I/O devices to directly transfer data to and from main memory (*see also* VDS).

DOS   MS-DOS (from Microsoft) or PC-DOS (the IBM version of MSDOS).

DOS Extender   A miniature operating system that allows you to create programs that are similar to conventional DOS programs (they can run under DOS, use interrupt 0x21, etc.). Unlike conventional DOS programs, extended programs can use special protected-mode features (access to extended memory, multitasking, etc.).

DOS Protected-Mode Interface (DPMI)   A protocol that allows protected-mode programs to cooperate. One program, the host (or server), provides an API for other programs (clients) to use. This API allows clients to switch to protected mode, allocate memory, etc. *See also*, VCPI.

DPL   Descriptor privilege level. The privilege level associated with a segment Descriptor. *Also see* CPL.

DPMI *See* DOS Protected-Mode Interface.

Dynamic Link Library A library that programs load at run time, as opposed to link time. Microsoft Windows uses DLLs extensively, as do several DOS extenders.

Easy-OMF A common object file format used for 32-bit programs.

EGA Enhanced Graphics Adapter.

EMS *See* Expanded Memory Specification

Enhanced Mode *See* 386 Enhanced Mode.

EPL Effective Protection Level. (*See* CPL).

Expanded Memory Additional memory available under the Expanded Memory Specification. A driver allows access to expanded memory by mapping 16K pages

Expanded Memory Specification (EMS) A standard API that provides Expanded Memory.

Extended Memory Memory above 1M. This memory is not directly accessible by conventional DOS programs. However, there are several ways to indirectly access extended memory. Chief among these methods is via Extended Memory Specification (XMS) drivers.

Extended Memory Specification (XMS) A standard API that allows programs to use an XMS driver to access Extended Memory.

Far Pointer A pointer that consists of a 16-bit segment (in real mode) or a 16-bit selector (in protected mode), joined with an offset (16-bits in real mode, 16- or 32-bits in protected mode). The compiler treats the two parts separately—arithmetic overflow (or underflow) in the offset does not affect the segment portion (contrast with Huge Pointer).

FCB File Control Block. Obsolete DOS data structure that manipulates files.

Flat Memory Model A method of constructing 32-bit programs that circumvent segmentation. The program uses a single, large segment for both code and data. Of course, the program must have two selectors (a code selector and a data selector), but they both refer to the same segment.

GDT Global Descriptor Table. (*See* Descriptor Table.)

Gigabyte 1,024 Megabytes.

GP Fault General Protection Fault (interrupt 13). A catch-all error raised by the processor to signal a variety of errors in protected mode.

GUI Graphical User Interface.

High Memory Area (HMA) A small region (64K-16 bytes) of extended memory that DOS programs can access with some hardware tricks. Most XMS drivers provide simplified access to the HMA.

HMA *See* High Memory Area.

Huge Pointer A 32-bit pointer that consists of a 16-bit segment (in real mode) or a 16-bit selector (in protected mode), joined with a 16-bit offset. The compiler understands how the two parts relate—arithmetic overflow (or underflow) in the offset causes the segment (or selector) portion to change accordingly (contrast with Far Pointer).

I/O Input/Output.

ICA *See* Interprocess Communications Area.

IDT Interrupt Descriptor Table.

Interprocess Communications Area A 16-byte region of memory at address 0x500 (0050:0000 in real mode). PC programs can use this area to store data that programs need to share.

Interrupt A hardware or software event that causes the CPU to execute a special type of subroutine (an ISR). When the ISR completes, execution resumes where it was interrupted.

Interrupt Vector The address of an ISR. When an interrupt occurs, its interrupt vector determines the address of the associated ISR.

IOPL I/O Privilege Level. The minimum required privilege to perform certain I/O instructions.

ISR Interrupt Service Routine.

LDT Local Descriptor Table. (*See* Descriptor Table.)

LE Linear Executable. A file format that supports linear protected-mode programs. Used by OS/2 and Windows virtual device drivers.

Linear Address A non-segmented address the CPU forms from a logical address. The processor adds the offset to the base address of the segment to form the linear address. The MMU, if active, will further convert this to a physical address. If the MMU is not active, linear addresses and physical addresses are equivalent.

Logical Address An address that consists of a segment selector and an offset. The CPU converts logical addresses to linear addresses.

Logo A graphics language developed by MIT.

LRU Least Recently Used. Virtual Memory systems move blocks of memory that are LRU out of real memory and into a Swap File.

MCB Memory Control Block. A data structure used by DOS to manage memory below 1 megabyte.

Memory Model The method a program uses to manage segmentation. For example, small model programs have a single code segment and a single data segment. Large model programs may use multiple code and data segments.

MMU Memory Management Unit. (*See* Linear Address.)

NE files New Executable. A file format that supports Windows and other protected-mode programs.

Near Pointer A pointer that contains only an offset (16- or 32- bit). The segment is implied by the pointer's use. For example, a near pointer to a function will automatically use the default code segment. A near pointer to a string will automatically use the default data segment.

NMI Non-maskable interrupt. The CPU can not disable this interrupt, although special hardware in the PC can.

Overlay A method to make more memory available to conventional DOS programs. Selected functions reside on disk. When the program uses a function that is not in memory, the overlay manager will load the function possibly removing other functions from memory.

Page Directory A list of Page Tables that the MMU uses to convert addresses (*see* Page Table).

Page Fault A special interrupt that the MMU generates when a program attempts to access a page of memory that is not present.

Page Table A table in memory that tells the MMU how to convert a Linear Address to a Physical Address. The Page Directory points to multiple page tables, each responsible for a certain range of Linear Addresses.

PDE Page Directory Entry. (*See* Page Directory.)

Physical Address A non-segmented address that corresponds to an actual physical memory location. The MMU, if active, generates physical addresses from linear addresses. If the MMU is not active, linear addresses and physical addresses are equivalent.

PL Privilege Level.

Protected Mode An operating mode present in 286, 386, and 486 processors. In this mode, the CPU can access Extended Memory, support multitasking, and virtualize memory and devices. Contrast with Real Mode.

Profiler A program that monitors the execution of programs. The profiler gathers performance statistics about the subject program. For example, a profiler can report the amount of time spent executing each function in a program.

PSP Program Segment Prefix. Microsoft often calls the PSP the Program Data Base (PDB).

PTE Page Table Entry.

RAM Random Access Memory.

Real Mode An operating mode present in 286, 386, and 486 processors. This mode causes the CPU to operate like an 8088 or 8086 CPU. DOS and DOS programs can only run in real mode. Contrast with Protected Mode.

Resources   Data used by Microsoft Windows programs. Menus, dialogs, bitmaps, and cursors are examples of resources. Also see binding.

ROM   Read only memory. ROM is preprogrammed and is difficult or impossible to modify. It is also non-volatile.

RPL   Requestor Privilege Level. *See also* CPL.

SCSI   Small Computer Systems Interface. A common interface for high-performance devices (i.e., disk drives, tape drives, etc.).

SDK   Software Development Kit.

Secondary Storage   Memory that is not directly accessible by the CPU. For example, disk drives are secondary storage.

Selector   The segment portion of a protected-mode pointer. Unlike a real-mode segment, a selector's value does not correspond to its memory location. Instead, it is an index into one of the descriptor tables (the GDT, or LDT).

Standard Mode   An operating mode for Microsoft Windows. In this mode, Windows requires a 286, 386 or 486 CPU and takes advantage of extended memory and 16-bit protected-mode features. *See also*, 386 Enhanced Mode.

Stub   A real-mode program you can store with a protected-mode program. If you attempt to run the protected-mode program from DOS, the stub program runs instead. Some stubs simply print an error message. More sophisticated stubs load the appropriate protected-mode environment.

Swap File   A file on a secondary storage device used to provide virtual memory. Memory that resides in the swap file is "swapped out" or "paged out."

Terminate Stay Resident (TSR)   A DOS program that remains in memory after it returns control to the operating system. Some stimulus (usually a hot key, or an interrupt) will cause the TSR to execute. The DOS print spooler (PRINT.EXE) and Borland's SideKick are both TSR programs.

TI   Table Indicator. A bit in each segment selector. When this bit is a 0, the selector refers to a Descriptor in the GDT. If the bit is 1, the Descriptor is in the LDT.

TSR   *See* Terminate Stay Resident.

TSS   Task State Segment.

UAE   Unrecoverable Application Error. An all-purpose error that Windows raises for many different errors. Often, a UAE corresponds to a GP Fault.

UMB   *See* Upper Memory Block.

Upper Memory Block (UMB)   A block of memory between 640K and 1M that DOS programs can access. Typically, users load TSRs and device drivers in UMBs to make more contiguous memory below 640K avaliable.

V86 Mode   *See* Virtual 86 Mode.

VCPI   *See* Virtual Control Program Interface.

VDS   Virtual DMA Specification. An API that DMA programs can use to coordinate memory accesses with the MMU.

VGA   Video Gate Array.

Virtual 86 Mode   A 386/486 mode that allows a program to operate in an environment that is similar to Real Mode. This allows protected-mode operating systems (like Microsoft Windows) to execute older software (like DOS) directly. DOS and the DOS program executes in a separate virtual machine with the same constraints as a Real-Mode program (1 megabyte memory limit, etc.).

Virtual Control Program Interface   A protocol that allows protected-mode programs to cooperate. One program, the host (or server), provides an API for other programs (clients) to use. This API allows clients to allocate memory, etc. *See also*, DPMI.

Virtual Machine   Protected-Mode systems can run multiple programs in a way that each runs unaware of each other or the underlying operating system. In this case, each program is said to run in its own virtual machine.

Virtual Memory   A technique for using memory in secondary storage to transparently simulate main memory.

VM   Virtual memory (in other books this may sometimes mean virtual machine).

VxD   Virtual device driver. Device drivers used by Windows in 386 Enhanced Mode. These drivers are true 32-bit programs that are privileged and can access all memory.

XMS   *See* Extended Memory Specification.

APPENDIX ▪ B

DOS Protected-Mode Interface (DPMI)

This Appendix contains a summary of the most useful DPMI functions. For a complete list, you can obtain the DPMI Specification (version 1.0: document 240977-001; version 0.9: document 240763-001) from:

Intel Literature
Box 58065
Santa Clara, CA 95051-8065
(800) 548-4725

Notes: You can only call the DPMI functions from protected-mode programs. To call a function, load the AX register with the function code and issue interrupt 0x31. Unless otherwise noted, all functions return with the carry flag clear when successful. If the carry flag is set, the function failed. A version 1.0 host also loads the AX register with an error code when a failure occurs.

Function 0x0000   **Allocate LDT Descriptors**

Input:
AX=0
CX=number of descriptors

Output:
AX=base selector

Returns one or more descriptors that your program can use. The descriptors are set to data segments. If this function returns more than one descriptor, you can determine selectors for subsequent descriptor by using the huge pointer increment (see function 3). Since the descriptors will have a zero base address and limit, you will need to use functions 7 and 8 to set the segments.

Version: 0.9
Equivalent Windows Function:
AllocSelector()

Function 0x0001   Free LDT Descriptor

Input:
AX=1
BX=Selector to free

Output: None

Frees allocated descriptors (see function 0). If function 0 returned multiple descriptors, you free each descriptor with a separate call to function 1.
    Under version 1.0, any segment register that contain the selector will be set to zero.

Version: 0.9
Equivalent Windows Function: FreeSelector()

Function 0x0002   Real-Mode Segment to Descriptor

Input:
AX=2
BX=real-mode segment address

Output:
AX=selector

Returns a data segment selector equivalent to the specified real-mode paragraph address. The descriptor will have a 64K limit. You can never modify or free selectors that function 2 creates. Therefore, only use function 2 to create "permanent" selectors (i.e., video memory, BIOS data, etc.).

Version: 0.9
Equivalent Windows Function: None (see __0000H, __B000H, and the other predefined selectors)

Function 0x0003   Get Huge Pointer Increment

Input:
AX=3

Output:
AX=selector increment
(This function never fails.)

Returns the value used to locate additional segments when huge allocations occur (see function 0).

Version: 0.9
Equivalent Windows Function: None (See the __AHINCR and __AHSHIFT constants)

Function 0x0006   Get Segment Base Address

Input:
AX=6
BX=selector

Output:
CX:DX=segment's 32-bit linear base address

This function returns the base address of a segment in the LDT. There is no DPMI function that returns a segment's limit—use the LSL instruction instead. From Windows, you can use GetSelectorLimit().

Version: 0.9
Equivalent Windows Function:
GetSelectorBase()

Function 0x0007   Set Segment Base Address
Input:
AX=7
BX=selector
CX:DX=32-bit linear base address

Output: None

Sets an LDT segment's base address. A version 1.0 host (and some 0.9 hosts) will automatically reload any segment registers that contain the selector.

Version: 0.9
Equivalent Windows Function:
SetSelectorBase()

Function 0x0008   Set Segment Limit
Input:
AX=8
BX=selector
CX:DX=32-bit limit
Output: None

Sets an LDT segment's limit. A DPMI 1.0 host (and some 0.9 hosts) will automatically reload any segment registers that contain the selector. To read a segment's limit, use the LSL assembly language instruction. Windows programs may also use GetSelectorLimit().

Version: 0.9
Equivalent Windows Function:
SetSelectorLimit()

Function 0x0009   Set Descriptors Access Right Byte
Input:
AX=9
BX=LDT selector
CL=access rights byte (see Chapter 4)
CH=80386 extended access rights byte (see Chapter 4)

Output: None

The CL register contains the descriptor bytes from bit 40 to bit 47. The top 4 bits of the CH register contains bits 55 to 52. A DPMI 1.0 host (and some 0.9 hosts) will automatically reload any segment register that contains the selector. To read a segment's access rights, use the LAR assembly language instruction.

Version: 0.9
Equivalent Windows Function: None (see AllocDStoCSAlias() and PrestoChangoSelector())

Function 0x000A   Create Alias Descriptor
Input:
AX=0xA
BX=selector

Output:
AX=data selector

This function returns a data selector that matches the supplied selector (which can be a data or executable segment). You can use this function to write into a code segment.

Version: 0.9
Equivalent Windows Function: None (see PrestoChangoSelector() and AllocDStoCSAlias())

Function 0x000B   Get Descriptor
Input:
AX=0xB
BX=LDT selector
ES:DI or ES:EDI=pointer to 8-byte buffer

Output:
Buffer contains descriptor

Function 0xB returns the 8-byte descriptor associated with the selector. See Chapter 4 for more details about descriptors.

Version: 0.9
Equivalent Windows Function: None (see GetSelectorBase() and GetSelectorLimit())

Function 0x000C   Set Descriptor
Input:
AX=0xC
BX=LDT selector
ES:DI or ES:EDI=pointer to 8-byte buffer

Output: None

The DPMI host directly copies the 8-byte buffer to the selector's descriptor. A DPMI 1.0 host (and some 0.9 hosts) will reload any segment register that contains the selector.

Version: 0.9
Equivalent Windows Function: None (see SetSelectorBase() and SetSelectorLimit())

Function 0x000D   Allocate Specific LDT Descriptor
Input:
AX=0xD
BX=selector

Output: None

This function attempts to allocate the specified LDT descriptor. DPMI 0.9 hosts reserve selectors 0x4-0x7C for this function and all clients share them. DPMI 1.0 hosts reserve the same selectors, but each client has a private LDT.

Version: 0.9
Equivalent Windows Function: None

Function 0x0100   Allocate DOS Memory

Input:
AX=0x100
BX=number of 16-byte paragraphs required

Output:
If carry flag is clear:
    AX=real mode segment allocated
    DX=base selector for allocated memory
If carry flag is set
    AX=error code
    BX=size of largest available block (in paragraphs)

Protected-mode programs use this DPMI function to allocate memory below 1M (similar to DOS interrupt 0x21, function 0x48). If a 16-bit program requestS more than 64K of memory, the DPMI host returns the first of a series of selectors. You can find the subsequent selectors by using the huge pointer increment (see function 3). You should not free or modify descriptors (using function 0x0001) you obtain with this function. Using function 0x101 will automatically free the descriptors and the associated DOS memory.

Version: 0.9
Equivalent Windows Function:
GlobalDosAlloc()

Function 0x0101   Free DOS Memory

Input:
AX=0x101
DX=DOS memory selector from function 0x0100

Output: None

Use this function to free memory you obtained from function 0x100.

Version: 0.9
Equivalent Windows Function:
GlobalDosFree()

Function 0x0102   Resize DOS Memory

Input:
AX=0x102
BX=new block size (in 16-byte paragraphs)
DX=DOS memory selector from function 0x0100

Output:
If carry flag is clear: None
If carry flag is set:
    AX=error code
    BX=size of largest available block (in paragraphs)

This function resizes memory blocks allocated via function 0x100. A DPMI 1.0 host will reload any segment registers that contain a selector modified by this function. Also, it will zero any segment registers that contain selectors that this function frees.

Version: 0.9
Equivalent Windows Function: None

Function 0x0200   Get Real-Mode Interrupt Vector
Input:
AX=0x200
BL=interrupt number

Output:
CX:DX=real-mode interrupt vector address
(This function never fails.)

The CX:DX register contains the address of the real-mode interrupt vector. The address is a real-mode segment and offset—not a protected-mode address. This is the equivalent of DOS interrupt 0x21, function 0x35 in real mode.

Version: 0.9
Equivalent Windows Function: None

Function 0x0201   Set Real-Mode Interrupt Vector
Input:
AX=0x201
BL=interrupt number
CX:DX=real-mode interrupt vector address

Output: None
(This function never fails.)

The CX:DX register contains the address of the real-mode interrupt vector. The address is a real-mode segment and offset—not a protected-mode address. Note that hardware interrupt handlers should be locked (see function 0x600). This function is equivalent to DOS interrupt 0x21, function 0x25 in real mode.

Version: 0.9
Equivalent Windows Function: None

Function 0x0202   Get Exception Vector
Input:
AX=0x202
BL=exception number

Output:
CX:DX or CX:EDX=address of exception handler

This function returns the address of an exception (i.e., general protection, page fault, etc.) handler. DPMI version 1.0 supports function 0x202 for backward compatibility, but function 0x210 is preferred.

Version: 0.9
Equivalent Windows Function: None

Function 0x0203   Set Exception Vector
Input:
AX=0x203
BL=exception number

CX:DX or CX:EDX=address of exception handler

Output: None

This function sets the exception (i.e., general protection, page fault, etc.) handler address. DPMI version 1.0 support function 0x203 for backward compatibility, but function 0x211 is preferred.

Version: 0.9
Equivalent Windows Function:
InterruptRegister( ) (TOOLHELP)

Function 0x0204 Get Protected-Mode Interrupt Vector

Input:
AX=0x204
BL=interrupt number

Output:
CX:DX or CX:EDX=address of exception handler
(This function never fails)

This function returns the specified protected-mode interrupt vector.

Version: 0.9
Equivalent Windows Function: None

Function 0x0205 Set Protected-Mode Interrupt Vector

Input:
AX=0x205
BL=interrupt number
CX:DX or CX:EDX=address of exception handler

Output: None
You can use this function to set the specified protected-mode interrupt vector.

Version: 0.9
Equivalent Windows Function: None

Function 0x0210 Get Protected-Mode Exception Vector

Input:
AX=0x210
BL=exception number

Output:
CX:DX or CX:EDX=address of exception handler

This DPMI 1.0 function reads the exception handler address for the specified protected-mode exception.

Version: 1.0
Equivalent Windows Function: None

Function 0x0211 Get Real-Mode Exception Vector

Input:
AX=0x211
BL=exception number

Output:
CX:DX or CX:EDX=address of exception handler

This DPMI 1.0 function reads the exception handler address for the specified real-mode exception. The address is a protected-mode address—when an exception occurs in real mode, a protected-mode handler gets control.

Version: 1.0
Equivalent Windows Function: None

Function 0x0212   Set Protected-Mode Exception Vector

Input:
AX=0x211
BL=exception number
CX:DX or CX:EDX=address of exception handler

Output: None

This DPMI 1.0 function sets the exception-handler address for the specified protected-mode exception.

Version: 1.0
Equivalent Windows Function: None (See TOOLHELP's InterruptRegister() function)

Function 0x0213   Set Real-Mode Exception Vector

Input:
AX=0x213
BL=exception number
CX:DX or CX:EDX=address of exception handler

Output: None

This DPMI 1.0 function sets the exception-handler address for the specified real-mode exception. The address is a protected-mode address—when an exception occurs in real mode, a protected-mode handler gets control.

Version: 1.0
Equivalent Windows Function: None (See InterruptRegister())

Function 0x0300   Simulate Real-Mode Interrupt

Input:
AX=0x300
BL=interrupt number
BH=0 (reserved for future use)
CX=number of works to copy between stacks
ES:DI or ES:EDI=pointer to register structure (see Figure B-1)

Output:
ES:DI or ES:EDI=pointer to modified register structure (see Figure B-1)

This function calls a real-mode interrupt (specified in the BL register). The CS and IP fields in the register structure are ignored. Before the interrupt gains control, the host can copy parameters from the protected-mode stack to the real-mode stack. If the SS and SP fields in the register structure are zero, the host will provide a real-mode stack. Be sure that the FLAGS field (offset 0x20) of the register structure contains a valid flag word. Random values can cause unexpected results. You must remove any parameters from the protected-mode stack.

Version: 0.9
Equivalent Windows Function: None

Figure B-1. Real-Mode Register Structure

Offset		
0	EDI	
4	ESI	
8	EBP	
12	Reserved (all 0's)	
16	EBX	
20	EDX	
24	ECX	
28	Flags	ES
32	DS	FS
36	GS	IP (ignored)
40	CS (ignored)	SP
44	SS	

Function 0x0301   Call Real-Mode Procedure (RETF)

Input:
AX=0x301
BH=0 (reserved for future use)
CX=number of works to copy between stacks
ES:DI or ES:EDI=pointer to register structure (see Figure B-1)

Output:
ES:DI or ES:EDI=pointer to modified register structure (see Figure B-1)

This function calls a real-mode procedure (specified in the CS and IP fields of the register structure). Before the procedure gains control, the host can copy parameters from the protected-mode stack to the real-mode stack. If the SS and SP fields in the register structure are zero, the host will provide a real-mode stack. Be sure that the FLAGS field (offset 0x20) of the register structure contains a valid flag word. Random values can cause unexpected results. The real-mode procedure must end with a far return (RETF) instruction. You must remove any parameters from the protected-mode stack.

Version: 0.9
Equivalent Windows Function: None

Function 0x0302   Call Real-Mode Procedure (IRET)

Input:
AX=0x301
BH=0 (reserved for future use)

CX=number of works to copy between stacks
ES:DI or ES:EDI=pointer to register structure (see Figure B-1)

Output:
ES:DI or ES:EDI=pointer to modified register structure (see FigureB-1)

This function calls a real-mode procedure (specified in the CS and IP fields of the register structure). Before the procedure gains control, the host can copy parameters from the protected-mode stack to the real-mode stack. If the SS and SP fields in the register structure are zero, the host will provide a real-mode stack. Be sure that the FLAGS field (offset 0x20) of the register structure contains a valid flag word. Random values can cause unexpected results. The real-mode procedure must end with an interrupt return (an IRET instruction). You must remove any parameters from the protected-mode stack.

Version: 0.9
Equivalent Windows Function: None

Function 0x0303   Allocate Real-Mode Callback

Input:
AX=0x303
DS:SI or DS:ESI=pointer to protected-mode routine
ES:DI or ES:EDI=pointer to 0x32 byte buffer for register structure (see Figure B-1)

Output:
CX:DX=real-mode pointer to callback address

Use function 0x303 to create callbacks—real-mode addresses that transfer control to a protected-mode routine (see Chapter 9 for more on callbacks). You can pass the callback address to real-mode programs (like network or mouse drivers) that expect a real-mode function pointer. When the real-mode program calls the callback, your protected-mode program gets control. The protected-mode program can access the buffer pointed to by ES:DI (or ES:EDI) points to read and write the real-mode registers. There may be as few as 16 callbacks available.

Version: 0.9
Equivalent Windows Function: None

Function 0x0304   Free Callback

Input:
AX=0x304
CX:DX=real-mode callback address

Output: None

Use this function to free a callback returned by function 0x305.

Version: 0.9
Equivalent Windows Function: None

Function 0x0400   Get Version

Input:
AX=0x400

Output:
AH=DPMI major version number
AL=DPMI minor version number (in hundredths)
BX=flags
 bit 0=set if 32-bit host
 bit 1=set if host uses V86 mode for real-mode interrupts
 bit 2=set if host supports virtual memory
CL=processor (2=286,3=386,4=486)
DH=master PIC base interrupt
DL=slave PIC base interrupt
(This function never fails.)

You can use function 0x400 to learn about the DPMI host. The Windows DPMI host's version numbers are in binary, not BCD. Some DPMI hosts may not follow this convention. Therefore, version 0.9 returns AH=0 and AL=0x5A (90 decimal = 0x5A).

Version: 0.9
Equivalent Windows Function: None

Function 0x0500   Get Free Memory Information
Input:
AX=0x500
ES:DI or ES:EDI=pointer to 48-byte buffer (see Table B-1)

Output:
Results returned in buffer
(This function never falls.)

This function fills the supplied buffer with information about the memory system. Some hosts will not supply each data field—hosts that don't supply a field will set that field to 0xFFFFFFFF. All hosts provide the first field (largest available block). DPMI 1.0 hosts support this function for compatibility only—DPMI 1.0 prefers function 0x50B.

Version: 0.9
Equivalent Windows Function: None

Table B-1. Free Memory Information Buffer

Offset Length	Description
0x00	Size of largest available block in bytes
0x04	Maximum unlocked page allocation in pages
0x08	Maximum locked page allocation in pages
0x0C	Number of pages in linear address space
0x10	Number of unlocked pages
0x14	Number of pages free
0x18	Number of physical pages
0x1C	Number of pages in free linear address space
0x20	Number of pages in swap file
0x24	Reserved—all bytes set to 0xFF

Function 0x0501   Allocate Memory Block

Input:
AX=0x501
BX:CX=non-zero minimum block size in bytes

Output:
BX:CX=block's linear address
SI:DI=block handle

You use function 0x501 to reserve memory for protected-mode programs. Note that the memory is not associated with a segment selector. You must allocate a descriptor (using function 0, for instance) and set the base address and size of that descriptor. You need to save the block's handle (in the SI:DI registers) if you need to resize or free the block later. Memory allocated with this function is committed—your program will not receive a page fault inside the memory region even if one occurs. The DPMI host transparently handles page faults on your behalf.

Version: 0.9
Equivalent Windows Function:
GlobalAlloc() (Note: GlobalAlloc() also associates memory with a selector)

Function 0x0502   Free Memory Block

Input:
AX=0x502
SI:DI=block handle

Output: None

You can use function 0x502 to free memory allocated with function 0x501. If you have associated the memory with a segment descriptor, you should free the descriptor prior to freeing the memory.

Version: 0.9
Equivalent Windows Function:
GlobalFree() (Note: GlobalFree() frees the memory and its selector)

Function 0x0503   Resize Memory Block

Input:
AX=0x503
BX:CX=new block size (non-zero)
SI:DI=block handle

Output:
BX:CX=new linear address of block
SI:DI=new block handle

Function 0x503 resizes memory blocks allocated with function 0x501. You must update any descriptors that you previously associated with the block. The block may move as a result of this call.

Version: 0.9
Equivalent Windows Function:
GlobalRealloc()

Function 0x0504   Allocate Linear Memory
Input:
AX=0x504
EBX=page-aligned linear address or zero
ECX=non-zero block size
EDX=0 to create uncommitted memory, 1 to commit

Output:
EBX=linear address
ESI=handle

Only 32-bit DPMI 1.0 hosts support this function. It can create memory that will cause your program to receive a page fault when it is accessed (uncommitted) or not (committed). If you set EBX to zero, the DPMI host will provide an unused address.

Version: 1.0 (32-bit only)
Equivalent Windows Function: None

Function 0x0505   Resize Linear Memory
Input:
AX=0x505
ECX=non-zero block size
EDX=flags
    bit 0=set to create committed pages
    bit 1=set to update segment descriptors
ESI=block handle
ES:EBX=pointer to array of selectors (if bit 1 of EDX set)
EDI=length of selector array (if bit 1 of EDX set)

Output:
EBX=new linear address
ESI=new block handle

Only 32-bit DPMI 1.0 hosts support this function. It resizes blocks created with function 0x504.

Version: 1.0 (32-bit only)
Equivalent Windows Function: None

Function 0x0506   Get Page Attributes
Input:
AX=0x506
EBX=base offset of page in block
ECX=number of pages
ESI=memory block handle
ES:EDX=pointer to page attribute buffer (16-bits per page)

Output:
Returns output in buffer. Each 16 bit word has the following format:
    bit 6=set if page has been modified (see bit 4)
    bit 5=set if page has been accessed (see bit 4)
    bit 4=set if bits 5 and 6 are valid

bit 3=set if page is read only
bit 2-0=page type
  0=uncommitted page
  1=committed page
  2=mapped page

Only 32-bit DPMI 1.0 hosts support this function. Each page is 4K long and the offset in EBX is relative to the start of the block specified by the ESI register.

Version: 1.0 (32-bit only)
Equivalent Windows Function: None

Function 0x0507   Set Page Attributes

Input:
AX=0x507
EBX=base offset of page in block
ECX=number of pages
ESI=memory block handle
ES:EDX=pointer to page attribute buffer (16-bits per page)

Output:
If function fails, the carry flag is set and:
 ECX=number of pages set

Only 32-bit DPMI 1.0 hosts support this function. This function is the inverse of function 0x506. Refer to function 0x506 for the format of the page attribute buffer. Function 0x507 also allows a page type of 3. Then the DPMI host only modifies the page's attributes (read only, modified, etc.) and doesn't modify its type. If bit 4 is clear, the host ignores the accessed and modified bits (bits 5 and 6).

Version: 1.0 (32-bit only)
Equivalent Windows Function: None

Function 0x050A   Get Memory Block Information

Input:
AX=0x50A
SI:DI=block handle

Output:
BX:CX=base address of block
SI:DI=size of block in bytes

You can use function 0x50A to learn the address and length of a memory block.

Version: 1.0
Equivalent Windows Function: None (see GlobalSize())

Function 0x050B   Get Memory Information

Input:
AX=0x50B
ES:DI or ES:EDI=pointer to 128-byte buffer

Output:
Returns output in buffer (see Table B-2). All lengths and amounts are in bytes.

Function 0x50A returns a variety of information pertaining to the DPMI 1.0 host's memory status.

Version: 1.0
Equivalent Windows Function: None

Table B-2. Memory Information Buffer

Offset Length	Description
0x00	Total allocated DPMI physical memory
0x04	Total allocated DPMI virtual memory
0x08	Total DPMI virtual memory free
0x0C	Total virtual memory allocated for this virtual machine
0x10	Total free virtual memory for this virtual machine
0x14	Total virtual memory allocated for this client
0x18	Total virtual memory available for this client
0x1C	Total locked bytes of memory for this client
0x20	Maximum locked bytes of memory for this client
0x24	Maximum linear address for this client
0x28	Size of largest free memory block
0x2C	Minimum allocation unit
0x30	Allocation alignment unit
0x34	Unused—set to 0

Function 0x0600   Lock Memory
Input:
AX=0x600
BX:CX=starting linear address
SI:DI=region length in bytes

Output: None

This function causes DPMI hosts that support virtual memory to refrain from swapping pages that contain the specified region. Since pages are 4K long, this function may lock more memory than you specify. Hardware interrupt routines and time critical functions should be locked. If a page is locked more than once, you will have to make the same number of calls to function 0x601 (unlock memory) to unlock it.

Version: 0.9
Equivalent Windows Function:
GlobalPageLock()

Function 0x0601   Unlock Memory
Input:
AX=0x601
BX:CX=starting linear address

SI:DI=region length in bytes

Output: None

This function causes DPMI hosts that support virtual memory to unlock the pages that contain the specified region (see function 0x600). If a page was locked more than once, you will have to make the same number of calls to this function to unlock it.

Version: 0.9
Equivalent Windows Function:
GlobalPageUnlock()

Function 0x0604   Get Page Size
Input:
AX=0x604

Output:
BX:CX=page size in bytes
You can get the virtual memory system's page size (usually 4K) with function 0x604. A 16-bit host will return an error for this function.

Version: 0.9 (32-bit only)
Equivalent Windows Function: None

Function 0x0702   Mark Pages for Swapping
Input:
AX=0x702
BX:CX=starting linear address
SI:DI=region length in bytes

Output: None

This function causes DPMI hosts that support virtual memory to consider the specified pages as prime candidates for swapping. Only pages that are entirely within the specified range are marked. This function doesn't swap the data, it only advises the host that the memory region is a good candidate for swapping.

Version: 0.9
Equivalent Windows Function: None (see GlobalDiscard())

Function 0x0703   Discard Pages
Input:
AX=0x703
BX:CX=starting linear address
SI:DI=region length in bytes

Output: None

This function causes DPMI hosts that support virtual memory to discard the pages that contain the specified region. The host can reuse the physical memory without swapping the contents to disk. The contents of the region become undefined. Only pages that are entirely within the specified range are discarded.

Version: 0.9
Equivalent Windows Function: None (see flags in GlobalAlloc() and GlobalDiscard())

Function 0x0800   Map Physical Address

Input:
AX=0x800
BX:CX=starting physical address
SI:DI=region length in bytes

Output:
BX:CX=equivalent linear address

You can use function 0x800 to obtain an address to directly access physical device memory above 1M (use function 2 for addresses below 1M). Under DPMI 0.9, there is no way to free this mapping.

Version: 0.9
Equivalent Windows Function: None

Function 0x0801   Free Physical Address

Input:
AX=0x801
BX:CX=linear address (from function 0x800)

Output: None

Function 0x801 frees addresses you obtain from function 0x800. Note that this function is only available on DPMI 1.0 hosts (function 0x800 is present in 0.9 hosts).

Version: 1.0
Equivalent Windows Function: None

Function 0x0900   Disable Interrupts

Input:
AX=0x900

Output:
AL=previous interrupt state (1=enabled)

This function disables interrupts. The host may virtualize the interrupt flag for each DPMI client. Therefore, you can only disable interrupts for your program—other programs may continue to receive interrupts. You can also use the CLI instruction (or the _disable() library call) to disable interrupts, but they do not return the previous interrupt state (which may not correspond to the IF flag in the processor's flag register). The DPMI specification warns that calling this function (or CLI) may be very slow since the host may execute many more instructions than you expect.

Version: 0.9
Equivalent Windows Function: None

Function 0x0901   Enable Interrupts

Input:
AX=0x901

Output:
AL=previous interrupt state (1=enabled)

This function enables interrupts. The host may virtualize the interrupt flag for each DPMI client. Therefore, you can only enable interrupts for your program—other programs may not be receiving interrupts. You can also use the STI instruction (or the _enable() library call) to disable interrupts, but they do not return the previous interrupt state. The DPMI specification warns that calling this function (or STI) may be very slow since the host may execute many more instructions than you expect.

Version: 0.9
Equivalent Windows Function: None

Function 0x0902 — Get Interrupts State

Input:
AX=0x902

Output:
AL=interrupt state (1=enabled)

This function returns the virtual interrupt flag for your program.

Version: 0.9
Equivalent Windows Function: None

APPENDIX ▪ C

Manufacturers of DOS Extenders and Related Tools

In alphabetical order:

Ergo Computing, Inc.
One Intercontinental Way
Peabody, MA 01960
Phone: (508) 535-7510
16- and 32-bit extenders

Flashtek
121 Sweet Avenue
Moscow, ID 83843
Phone: (208) 882-6893
        (800) 397-7310
32-bit extender

IGC P3
1754 Technology Drive, Suite 108
San Jose, CA 95110
Phone: (408) 441-0366
32-bit extender

Intel
P.P. Box 58119
Santa Clara, CA 95052-8119
Phone: (800) 548-4725
        (503) 696-4787
32-bit C and extender

Lahey Computer Systems
Box 6091
Incline Village, NV 89450
Phone: (800) 548-4778
        (702) 831-2500
Extended FORTRAN

Metaware, Inc.
2161 Delaware Ave.
Santa Cruz, CA 95060-5706
Phone: (408) 429-6382
*32-bit C, C++, and Pascal; 32-bit
Windows Development Tools*

MicroWay
(mailing address)
Box 79
Kingston, MA 02364

(shipping address)
Cordage Park
Building 20
Plymouth, MA 02360
Phone: (508) 746-7341
*Extended C, C++, FORTRAN,
and Pascal*

Phar Lap Software, Inc.
60 Aberdeen Ave.
Cambridge, MA 02138
Phone: (617) 661-1510
16- and 32-bit DOS extenders

Rational Systems
220 North Main St.
Natick, MA 01760
Phone: (508) 653-6006
16- and 32-bit DOS extenders; 32-bit Windows development tools

Silicon Valley Software (SVS)
1710 South Amphlett Blvd. Suite, 100
San Mateo, CA 94402
Phone: (415) 572-8800
Extended C, FORTRAN, Pascal

Symantec
10201 Torre Avenue
Cupertino, CA 95014
Phone: (800) 554-4403
        (408) 252-3570 P3
Extended C, C++

WATCOM Systems Inc.
415 Phillip Street
Waterloo, Ontario
Canada N2L3X2
Phone: (800) 265-4555
        (519) 886-3700
Extended C, FORTRAN; 32-bit Windows development tools

OTHER RESOURCES:

GNU C/C++
The Delorie GNU C/C++ compiler is available from a variety of sources. The compiler and extender are nominally free, but you may have to pay a copy fee for disks or network connect time. If you have access to the Internet, you can obtain it via anonymous FTP from the grape.ecs.@clarkson.edu or archive-server@sun.soe.clarkson.edu machines. The Dr. Dobb's Journal forum on CompuServe also has the Delorie GNU C/C++ package (GO DDJFORUM from any ! prompt).

Several vendors will send you copies of the GNU C/C++ programs on disks for a fee. The most reasonable of these is the C User's Group, which charges about $50 for a set of disks. You can reach the C User's Group at:

C User's Group
1601 West 23rd Street Suite 200
Lawrence, KS 66046-2743
Phone: (913) 841-1631

If you have a CD-ROM drive, you can find GNU C/C++ for DOS (and 500 megabytes of other interesting things) on the excellent SIMTEL-20 MS-DOS CD-ROM from Walnut Creek for about $25 (half of the $50 copy fee to get it on floppies). You can reach Walnut Creek at:

Walnut Creek CD-ROM
1547 Palos Verdes Mall, Suite 260
Walnut Creek, CA 94596
Phone: (800) 786-9907
        (510) 947-5996

PROT
There are two versions of PROT. You can find the most recent version in *DOS 5: A Developer's Guide*. A less capable edition of PROT appeared in two issues of *Dr. Dobb's Journal* (August and September 1990). See the bibliography for more information on these publications.

APPENDIX ∙ D

286|DOS-Extender Lite User's Guide

*See companion disk for online text.

Introduction

Welcome to the world beyond 640K!

Now, with your FREE 286|DOS-Extender Lite, it's easy to build multi-megabyte Microsoft C/C++ and Borland C++ programs! 286|DOS-Extender Lite is a special trial size version of Phar Lap Software's award-winning 286|DOS-Extender Software Development Kit (SDK). It enables your program to break the 640K DOS barrier and access up to 2 MB of memory, with no need for overlays or EMS. Your Extended-DOS programs will run under DOS, DESQview and Windows.

286|DOS-Extender Lite includes all the capabilities you need to build and run Extended-DOS programs with either Borland C++ 3.1 or Microsoft C/C++ 7.0. However, you may want to purchase Phar Lap's 286|DOS-Extender SDK if you would like the following features: debugger support, access to up to 16 MB of memory, Phar Lap's technical support and extensive documentation, and the ability to deliver your Extended-DOS application to customers with Phar Lap's 286|DOS-Extender Run-Time Kit (RTK). The following chart outlines the differences between 286|DOS-Extender Lite and 286|DOS-Extender SDK. To order your SDK, just fill out the coupon at the back of this book or contact Phar Lap.

A Quick Tour of 286|DOS-Extender Lite

Computers with Intel and Intel-compatible 80286, 80386, or 80486 microprocessors hold a majority share of the IBM PC-compatible marketplace. These machines typically have two or more megabytes of memory. This is in sharp contrast to the situation just a few years ago, when the typical PC had an 8088 and less than a megabyte of memory.

But MS-DOS has not kept up with these sweeping changes. While PCs are shipping with more memory and better processors, more DOS applications than ever run out of memory.

Many users have found that a 2 MB machine, for example, does not actually give their applications 2 MB of memory: applications are held back by the 640K limitation imposed by MS-DOS. You can add memory to an IBM AT, PS/2, or 386 clone until you're blue in the face, and many DOS applications will nonetheless run out of memory.

These machines have untapped resources. 286|DOS-Extender Lite, PharLap's 16-bit DOS extender for 80286, 80386, and 80486 PCs, puts all this potential energy to work while fully preserving your investments in MS-DOS, Microsoft C/C++, and Borland C++.

Let's look at an example. Many manuals begin with the "hello world" sample program, but to show the power of 286|DOS-Extender Lite we need a sample program that suffers from the 640K confines of MS-DOS. Such programs are plentiful; almost any DOS program that uses large model, huge model, overlays, expanded memory (EMS), or the eXtended Memory Specification (XMS), is a good example. Any such program is also a likely candidate for using 286|DOS-Extender Lite!

But short of including 50,000 lines of code in our manual, how can we provide a quick look at the problem of running old DOS on the new machines?

We can simulate some "programming in the large" issues by using a small C program that requires a large amount of memory. The program shown below, BIG.C, attempts to use one megabyte of memory by declaring a 512 x 512 two-dimensional array of longs:

```
/* BIG.C */

#include <stdlib.h>
#include <stdio.h>

#define SIZE    512

static long huge array[SIZE][SIZE] ;  /* one-megabyte array */

main()
{
    int i, j;

    printf("Using %lu-byte array\n",
      (long) SIZE * SIZE * sizeof(long));

    for (i=0; i<SIZE; i++)
    {
      for (j=0; j<SIZE; j++)
          array[i][j] = (long) i * j; /* touch every element */
      printf("%d\r", i);              /* display odometer */
    }

    printf("done\n");
    return 0;
}
```

The Borland C++ command-line compiler, BCC, can be used to compile and link this straightforward C program for plain-vanilla, real-mode MS-DOS. The -ml (large model) switch is used in the BCC command line to get the maximum amount of available memory:

```
C:\>bcc -ml big.c
```

While BCC compiles BIG.C without error, the Borland linker, TLINK, refuses to link the program, and produces the following error message:

Fatal: Relocation item exceeds 1Meg DOS limit.

This isn't a problem with TLINK, because the Microsoft linker has the same limitation. The problem is that real-mode MS-DOS really does have a one-megabyte barrier! Even if TLINK did somehow produce BIG.EXE, it wouldn't run properly under real-mode MS-DOS.

But to run BIG.EXE you don't have to switch to a different operating system. 286IDOS-Extender Lite removes the one-megabyte DOS barrier, while continuing to run under DOS. You get to have your cake and eat it too.

To produce a 286IDOS-Extender Lite version of the BIG program, simply compile and link with BCC286, which is one of the programs included with 286IDOS-Extender Lite. BCC286 runs BCC and TLINK, taking care of all the details of producing a protected-mode executable. Protected mode executable? Under DOS? That's right:

```
C:\>bcc286 big.c

C:\>big
Using 1048576-byte array
done
```

The Microsoft C/C++ 7.0 compiler can produce protected-mode executables almost as easily (the -f- switch is required for the huge keyword):

```
C:\>cl -Lp -AL -f- big.c

C:\>bind286 big

C:\>big
Using 1048576-byte array
done
```

We just allocated and accessed one megabyte under MS-DOS, in a program whose name we typed on the DOS command line—just like any other regular DOS program. The source code for the program, as we've seen, used absolutely standard PC constructs: no messing with special interfaces like EMS or XMS, and no overlays.

It's as if MS-DOS had been turned into a protected-mode operating system, or at least into an operating system that can run protected mode programs! This in fact is exactly what 286IDOS-Extender Lite does. Behind the scenes, when BIG is run from the DOS command line, the program reinvokes itself under 286IDOS-Extender Lite, which resides in a program named LITE286.EXE. (Incidentally, LITE286.EXE plus another file, DOSCALLS.DLL, must be somewhere on the path.)

Running BIG is equivalent to running LITE286 BIG. LITE286 puts themachine into protected mode, runs BIG, then puts the machine back into real mode.

Clearly, BIG is not a typical real-mode DOS program. BCC286 and CL take advantage of their respective linkers' ability to produce protected-mode Windows programs, using it instead to produce protected-mode DOS programs. Chapter 2 of this manual explains precisely how this happens; if you prefer, you can run the compile and link steps yourself (from MAKE, for example).

Big Malloc

The huge array used in BIG.C provides a simple first example of 286|DOS-Extender Lite. In the same way that LITE286 can load a program with large amounts of data, it can also load programs with large amounts of code, so the huge array is a good simulation of a large program. Most C programs do not create huge static arrays, but many DOS programs do contain enormous amounts of code. Such programs often resort to performance-crippling overlays; BIG shows that, on an 80286 or higher machine with extended memory, this workaround is not necessary.

BIG.C made life easy for itself by using the "huge" keyword, but due to its often poor performance, "huge" is usually avoided in commercial PC software. More typically, large PC applications dynamically allocate memory via the C malloc() function, via operator new in C++, or directly via the MS-DOS Allocate Memory Block function (INT 21h AH=48h).

Our next example program, MEMTEST, does nothing more than run malloc() in a loop and touch every byte of the allocated memory. When malloc() eventually returns NULL, indicating that memory is exhausted, MEMTEST breaks out of the loop. While clearly the program does not do anything useful with the memory it allocates, its insatiable appetite for memory is a very good simulation of a large application:

```
/* MEMTEST.C */

#include <stdlib.h>
#include <stdio.h>

main()
{
    char *p;
    unsigned long allocs;

    for (allocs = 0; ; allocs++)
       if ((p = malloc(1024)) != 0)      /* in 1k blocks */
       {
         memset(p, 0, 1024); /* touch every byte */
         *p = 'x';             /* do something, anything with */
         p[1023] = 'y';        /* the allocated memory        */

         if (allocs && (allocs % 1024) == 0)   /* odometer */
             printf("Allocated %u megabytes\r", allocs >> 10);
       }
       else
         break;

       printf("Allocated %lu bytes\n", allocs << 10);
       return 0;
}
```

Using Borland C++ 3.1 or Microsoft C/C++ 7.0, this program can be compiled for real-mode MS-DOS with the following command lines:

```
C:\>bcc -ml memtest.c
```

```
C:\>cl -AL memtest.c
```

These commands produce a large model version of MEMTEST.EXE, allowing maximum memory allocation under real-mode MS-DOS. On a COMPAQ 386 with 2 MB of memory, MEMTEST should allocate around 2 MB of memory (if you don't think this is what MEMTEST should do, you've been programming in real mode for too long!). But of course, here is what real-mode large model MEMTEST does instead:

```
C:\>memtest
Allocated 417792 bytes
```

Only 408 KB available on a 2 MB machine?! By making better use of the DOS 5.0 LOADHIGH, DEVICEHIGH, and DOS=HIGH,UMB statements, or by using superb expanded memory managers such as Quarterdeck QEMM or Qualitas 386MAX, we could probably have created a better configuration, in which MEMTEST might get as much as 610 KB or so. But no matter how much we huffed and puffed and fooled with CONFIG-.SYS, real-mode MEMTEST would never allocate more than one megabyte of memory.

Furthermore, even if you do maximize the available DOS memory on one machine, there is no guarantee that all (or even most) of a program's users will have such an "ideal" configuration. By developing for protected-mode DOS, you can bypass a lot of these messy user-configuration issues.

Now, to produce a version of MEMTEST that behaves more sensibly, the only thing you need to differently is to run in protected mode:

```
C:\>cl -Lp -AL memtest.c

C:\>bind286 memtest
```

or:

```
C:\>bcc286 memtest.c

C:\>memtest
Allocated 2193408 bytes
```

We allocated almost 2 MB of memory under MS-DOS! This is dramatically different behavior from the first version of MEMTEST we produced, yet we're using the same source code. Simply recompiling for 286|DOS-Extender Lite, without source code changes, gives us a program that runs under DOS yet breaks the 640K barrier, without EMS, overlays, or other workarounds. Using 286|DOS-Extender Lite with Microsoft C/C++ or Borland C++ provides a version of malloc() that transparently uses extended memory, plus functions such as memset() and pointer dereferences such as *p and p[1023], which transparently access extended memory.

Protected Mode C++

286|DOS-Extender Lite is not limited to programs written in C; C++ programs can just as easily run under protected-mode DOS. For example, the C++ new operator in protected-mode DOS works exactly the same as the C malloc() function: instead of halting somewhere around 640K, operator new can be used to allocate up to 2 MB of memory under 286|DOS-Extender Lite. (286|DOS-Extender SDK can allocate up to 16 MB.)

Other C++ features, such as the iostream input and output operators and static constructors and destructors, work just the way one would expect from having used C++ in real-mode DOS.

The next sample program, MEMTEST2.CPP, uses a number of C++ features. The C++ set_new_handler() function is particularly useful; it lets MEMTEST2 install a handler that will automatically be called when operator new fails. This considerably simplifies the program's main loop:

```
/* MEMTEST2.CPP */

#include <stdlib.h>
#include <iostream.h>
#include <new.h>

class msg {
public:
    msg()    { cout << "hello from " << __FILE__ << "\n" ; }
    ~msg()   { cout << "bye\n" ; }
    } ;

static msg banner;  // test C++ static constructors, destructors

static unsigned long bytes = 0;
static unsigned long allocs = 0;
static unsigned blk_size = 10240;

void new_fail(void)
{
    if (blk_size)
      blk_size >>= 1;  // try to allocate a smaller block
    else
    {   // memory exhausted
      cout << "Allocated " << bytes << " bytes\n" ;
      exit(1);
    }
}

main()
{
    char *p;

    set_new_handler(new_fail);    // called when new fails

    for (;;)
    {
      p = new char[blk_size];    // allocate memory
      memset(p, 0, blk_size);    // touch every byte
      *p = 'x';                  // do something, anything with
      p[blk_size-1] = 'y';       //    the allocated memory

      bytes += blk_size;
      allocs++;
      if ((allocs % 25) == 0)    // odometer
        cout << "Allocated " << bytes << " bytes\r";
    }
}
```

We won't even bother showing the real-mode version this time, since by now it's pretty obvious how limited real mode is. To compile this C++ program for protected-mode DOS, all you need to do is BCC286. (Please note the version presented here compiles only with Borland C++; the version in the EXAMPLES directory can be compiled with either Borland C++ or Microsoft C/C++ 7.0):

```
C:\>bcc286 memtest2.cpp

C:\>memtest2
hello from memtest2.cpp
```

```
Allocated 2027520 bytes
bye
```

Because 286|DOS-Extender Lite is compatible with the DPMI specification (as well as with every other major memory-management specification, including VCPI, XMS, VDS, and INT 15h), this protected mode C++ program can allocate up to 2 MB of memory under all modes of Windows 3.x:

```
C:\>memtest2
hello from memtest2.cpp
Allocated 2027520 bytes
bye
```

Protected Mode MS-DOS

What's really happening here? We've seen that 286|DOS-Extender Lite can load programs with huge arrays, or enormous amounts of code, and that protected-mode DOS versions of C functions such as malloc( ), and of operator new in C++, can dynamically allocate large amounts of memory. How does all this work?

While generally used with C or C++ programs, 286|DOS-Extender Lite is not a C or C++ library. 286|DOS-Extender Lite does replace some startup code and library functions, but this is simply to make the code protected-mode "clean." The real magic occurs at a lower level.

In essence, 286|DOS-Extender Lite provides MS-DOS (INT 21h) functions in protected mode. Since your program runs in protected mode, any software interrupts your program generates—such as DOS calls made by the C run-time library when you call a function such as printf( )—occur in protected mode too, and are caught by 286|DOS-Extender Lite.

In most cases, 286|DOS-Extender Lite passes the call down to MS-DOS, which is still running in real mode. DOS file I/O functions are handled this way, for example: the 286|DOS-Extender Lite handler for these functions reissues (or "reflects") the call in real mode.

Merely by providing protected-mode surrogates for these functions, 286|DOS-Extender Lite allows your program to think that it is running under a protected-mode version of MS-DOS. The program can call INT 21h in protected mode without worrying about the fact that its file I/O buffers are probably located in extended memory. 286|DOS-Extender Lite automatically takes care of all the details of transferring data between conventional memory (where real-mode DOS can get at it) and extended memory (where your protected-mode program probably allocated it).

Because 286|DOS-Extender Lite acts as a protected-mode "wrapper" around real-mode MS-DOS, you have a completely compatible environment. 286|DOS-Extender Lite isn't replacing DOS, so it will work with whatever version of DOS you or your customers already have.

Of course, real-mode MS-DOS does not know how to do things like run protected-mode programs, allocate extended memory, load dynamic link libraries (DLLs), or install protected-mode interrupt handlers. Requests such as these are handled by 286|DOS-Extender Lite entirely in protected mode.

Memory allocation is a good example. Rather than use C or C++ constructs to allocate memory, the next sample program, DOSMEM.C, goes directly to DOS using INT 21h Function 48h (Allocate Memory Block). Typically, a DOS program finds out how much memory is available by asking this function for 0FFFFh paragraphs (one megabyte). Real-mode DOS will naturally fail such a request, but it will also return the actual number of paragraphs available in the largest block of free memory:

```
/*  DOSMEM.C */

#include <stdlib.h>
#include <stdio.h>
#include <dos.h>

main()
{
    unsigned segment, avail;
    char far *fp;
    _asm mov ah, 48h
    _asm mov bx, OFFFFh
    _asm int 21h
    _asm jc error
    _asm mov segment, ax
    fp = MK_FP(segment, 0);
    *fp = 'x';   /* make sure it's genuine */
    printf("Allocated OFFFFh paragraphs: %Fp\n", fp);
    return 0;
error:
    _asm mov avail, bx
    printf("Only %04Xh paragraphs available\n", avail);
    return 1;
}
```

```
C:\>bcc dosmem.c

C:\>dosmem
Only 4FE9 paragraphs available
```

Or with Microsoft C/C++:

```
C:\>cl dosmem.c

C:\>dosmem
Only 4FE9 paragraphs available
```

In protected mode, an amazing thing happens: a request for OFFFFh paragraphs easily succeeds:

```
C:\>bcc286 dosmem.c

C:\>dosmem
Allocated OFFFFh paragraphs: 0A3D:0000
```

or:

```
C:\>cl -AL -Lp dosmem.c

C:\>bind286 dosmem

C:\>dosmem
Allocated OFFFFh paragraphs: 0A3D:0000
```

Using the exact same INT 21h functional interface as real-mode DOS, 286|DOS-Extender Lite provides functionality that DOS alone can't provide. This new functionality is provided to every protected mode program running under 286|DOS-Extender Lite. Thus,

286|DOS-Extender Lite isn't a library, but an extension to the operating system. (That's why it's called a DOS extender.)

When protected-mode DOSMEM allocates 0FFFFh paragraphs, where does this memory come from? In general, this doesn't matter to the program, because it has asked INT 21h Function 48h for memory, and has received a value back in the AX register which it can use as the basis for a far segment:offset pointer. In DOSMEM.C, note how a far pointer is created with the Borland MK_FP() macro, and poked with the C * dereferencing operator. (In Borland C++, MK_FP is defined in dos.h.)

With Micrsoft C/C++, it must be defined in dosmem.c.) Thus, we have immediately usable memory; it doesn't really matter where it "comes from," nor for that matter what value INT 21h Function 48h returns in AX. All we need to know is that we can use it.

However, the pointer 0A3D:0000 displayed above by DOSMEM in protected mode is a little strange. Paragraph 0A3Dh seems to be too low in memory, for example. But in protected mode the address 0A3D:0000 has nothing whatever to do with absolute memory location 0A3D0h. Instead, 0A3Dh is a protected-mode selector that is essentially an index into a table of segment descriptors used by the chip. These descriptors in turn contain the base address, size, and protection "access rights" of the corresponding segment. Thus, memory management in protected mode is somewhat indirect, but all the indirection is managed entirely by the chip, "inside" an instruction such as MOV AX, ES:[BX].

BIOS Calls in Protected Mode

To create a useful environment for PC software, it is not sufficient merely to provide INT 21h in protected mode. The ROM BIOS calls (INT 10h, INT 16h, and so on) need to be available in protected mode too.

C run-time library functions such as _bios_serialcom(), _bios_printer(), and _bios_keybrd() are available in protected mode. Furthermore, protected-mode DOS programs can call BIOS functions from separate .ASM modules assembled with TASM or MASM, or using inline assembler, the int86() and int86x() functions, or Borland register pseudo-variables.

For example, if our MEM sample program did direct screen writes (which we will discuss in more detail later in this chapter), it might include initialization code such as the following, which uses INT 10h Function 0Fh (Get Video Mode):

```
#include <dos.h>

#define GET_VIDEO_MODE     0x0F

int video_mode(void)
{
    union REGS r;
    r.h.ah = GET_VIDEO_MODE;
    int86(0x10, &r, &r);
    return r.h.al;
}
```

or, using inline assembler, something like this:

```
int video_mode(void)
{
    _asm mov ah, GET_VIDEO_MODE
    _asm int 10h
    _asm xor ah, ah
    // 2 byte quantity returned in AX
}
```

or, using Borland register pseudovariables:

```
int video_mode(void)
{
    _AH = GET_VIDEO_MODE;
    geninterrupt(0x10);
    _AH = 0;
    // 2 byte quantity returned in AX
}
```

All these varieties of the video_mode() function run just fine in protected mode, because 286|DOS-Extender Lite supports INT 10h (BIOS Video) in protected mode.

The following list shows all interrupts and functions that are supported in protected mode—the vast majority of DOS (INT 21h) and BIOS (INT 10h, INT 16h, etc.) calls:

INT 10h (BIOS Video)
Functions 0 through 1Ch
INT 11h (BIOS Equipment Check)
INT 12h (Conventional Memory Size)
INT 14h (BIOS Communications)
Functions 0 through 5
INT 16h (BIOS Keyboard)
Functions 0 through 12h
INT 17h (BIOS Printer)
Functions 0 through 2
INT 1Ah (BIOS Time)
Functions 0 through 80h
INT 21h (MS-DOS Functions)
Functions 0 through 0Eh
Functions 19h through 30h
Functions 32h through 43h
Function 44h (IOCTL)
Subfunctions 0, 1, 6, 7, 8, 9, 0Ah, 0Bh, 0Eh, and 0Fh
Functions 45h through 63h
Because a request to INT 21h Function 48h (Allocate Memory Block) for FFFFh paragraphs can succeed in protected mode, this function should be used only for memory allocation, not to determine the amount of available memory. Use the DosMemAvail() and DosRealAvail() functions instead for this purpose.
Functions 66h through 6Ch
INT 33h (Microsoft Mouse)

Compatibility with Industry Standards

We have seen that 286|DOS-Extender Lite (that is, LITE286.EXE) manages the interface between your protected-mode program and real-mode MS-DOS. At the DOS command line, when you type the name of a protected-mode .EXE file, LITE286 puts the machine into protected mode and launches your program. Whenever your program makes DOS or BIOS calls from protected mode, 286|DOS-Extender Lite handles them and/or passes them down to MS-DOS or the ROM BIOS. When your program exits, 286|DOS-Extender Lite puts the computer back into real mode.

But what if the machine wasn't in real mode to begin with? Many 80386 and 80486 computers, for example, will be running software such as Microsoft Windows 3.x (Enhanced mode), Microsoft EMM386, Quarterdeck DESQview/386, or Qualitas

386MAX. When these are loaded, MS-DOS is running not in real mode but in a one-megabyte protected mode that Intel calls "virtual 8086" mode. Furthermore, users may be running programs that use extended memory, such as VDISK, HIMEM, or SMARTDrive.

286|DOS-Extender Lite handles all these situations gracefully. It is compatible with all the PC industry standards for protected mode, expanded memory (EMS), and extended memory (XMS). It supports the Virtual Control Program Interface (VCPI) and DOS Protected Mode Interface (DPMI). VCPI, a specification developed jointly by Quarterdeck Office Systems and Phar Lap Software, allows EMS emulators and DOS extenders to coexist; it is an extension to EMS 4.0. DPMI is a specification whose primary goal is compatibility between DOS extenders and DOS multitasking environments; DPMI was jointly developed by a committee including Microsoft, Intel, IBM, Phar Lap, Quarterdeck, Borland, Lotus, Rational Systems, and other companies.

This means that programs developed with 286|DOS-Extender Lite can run in a wide variety of DOS environments.

All this compatibility requires no work from you. There is no configuration or "tune" program to run. 286|DOS-Extender Lite automatically configures itself each time it runs. If run under Windows 3.x Enhanced mode, for example, the program will automatically get virtual memory with no additional effort. Or if you switch from HIMEM.SYS to QEMM386.SYS, you don't have to reconfigure 286|DOS-Extender Lite in any way.

What's So Protected About Protected Mode?

So far we have described the process of compiling for protected mode and running under MS-DOS. The next step in the development cycle is debugging.

Returning to the MEM sample program, for example, suppose we forgot to check the return value from malloc(). In the C++ version, we could use set_new_handler() to catch failed memory allocations.

But in C, it's simply a mistake to forget to check the return value from malloc():

```
for (allocs = 0; ; allocs++)
{
    p = malloc(1024);
    /* BUG:  not checking return value from malloc!*/
    memset(p, 0, 1024);
    *p = 'x';
    p[1023] = 'y';
}
```

This horrible code runs without complaint in real mode. In a large model program, its probable effect is to repeatedly bash the low-memory interrupt vector table.

What happens in protected mode when malloc() fails and we then try to dereference (peek or poke) the resulting NULL pointer? Instead of trashing memory, the program halts with a message like this:

```
Fatal error 286.3330: General protection fault detected.
PID=0001  TID=0001  SID=0001  ERRORCODE=0000
AX=0000  BX=0000  CX=0200  DX=0000  SI=056C  DI=0000  BP=2DCC
CS:IP=014F:0CC5  DS=0157  ES=0000  SS:SP=0157:2DCA  FLAGS=3216
```

The message "General protection fault detected" is an indication that the program has in some way violated the rules of protected mode. These rules prevent writing into code segments, executing data segments, reading or writing past the end of a segment, or using a segment that doesn't belong to you.

A general protection violation, or GP fault, shows either a bug in your program, or an area that needs to be converted so that it will work in protected mode. In either case, the CPU signals a GP fault when your program tries to violate protection. This makes protected mode a superb environment for software development: the hardware will help you find bugs and trouble spots.

In the case of the buggy version of MEM, the message "General protection fault detected" message alerts us to a bug that the CPU found for us: the program dereferences pointers without checking if malloc() succeeded. If you examine the register dump produced by 286|DOS-Extender Lite, you will note that the ES register is set to zero, suggesting we tried to dereference a NULL pointer. This NULL pointer checking is not inserted by the compiler: the Intel processor takes care of it in hardware, making it just one example of the many checks that the CPU does in protected mode, with no extra work on our part.

Debugging with TDW or CVP7 Under MS-DOS (With the 286|DOS-Extender Software Development Kit)

As explained at the beginning of this file, 286|DOS-Extender Lite does not support debugging. The 286|DOS-Extender SDK, however, supports the powerful debugging features of both the protected-mode Windows version of Turbo Debugger (TDW) that comes with Borland C++, and CodeView for Windows (CVW). (286|DOS-Extender includes a front-end program for CVW, called CVP7. That's the executable used in the following examples.) We would like to take this opportunity to illustrate the debugging support available with the 286|DOS-Extender SDK.

Let's look at the buggy MEM program. A protected-mode symbolic debugger like TDW would let us pinpoint the exact location of the bug in the MEM program (if we didn't already know it).

We wouldn't run either TDW or CVP7 under Windows, though. Rather, we would use 286|DOS-Extender to run TDW or CVP7 under MS-DOS, right from the DOS prompt, without Windows.

Just as 286|DOS-Extender runs your protected-mode applications under MS-DOS, it can run protected-mode debuggers such as TDW and CVP7. (286|DOS-Extender makes this possible through its support for dynamic link libraries (DLLs). This feature is explained in the documentation for the 286|DOS-Extender SDK.) CVP7 and TDW run under

DOS because 286|DOS-Extender supplies Windows-emulation libraries such as KER-NEL.DLL, USER.DLL, and WINDEBUG.DLL.

Why can't we just use the protected-mode TD286 debugger? Because TD286 merely runs in protected mode: it doesn't know how to debug protected-mode programs. In a way, TD286 is a "cross-development tool": it's a protected-mode debugger, used to debug real-mode programs. When running under 286|DOS-Extender, TDW is a protected mode DOS debugger, used to debug protected-mode DOS programs.

To make symbolic information available for TDW under DOS, we would use the Borland C++ -v switch:

```
C:\>bcc286 -v buggymem.c
```

To make symbolic information available for CVP7 under DOS, we would use the Microsoft C/C++ -Zi switch:

```
C:\>cl -Zi -AL -Lp buggymem.c
```

The two following sections provide specifics for debugging with TDW and CVW, respectively.

The Nuts and Bolts of TDW

To debug a protected-mode program under DOS, run TDW, together with your program, under 286|DOS-Extender:

```
C:\>RUN286 \borlandc\bin\tdw buggymem
```

You would probably tire of typing such a long command line each time you want to debug a protected-mode DOS program. The Phar Lap BIND286 utility can be used to create a new executable, TDP.EXE, whose name you would then type on the DOS command line instead of RUN286 TDW. To build TDP.EXE:

```
C:\>bind286 \borlandc\bin\tdw -exe \RUN286\bin\tdp.exe
```

Whether you run TDP or RUN286 TDW, you can do source-level debugging of protected-mode DOS programs without having to learn a new debugger. For the remainder of this discussion, we shall refer to TDW running under 286|DOS-Extender as TDP. If you do not already know how to use or Turbo Debugger, refer to the Borland documentation, or to one of several third-party books, such as Tom Swan's Mastering Turbo Debugger (Carmel IN: Hayden Books, 1990, 618 pp., ISBN 0-672-48454-4).

TDP displays just a few differences from real-mode TD. The major difference is that TDP can debug multimegabyte applications, whereas real-mode TD can't. TDP can also be extended using Phar Lap's PMON, which provides the ability to walk the protected-mode descriptor tables, display DPMI interrupt and exception vectors, and so on.

Inside TDP, you can press F9 to run a program, F8 to step, F7 to trace, F2 to set a breakpoint, CTRL-W to watch an expression, F1 to get help, and so on. Alternatively, you can use the pull-down menus and the mouse. TDP can be run in 25-line or 43/50-line mode.

When debugging BUGGYMEM, if you press F9, malloc would eventually run out of memory. TDP would run into our offending code, and place the cursor on the REP STOSW instruction and display this message:

```
Exception 13, error code 0
```

Sure enough, forgetting to check the return value from malloc() causes an "exception 13" (also known as an INT 0D, a General protection violation, or a GP fault). The CPU window would show that the ES segment register holds a value of zero, indicating that we're trying to do something with a NULL pointer.

In real mode, the interpretation of 0:0 as a NULL pointer is an arbitrary convention, because in real mode, 0:0 is a completely legitimate address (it holds the address of the divide-by-zero interrupt handler). Protected mode, however, provides hardware support for the notion of a NULL pointer.

Where would we be? By selecting the "Stack" option from the TDP "View" menu, and then navigating the stack view window, we would see that we're somewhere inside the call to memset() inside main(). This is not surprising, given that the call to memset() immediately follows the incorrect use of malloc().

Can you imagine debugging this code without TDW? We hope you will see from this example how much easier protected-mode programming can be with the features available in the 286|DOS-Extender SDK.

The Nuts and Bolts of CVW

To debug a protected-mode Microsoft program under DOS, run CVP7, together with your program, under 286|DOS-Extender:

    C:\>cvp7 buggymem

Unlike TDW (which can be invoked directly by 286|DOS-Extender SDK), CVW requires a little help to get started. CVP7 is a "wrapper" program supplied with the 286|DOS-Extender SDK. CVP7 changes the video mode, adjusts certain aspects of CVW's execution environment, filters out dangerous CVW switches, and (finally) invokes CVW4.EXE.

If you are familiar with either CodeView or CodeView for Windows, you can do source-level debugging of protected-mode programs without having to learn a new debugger. If you are not familiar with CodeView, then using 286|DOS-Extender is an excellent way to get started. Running CodeView in protected mode helps you to catch bugs as they happen, by signaling General protection ("GP") faults. This is in contrast to what occurs in real mode, where programs are allowed to dereference pointers willy-nilly, often corrupting data structures in obscure, hard-to-find ways. However you learn CodeView, you will want to read Microsoft's documentation to completely understand each command.

If you've used real-mode CV, but have not done much protected-mode programming, there's only one thing you should be aware of: protected-mode selectors don't look quite the same as the real-mode paragraph addresses you're used to. The first time you use CVP7, you might find yourself asking "What is this strange value I get back from malloc()?" For example, if the value in ES is 049F, don't assume it's a bad value: that's a typical number for a protected mode selector.

Additionally, the switches allowed for real- and protected-mode CodeView differ. CV's /R switch, which enables the use of 80386 ,debug registers is not allowed with CVP7. Similarly, /E and /X (expanded and extended memory support, respectively) are not allowed; CVP7, running as a 286|DOS-Extended program in protected mode, has no need for these switches.

Two features of real-mode CodeView that are lacking in CVP7 are the ability to launch a sub-shell via the "!" command or the "FILE" menu, and the ability to view the programs output with the "F4" command.

Essentially all the other commands in real-mode CodeView work exactly as you would expect. Inside CVP7, you can switch between displaying source code and object code with F3, you can use F2 to display the current register set, and you can use F9 and F5 to set a breakpoint and run your program. If the HELPFILES environment variable is set correctly, F1 invokes CodeView's built-in help system. Of course you may invoke all functions either by pulling down menus or by typing in the command window, just like real-mode CodeView or CodeView for Windows.

Using CVP7 to debug protected-mode programs is, in essence, very similar to using TDP. The steps you would take to debug buggymem.exe, for example, are nearly identical to the steps outlined above for TDP. When debugging BUGGYMEM, if you type "g", malloc would eventually run out of memory. CVP7 would run into our offending code, and place the cursor on the REP STOSW instruction and display this message:

Exception #13

Sure enough, forgetting to check the return value from malloc() causes an "exception 13" (also known as an INT 0D, a General protection violation, or a GP fault). The register window would show that the ES segment register holds a value of zero, indicating that we're trying to do something with a NULL pointer.

In real mode, the interpretation of 0:0 as a NULL pointer is an arbitrary convention, because in real mode, 0:0 is a completely legitimate address (it holds the address of the divide-by-zero interrupt handler). Protected mode, however, provides hardware support for the notion of a NULL pointer.

Where would we be? By selecting the CVP7 "Calls" menu, and then navigating the stack view window, we would see that we're somewhere inside the call to memset() inside main(). This is not surprising, given that the call to memset() immediately follows the incorrect use of malloc().

Can you imagine debugging this code without CodeView? We hope you will see from this example how much easier protected-mode programming can be with the features available in the 286|DOS-Extender SDK.

See Microsoft's C/C++ Environment and Tools manual for more information on using CVW4.

What About Direct Screen Writes?

So far we have seen that straightforward C or C++ code can be run, without source-code changes, under Phar Lap's 286|DOS-Extender Lite.

But while they allocated large amounts of memory, and showed some of the benefits of 286|DOS-Extender Lite and the basic process of developing applications with 286|DOS-Extender Lite, our MEMTEST sample programs are too simple to illustrate all the issues involved in PC software development. The remainder of this chapter quickly examines some of the issues pertinent to Microsoft C/C++ and Borland C++.

Clearly, MEMTEST is not a typical PC program. For example, it uses the portable printf() function to display output. With the exception of programs such as compilers and linkers, however, applications for the PC tend to use direct screen writes or other low-level code. How well do such programs run under 286|DOS-Extender Lite?

We saw earlier that DOS (INT 21h) and BIOS calls are supported in protected mode. Thus, low-level PC code runs as is under 286|DOS-Extender Lite.

However, the PC programming interface doesn't consist only of DOS and BIOS calls. The ability to peek and poke absolute memory locations is also part of the PC programming interface, and this ability normally assumes that the program is running in real mode.

Direct screen writes are a good example, because these assume that absolute memory locations such as B8000h can be addressed through pointers such as B800:0000. When a program is manipulating an address such as B800:0000, it's really interested in absolute memory location B8000h. Similarly, when it manipulates an address such as 0040:006C, it's really interested in absolute memory location 46Ch. In protected mode the equivalence of B8000h and B800:0000 no longer holds. It is precisely because protected mode throws out this equivalence that it can provide more than one megabyte of memory.

Besides the tiny video_mode() function we saw in the discussion of DOS and BIOS calls, a program that does direct screen writes probably would also include code such as the following, which puts the paragraph address of the text mode video display memory (0xB000 or 0xB800) into a global variable. This code also uses the MK_FP() macro from DOS.H in Borland C++ to create a far pointer to B000:0000 or to B800:0000:

```
unsigned short get_vid_mem(void)
{
    int vmode = video_mode();
    unsigned short seg;

    if (vmode == 7) /* monochrome */
      seg = 0xB000;
```

```
    else if ((vmode == 2) || (vmode == 3))
      seg = 0xB800;
    else
      return 0;

    return seg;
}

static BYTE far *vid_mem;    /* use far pointer */

video_init(void)
{
    vid_mem = MK_FP(get_vid_mem(), 0);
}

#define SCR(y,x)    (((y) * 160) + ((x) << 1))

void wrt_str(int y, int x, ATTRIB attr, unsigned char *p)
{
    BYTE far *v = vid_mem + SCR(y, x);
    while (*p)
    {
      *v++ = *p++;
      *v++ = attr;
    }
}
```

But if we now try to run a program that includes this code under 286|DOS-Extender
Lite, we get another one of those "General protection fault detected" messages, just as if
our code contained a bug:

```
C:\>cl -AL -Lp memtest3.c

C:\>bind286 memtest3

C:\>memtest3
Fatal error 286.3330: General protection fault detected.
PID=0001  TID=0001  SID=0001  ERRORCODE=B800
AX=0041  BX=0098  CX=01ED  DX=0000  SI=042E  DI=042E  BP=0F08
CS:IP=022F:01FD   DS=024F  ES=024F  SS:SP=024F:0F06   FLAGS=3206
```

or:

```
C:\>bcc286 memtest3.c

C:\>memtest3
Fatal error 286.3330: General protection fault detected.
PID=0001  TID=0001  SID=0001  ERRORCODE=B800
AX=0041  BX=0098  CX=01ED  DX=0000  SI=042E  DI=042E  BP=0F08
CS:IP=022F:01FD   DS=024F  ES=024F  SS:SP=024F:0F06   FLAGS=3206
```

Our code doesn't contain a bug. However, ERRORCODE=B800 suggests that simply
loading the paragraph address of the video display memory into a segment register such as
DS or ES isn't going to work in protected mode.

It's extremely simple to get this code working in protected mode. To write directly to
video memory from protected mode, you need a function call that "maps" absolute memory locations into the address space of your protected-mode program. The only function
that needs to be changed is get_vid_mem(), so that instead of returning 0xB000 or

0xB800, it returns a protected-mode selector that maps one of these real-mode paragraph addresses. To do this, we use the Phar Lap API (PHAPI) function DosMapRealSeg(), whose prototype is in PHAPI.H.

```
#ifdef DOSX286
// symbol DOSX286 automatically defined by BCC286
#include <phapi.h>
#endif

unsigned short get_vid_mem(void)
{
    int vmode = video_mode();
    unsigned seg;

    if (vmode == 7)
      seg = 0xB000;
    else if ((vmode == 2) || (vmode == 3))
      seg = 0xB800;
    else
      return 0;


#ifdef DOSX286
{
    unsigned short sel;
    /*
       DosMapRealSeg() takes a real mode paragraph address
       and a count of bytes, and gives back a selector that
       can be used to address the memory from protected
       mode. Like all PHAPI functions, DosMapRealSeg()
       returns 0 for success, or a non-zero error code. Any
       other information (such as the selector we're
       interested in) is returned via parameters.
    */
    if (DosMapRealSeg(seg, (long) 25*80*2, &sel) == 0)
      return sel;
    else
      return 0;
}
#endif

    return seg;
}
```

In the larger program from which this code was extracted, this was the only source-code change needed to get the program running under 286IDOS-Extender Lite. All the actual direct screen writes ran in protected mode without modification. Most graphics code can be ported to 286IDOS-Extender Lite in the same way, simply by changing the function that returns the segment number of video memory, to use DosMapRealSeg (0xA000, ...). Since the PHAPI-specific or protected-mode code is inside an #ifdef, the same code can be compiled for real mode. (Note that BCC286 automatically defines DOSX286. To get similar behavior from CL, you would specify -DDOSX286.)

When the program is finished with the selector to video memory, it should free it by calling DosFreeSeg():

```
DosFreeSeg(FP_SEG(vid_mem));     // segment of far pointer
```

That's all it takes to get direct screen writes working in protected mode.

Summary

Any given program probably will require only a few PHAPI functions; the vast majority of your DOS code will work "as is" under 286|DOS-Extender Lite. You can preserve your investment and your customer's investment in MS-DOS.

286|DOS-Extender Lite turns Microsoft C/C++ and Borland C++ into toolkits for protected-mode DOS development. Just by adding the -Lp switch to CL, or using BCC286 rather than BCC, your Borland C++ programs break the 640K barrier.

Using 286|DOS-Extender Lite with Borland C++

The easiest way to compile and link 286|DOS-Extender Lite programs with Borland C++ is to use BCC286, available with 286|DOS-Extender Lite:

```
C:\TEST>bcc286 memtest.c
```

```
C:\TEST>memtest
```

C++ programs can also be compiled and linked for 286|DOS-Extender Lite:

```
C:\TEST>bcc286 memtest.cpp
```

```
C:\TEST>memtest
```

BCC286.EXE will usually be installed in C:\LITE286\BIN, which must be on your path. BCC286 uses Borland's BCC.EXE and TLINK.EXE; these must also be on the path. For example:

```
C:\TEST>set path=c:\LITE286\bin;c:\borlandc\bin;c:\bin
```

286|DOS-Extender Lite requires TLINK version 4.0 or higher, shipped with Borland C++; it will not work with the earlier Turbo C or Turbo C++ versions of TLINK. 286|DOS-Extender Lite also requires the Borland C++ command-line tools, and will not work with the BC integrated development environment (IDE).

BCC286 also uses C0PL.OBJ and PHAPI.LIB, which come with 286|DOS-Extender Lite, and BCL286.LIB, which is built when you install 286|DOS-Extender Lite. These files must be located on the path, or in a directory named in an optional LIB environment variable, or in the library path specified with a BCC286 -L command-line parameter. These files are usually installed in C:\LITE286\BC3.LIB. If you receive a message from BCC286 such as "Cannot find C0PL.OBJ", you need to specify a library search path. For example:

```
C:\TEST>bcc286 -L\LITE286\bc3\lib;\borlandc\lib phoo.c
```

or:

```
C:\TEST>set lib=\LITE286\bc3\lib;\borlandc\lib
```

```
C:\TEST>bcc286 phoo.c
```

A good place to put switches such as -L and -I (include file path) is inside the Borland C++ TURBOC.CFG file. For example:

```
C:\TEST>type turboc.cfg
-L\LITE286\bc3\lib;\borlandc\lib;\borlandc\classlib\lib

-I\borlandc\include;\LITE286\inv
-G
-O
```

BCC286 does a large model compile with BCC and then creates a module-definition (.DEF) file which is passed to TLINK, along with protected-mode object modules and libraries, to create a protected mode executable which can be run from the DOS command line. BCC286 places a loader inside each protected-mode executable; this loader automatically runs 286|DOS-Extender Lite (LITE286.EXE) each time you start the protected-mode executable from the DOS command line.

BCC286 Usage in Detail

If you run BCC286 without any command-line arguments, it displays the standard BCC options followed by the additional options supplied by BCC286:

BCC286 Version 2.1 Copyright (c) 1991 Phar Lap Software, Inc.
Borland C++ Version 3.1 Copyright (c) 1991 Borland International
Syntax is: BCC [options] file[s]   * = default; -x- = turn switch x off

-1	80186/286 Instructions	-2	80286 Protected Mode Inst.
-Ax	Disable extensions	-B	Compile via assembly
-C	Allow nested comments	-Dxxx	Define macro
-Exxx	Alternate Assembler name	-G	Generate for speed
-Hxxx	Use pre-compiled headers	-Ixxx	Include files directory
-K	Default char is unsigned	-Lxxx	Libraries directory
-M	Generate link map	-N	Check stack overflow
-Ox	Optimizations	-P	Force C++ compile
-Qxxx	Memory usage control	-S	Produce assembly output
-Txxx	Set assembler option	-Uxxx	Undefine macro
-Vx	Virtual table control	-Wxxx	Create Windows application
-X	Suppress autodep. output	-Yx	Overlay control
-Z	Suppress register reloads	-a	Generate word alignment
-b	* Treat enums as integers	-c	Compile only
-d	Merge duplicate strings	-exxx	Executable file name
-fxx	Floating point options	-gN	Stop after N warnings
-iN	Max. identifier length	-jN	Stop after N errors
-k	Standard stack frame	-lx	Set linker option
-mx	Set Memory Model	-nxxx	Output file directory
-oxxx	Object file name	-p	Pascal calls
-r	* Register variables	-u	* Underscores on externs
-v	Source level debugging	-wxxx	Warning control
-y	Produce line number info	-zxxx	Set segment names

BCC286: Phar Lap 286|DOS-Extender driver for Borland C++ produces protected-mode DOS executables

usage: bcc286 [options] [filenames]
options: any bcc option or:
-stack=n   set stack size
-nostub   for smaller file without stub loader
-keep   keep BCC286's RSP, LNK, and DEF files

BCC286 Input Files

BCC286 accepts the following file types:

- C source files (default extension .C)
- C++ source files (default extension .CPP)
- Assembly-language source files (default extension .ASM)
- .OBJ object modules
- .LIB object libraries
- .DEF module-definition files

Pathnames can be specified using either backslashes or forward slashes:

```
C:\TEST>bcc286 \phoo\bar\hello.cpp
```

```
C:\TEST>bcc286 /phoo/bar/hello.cpp
```

In addition to standard BCC operation (described in the Borland C++ User's Guide) BCC286 handles .DEF and .ASM files in the following way: .DEF files are passed to TLINK, and override the standard BCC286 module-definition file. For example:

```
C:\TEST>bcc286 hello.c hello.def
```

If an .ASM file is the first file passed to BCC286, then no startup code is linked in. For example:

```
C:\TEST>bcc286 hello.asm phoo.c bar.c
```

Like BCC, BCC286 also accepts response files and configuration files, including TURBOC.CFG. For example:

```
C:\TEST>type hello.rsp
-v
-DDEBUGGING
-L\LITE286\bc3\lib;\borlandc\lib
hello.c
```

```
C:\TEST>bcc286 @hello.rsp
```

```
C:\TEST>type hello.cfg
-v -DDEBUGGING -L\LITE286\bc3\lib;\borlandc\lib
```

```
C:\TEST>bcc286 +hello.cfg hello.c
```

Response and configuration files do not suffer from the 128-byte limitation of the DOS command line.

BCC286-specific switches such as -stack should not be placed in configuration files. They can, however, be placed in response files.

Environment Variables

BCC286 switches can also be placed in an optional BCC286 environment variable. Except for BCC286-specific switches such as -stack or -nostub, switches placed in the BCC286 environment variable will also be passed on to BCC. For example:

```
C:\TEST>set bcc286=-v -DDEBUGGING -L\LITE286\bc3\lib;\borlandc\lib
```

```
C:\TEST>bcc286 phoo.c bar.c
```

As noted earlier, in addition to the BCC -L switch for specifying a library search path, BCC286 will also use an optional LIB environment variable. For example:

```
C:\TEST>set lib=\borlandc\lib;\LITE286\bc3\lib

C:\TEST>bcc286 phoo.c bar.c phoobar.lib
```

BCC286 Switches

BCC286 provides a number of features not found in BCC, including the ability to specify .DEF files on the command line and to set the stack size.

Most BCC286 switches, whether specified on the command line, in the BCC286 environment variable, or in a response or configuration file, are passed down to BCC. The following switches are not passed down, and are unique to BCC286:

-keep

Normally, BCC286 removes the three temporary files it creates: the BCC response file, TMP.RSP; the TLINK response file, TMP.LNK; and the module-definition file, TMP-.DEF. If you use the -keep switch, BCC286 won't remove these files; you'll be able to examine, copy, or edit them for your own use with BCC and TLINK.

-nostub

286IDOS-Extender Lite programs produced with BCC286 can be run directly from the DOS command line because they include a "real-mode stub" called GORUN286.EXE, which reinvokes the program under LITE286.EXE. This GORUN286 stub increases the size of the program by about 10 KB. The BCC286 -nostub switch suppresses the use of this stub, resulting in smaller executable files which, however, can only be run from the DOS command line by explicitly using LITE286; otherwise they produce a confusing message and exit back to DOS. For example:

```
C:\TEST>bcc286 hello.c

C:\TEST>hello
hello world!

C:\TEST>bcc286 -nostub hello.c

C:\TEST>hello
This program must be run under OS/2.

C:\TEST>LITE286 hello
hello world!
```

Note, however, that under the full-fledged 286IDOS-Extender, the DosExecPgm() function and the spawn() family of functions in the C run-time library can directly invoke protected-mode programs without a real-mode stub.

If you want to specify a real-mode stub other than GORUN286, use a .DEF file. As noted earlier, .DEF files can be specified on the BCC286 command line. For example:

```
C:\TEST>type hello.def
PROTMODE
STUB 'mystub.exe'
EXPORTS BCC286_EXE

C:\TEST>bcc286 hello.c hello.def
```

-stack=xxx

This switch can be used to set the stack size of a program. For example:

```
C:\TEST>bcc286 -stack=10240 hello.c
```

Stack size can alternatively be specified inside a .DEF file. For example:

```
C:\TEST>type hello.def
PROTMODE
STUB 'gorun286.exe'
STACKSIZE 10240
EXPORTS BCC286_EXE

C:\TEST>bcc286 hello.c hello.def
```

The default stack size defined by BCC286 is 4 KB. If you receive a TLINK "Group DGROUP exceeds 64K" error message, you can try reducing the stack size.

BCC286 Differences from BCC

BCC286 has the following differences from BCC:

The only supported memory model switch is -ml (large model). If you need near or huge data, use the near, far, and huge keywords in your source code to create "mixed model" programs.

Because 286|DOS-Extender Lite, like Windows, does not support overlays, the BCC -Yo and TLINK -o overlay switches cannot be used when creating 286|DOS-Extender Lite programs. 286|DOS-Extender Lite does not suffer from the 640K limitations of MS-DOS, so overlays are usually unnecessary.

Using BCC and TLINK

If you would prefer to use BCC and TLINK directly to compile and link 286|DOS-Extender Lite programs, instead of using BCC286, there are certain command-line options, object modules, libraries, and module-definition files which you must use. These are normally taken care of automatically by BCC286.

For example, to produce a protected-mode DOS version of HELLO.EXE, without BCC286:

```
C:\TEST>bcc -c -ml -2 -DDOSX286 -h hello.c

C:\TEST>type protmode.def
PROTMODE
STUB      'gorun286.exe'
EXPORTS   BCC286_EXE

C:\TEST>type hello.lnk
\LITE286\BC3\lib\c0pl hello
hello
nul
phapi bcl286
protmode
C:\TEST>tlink /L\LITE286\BC3\lib @hello.lnk
```

The following briefly describes each switch, statement, or file. This description is necessary only if you are compiling and linking directly with BCC and TLINK, rather than using BCC286.

BCC Switches

-c (compile only): A module-definition (.DEF) file must be specified when using Borland TLINK to produce 286|DOS-Extender Lite programs, but BCC (unlike BCC286) does not accept .DEF files on its command line. Therefore, TLINK must be run as a separate step.

-ml (large model): Large model is required when using Borland C++ to produce 286|DOS-Extender Lite programs. The near, far, and huge keywords can be used in source code to produce a "mixed model" program.

-2 (80286 protected-mode instructions): This switch is usually not necessary, but BCC produces better code when it is used. Since 286|DOS-Extender Lite programs run only on 80286 and higher machines, it makes sense to use this switch. If a user attempts to run a 286|DOS-Extender Lite program on an 8086 or 8088 machine, LITE286 detects the error before your program starts.

The -2 switch is necessary if your C or C++ program includes inline assembly-language statements that use 286-based protected-mode instructions such as LAR or LSL.

-DDOSX286 (define the symbol DOSX286): This symbol is not strictly necessary, but BCC286 automatically defines it, and some of the examples in this manual assume that it has been defined.

.DEF File Statements A .DEF file provides information to the linker about the contents and system requirements of a protected-mode program, including Windows and 286|DOS-Extender Lite programs. A .DEF file is needed to produce a 286|DOS-Extender Lite program with Borland C++. BCC286 automatically produces a standard .DEF file that contains the following statements (the line that begins with a semicolon is a comment):

```
; protmode.def
PROTMODE
STUB 'gorun286.exe'
EXPORTS BCC286_EXE
```

If you are running BCC and TLINK directly without using BCC286, then you must specify your own .DEF file. You can create one standard PROTMODE.DEF for use with all your programs, or create a separate customized .DEF file for each program.

The statements used in the default .DEF file created by BCC286 are explained below:

PROTMODE: The PROTMODE statement should almost always be used. Only omit this statement when you are creating a real-mode DLL.

STUB 'gorun286.exe': The STUB statement embeds the specified real-mode DOS executable at the beginning of the protected-mode executable. This real-mode DOS executable then becomes the "stub" which is run whenever the program is invoked from the DOS command line.

GORUN286.EXE is a real-mode program which reinvokes 286|DOS-Extender Lite programs under LITE286.EXE, creating the useful illusion that MS-DOS is capable of running protected-mode programs. If a different real-mode stub is specified, the 286|DOS-Extender Lite program may have to be run from the DOS command line with an explicit LITE286 statement.

If the STUB statement is omitted and the 286|DOS-Extender Lite program is run directly from the DOS command line, it will print out the confusing and untrue statement "This program must be run under OS/2."

EXPORTS BCC286_EXE: Currently, this is required only for Borland C++ executables that use floating-point math. However, it is safest to include this statement in all Borland C++ executables.

TLINK Switches and Files

/L\lite286\bc3\lib: The TLINK /L switch specifies a library search path. The libraries PHAPI.LIB and BCL286.LIB, and the C0PL.OBJ startup object module, are usually located in C:\LITE286\BC3\LIB.

@hello.lnk: While TLINK can be run with all necessary files and switches named right on the command line, in most genuine programs this will run up against the 128-byte DOS command line limit. For example, even protected-mode HELLO requires a long command line if you're not using BCC286:

```
C:\TEST>tlink /L\LITE286\bc3\lib c0pl hello,hello,,bcl286 phapi,protmode
```

The alternative is to put TLINK input in a response file. Newlines are used to delimit fields, and a + sign is used to continue fields across multiple lines. The TLINK fields are obj, exe, map, lib, def. For example:

```
C:\TEST>type hello.lnk
c0pl +
hello
hello
nul
bcl286 phapi
protmode

C:\TEST>tlink /L\LITE286\bc3\lib @hello.lnk
```

00PL.OBJ: This is 286|DOS-Extender Lite protected-mode large model startup code for Borland C++. This file is shipped with 286|DOS-Extender Lite SDK and will generally be located in C:\LITE286\BC3\LIB.

PHAPI.LIB: This library contains import references for Phar Lap application program interface (PHAPI) functions exported from the 286|DOS-Extender Lite DLLs.

BCL286.LIB: This library contains a protected-mode compatible version of the Borland C++ run-time library. This file is built during installation of 286|DOS-Extender Lite, from Borland's CL.LIB, and will generally be located in C:\LITE286\BC3\LIB.

Building Floating-Point Programs

By default, BCC286 compiles program with the -f flag, for floating-point emulation. If a program does not in fact require floating-point math, this makes the executable about 16 KB larger than necessary. To generate smaller executables, use the BCC286 -f- (no floating point) option. For example:

```
C:\TEST>bcc286 -f- hello.c
```

If you are using floating-point math, there are several issues which may be important:

If you will be running floating-point protected-mode applications under Windows Enhanced mode, you must install the virtual device driver PHARLAP.386, included with 286 I DOS-Extender Lite. Insert the statement "DEVICE=C:\LITE286\BIN\PHARLAP-.386" (or whatever path is appropriate) in the [386Enh] section of the SYSTEM.INI file.

BCC286 generates a protected-mode floating-point program when the -f (floating point emulation), -ff (fast emulation), -f87 (8087 hardware) or -f287 (80287 hardware) option is used. When linking such programs directly with TLINK, however, you must specify the correct library modules. For example, if sqrt.exe uses floating-point emulation:

```
C:\TEST>bcc286 -f sqrt.c
```

or:

```
C:\TEST>bcc -c -f -ml -2 -h -DDOSX286 sqrt.c

C:\TEST>tlink c0pl sqrt emu286.lib,sqrt,,emu mathl phapi bcl286,protmode
```

If sqrt2.exe uses 80287 floating-point hardware instructions:

```
C:\TEST>bcc286 -f287 sqrt2.c
```

or:

```
C:\TEST>bcc -c -f287 -ml -2 -h -DDOSX286 sqrt2.c

C:\TEST>tlink c0pl sqrt fp286.lib,sqrt2,,fp87 mathl phapi bcl286,protmode
```

Note that floating-point emulation requires EMU286.LIB (linked in as an object module) and EMU.LIB, while programs that use floating-point hardware instructions require FP286.LIB (linked in as an object module) and FP87.LIB.

If you build floating-point applications without BCC286, you must export the symbol BCC286_EXE. Simply insert the statement "EXPORTS BCC286_EXE" in your module-definition (.DEF) file. For example:

```
C:\TEST>type protmode.def
PROTMODE
EXPORTS   BCC286_EXE
```

If you have a floating point coprocessor, but need to test floating-point emulation, set 87=NO in the DOS environment.

Using 286 I DOS-Extender with Microsoft C/C++ 7.0

The easiest way to build Microsoft C/C++ protected-mode programs is to use the CL command, with which you are probably already familiar:

```
C:\TEST> cl -Lp -AL memtest.c

C:\TEST> bind286 memtest

C:\TEST> memtest
```

The -Lp switch instructs CL to link against the protected-mode library LLIBCEP.LIB, which should already be installed in \LITE286\MSC700\LIB. The -AL switch instructs CL to create a large-model program. Using large model is not a requirement to run in protected mode, but it offers the best combination of speed and data-segment size under most conditions. If your program can fit into small model, however, you will obtain better performance by running in real mode.

Protected-mode programs are linked against LLIBCEP.LIB and PHAPI.LIB, both of which should be in the sub-directory MSC700\LIB of your LITE286 directory. (If LLIBCEP.LIB is not present, please review the installation instructions, and re-run MKLIB.BAT.)

In order for CL to find the 286|DOS-Extender Lite libraries,include files, and programs, you must edit three of your environment variables. The LIB environment variable specifies a list of directories in which to search for libraries. The INCLUDE environment variable lists the directories containing include files. You must add the LITE286 subdirectory BIN to you PATH variable. A typical set of environment variables would include:

```
C:\> set PATH=c:\;c:\dos;c:\bin;c:\c700\bin;c:\lite286\bin
C:\> set LIB=c:\c700\lib;c:\lite286\msc700\lib
C:\> set INCLUDE=c:\c700\include;c:\lite286\inc
```

Differences Between Real and Protected-Mode CL

With 286|DOS-Extender Lite, programming for protected mode issurprisingly similar to programming for real mode. This includes, for instance, providing switches to CL. There are, however, slight differences in the command line used to build a protected-mode program:

The -AH (huge model) and -AT (tiny, or COM model) switches are not supported in protected mode. You may not build p-code programs. This means you will not use the -Of, -Ov, -Oq, -Gn, -Gp, and -NQ switches in building protected-mode programs.

The various -G switches that specify Windows entry/exit code generation should not be used when compiling 286|DOS-Extender Lite programs.

Linking by Hand

Ordinarily, you would use CL to build protected-mode programs. CL invokes the various compiler passes, and then optionally invokes the linker. You may want, however, to run the Microsoft C/C++ linker, LINK.EXE, by hand. If you want to replicate exactly the action of CL, the command line is fairly simple:

```
C:\> cl -c -AL hand.c
C:\> link hand.obj,hand.exe/noi,,/nod:llibce.lib llibcep.lib;
C:\> bind286 hand
```

The following sections briefly describe each switch, statement, and file. This information is necessary only if you are linking with LINK rather than using CL.

CL Switches

-c (compile only):   This switch instructs CL to create on object file, but to not run the linker. The object file that you link against might be created by CL, MASM, or any other tool compatible with the C7 linker and run-time libraries.

-AL (large model):   While not strictly required, large model and protected-mode programming go hand in hand. Real-mode DOS provides a more space-efficient execution environment for small model than does 286|DOS-Extender Lite.

-Lp (protected mode):   Note that this switch is absent from the CL command line. Since CL is not running LINK, -Lp is not required.

LINK Switches

Refer to the manual Microsoft C/C++ Environment and Tools for information on LINK command line specifiers.

The following sample command line links a protected-mode program:

```
C:\> link hand.obj,hand.exe/noi,nul,/nod:llibce.lib llibcep.lib;  hand.obj
(object list):
```

All the names that precede the first comma comprise a list of objects to be included in the resulting executable image. If any file name in this list does not have an extension, .OBJ is assumed.

hand.exe (executable image):   The file name in this position specifies the name of the resulting image. The default extension here is .EXE.

/noi (no ignore case):   This switch determines the case-significance of external symbols.

nul (map file):   LINK can optionally generate a map file. By naming the NUL device file NUL.MAP, no file is generated.

/nod:llibce.lib (no default search):   LINK will search, by default, the set of library names embedded in the object files. /nod:llibce instructs LINK to avoid searching that library.

llibcep.lib (library list):   LLIBCEP is the protected-mode library created during the installation process. It completely replaces, and is built from, LLIBCE.LIB.

For more information about each of the CL and LINK options, please consult the manual Microsoft C/C++ Environment and Tools.

Running Protected Mode Applications Under MS-DOS

So far we have seen that a program produced by BCC286 can be run directly from the DOS command line simply by typing its name, like any other DOS program. 286|DOS-Extender Lite programs can also be run under DOS without a command line, using any of the many alternatives to COMMAND.COM such as the DOSSHELL in DOS 5.

By default, a protected-mode program produced by BCC286 includes a real-mode "stub" program called GORUN286. When compiled with Microsoft C/C++, BIND286 is used to attach the stub. When one of these programs is started under DOS, an embedded copy of GORUN286.EXE actually runs initially. GORUN286 is called a stub because its sole job is to restart the program under 286|DOS-Extender Lite, (LITE286.EXE). In other words, if PHOO.C is compiled with either:

```
C:\TEST>bcc286 phoo.c
```

or:

```
C:\>cl -AL -Lp phoo.c
```

```
C:\>bind286 phoo
```

then running the program by typing its name:

```
C:\TEST>phoo
```

is equivalent to typing LITE286 followed by the name of the program:

```
C:\TEST>lite286 phoo
```

This seems like no big deal: after all, we've saved only six letters and a space. However, by eliminating the need to type those seven keystrokes, we have effectively hidden the DOS extender, and created the useful illusion that MS-DOS is an operating system that runs protected-mode executables.

Though usually hidden, the key components of 286|DOS-Extender Lite are LITE286.EXE, which loads 16-bit protected-mode .EXE files under MS-DOS, and DOSCALLS.DLL, a dynamic link library (DLL) which contains some of the functions used by the protected-mode startup code and run-time library. The directory containing LITE286.EXE, for example C:\LITE286\BIN, must be located somewhere on the DOS file-search path when you start an executable produced by BCC286.

LITE286.EXE puts the computer into protected mode and loads your protected-mode program. Whenever your program makes DOS (INT 21h) or BIOS requests from protected mode, the DOS extender quickly and invisibly does the work of sending the requests off to MS-DOS or the ROM BIOS, which are running in real mode. Thus, 286|DOS-Extender Lite is 100% compatible with DOS: it's not an emulation, but literally an extension of DOS.

Compatibility

There is another side to extending MS-DOS. One of the key services of 286|DOS-Extender Lite, in contrast to any "roll your own" approach to protected mode, is compatibility.

We've been assuming that the computer is in real mode, that LITE286 switches it into protected mode, installs some interrupt handlers, spawns your protected-mode program and, when your program completes, puts the computer back into real mode.

But that would involve a simplistic view of the PC world in the 1990s. Most users of 80386 and 80486 machines are employing memory managers such as EMM386, 386MAX and QEMM, or multitasking window systems such as DESQview or Microsoft Windows 3.x. When such programs are running, the computer is not in real mode; it's running in a one-megabyte protected mode called virtual 8086 mode. The assumption that a DOS extender can simply switch the machine from real mode to protected mode does not take into account the fact that many machines won't be in real mode. Furthermore, users may be running programs such as VDISK or HIMEM or SMARTDrive, which use extended memory. LITE286 must be able to run your protected-mode program under DOS, yet be highly compatible with any other memory-management software a user might be running.

One of the key questions about any protected-mode MS-DOS solution is how compatible it is with all this different software. Is it compatible with EMM386, 386MAX, and QEMM? Does it run in a window inside DESQview/386 or Microsoft Windows 3.x

Enhanced mode? What if the machine is already running an expanded memory (EMS) or extended memory (XMS) manager? What if there are VDISKs or a SMARTDrive? What if your protected-mode program has been spawned from within a 386|DOS-Extender program such as IBM Interleaf Publisher, Mathematica, or AutoCAD/386?

286|DOS-Extender Lite handles all these situations gracefully. It is compatible with all the PC industry standards for protected mode and extended memory. In particular, it supports the Virtual Control Program Interface (VCPI) and DOS Protected Mode Interface (DPMI). VCPI is a specification developed jointly by Quarterdeck Office Systems and Phar Lap Software that allows EMS emulators and DOS extenders to coexist; it is an extension to EMS 4.0. DPMI is a specification whose primary goal is compatibility between DOS extenders and DOS multitasking environments; DPMI was jointly developed by a committee including Microsoft, Intel, IBM, Phar Lap, Quarterdeck, Borland, Lotus, and other companies. For more details on VCPI and DPMI, plus the old INT 15h and XMS standards, we recommend the book Extending DOS, Second Edition, edited by Ray Duncan (Reading MA: Addison-Wesley, 1991, 538 pp., ISBN 0-201-56798-9).

To summarize, programs developed with 286|DOS-Extender Lite can run in a wide variety of environments. LITE286 takes care of all the messy details of compatibility. There is no separate configuration or "tune" program to run.

LITE286 Requirements

LITE286 does have a few requirements, however.

If an expanded memory (EMS) handler is installed, it must follow the EMS 4.0 and VCPI specifications. Almost all EMS managers shipping today are VCPI-compatible; if yours isn't, contact the manufacturer about upgrading to a new version. (The exception is IBM PC-DOS 4.01, which has an EMS manager that is not VCPI-compatible.)

Microsoft's EMM386, included with DOS 5.0 and Windows 3.x, is VCPI-compatible, and can therefore be used with 286|DOS-Extender Lite. However, the EMM386 NOEMS switch effectively disables VCPI support, and therefore cannot be used.

If an extended memory (XMS) manager such as HIMEM.SYS is installed, we recommend setting a fairly large handle count. For example:

```
DEVICE=C:\WIN30\HIMEM.SYS /NUMHANDLES=127
```

LITE286 will not run in the DOS compatibility box of OS/2 1.x, because that environment is limited to a maximum of 640K. However, it will run in the DOS compatibility boxes of OS/2 2.0, which provide DPMI support.

One important word of warning: Even though you don't have to explicitly type "LITE286" to run an executable produced by BCC286 under MS-DOS, the LITE286-.EXE file is necessary. The directory containing both this file and DOSCALLS.DLL (for example C:\LITE286\BIN) must be located somewhere on the DOS file-search path. If GORUN286 cannot find LITE286.EXE, it will display the message:

```
This program requires Phar Lap's 286|DOS-Extender
```

If LITE286.EXE cannot find DOSCALLS.DLL (which should be located in the same directory as LITE286.EXE), it will display the message:

```
Fatal error 286.2190: Load program failed -- File not found --
DOSCALLS.DLL.
```

If you receive either of these messages when trying to run a 286|DOS-Extender Lite executable, ensure that your path is correct. For example:

```
C:\TEST>set path=c:\bin;c:\LITE286\bin;c:\dos
```

Note that neither LITE286.EXE nor the 286|DOS-Extender Lite DLLs can be shipped to end-users. In order to prepare programs for redistribution, you must purchase the 286|DOS-Extender Run time Kit (RTK), which lets you bind 286|DOS-Extender plus any necessary DLLS into your application (an application may consist of multiple executable files, all of which are covered by a single license agreement).

With these details out of the way, protected-mode programs will run under MS-DOS.

Error Messages

The most common fatal error messages are described briefly in the following sample sessions.

```
C:\TEST>LITE286 phoobar
Fatal error 286.2190: Load program failed -- File not found -- phoobar.exe.
```

There is no program named PHOOBAR.EXE. Either you have misspelled the program's name, or it is not located on the path.

```
C:\DOS>LITE286 bad
Fatal error 286.3330: General protection fault detected.
PID=0001  TID=0001  SID=0001  ERRORCODE=0000
AX=0004  BX=0000  CX=0019  DX=008B  SI=00DA  DI=00DA  BP=0BE2
CS:IP=0237:001D   DS=024F  ES=0000  SS:SP=024F:0BDE   FLAGS=3246
```

Your program violated a rule of protected mode, causing a General protection fault (GP fault). There is a bug in your program, or a piece of code which must be modified before it can be run in protected mode, or you have unintentionally included real-mode code (for example, real-mode libraries) in the program.

```
C:\DOS>LITE286 mem
Fatal error 286.1000: System does not have an 80286 (or newer) processor.
```

You have attempted to run a 286|DOS-Extender Lite program on a machine which does not have an 80286, 80386, or 80486 processor.

```
C:\DOS>LITE286 mem
Fatal error 286.1020: This program requires VCPI or DPMI in V86 mode.
```

A program, probably an expanded-memory manager, has put the computer into virtual 8086 mode, but the program does not support either the Virtual Control Program Interface (VCPI) or the DOS Protected Mode Interface (DPMI). Contact the manufacturer about upgrading to a later version which does support VCPI or DPMI, or remove the program. Some of the expanded memory simulators with which LITE286 works are:

- QEMM 4.1 or later (Quarterdeck)
- 386MAX 4.02 or later (Qualitas)
- EMM 4.02 or later (COMPAQ)
- EMM386 (DOS 5.0, Microsoft Windows 3.x versions)

LITE286 Command Line Options

What if you want to run your 286|DOS-Extender Lite program on hardware that is not 100% IBM-compatible? What if you need to reserve a certain amount of extended memory because some other program doesn't adhere to any of the PC industry's standards for extended memory usage? What if your program does a large amount of file I/O and you want LITE286 to use a larger conventional-memory "transfer buffer" for DOS and BIOS calls?

LITE286 has a number of command line options which can be used in (frankly, rather rare) situations such as these. If you type LITE286 -help on the DOS command line, a list of these command line options is displayed (the following display is not complete):

```
C:\DOS>LITE286 -help
286|DOS-Extender Lite: 2.5 -- Copyright (C) 1986-92 Phar Lap Software, Inc.
    LITE286  switch(es) filename

        -EXTLIMIT n        Set max. bytes of extended memory used
        -EXTLOW addr       Set lowest extended memory address used
        -EXTHIGH addr      Set highest extended memory address used
        -ISTKSIZE n        Set size of interrupt stacks (1K blocks)
        -LDTSIZE n         Set number of LDT entries
        -NISTACK n         Set number of interrupt stacks
        -REALIMIT n        Set max. bytes of real memory used
        -SWITCH name       Select mode switch method (AUTO, AT, 386,
                              SURESWITCH, PS2, INBOARD, 6300, ACER,
                              VECTRA, VCPI, or FAST)
        -SWITCHFILE name   Select external switching .BIN file
        -XFERSIZE n        Set size of transfer buffer (1K blocks)
```

Any LITE286 switch can be set on the DOS command line. For example, the following runs MYPROG.EXE with a transfer buffer of 16 KB:

```
C:\TEST>LITE286 -xfersize 16 myprog
```

However, since normally we don't bother typing "LITE286" to run a program produced by BCC286, we need another way to set LITE286 command-line options. For example, the following is equivalent to the LITE286 command line just shown:

```
C:\TEST>set phoo=-xfersize 16
```

```
C:\TEST>set bar=-xfersize 32
C:\TEST>phoo
```

```
C:\TEST>bar
```

Of course, you must have sufficient room in your DOS environment. If you receive an "Out of environment space" message, you need a larger DOS environment. Add a line such as the following to your CONFIG.SYS file, and reboot:

```
SHELL=c:\dos\command.com /p /e:512
```

Note that only LITE286 switches are processed in the LITE286 or application-specific DOS extender environment variables, or in the "configuration block" in an executable. Any command line switches specific to your program must be handled by your program in the usual way.

The Phar Lap Application Program Interface (PHAPI)

The full-blown 286|DOS-Extender SDK comes with extensive support for the Phar Lap Application Program Interface (PHAPI), which provides protected-mode DOS programs with a set of services in the following areas:

- Creating and changing protected-mode selectors
- Communication between real and protected mode
- Dynamic Link Library (DLL) support
- Interrupt and exception handling
- DOS memory management
- 80386 paging functions

The following functions are part of PHAPI; prototypes for these functions appear in PHAPI.H:

Selector and Memory Management

DosAllocHuge	Allocate huge (> 64k) segment
DosAllocRealSeg	Allocate segment in conventional memory
DosAllocSeg	Allocate segment
DosCreateCSAlias	Create code alias to a data segment
DosCreateDSAlias	Create data alias to a code segment
DosFreeSeg	Free segment
DosGetBIOSSeg	Get selector to the BIOS data area
DosGetHugeShift	Get selector increment for huge segments
DosGetPhysAddr	Convert selector:offset to physical address
DosGetSegDesc	Get segment descriptor
DosLockSegPages	Lock pages of a segment
DosMapLinSeg	Map linear address
DosMapRealSeg	Map real-mode address into protected mode
DosMapPhysSeg	Map physical address
DosMemAvail	Get amount of available extended memory
DosRealAvail	Get amount of available conventional memory
DosReallocHuge	Resize a huge segment
DosReallocSeg	Resize a segment
DosSetSegAttrib	Set access rights of a segment
DosUnlockSegPages	Unlock pages of a segment
DosVerifyAccess	Verify segment for read, write, execute

Interrupts and Exceptions

DosChainToProtIntr	Chain to a protected-mode interrupt handler
DosChainToRealIntr	Chain to a real-mode interrupt handler
DosGetExceptionHandler	Get exception (e.g., GP fault) handler
DosGetProtVec	Get protected-mode interrupt vector
DosGetRealProtVec	Get real- and protected-mode interrupt vector
DosGetRealVec	Get real-mode interrupt vector
DosIsProtIntr	Test if interrupt is from protected mode

DosIsRealIntr   Test if interrupt is from real mode
DosProtIntr   Generate a protected-mode interrupt from real mode
DosRealIntr   Generate a real-mode interrupt from protected mode
DosSetExceptionHandler   Set exception handler
DosSetPassToProtVec   Set interrupt vector to go to protected-mode handler
DosSetPassToRealVec   Set interrupt vector to go to real-mode handler
DosSetProtVec   Set protected-mode interrupt vector
DosSetRealProtVec   Set real- and protected-mode interrupt vectors
DosSetRealVec   Set real-mode interrupt vector
DosVProtIntr   Generate a protected-mode interrupt from real mode
DosVRealIntr   Generate a real-mode interrupt from protected mode

Mixing Real- and Protected-Mode Code

DosFreeProtStack   Free a protected-mode stack
DosFreeRealStack   Free a real-mode stack
DosProtFarCall   Call a protected-mode function from real mode
DosProtFarJump   Jump to protected mode from real mode
DosProtToReal   Convert a protected- to a real-mode address
DosRealFarCall   Call a real-mode function from protected mode
DosRealFarJump   Jump to real-mode from protected mode
DosRealToProt   Convert a real- to a protected-mode address
DosVProtFarCall   Call a protected-mode function from real mode
DosVProtFarJump   Jump to protected mode from real mode
DosVRealFarCall   Call a real-mode function from protected mode
DosVRealFarJump   Jump to real-mode from protected mode

Dynamic Linking

DosEnumMod   Enumerate the currently-loaded modules
DosEnumProc   Enumerate the functions in a DLL
DosFreeModule   Free a DLL
DosGetModHandle   Get the module handle of a DLL
DosGetModName   Get the filename of a DLL
DosGetProcAddr   Get the selector:offset of a function in a DLL
DosGetRealProcAddr   Get the real-mode address of a function in a DLL
DosLoadModule   Load a DLL
DosSetProcAddr   Set the address of a function in a DLL

Miscellaneous

DosExecPgm   Start a new protected- or real-mode process
DosExit   Exit from a program
DosExitList   Register an exit routine
DosGetMachineMode   Get processor mode
DosIsPharLap   Test if running under 286IDOS-Extender
DosPTrace   Debug a child program

Run-Time Library

Keep in mind the following points when using the Borland C++ run-time library in protected mode:

The farmalloc( ) call in protected mode is not the same as large-model malloc( ). farmalloc( ) takes an unsigned long parameter, and can be used to allocate huge (> 64 KB segments); consequently, it has additional overhead not present when using plain malloc( ). Only use farmalloc( ) if you really want to allocate huge segments.

The biosdisk( ) function is not supported, because 286|DOS-Extender Lite does not support INT 13h (BIOS disk services) in protected mode.

The setvect( ) function is not supported. setvect( ) is equivalent to an INT 21h AH=25h (Set Interrupt Vector). While INT 21h AH=25h is fully supported under 286|DOS-Extender Lite, it is almost never what one would want in a protected mode program. All the most-common interrupts, such as Ctrl-C, Ctrl-Break, and Critical Error, require that real-mode interrupts be passed on to protected mode. This functionality is provided by the DosSetPassToProtVec( ) function, available only with the full-fledged 286|DOS-Extender SDK.

ANNOTATED
BIBLIOGRAPHY

DPMI and VCPI

Chui, Paul. "Undocumented DOS from Protected-Mode Windows 3," *Dr. Dobb's Journal*, February 1992.
  Chui uses DPMI to call undocumented DOS functions from Windows.

Davis, Ralph. *Windows Network Programming*, Reading MA: Addison-Wesley, 1992.
  Davis uses DPMI to call network TSRs and drivers.

Intel Corporation, et al., *DOS Protected Mode Interface (DPMI) Specification*, Santa Clara, CA: Intel Corp., 1990.

Phar Lap Software, et al., *Virtual Control Program Interface*, Cambridge, MA: Phar Lap Software, 1989.
  These two specifications document the two primary standards that allow DOS extenders to coexist with each other (and with other protected-mode programs). These documents are free of charge. The DPMI specification comes in two flavors: version 0.9 (order number 240763-001) and version 1.0 (order number 240977-001).

Schulman, Andrew. "The Programming Challenge of Windows Protected Mode," *PC Magazine*, June 25, 1991.
  Undocumented DOS calls from Windows using DPMI.

General DOS Programming (including TSRs)

Duncan, Ray. *IBM ROM BIOS*, Redmond, WA: Microsoft Press 1988

Duncan, Ray. *MS-DOS Functions*, Redmond, WA: Microsoft Press 1988
  These books are small, handy, and inexpensive. While they don't contain much detail, they are excellent as quick references.

Schulman, Andrew, et al., *Undocumented DOS*, Reading MA: Addison-Wesley, 1990
This book contains a great deal of information that had previously been undocumented or poorly documented. Many pearls for TSR programming here. A second edition is scheduled for early 1993.

Williams, Al. *DOS 5: A Developer's Guide*, Redwood City, CA: M&T Books, 1991
Parts 1 and 2 are about DOS programming in general, including details about graphics, EMS, TSRs, and device drivers. Many of the chapters contain practical toolkits that you can use right away. Part 3 covers protected-mode techniques for DOS programmers. You'll find chapters on extended memory techniques and the complete source for PROT, a 386 DOS extender. Part 3 also contains chapters on using extended memory, accessing 4 gigabytes from real mode (its true), and using 386 hardware debugging. A new edition is scheduled to be available during 1993.

General Protected-Mode DOS Programming

Duncan, Ray, et al., *Extending DOS*, Second Edition, Reading MA: Addison-Wesley, 1992
Good chapters on DOS extenders, DPMI, and other topics of interest to protected-mode programmers.

Intel Corporation, *80386 Programmer's Reference Manual*, Santa Clara, CA: Intel Corp., 1986

Intel Corporation, *80386 System Software Writer's Guide*, Santa Clara, CA: Intel Corp., 1987
These books (and their 286 and 486 counterparts) are well worth having. However, some of the techniques these manual illustrate are not often used in practice for performance reasons.

Turley, James. *Advanced 80386 Programming Techniques*, Berkeley, CA: Osborne/-McGraw-Hill, 1988
An excellent book that covers "pure" 386 programming (in other words, on some platform other than the PC). None of the code will run on a DOS machine, but Turley's explanations of protected mode are extraordinarily lucid.

General Windows Programming

Norton, Daniel. *Writing Windows Device Drivers*, Reading MA: Addison-Wesley, 1992.
This is a great reference for writing VxDs—Windows 32-bit flat device drivers.

Petzold, Charles. *Programming Windows*, Redmond WA: Microsoft Press, 1990
The book from the man who taught practically everyone how to write Windows programs. If you are one of the nine Windows programmers who still haven't read this book, go get it now.

Schulman, Andrew, et al., *Undocumented Windows*, Reading, MA: Addison Wesley, 1992
A must have reference that documents the midnight exploration of Windows

internals by Andrew Schulman, David Maxey, and Matt Pietrek. If you ever wondered what a global handle really is and how it relates to a protected-mode selector, then this is the book.

WIN32

Microsoft, *WIN32 Application Programming Interface*, Redmond, WA: Microsoft Press, 1992

A two volume reference for the WIN32 API. WIN32 is going to be increasingly important for protected-mode DOS and Windows programmers alike—don't let it sneak up on you.

INDEX

Attention 3 1/2" Disk Drive Users:

The *DOS and Windows Protected Mode* disk is available in 3 1/2" high density format. Please return the order form below with a check for $10.00 payable to Addison-Wesley to:

Addison-Wesley Publishing Company
Order Department
1 Jacob Way
Reading, MA 01867-9984

Please send me the 3 1/2" high density disk to accompany *DOS and Windows Protected Mode* by Al Williams (ISBN 0-201-62297-1). I am enclosing a check for $10.00.

Name:

Address:

City: State: Zip:

WITH LOVE AND BABKA

WITH LOVE AND
BABKA

50
Sweet and Savory
Recipes for
Everyone's Favorite
Braided Bread

ELANA PEARLMAN

PHOTOGRAPHY BY CAITLIN BENSEL

SIMON ELEMENT

NEW YORK | LONDON | TORONTO | SYDNEY | NEW DELHI

SIMON
ELEMENT

An Imprint of Simon & Schuster, LLC
1230 Avenue of the Americas
New York, NY 10020
Copyright © 2024 by Elana Pearlman

Photography Copyright © 2024 by Caitlin Bensel
Food Styling: Torie Cox
Food Styling Assistant: Carrie Sawyer
Props: Christine Keely

First Simon Element hardcover edition November 2024

SIMON ELEMENT is a trademark of Simon & Schuster, LLC

Simon & Schuster: Celebrating 100 Years of Publishing in 2024

For information about special discounts for bulk purchases, please contact Simon & Schuster Special Sales at 1-866-506-1949 or business@simonandschuster.com.

The Simon & Schuster Speakers Bureau can bring authors to your live event. For more information or to book an event, contact the Simon & Schuster Speakers Bureau at 1-866-248-3049 or visit our website at www.simonspeakers.com.

Interior design by Kristina Juodenas

Manufactured in China

1 3 5 7 9 10 8 6 4 2

Library of Congress Cataloging-in-Publication Data has been applied for.

ISBN 978-1-6680-5108-5
ISBN 978-1-6680-5109-2 (ebook)

To my mom, Leslye,
for teaching me how to bake,
passing down traditions,
and always igniting the flame within me

Contents

Sweet Inspirations

Sweet Final Touches

Savory Inspirations

Savory Final Touches

Acknowledgments

I would love to acknowledge the amazing team that helped put this book together. Caitlin Bensel, who took the vision of this book and truly brought it to life through the lens of her camera. Torie Cox and Carrie Marie Sawyer, who styled every image beautifully and truly made my dreams into a reality. Samantha Weiner, my editor and the main reason why this book has come to fruition, I am so grateful for all your direction as well as your enthusiasm for all things babka.

To Nathan, my husband, who never stops believing in me and always sees me in the best light—thank you for trying countless babka flavors until I got them just right. Your patience, kindness, and unwavering support is something I will never be able to thank you enough for. I love you always.

To my crazy, loud, and food-oriented family. Mom, Dad, and Zachary, thank you all for being my taste testers and even eating the terrible babkas and telling me they were delicious. I am so lucky to call you all my family and to have your loving support. Mom and Dad, thank you for having our household always re-volve around food; I don't know if I would have ever found this career path if it was not for the two of you.

To my babka enthusiasts, we have finally found each other and are here to celebrate babka and the incredible twisted bread that it is. Because no one should ever go a day without a slice of babka.

Introd

uction

1/2 t salt
2 t Baking Powder
Beat eggs well, add sugar beat, add
all beat add flour. Sift with BP
and salt. Knead well and Roll

Spritz Cookies
lb Shorting
c. sugar
t. salt - If you don't use salt but[ter]
eggs
t. Van.
c. flour
t. B. P.
Melt Shortening then
bowl add all ingred
and well.
Bake 350° until
...

mix with p...
pan add cheese mixt...
1 et c. cheese
2 egg yolks
1/2 c. sugar
mix first...
well, add b...
2 egg whites S...

1 1/2 c.
2 t. B...

Lemon Bread Pudding
Bread Crumbs
scalded milk
sugar   3 eggs
salt   1 Tb. melted Butter

... stale bread crumbs
... milk until cool
add sugar, melted butter
grated lemon rind and
beaten egg yolks. Turn
... greased pan and

Pound Cake
5 eggs
1 1/2 c. sugar
1 stick...

Baking has always been the center of my world. My great-grandmother Nana Mary was an amazing baker and dreamed of one day opening her own bakery. She worked tirelessly in bakeries all over New York City, learning everything that she could from as many people as possible. Sadly, the day for her to open her own shop never came, but she did pass her love of baking all the way down to my mother—her granddaughter—and then eventually down to me.

I grew up baking with my mom, and dessert was always the part of the meal that I looked forward to most, no matter what the occasion. I was twelve years old when I knew that I wanted to pursue baking as a career. I was fascinated with all the baking shows on the Food Network, and when *Ace of Cakes* came out, I knew I wanted to go to the Culinary Institute of America just like Duff Goldman had. I even started my own cake company, Elana's Cakery, where I baked cakes for neighbors and friends. I applied to the Culinary Institute of America in New York as soon as I graduated from high school, making it my one and only option for college. Now I get to live my passion every day, and I couldn't imagine my life any other way.

Both of my parents grew up in Jewish families on Long Island, and while I was born in New Jersey, my family moved to Southern California when I was just four years old. With my curly dark hair and boisterous family, I stuck out like a sore thumb in a sea of straight blond hair. We traveled back to New York often, though, and it was on those trips that I was introduced to and fell in love with the classic baked goods that Nana Mary had been baking all those years ago.

One day, my mom came across a box filled with Nana Mary's old recipes all written on small index cards. As we sifted through the dozens and dozens of recipes, memories flooded back of all the times we would bake together, and I decided to shift my focus to reinventing some of those recipes. I felt somehow drawn to babka, and I began to think of new and exciting ways to present the delicious, twisted loaf. How could we make this bread more exciting and make it an everyday item rather than the holiday-specific bread that it has always been? I started to brainstorm, and the list of flavor combinations, both sweet and savory, grew. In this book you'll find the culmination of that work, with both the classic babkas that I grew up eating and those for any occasion.

Spritz Cookies

1 lb Shortening
2 c. sugar
1 t. salt - if you dont use salt butter
4 eggs
2 t. Van.
5 c. flour
5 t. B. P.
melt Shortening then
in bowl add all ingred
Blend well.
   Bake 350° until
brown

Lemon Bread Pudding

2 c. bread Crumbs
4 " scalded milk
1 " sugar   3 eggs
1/2 t. salt   1 Tb. melted Butter
1 lemon

   Soak stale bread Crumbs
in milk until cool
add sugar, melted butter
grated lemon rind and
beaten egg yolks. Turn
into a greased pan and
bake 50 min. slow oven
remove from oven, cool
slightly spread with filling
merange. Beat white of
eggs, gradually add the sugar
and juice of the lemon
Return to oven to brown.
              (over)

Raisin Cake

Boil 1 box raisins
in 2 1/2 qt. water for
10 min.
1/2 c. oil   4 cups flour
1 sugar   1 T. B. S.
3 eggs   1 t. B. P.
mix well ad raisins
Bake 45 min.

Crumb Cake
1/4 lb butter - 2 t B. P.
1/2 qt. sugar   3/4 c. milk
2 c. flour   2 eggs
      1 ts. Van.
Work dry ingred with
fingers into butter. take some
off for top. add eggs. milk
van.

8 cups flour
4 t yeast
2 tb. salt
5 tb. sugar
a little less
2" luke warm water
1 tsp. baking powder
Heat oven 10 min then put
chall in hot oven turn to medial
heat

History of Babka

The babka we know today is a far cry from the ones that my grandmother, mother, and I grew up eating. Most Jewish bakeries keep parve, meaning they make their baked goods dairy-free so that they can be eaten after a meal containing meat to abide by kashrut (kosher law). Not being able to use dairy products in baked goods requires the substitution of margarine or vegetable shortening, which I personally find results in a denser and drier final product.

Babka originated in Eastern Europe and was brought to the United States somewhere between the late 1800s and early 1900s. At first, it was made by simply taking leftover challah dough and spreading chocolate or whatever other topping might be available. Most people knew babka as something that was eaten during the holidays more out of tradition than the desire for a tasty treat. Over time, though—starting with the famous *Seinfeld* episode in which Elaine decides that cinnamon babka is "the lesser babka"—a shift began to occur. In 2013, Breads Bakery in New York City showcased their updated take on babka. *New York* magazine deemed them the best babka in New York City, and with the help of social media, the rest is history.

How to Navigate This Book

I have divided this book into different sections, so you have everything you need in one place. I highly recommend reading through the equipment and pantry list as it is so important to have your mise en place together before you begin.

THE DOUGH

This section covers everything you need to know about the base of a babka. There are a few different options; each mix-in recipe calls for a certain type of dough, but feel free to color outside the lines here and go with a dough that sounds great to you. There is also a recipe for Butter Blocked Dough (page 44). This is a delicious option if you have the time for it. Just like making croissants, this is a lengthy process but so worth the buttery outcome.

SWEET INSPIRATIONS

All the sweet fillings as well as any tweaks to the base dough recipes are in this section. Once you have your dough ready, this is your next step. Be sure to glance over the recipe you decide to make before you prepare your dough as some of the fillings require cooling time.

SWEET FINAL TOUCHES

Here you will find the basic recipes that are used multiple times throughout this book. These are your basics, such as whipped cream and glazes.

SAVORY INSPIRATIONS

This is where you will find all the fun savory combinations, such as bacon jam paired with caramelized onions and beer jam. As with the sweet inspirations, this is the next stop after you've made your dough.

SAVORY FINAL TOUCHES

As with the sweet final touches, these are recipes called for frequently for savory babkas, such as garlic butter or caramelized onions.

Recommended Equipment

STAND MIXER

Can babka dough be mixed by hand? Yes, of course! Will your muscles thank you if you use a mixer instead? Most definitely. I recommend a 5- or 7-quart stand mixer with a dough hook attachment. This will make mixing easier, faster, and more consistent, and will create the desired gluten formation that makes babka so delicious and pillowy soft.

ROLLING PIN, PREFERABLY WOODEN

Nana Mary passed down her rolling pin to her daughter, then to my mother, and my mother passed it down to me. There is even a small "M" that she engraved on one end. This particular "rolling pin" was actually at one point a table leg that my great-grandfather cut and sanded down for her, and it works perfectly. So, don't get caught up in finding the perfect rolling pin. Any will do with a little bit of practice. Maybe you've got a table somewhere that really doesn't need that fourth leg (just remove any paint or varnish before use).

DIGITAL SCALE

Accurately measuring your ingredients (especially in baking) is vital to guaranteeing consistency and quality. If I were to say 1 cup of flour, is that packed down or not? Leveled with the top or just eyeballed? Conversely, 100 grams of flour is the same every time you measure it on a scale. You can get a digital scale on Amazon or at a local grocery store. It will change the outcome of your baked goods for the better!

LOAF PAN

Babkas can be baked in all shapes and sizes, and we'll get into that later. The traditional way is in an 8½ × 4½-inch loaf pan, so that it can be sliced evenly for serving. The taller sides of these pans also help to guide the babka into the right shape as it bakes. The recipes in this book are scaled to fit that size pan, so measure yours before you bake to determine whether or not you need to adjust your ingredient quantities.

RULER

Eyeballing doesn't really ever work out well for me, so I use a 12-inch ruler to ensure that my babka dough has been rolled out to the correct size and thickness before I add my fillings.

DOUGH/BOWL SCRAPER

One of my favorite kitchen tools! This flexible piece of plastic will aid you in getting the dough cleanly out of the bowl onto a work surface, and you can also use it to spread fillings onto the babka dough. This is a common method in commercial baking operations.

BENCH SCRAPER/BENCH KNIFE

The bench scraper is a rectangular piece of metal with a handle on one side typically used to clean a work surface of flour, dough, and any other ingredients before you add water and scrub to avoid creating a paste that will just leave you with a bigger mess. It can also be used to trim the tails off the babka dough once you've rolled it out.

Ruler

Mixing Bowls

Digital Scale

Rolling Pin

Skillet

Wire Rack ↘

Saucepan

Stand Mixer

Blender

Offset Spatula

Dough Scraper

Bench Scraper

Loaf Pan

Food Processor

Rubber Spatula

Pastry Brush

RUBBER SPATULAS

The flexibility of a rubber spatula helps to ensure that you can get every last bit of an ingredient out of the container. They also come in handy for scraping down the side of a mixing bowl to ensure that all of the ingredients are being properly incorporated.

METAL OFFSET SPATULAS

For spreading babka filling onto the dough, the offset's angle helps you spread more evenly without poking any holes in the dough or dragging your knuckles through the filling.

PASTRY BRUSH

While these come in two options, I prefer the silicone brushes as the traditional pastry brush tends to start shedding bristles over time and you will inevitably end up with some in your food. I use this brush for soaking my babka after it comes out of the oven with either simple syrup or olive oil.

MIXING BOWLS

I prefer a metal mixing bowl, but my mom prefers glass. Either option is fine; it is really up to you and what you are most comfortable using. Get a variety of sizes for measuring out ingredients as well as mixing fillings and glazes.

SAUCEPANS

In this book you will probably only need a small and medium saucepan. I like stainless steel ones with a heavy bottom, as that helps to prevent scalding.

SKILLETS

A small skillet will be perfect for the few items that are toasted or sautéed in this book.

WIRE COOLING RACKS

After the babka has cooled in the pan for 30 minutes, I like to take it out and let it finish cooling on a wire rack. This allows the hot air to flow out the bottom and sides of the babka, cooling it faster and more evenly.

SMALL KITCHEN TORCH

This comes in handy with the toasted marshmallow cream for the S'mores babka (page 101) as you can torch the marshmallow while whipping to get that campfire taste. There are also so many other fun cooking and baking uses for a torch.

FOOD PROCESSOR

Instead of chopping away, most items can be put into a food processor to speed along the process. If using a small food processor, do not overrun it and try to fill it to the top; instead process everything in smaller amounts.

BLENDER

For two of the savory babkas you will need a blender to create a silky-smooth puree. I prefer Vitamix, which is the brand you will find in most professional kitchens.

PROBE THERMOMETER

While many cooks and bakers eyeball doneness for their food, the only way to be absolutely sure that a babka is done is by taking the internal temperature of the center of the loaf while it is in the oven.

Pantry List

BUTTER

I use unsalted European butter to bake all my babkas. Many bakers prefer European butters as they have a higher fat content than American butters, making baked goods more flavorful and giving a slightly creamier final texture. My personal favorite brand is Plugrà, which can be found in many grocery stores. If you can't find it, look for brands such as Kerrygold or any other higher fat content European butter.

ALL-PURPOSE FLOUR

All these recipes were developed using King Arthur's all-purpose flour with a protein content of 11.7%. If you plan to use locally milled flour, please note that you may need to adjust the ratio of wet to dry as the absorption rate of hyperfresh flours tends to be higher. Here in Central Texas, I love using Barton Springs Mill all-purpose flour, which is a blend of hard red and soft white wheats. When I use this flour, I generally increase the amount of milk that I am mixing into the dough by 10 percent to 15 percent.

Favorite Flour

Over the past decade, locally milled flours have become more prominent both in restaurants and home kitchens. I'm a huge believer in supporting local and using products that have been minimally processed. This is why I love both Barton Springs Mill as my local flour and King Arthur as a commercial and readily available flour. Both brands process their wheat as little as possible, and the quality shines through.

YEAST

Active dry yeast is generally the most readily available and easy to use, so that's what you'll find in all the following dough recipes. If you can only find instant (fast-acting) yeast, simply use 25 percent less by weight than what the recipe calls for. No need to adjust the method, just follow the instructions as written.

VANILLA

Most people don't know this, but vanilla is one of the most chemically complex spices in the world with more than 250 different taste and aroma compounds. In short, vanilla is anything but plain. While vanilla extract and imitation vanilla are both readily available and inexpensive relative to whole vanilla beans or paste, the difference in taste is profound. This is an ingredient whose quality I never sacrifice, and I encourage you to do the same whenever possible. As a quick and easy conversion if you have whole vanilla beans, 1 vanilla bean equals 2 teaspoons of extract or paste.

CHOCOLATE/COCOA POWDER

Chocolate has always been at the center of my universe even when I was a little kid. Please believe me when I say that the chocolate and cocoa powder you use makes a huge difference. While it's a splurge compared to Hershey's or Ghirardelli, I highly recommend Valrhona and Cacao Barry brands.

SALT

All the recipes in this book have been tested using Morton kosher salt. Please know that all salt varieties differ and that some can be stronger (meaning bigger crystals) than others. For the best result, I recommend using Morton kosher salt, unless otherwise specified in a recipe.

Techniques

There are a number of techniques that you will be asked repeatedly to perform, so I've included them here in great detail. Once you've made the dough, you will first knead it (see The "Tearing" Method below) and then set aside to rest. When ready to use the dough, it gets rolled out to a rectangle, filled, and then rolled up (see How to Roll Up and Cut Babka Dough on page 30). After that, the babka gets proofed, baked, and then generously lathered in either a simple syrup or olive oil (see Proofing and Baking on page 34).

THE "TEARING" METHOD

Traditional kneading is the act of folding dough onto itself over and over in order to strengthen the gluten structure and form a cohesive, fully mixed dough. The "Tearing" method is similar in concept but rather than just folding the dough, you use one hand to anchor the dough to the table and the other to push the dough down and away from you, tearing it with each movement. This accelerates the gluten structure formation without risking accidentally overworking the dough and ending up with a tough, chewy babka.

INSTRUCTIONS:

Remove the babka dough from the mixer bowl to a lightly floured surface. Use your nondominant hand to anchor the half of the dough closer to you to the table.

With your dominant hand, put pressure down on the dough just in front of the anchor hand using your palm. Push down and away from your body, effectively spreading the dough out behind your dominant hand. Please note, you don't want to actually tear the dough in half. What you're looking for is to expose the center of the dough, and it should look sort of ragged.

Using your dominant hand, fold the torn dough back on top of the anchored dough. Give the dough a quarter turn and repeat this sequence for about 2 minutes, or until you can take a small piece of dough, stretch it thin, and see the formed gluten strands in the light. This is called the windowpane test. As you tear the dough, it will begin to feel harder and tougher. This is what you want at this stage. The increased resistance is a sign of the gluten development. It is also why you will rest the dough for a long time following this step, to allow the gluten to relax again before you roll the dough out.

HOW TO ROLL UP AND CUT BABKA DOUGH

To create those stunning swirls on the inside and top of a babka, you must roll up and cut your dough a specific way. Following are the steps to achieve a beautiful babka every time. I recommend taking your time and reading over the instructions completely before beginning so you can have everything ready, and remember to have fun! Either way, you will be eating a delicious babka at the end of the process.

Once you have rolled the dough into a rectangle and added the filling, set the dough with the long side facing you (the dough should be horizontal to your body). Start at the top left corner of the dough and begin rolling the dough down. Work across the length of dough from left to right and then start moving back again, rolling as you go. Roll tightly enough to avoid large air pockets and to seal the filling in, but not so tight that the filling bunches up and starts spreading toward you.

Once the dough is rolled up, roll the log on the table one or two more times to make sure it is nice and tight inside. Measure the length of the dough log. It should be slightly longer than the loaf pan. If it is too short, place your hands in the center of the log 3 to 4 inches apart and roll the log from the center outward with gentle pressure to increase the length. If it is too long, you can pat the dough using your palms on either end of the log to shorten it.

Use a pizza cutter or sharp knife to slice the roll in half lengthwise (from left to right). Take the two halved lengths of dough and with the exposed layers facing up, turn one of the pieces 180 degrees so that the opposite ends are now touching. Then cross one length over the other to form an X.

Starting on one side of where the X meets, twist the two lengths together until you reach the end. Then do the same on the other side. You should be able to do two to three twists per side.

Remeasure the twisted babka dough. At this point, you want the dough to be the same length as the loaf pan. Any excess can be cut off and placed into a buttered muffin tin for a quick babka muffin.

Rub room-temperature butter on the inside of the loaf pan so that the babka will come out of the pan easily.

Place the twisted babka dough into the pan. Don't fuss with making it look perfect at this point, as it will rise and expand as it proofs.

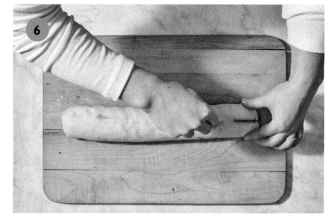

Cover the pan of babka dough with a towel and set aside in a warm draft-free area until the dough has risen and looks puffy. Depending on the temperature this will take 2 to 3 hours. Room temperature will work, but if your oven has a proof setting, this will speed up the process significantly. It is very important that you are not impatient at this stage, as an underproofed dough will end up tough and chewy.

Once the babka has proofed, arrange an oven rack in the center of the oven and preheat the oven to 350°F standard or 325°F convection. (If you used the oven to proof, make sure you take the babka out before heating.) If there is a rack above the center rack, be sure that there will be plenty of room for the babka to expand without hitting it.

Place the babka in the oven with a sheet pan underneath in case any filling overflows. Bake for 25 minutes, and then rotate the babka 180 degrees in the oven so it bakes evenly. Bake until the top is a deep golden brown and a probe thermometer reads 185°F in the center of the babka, another 20 to 30 minutes.

When the babka is done, generously brush the top with simple syrup for sweet or olive oil for savory. This will help to retain moisture and give it a beautiful sheen.

After it has cooled for 30 minutes, gently flip the babka out of the pan and place it right-side up on a wire rack to cool completely.

Reheating Options

SKILLET

Have some extra babka slices lying around? This is my personal favorite method for reheating babka. It creates a delicious golden brown exterior with a soft, melty inside.

Heat a nonstick skillet over medium heat. Add 3 to 5 tablespoons of salted butter and allow it to melt and begin to bubble. Place a babka slice in the pan, let it toast, and flip once golden brown, 2 to 3 minutes. At this point, you can either add more butter to the pan to fry the other side or simply allow it to warm through. Remove from the pan and enjoy! For sweet babkas, I love to top the slices with whipped cream, ice cream, or chocolate ganache.

OVEN

We've all been there. Life is busy, sometimes we don't have time to bake day of or even the day before. This is a great method for getting that babka refreshed and tasting like it just came out of the oven. After the babka has been baked and fully cooled, wrap it tightly in two to three layers of plastic wrap, then store in a freezer-grade plastic bag. Be sure to get as much air out of the bag as possible. Freezer burn occurs more rapidly when your food is exposed to too much air. Packing the babka tightly will allow you to store it frozen for up to 2 months.

On the day you would like to eat the babka, remove it from the freezer and let it thaw at room temperature for 3 to 4 hours (keep the plastic wrap on during the thawing period). Unwrap the babka, then wrap it in aluminum foil and place on a sheet pan in a 350°F standard or 325°F convection oven for 10 to 15 minutes to warm through. For the final 5 minutes, remove the foil so that the babka can get crispy on the exterior. Remove from the oven and serve.

MICROWAVE

Don't feel like putting in too much effort? I won't judge! Slice up the babka and place the slices on a plate (or, if you're like me, just use some paper towels). Microwave on high for 15 to 20 seconds, long enough to warm the slices through, but not so long that you double cook the dough. Enjoy right from the microwave—usually in our house this looks like eating while standing at the kitchen island as you gobble away your delicious slice of babka.

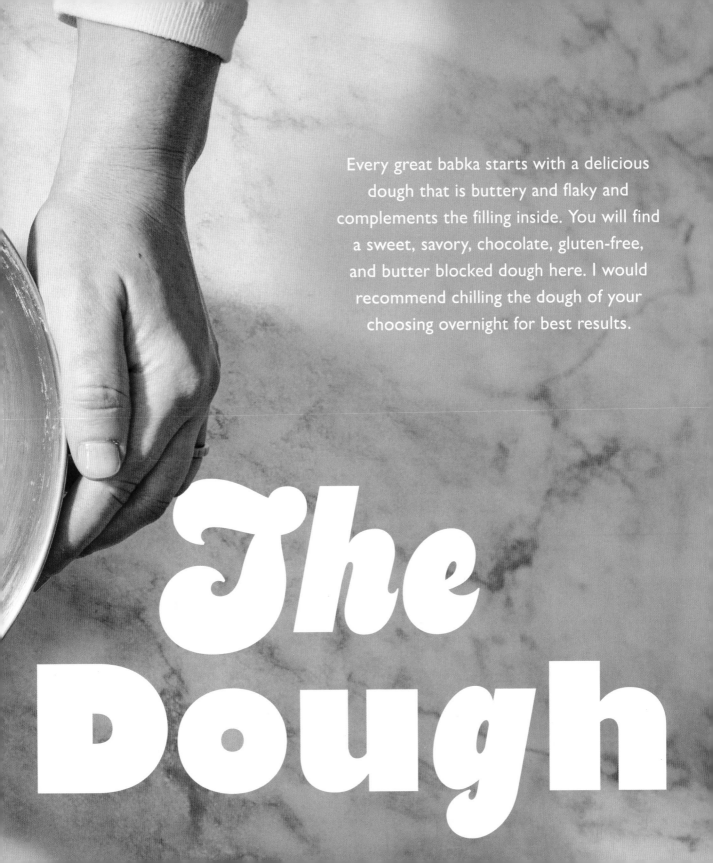

Every great babka starts with a delicious dough that is buttery and flaky and complements the filling inside. You will find a sweet, savory, chocolate, gluten-free, and butter blocked dough here. I would recommend chilling the dough of your choosing overnight for best results.

The Dough

Sweet Babka Dough

This is my go-to, make-in-a pinch babka dough recipe. You will be eating babka just a few hours after starting, so when the craving comes, this is the perfect place to start. The dough is buttery and delicious in every way, and works great with any of the fillings you'll find in the book.

Makes 1 babka

176 grams (¾ cup) whole milk, plus more as needed

7 grams (2¼ teaspoons) active dry yeast

80 grams (⅓ cup + 1 tablespoon) sugar

½ teaspoon vanilla bean paste or extract

450 grams (3¾ cups) all-purpose flour, sifted, plus more as needed

½ teaspoon kosher salt

1 large egg (50 grams)

1 large egg yolk (18 grams)

68 grams (5 tablespoons) unsalted butter, at room temperature

Continued . . .

Warm the milk in the microwave until it reaches 80°F and then pour it into a stand mixer bowl. Whisk in the yeast, sugar, and vanilla until combined. Let sit for 5 minutes, until frothy and bubbly. If nothing has happened this means the yeast did not activate. If this is the case, you will need to make the mixture again and be sure to check these two things: Is your yeast expired? Is your milk at the correct temperature? If your milk was too cold, the yeast may still be dormant. If it was too hot, the yeast likely died off before it had a chance to activate.

Attach the dough hook. Add the flour, salt, whole egg, egg yolk, and butter and mix on low speed until combined, about 2 minutes. Scrape down the sides of the bowl as needed. Check the dough. If it looks very dry and is not coming together, then add 1 tablespoon milk. If it is too wet, then add 1 tablespoon flour until a shaggy dough forms.

Increase the mixer speed to medium and mix until a cohesive dough forms, another 4 minutes.

Transfer the dough to a lightly floured surface. Knead the dough for 2 minutes using the "Tearing" method (see page 29).

Form the dough into a rectangular shape about 1 inch thick using a rolling pin and your hands. Wrap tightly in plastic wrap and refrigerate for at least 3 hours and up to 24 hours.

The dough is now ready to use for any of the recipes in the book.

Savory Babka Dough

This recipe is almost identical to the sweet babka dough, except this one has more salt and less sugar. I prefer to use this for my savory babkas as it balances out the flavor profile of the bread so the fillings can really shine.

Makes 1 babka

---

176 grams (¾ cup) whole milk, plus more as needed

---

7 grams (2¼ teaspoons) active dry yeast

---

40 grams (3 tablespoons) sugar

---

450 grams (3¾ cups) all-purpose flour, sifted, plus more as needed

---

10 grams (2½ teaspoons) kosher salt

---

1 large egg (50 grams)

---

1 large egg yolk (18 grams)

---

68 grams (5 tablespoons) unsalted butter, at room temperature

---

Continued . . .

Warm the milk in the microwave until it reaches 80°F and then pour it into a stand mixer bowl. Whisk in the yeast and sugar until combined. Let sit for 5 minutes, until frothy and bubbly. If nothing has happened this means the yeast did not activate. If this is the case, you will need to make the mixture again and be sure to check these two things: Is your yeast expired? Is your milk at the correct temperature? If your milk was too cold, the yeast may still be dormant. If it was too hot, the yeast likely died off before it had a chance to activate.

Attach the dough hook. Add the flour, salt, whole egg, egg yolk, and butter and mix on low speed until combined, about 2 minutes. Scrape down the sides of the bowl as needed. Check the dough. If it looks very dry and is not coming together, then add 1 tablespoon milk. If it is too wet, then add 1 tablespoon flour until a shaggy dough forms.

Increase the mixer speed to medium and mix until a cohesive dough forms, another 4 minutes.

Transfer the dough to a lightly floured surface. Knead the dough for 2 minutes using the "Tearing" method (see page 29).

Form the dough into a rectangular shape about 1 inch thick using a rolling pin and your hands. Wrap tightly in plastic wrap and refrigerate for at least 3 hours and up to 24 hours.

The dough is now ready to use for any of the recipes in the book.

Butter Blocked Dough

Want to level up the babka game? This croissant-style babka dough is my personal favorite, though it does require some elbow grease if you don't happen to have a dough sheeter lying around. I promise you, though, it is so worth it.

Makes 1 babka

Sweet Babka Dough (page 39) or Savory Babka Dough (page 41)

185 grams (½ cup + 5 tablespoons) unsalted butter, cold

Make the dough as directed and refrigerate overnight.

The following day, slice the cold butter into ½-inch-thick slices and place on a sheet of parchment paper, making a square/rectangle shape. Make sure you are working on a strong, stable surface. Take another sheet of parchment paper and lay it on top of the butter. Take a rolling pin and smack the butter with it to make it more pliable. Hit it until the pieces start to smoosh a bit and you can begin to see the indentation from the rolling pin. Then roll over the pliable butter to flatten slightly. It should be about ¼ inch thick. Take off the top piece of parchment and using a bench scraper and ruler, cut the butter block into a 7-inch square, taking any butter that is larger than the size needed and adding it back into the square. Place aside.

After the dough has rested for 24 hours, take it out of the refrigerator and roll it into an 8 × 18-inch rectangle, with the long side facing you. Place the butter block on the far right side of the dough, leaving about a ¼-inch border around the sides. Flip the other half of the dough over the butter and lightly seal it closed. Rotate the dough 90 degrees so the seal is now facing up.

Roll the dough, east and west, into a 9 × 16-inch rectangle. Square off the dough by using your bench scraper to cut off any parts that are not straight (save the scraps).

Using your finger to make indentations, divide the dough into thirds. Take the scraps and place them in the center. Take the right edge and bring it to the first indentation line, and then take the left edge and fold it over the piece you just folded. This is called a letter fold. Press down gently with your rolling pin to flatten slightly, wrap in plastic wrap, and refrigerate for 30 minutes.

Do this fold two more times, resting for 30 minutes after each fold. Wrap tightly in plastic wrap and refrigerate overnight.

The dough is now ready to be used for any of the recipes in this book.

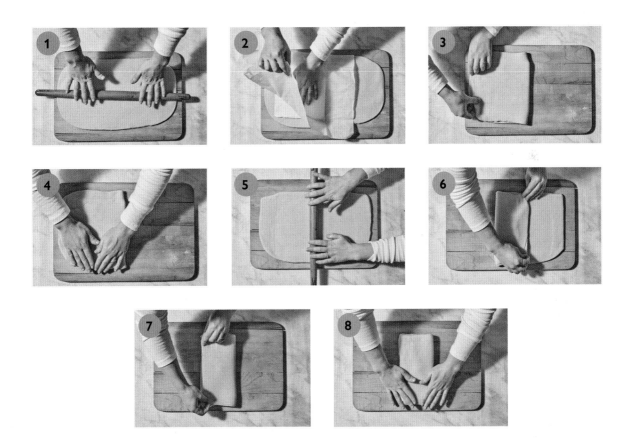

Gluten-Free Dough

This recipe is based off of a recipe from one of my favorite chefs in culinary school, Chef Richard Coppedge. His knowledge of allergies and food sensitivities is unparalleled, and he has helped countless people to be able to enjoy delicious baked goods that would have otherwise been inaccessible to them due to their allergies and intolerances.

Makes 1 babka

5 grams (1¼ teaspoons) instant (fast-acting) yeast

99 grams (½ cup) sugar

255 grams (1½ cups) GF Flour Blend #1 (recipe follows)

255 grams (1½ cups) GF Flour Blend #2 (recipe follows)

20 grams (2 tablespoons) guar gum

10 grams (2 tablespoons) psyllium husk

120 grams (½ cup + 2 teaspoons) warm water

340 grams (1½ cups) whole milk

2 large eggs (100 g)

7 grams (1 teaspoon) honey

½ teaspoon kosher salt

84 grams (6 tablespoons) unsalted butter, melted

In a stand mixer fitted with the paddle attachment, combine the yeast, sugar, flour blends, and guar gum. Mix on low to combine.

In a small bowl, stir together the psyllium husk and warm water. After about 30 seconds it should form a gel-like texture.

In a separate bowl, whisk together the milk, eggs, honey, salt and melted butter. Add the psyllium husk gel and whisk to combine.

Stream the wet ingredients into the flour mixture with the mixer on low. Paddle until smooth.

Cover the bowl with plastic wrap and refrigerate for 1 hour.

The dough is now ready to be used in any recipe that calls for it.

Gluten-Free Flour Blends

GF Flour Blend #1

MAKES 284 GRAMS (SCANT 2 CUPS)

142 grams (½ cup + ⅓ cup) white rice flour

99 grams (⅔ cup) brown rice flour

43 grams (⅓ cup) potato starch

Whisk all ingredients together in a bowl.

GF Flour Blend #2

MAKES 342 GRAMS (GENEROUS 2½ CUPS)

74 grams (⅓ cup) white rice flour

202 grams (2 cups) potato starch

18 grams (5¼ teaspoons) guar gum

48 grams (¼ cup) albumen powder

Whisk all ingredients together in a bowl.

Chocolate Babka Dough

I could eat chocolate every day—breakfast, lunch, and dinner. My mom has photos of me as a little girl, face covered in chocolate after I had snuck into the pantry and found my way to the chocolate chips. This dough is one of my favorites and can be used in place of the regular dough anytime you feel a chocolate craving coming on (which, if you're like me, is two to three times a day).

Makes 1 babka

176 grams (¾ cup) whole milk, plus more as needed

7 grams (2¼ teaspoons) active dry yeast

80 grams (⅓ cup + 1 tablespoon) sugar

½ teaspoon vanilla bean paste or extract

80 grams (⅓ cup + 1 tablespoon) hot water (100°F–120°F)

35 grams (7 tablespoons) unsweetened cocoa powder

450 grams (3¾ cups) all-purpose flour, sifted, plus more as needed

½ teaspoon kosher salt

1 large egg (50 grams)

1 large egg yolk (18 grams)

68 grams (5 tablespoons) unsalted butter, at room temperature

56 grams (⅓ cup) dark chocolate chips, melted

Warm the milk in the microwave until it is about 80°F and pour it into a stand mixer bowl. Add the yeast, sugar, and vanilla and whisk until combined. Let sit for 5 minutes, until frothy and bubbly. If nothing has happened this means the yeast did not activate. If this is the case, you will need to make the mixture again and be sure to check these two things: Is your yeast expired? Is your milk at the correct temperature? If your milk was too cold, the yeast may still be dormant. If it was too hot, the yeast likely died off before it had a chance to activate.

In a bowl, whisk together the hot water and the cocoa powder to form a paste. Add to the stand mixer bowl along with the flour, salt, whole egg, egg yolk, butter, and melted chocolate. Attach the dough hook and mix on low speed for 2 minutes, until combined. Scrape down the sides of the bowl as needed. Look at your dough. If it looks very dry and is not coming together, then add 1 tablespoon milk. If it is too wet then add 1 tablespoon flour until a shaggy dough forms.

Increase the mixer speed to medium and mix for another 4 minutes, until a dough forms. This dough is wetter than the basic babka dough, so don't worry if it looks different.

Turn the dough out on a lightly floured surface. Knead the dough for 2 minutes using the "Tearing" method (see page 29).

Form into a rectangular block about 1 inch thick. Wrap tightly in plastic wrap and refrigerate for at least 3 hours and up to 24 hours.

The dough is now ready to be used for any of the recipes in this book.

Playing

This section is intended to give some
inspiration for ways to prepare babka outside
of the traditional loaf. In the following pages
you'll find instructions on how to make
your babka into muffins, bread pudding,
and even French toast!

ound

Babkins

Want to make individual babkas but don't have any miniature loaf pans? This is a great way to allow everyone to enjoy their own babka while showing off a fun technique. This is one of my favorite ways to eat babka since you can munch away without any silverware, and everyone gets all the best parts: the crunchy top, the silky center, and the caramelized bottom.

Makes 6 babkins

Sweet Babka Dough (page 39) or Savory Babka Dough (page 41)

Filling of choice from the Sweet and Savory Inspiration chapters

---

Softened butter for the pan

Simple Syrup (page 143) or olive oil

Make the dough as directed and prepare the filling.

Butter 12 cups of a muffin tin, making sure to really coat the edges.

Roll out the dough to a 12½ × 24¼-inch rectangle a little thicker than ¼ inch, making sure the longer side is horizontal to your body.

Spread the filling all over the dough, making sure to get the edges. If the filling requires something sprinkled on top, do that now.

Take the bottom third of the dough and lift it up to the middle, then take the top third and cover the fold you just made. Your dough should be approximately 8 x 12½ inches.

Continued . . .

Using a rolling pin, gently press down on your dough and roll to about ½ inch thick, going from east to west, doing your best to keep the filling from oozing out. It is okay if some comes out, just clean as you go to keep your workstation clean.

Cut from north to south (the short way) into 2½-inch sections. You should get about 6 sections and then divide each section into quarters. Each strand that you are cutting should be ⅝ inch wide.

Make a basket weave (see page 55). Once completed take your hands on either side of the weaved dough and gently push the dough under itself to fluff it up and create a slight ball. Take this and place it into a prepared muffin cup.

Cover the muffin tin with a towel and set aside in a warm draft-free area until the dough has risen and looks puffy, about 1 to 2 hours. Remove the towel when ready to bake.

Preheat the oven to 350°F standard or 325°F convection.

Place the muffin tin in the oven with a sheet pan on the shelf below it to catch any drips. Bake for 15 minutes, rotate 180 degrees, and then bake for an additional 15 to 20 minutes, until golden brown and a thermometer inserted reads 190°F.

Remove from the oven and immediately glaze with simple syrup for sweet babka or olive oil for savory. Let cool, then remove from pan and let cool completely on a wire rack and serve.

Storage: I recommend eating these the same day you make them, but they will last for 3 days in an airtight container at room temperature or for 3 months wrapped in two layers of plastic wrap in the freezer. For reheating instructions, follow the steps on page 34.

How to Basket Weave Babka Dough

Take the 4 strands and lay them like you would for a basket weave: Take 2 strips and place them vertically on the table. Take the other 2 strips and place them horizontally over the 2 vertical strips, weaving your strips so that each strand goes over one and then under the next. It should look like a hashtag.

Pick a piece that is underneath a strand and start with it, taking it and placing it over the one above it. Repeat with the other strands that are underneath a previous layer until you do all 4. It should begin to look like a windmill now.

Take the pieces that have not been moved from the original hashtag and go the opposite way you just went (to the left), putting these "straight" strips over the ones you just weaved. Continue with the left and right, weaving until it is completely weaved. Tuck in/under any rogue ends.

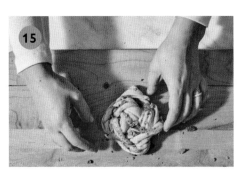

THE DOUGH

Babka Cake

For seven years, I owned and operated a boutique wedding cake business. When I would tell people that I don't particularly enjoy cake (which is true), they were understandably confused. Babka and ice cream for my birthday, though? Count me in. You can leave this babka as is after baking, or top with buttercream and/or frosting.

Makes one 8-inch cake

Sweet Babka Dough (page 39)

Filling of choice (pages 67 to 140)

Softened butter for the pan

Make the babka dough and filling as directed.

Butter an 8 × 3-inch cake pan.

Roll out the dough to a 12½ × 24¼-inch rectangle a little thicker than ¼ inch. Spread the filling all over the dough, making sure to get the edges. If the filling requires something sprinkled on top, do that now.

Roll up the babka dough as if you were rolling up two scrolls, taking the left side and rolling it toward the center and stopping at the middle. Repeat with the right side. Take a knife and slice through the center where they both meet, separating the two.

Take a pizza cutter or a sharp chef's knife and slice the rolls lengthwise, to expose the filling. Take the 4 strands and make a basket weave (see page 55). Once weaved together, place in the buttered cake pan.

Cover the cake pan with a towel and proof as directed on page 34.

Preheat the oven to 350°F standard or 325°F convection.

Bake the cake as directed on page 34, baking for 30 minutes, rotating 180 degrees, and then baking for another 15 to 20 minutes.

French Toast

French toast brings up some core memories for me. My mom had a knack for treating us to a good breakfast, and French toast was always a favorite of mine. Go all out for this one. Make a fruit salad, whip up some eggs, and dig into a big hunk of French toast. You deserve it!

Makes 9 slices of French toast

226 grams (1 cup) whole milk

4 eggs (200 grams)

28 grams (2 tablespoons) sugar

2 teaspoons vanilla extract

1 teaspoon ground cinnamon

½ teaspoon kosher salt

1 loaf babka, cut into 1-inch-thick slices

70 grams (5 tablespoons) butter, for cooking

Powdered sugar, syrup, or jam, for serving

Continued . . .

Preheat the oven to 250°F. Line a sheet pan with parchment paper.

Preheat a griddle to 350°F or place a skillet over medium heat.

In a bowl, whisk together the milk, eggs, sugar, vanilla, cinnamon, and salt until it is a homogeneous mixture. Pour into an 8-inch square baking dish or a shallow dish.

Add the butter to the griddle or skillet and let it heat up as you take one slice at a time and dredge it in the egg mixture, making sure to get both sides and all parts of the babka slice.

Place on the hot griddle and cook until golden brown on one side, then flip over and repeat on the opposite side. Remove and place on the lined sheet pan and put in the oven to keep warm.

Repeat with all the babka slices. Top with powdered sugar, syrup, or your jam of choice.

Storage: If you have any leftovers, those can be kept in the refrigerator for 5 days, but let's be completely honest with each other: French toast really should only be eaten the day it is made. It never lives up to its utmost potential once it has been reheated.

Bread Pudding

A classmate of mine from culinary school shared this recipe with me, and I will forever be grateful to her for it. I have made some tweaks to make it my own, but this is one of the best bread puddings I have ever had. It is not too watery, not too dry, and is great topped with a bourbon anglaise or ice cream. Feel free to change out the spices, chocolate, and dried fruit to make it your own. There really are unlimited options.

Makes one 8-inch square; sixteen 2-inch servings

425 grams (4½ cups) babka

319 grams (1¾ cups) white chocolate chips

532 grams (2¼ cups) heavy cream

213 grams (1 cup) whole milk

92 grams (7½ tablespoons) sugar

Pinch of salt

¾ teaspoon ground cinnamon

6 eggs (300 grams)

Softened butter for the pan

138 grams (1 cup + 1 tablespoon) dried cherries

Day before: Cut the babka into ½-inch cubes. Place in a single layer on a sheet pan lined with parchment paper and let it stale out overnight.

Day of: Place the white chocolate in a large bowl with a fine-mesh sieve over the top.

In a medium pot, combine the heavy cream, milk, 46 grams of the sugar, the salt, and cinnamon. Bring to a simmer over medium heat.

While the heavy cream mixture is heating, in a large bowl, whisk the eggs with the remaining 46 grams sugar (make sure this bowl is large enough to hold the egg mixture as well as the heavy cream mixture).

Once the heavy cream mixture is simmering, remove it from the heat and slowly stream it into the egg mixture while whisking. This can be a bit challenging to do by yourself. You can always find a friend to stream in the hot mixture for you as you whisk (I always put down a damp towel under my bowl so it stays in place while I whisk). This method of slowly warming the eggs is called tempering and is used in a variety of baking recipes.

After all the liquid is tempered in, immediately pour it into the sieve over the white chocolate. Remove the sieve and stir to combine.

Add the dried babka pieces to the bowl and lightly mix together. Let this mixture soak for 2 hours, stirring every 20 minutes.

Preheat the oven to 350°F standard or 325°F convection. Generously butter an 8-inch square pan.

As soon as the 2 hours are up, add the dried cherries, making sure they are evenly distributed. Scrape the bread pudding mixture into the prepared pan and bake until a thermometer inserted reads 170°F, about 1 hour.

Let cool to room temperature before slicing.

Storage: This keeps well in the refrigerator in an airtight container for up to 5 days.

Fun Babka Shapes

Looking to make the babka into a fun shape for a holiday or special occasion?
Below are some ideas, and feel free to get creative and make your own shapes too.

Heart Shape

Roll the babka dough on a lightly floured
surface to a 9 × 20-inch rectangle.

Fill the babka with your choice of filling
and roll up as described on page 30.

Slice the babka lengthwise so you have 2 long
pieces. Now cut those pieces in half lengthwise
again so you now have 4 long strands. Take
2 of the strands and create an X shape.
Corkscrew one half of the strands together,
then repeat on the other half.
Repeat with the remaining 2 strands.

Take both twisted pieces and put them parallel
to each other on a sheet pan lined with
parchment. Take the top right piece and start
to roll it like a snail shell in on itself, toward the
center to create the top right part of the heart.
Do the same on the left. Put these 2 pieces
together and then gently push the rest of the
strands together until you get to the bottom
where you are going to take 1 piece and put it
over the other to create the "tail" of the heart.

Proof, bake, and cool as described on page 34.

Wreath

Roll the babka dough on a lightly floured
surface to a 9 × 20-inch rectangle.

Fill the babka with your choice of filling
and roll up as described on page 30.

Slice the babka lengthwise so you have 2 long
pieces. Now cut those pieces in half lengthwise
again so you have 4 long strands. Take 2 of the
strands and create an X shape. Corkscrew one
half of the strands together, then repeat on the
other half. Repeat with
the remaining 2 strands.

Place both twisted strands on a sheet pan
lined with parchment and connect both
ends to form a circle. Twist together the
ends so they do not come apart.

Proof, bake, and cool as described on page 34.

Sandwich Bread

No instructions needed here, this is just to remind
you that you can take any of the babkas, sweet or
savory, and turn them into the base for your favorite
sandwich! I did a collab with a friend who took my
Hatch Pimento Cheese babka (page 153), toasted it
on the griddle, and finished it with the toppings of
a croque madame. I personally love the PB&J babka
(page 95) toasted in butter and then made into a
PB&J sandwich. As you can see, there are endless
options. Have fun and enjoy a delicious sandwich!

Inspir

Sweet

ations

The following inspirations were created based on my own tastes and memories, and I wanted to share them all with you. If a part of a recipe doesn't sound delicious to you—perhaps you prefer blueberry jam over strawberry jam— then please feel free to change it out. These recipes are here to satisfy your sweet tooth in the best way possible.

Pantry Staple

Have you ever bought a cookbook and instantly felt inspired to bake something from it just to find out you need about twenty ingredients you don't have? I know I have, and then the deflation kicks in when you realize you are going to have to go to the grocery store and it's probably really cold outside, too, which means you have to put on pants. . . . This is the babka for that moment when inspiration sparks and you are ready to bake. An ode to growing up going to friends' homes and having butter tortillas with sugar—salty and sweet. Enjoy the simple things in life!

Makes 1 babka

Sweet Babka Dough (page 39) or
Butter Blocked Dough (page 44), made with sweet dough

Softened butter for the pan

75 grams (⅓ cup) sugar

5 grams (¾ teaspoon) sea salt

All-purpose flour, for dusting

75 grams (5½ tablespoons) butter, at room temperature

Simple Syrup (page 143), for generously brushing on after baking

Continued . . .

Make the dough as directed.

Brush softened butter into an 8½ × 4½-inch loaf pan, making sure to get the corners.

In a small bowl, mix together the sugar and salt.

Lightly dust a work surface with flour and roll the dough to a 9 × 14-inch rectangle. Spread the 75 grams butter all over the rolled-out dough, reaching the edges. Sprinkle the sugar and salt mixture over the butter. With a rolling pin, lightly press the sugar into the dough.

Roll up and cut the babka as directed on page 30.
(For a more playful babka, see the variation on the next page.)

Proof, bake, and cool as directed on page 34. Generously brush the babka with the simple syrup after baking.

Wild Babka:

Take the rolled-up babka, and using your bench scraper or a sharp knife cut it into 4 or 5 sections. Take each section and place it with the swirl facing up in your buttered loaf pan, in no particular order.

Cinnamon Raisin Pecan

My husband, Nate, is a die-hard oatmeal raisin cookie person. He was the kid growing up whose favorite candy was Raisinets. He is the definition of a raisin person. When I was coming up with my play on the cinnamon babka, the first thought that came to mind was Nate and his love for raisins and how perfectly that would go with cinnamon, and then I added in candied pecans for a good crunch.

Makes 1 babka

Sweet Babka Dough (page 39) or
Butter Blocked Dough (page 44), made with sweet dough

---

75 grams (½ cup + 3 tablespoons) Candied Pecans (page 146)

---

75 grams (½ cup) golden raisins

---

1 teaspoon ground cinnamon

---

50 grams (¼ cup) sugar

Softened butter, for the pan

All-purpose flour, for dusting

---

50 grams (3½ tablespoons) unsalted butter, at room temperature

---

Simple Syrup (page 143), for generously brushing on after baking

---

Continued . . .

Make and chill the dough as directed.

Make the candied pecans. Break up and roughly chop into $\frac{1}{4}$-inch pieces.

Soak the raisins in hot water while you measure the rest of the ingredients, making sure that they are fully submerged. If you have jumbo raisins, give them a rough chop once they've been strained and set aside.

In a small bowl, combine the cinnamon and sugar to make a homogenous mixture.

Butter an $8\frac{1}{2} \times 4\frac{1}{2}$-inch loaf pan, using a pastry brush to get into the corners.

Lightly dust a work surface with flour and roll the dough to a 9×14-inch rectangle. With an offset spatula, spread the 50 grams of butter all over the dough, spreading it evenly to all the edges. Sprinkle the cinnamon-sugar mixture on top. Sprinkle the raisins and pecans over the cinnamon-sugar mixture. With a rolling pin, lightly roll over everything, securing all fillings in place.

Roll up and cut the babka as directed on page 30.

Proof, bake, and cool as directed on page 34.
Generously brush the babka with the simple syrup after baking.

Chocolate Cinnamon

Traditional babka usually comes in chocolate or cinnamon. I love a good revamp of an old classic, so I use milk and dark chocolate as well as chopped chocolate to get all different chocolate bits in each bite. This one will always be my favorite babka since this was the babka that started it all.

Makes 1 babka

Chocolate Babka Dough (page 48), Sweet Babka Dough (page 39), or Butter Blocked Dough (page 44), made with sweet dough

---

160 grams Chocolate Cinnamon Filling (recipe follows)

Softened butter for the pan

All-purpose flour, for dusting

---

25 grams (3 tablespoons) chopped milk chocolate chips

---

25 grams (3 tablespoons) chopped dark chocolate chips

Simple Syrup (page 143), for generously brushing on after baking

---

Make and chill the dough as directed. Make and cool the filling as directed.

Butter an 8½ × 4½-inch loaf pan, using a pastry brush to get into the corners.

Lightly dust a work surface with flour and roll the dough to a 9 × 14-inch rectangle. Using an offset spatula, dollop the filling all over the dough and spread it evenly to the edges. Sprinkle the chopped chocolates on top. Roll up and cut the babka as directed on page 30.

Proof, bake, and cool as directed on page 34.
Generously brush the babka with the simple syrup after baking.

Continued . . .

Chocolate Cinnamon Filling

MAKES ENOUGH FOR 1 BABKA

114 grams (½ cup + 3 tablespoons) milk chocolate chips

114 grams (½ cup + 3 tablespoons) dark chocolate chips

32 grams (2½ tablespoons) unsalted butter

1 teaspoon ground cinnamon

Make a double boiler: Fill a pot with 1 inch of water and find a heatproof bowl that can sit over the pot without touching the water. Bring the water to a boil without the bowl.

In the bowl, combine the chocolate chips, butter, and cinnamon. Place the bowl on top of the pot and turn off the heat. Stir until melted. Remove the bowl from the pot. Let cool slightly, so it is no longer hot to the touch but not so cool that the chocolate has begun to harden.

Coffee Cake

This babka has it all: the sweet from a caramelized white chocolate (which has toasty notes to it), the espresso powder (which resembles a cup of coffee), and then the streusel—no need to skimp on that. Pile it on and if some falls off while baking, no worries, you now have delicious streusel bites to snack on!

Makes 1 babka

Sweet Babka Dough (page 39) or Butter Blocked Dough (page 44), made with sweet dough

Streusel (recipe follows)

171 grams (1 cup) Caramelized White Chocolate (recipe follows)

150 grams (¾ cup) white chocolate chips

48 grams (3½ tablespoons) unsalted butter, at room temperature

¾ teaspoon espresso powder

Softened butter, for the pan

All-purpose flour, for dusting

Simple Syrup (page 143), for generously brushing on after baking

Continued . . .

Make and chill the dough as directed.
Make the streusel and the caramelized white chocolate.

Make a double boiler: Fill a pot with 1 inch of water and find a heatproof
bowl that can sit over the pot without touching the water.
Bring the water to a boil without the bowl.

Place the chocolate chips, caramelized chocolate, butter, and espresso powder in the
bowl. Place the bowl on top of the pot and turn off the heat. Stir until melted and
combined. Remove the bowl from the pot, and let cool slightly while you
roll out the dough.

Butter an 8½ × 4½-inch loaf pan, using a pastry brush to get into the corners.

Lightly dust a work surface with flour and roll the dough to a 9 × 14-inch rectangle.
Spread the white chocolate mixture all over the rolled-out dough, reaching the edges.
Sprinkle one-third of the streusel mixture over the chocolate and use a rolling pin to
lightly push it in.

Roll up and cut the babka as directed on page 30.

Proof the dough as directed on page 34. Once the babka is done proofing, take the
remaining streusel and pile it on top of the dough, pressing it lightly into place.

Bake and cool as directed on page 34.
Generously brush the babka with the simple syrup after baking.

Streusel

MAKES 414 GRAMS (2¾ CUPS)

159 grams (1 cup + 3 tablespoons) all-purpose flour

120 grams (1 cup + 1 tablespoon) packed brown sugar

5 grams (2 teaspoons) ground cinnamon

½ teaspoon sea salt

129 grams (9 tablespoons) unsalted butter, cold and cut into ½-inch cubes

In a bowl, whisk together the flour, brown sugar, cinnamon, and salt.

Toss in the cold butter and use a pastry cutter, fork, or your hands to blend the butter into the dry ingredients. You know when it is properly combined when you squeeze some streusel in your hand and it stays together. Refrigerate until ready to use.

Caramelized White Chocolate

MAKES 188 GRAMS (¾ CUP)

188 grams (1 cup + 2 tablespoons) white chocolate chips

Preheat the oven to 200°F. Line two sheet pans with silicone baking mats or parchment paper.

Spread the white chocolate on one of the sheet pans and bake until it reaches a nice golden brown dulce de leche color, about 1 hour, checking every 20 minutes and using an offset spatula to spread around the chocolate so it caramelizes evenly.

Scrape into a food processor and process until smooth. Spread onto the second sheet pan and let cool. Break up and place in a container at room temperature until ready to use.

Birthday Cake

This play on a classic confetti birthday cake comes with a choose-your-own-adventure option for the icing: vanilla or chocolate buttercream. You can get creative and make half batches of both and top one half with chocolate and one half with vanilla for the best of both worlds. And don't forget the candles!

Makes 1 babka

Sweet Babka Dough (page 39)

75 grams (5 tablespoons) sprinkles

Softened butter, for the pan

75 grams ($\frac{1}{3}$ cup) sugar

3 grams ($\frac{1}{4}$ teaspoon) sea salt

1 vanilla bean or 1 teaspoon vanilla bean paste

All-purpose flour, for dusting

75 grams ($5\frac{1}{2}$ tablespoons) unsalted butter, at room temperature

Simple Syrup (page 143), for generously brushing on after baking

Vanilla Buttercream (recipe follows) or Chocolate Buttercream (recipe follows)

Make the babka dough just until the cohesive dough forms in the mixer. Turn the dough out onto a work surface and knead the dough for 2 minutes using the "Tearing" method (see page 29). Place sprinkles on the table and begin to knead for 1 minute. Don't worry if all the sprinkles don't end up in the dough.

Form into a rectangular block about 1 inch thick. Wrap tightly in plastic wrap and refrigerate for at least 3 hours and up to 24 hours.

Butter an 8½ × 4½-inch loaf pan, using a pastry brush to get into the corners.

In a small bowl, combine the sugar and salt. Split the vanilla bean open and scrape in the seeds (or add the vanilla bean paste) to the mixture, and stir to combine.

Lightly dust a work surface with flour and roll the dough to a 9 × 14-inch rectangle. Spread the 75 grams of butter all over the rolled-out dough, reaching the edges. Sprinkle the vanilla sugar over the butter and use a rolling pin to lightly push it in.

Roll up and cut the babka as directed on page 30.

Proof, bake, and cool as directed on page 34. Meanwhile, make the buttercream.

Once the babka has cooled completely and right before you are ready to serve, place the buttercream into a pastry bag fitted with an 825 piping tip. Pipe the buttercream along the top of your babka, starting at the back and creating a snake shape, going back and forth until you get to the other end. Top with sprinkles, put on a serving tray, insert candles, and enjoy!

Continued . . .

Vanilla Buttercream

MAKES 500 GRAMS (2 CUPS)

170 grams (12 tablespoons) unsalted butter, at room temperature

85 grams (heaping ⅓ cup) mascarpone

255 grams (2 cups) powdered sugar, sifted

¾ teaspoon vanilla bean paste or extract

Pinch of salt

In a stand mixer, beat the butter on medium speed until broken up and beginning to cream. Add the mascarpone and mix on medium until combined (depending on the temperature of your mascarpone, it may break and look curdled—do not worry it will come back together!).

Add the powdered sugar, vanilla, and salt. Begin on low speed and then once incorporated enough to not go everywhere, increase the speed to high and beat for 2 to 3 minutes, scraping down the bowl occasionally (be sure to turn off the mixer before scraping). Taste to see if you would like to adjust anything. Want it sweeter? Add more powdered sugar. Is it too sweet? Add a bit more salt.

Place in a covered container until ready to use. If not using it right away, store in the refrigerator overnight and bring to room temperature. Rewhip it with the paddle attachment for 2 to 3 minutes until light and fluffy again.

Chocolate Buttercream

170 grams (12 tablespoons) unsalted butter, at room temperature

85 grams (heaping ⅓ cup) mascarpone

255 grams (2 cups) powdered sugar, sifted

85 grams (1 cup) unsweetened cocoa powder, sifted

¾ teaspoon vanilla bean paste or extract

Pinch of salt

40 grams (3 tablespoons) heavy cream

In a stand mixer, beat the butter on medium speed until broken up and beginning to cream. Add the mascarpone and mix on medium until combined (depending on the temperature of your mascarpone, it may break and look curdled—do not worry it will come back together!).

Add the powdered sugar, cocoa, vanilla, and salt. Begin on low speed and then once incorporated enough to not go everywhere, increase the speed to high and beat for 2 to 3 minutes, scraping down the bowl occasionally (be sure to turn off the mixer before scraping). Stream in the heavy cream and beat to incorporate. Taste to see if you would like to adjust anything. Want it sweeter? Add more powdered sugar. Is it too sweet? Add a bit more salt.

Place in a covered container until ready to use. If not using it right away, store in the refrigerator overnight and bring to room temperature. Rewhip it with the paddle attachment for 2 to 3 minutes until light and fluffy again.

Strawberry Shortcake

Sweet Babka Dough (page 39) or Butter Blocked Dough (page 44), made with sweet dough

---

Softened butter, for the pan

All-purpose flour, for dusting

---

200 grams (⅔ cup) strawberry jam

Simple Syrup (page 143), for generously brushing on after baking

---

Powdered sugar, for dusting

Whipped Cream (page 143)

Sliced strawberries, for garnish

Make and chill the dough as directed.

Butter an 8½ × 4½-inch loaf pan, using a pastry brush to get into the corners.

Lightly dust a work surface with flour and roll the dough to a 9 × 14-inch rectangle. Spread the strawberry jam all over the rolled-out dough, reaching the edges.

Roll up and cut the babka as directed on page 30.

Proof, bake, and cool as directed on page 34.

Once the babka is fully cooled, place on a serving dish and dust with powdered sugar.

Serve each slice of babka with a dollop of whipped cream and fresh cut strawberries.

Black Forest

Boozy with a hint of chocolate and cherries, this one is a fun babka flavor. You will have extra cherries jubilee, so save it to use as an ice cream topping!

Makes 1 babka

Chocolate Babka Dough (page 48)

Chocolate Filling (recipe follows)

223 grams (¾ cup) Cherries Jubilee (recipe follows)

Softened butter, for the pan

All-purpose flour, for dusting

Kirschwasser Simple Syrup (page 143)

Dark Chocolate Glazing Ganache (page 147)

Whipped Cream (page 143), flavored with Kirschwasser to taste

Make and chill the dough as directed. Make the chocolate filling and cherries jubilee.

Butter an 8½ × 4½-inch loaf pan, using a pastry brush to get into the corners.

Lightly dust a work surface with flour and roll the dough to a 9 × 14-inch rectangle. Spread the chocolate filling all over the rolled-out dough and spread the cherries jubilee on top of the chocolate, reaching the edges.

Roll up and cut the babka as directed on page 30.

Continued . . .

Proof and bake as directed on page 34. Meanwhile, make the simple syrup.

Immediately after the babka comes out of the oven, heavily brush with the Kirschwasser simple syrup.

Once the babka has fully cooled, take it out of the pan and place on a wire rack. Make the ganache and glaze the babka. Let set and then move it to a serving platter.

Serve slices with Kirschwasser whipped cream and extra cherries jubilee.

Chocolate Filling

MAKES ENOUGH FOR 1 BABKA

114 grams (½ cup + 3 tablespoons) milk chocolate chips

114 grams (½ cup + 3 tablespoons) dark chocolate chips

32 grams (2½ tablespoons) unsalted butter

Make a double boiler: Fill a pot with 1 inch of water and find a heatproof bowl that can sit over the pot without touching the water. Bring the water to a boil without the bowl.

In the bowl, combine the chocolate chips and butter. Place the bowl on top of the pot and turn off the heat. Stir until melted. Remove the bowl from pot. Let cool slightly before using.

Notes:

If using frozen cherries there will be extra liquid, so double the cornstarch and water amounts.

Make sure to give your slurry a good whisk before adding it. If it is not fully incorporated you will end up with pockets of cornstarch, and no one wants that!

The cherries must be completely cool before using. A little trick of the trade: Place in a metal bowl in the freezer (with a towel underneath if you have glass shelves) and stir it every 10 minutes, until cooled.

Cherries Jubilee

MAKES 670 GRAMS (2¼ CUPS)

---

396 grams (3½ cups) dark cherries, frozen (see Notes) or fresh

---

14 grams (1 tablespoon) fresh lemon juice

---

167 grams (¾ cup + 1 tablespoon) granulated sugar

---

178 grams (¾ cup + 1 tablespoon) packed brown sugar

¼ teaspoon salt

---

57 grams (¼ cup) Kirschwasser

½ teaspoon vanilla bean paste or extract

---

28 grams (¼ cup) cornstarch

---

28 grams (2 tablespoons) water

In a saucepan, combine the cherries, lemon juice, both sugars, and salt and cook over medium heat, stirring constantly with a wooden spoon. Once the cherries have released their juice and the sugar has dissolved, about 3 minutes, remove from the heat.

Add the Kirschwasser, and with either a match or a long-handled lighter, set the cherries on fire and return the pan to low heat. When the flames have died out, add the vanilla and stir the cherries to coat.

If there are still large chunks of cherries, either carefully place into the bowl of a food processor and process to a jam-like consistency or take an immersion blender and carefully blend to break the fruit into smaller pieces. You don't want to puree your mixture, and you don't want large chunks, either. Place back into the saucepan.

In a small bowl, whisk together the cornstarch and water to make a homogenous slurry. It should be the consistency of Elmer's glue. If too thick add more water, if too thin add more cornstarch.

Bring the cherry mixture to a boil. Once boiling, whisk in the slurry (see Notes) and continue to whisk as you bring it to a full rolling boil for 2 minutes. The mixture should have thickened to a jam-like consistency.

Scrape into a heatproof bowl to cool completely before using (see Notes).

PB&J

Forever a classic sandwich for me is the peanut butter and jelly. I grew up eating them for lunch and will pack them on hikes to this day. Feel free to change out the jam on this to suit your taste.

Makes 1 babka

Sweet Babka Dough (page 39) or
Butter Blocked Dough (page 44), made with sweet dough

Peanut Butter Filling (recipe follows)

Softened butter, for the pan

All-purpose flour, for dusting

120 grams (⅓ cup) strawberry jam, or your jam of choice

Simple Syrup (page 143), for generously brushing on after baking

Peanut Butter Glaze (page 146)

Continued . . .

Make and chill the dough as directed. Make the peanut butter filling.

Butter an 8½ × 4½-inch loaf pan, using a pastry brush to get into the corners.

Lightly dust a work surface with flour and roll the dough to a 9 × 14-inch rectangle. Place the peanut butter filling in the microwave for 20 seconds, not to melt it but to soften it and make it a bit easier to spread. Spread it on the rolled-out dough. Follow with the strawberry jam, making sure both are to the edges.

Roll up and cut the babka as directed on page 30.

Proof, bake, and cool as directed on page 34. Brush the babka generously with the simple syrup.

Once cooled, take out of the pan and place the babka on a wire rack. Pour the peanut butter glaze on top and let set before moving to a serving dish.

Peanut Butter Filling

MAKES ENOUGH FOR 1 BABKA

150 grams (½ cup) creamy peanut butter (I recommend Jif)
23 grams (3 tablespoons) powdered sugar, sifted
¼ teaspoon fine sea salt

Combine all the ingredients in a bowl with a spatula. Set aside until ready to use.

Cinnamon Bun

A sinful and gooey center, frosted with a tangy cream cheese buttercream—it really is divine. Please do note that since this is so gooey you should not cut this and twist it; leave it as a log instead so the filling can stay inside the babka.

Makes 1 babka

Sweet Babka Dough (page 39) or
Butter Blocked Dough (page 44), made with sweet dough

Cinnamon Filling (recipe follows)

Softened butter, for the pan

All-purpose flour, for dusting

Simple Syrup (page 143), for generously brushing on after baking

Cream Cheese Icing (recipe follows)

Make and chill the dough as directed. Make the cinnamon filling.

Butter an 8½ × 4½-inch loaf pan, using a pastry brush to get into the corners.

Lightly dust a work surface with flour and roll the dough to a 9 × 14-inch rectangle. Spread the cinnamon filling mixture all over the rolled-out dough, reaching the edges.

Follow steps 1 and 2 of How to Roll Up and Cut Babka Dough (page 30) and do NOT cut this in half lengthwise; the filling will ooze everywhere. Instead leave it as a log, cut in half crosswise, and then twist the two closed logs together.

Continued . . .

Proof and bake as directed on page 34. Brush the babka generously with the simple syrup. Make the cream cheese icing.

Once the babka is slightly cooled, you should be able to put your hand on it and still feel the warmth but it should not be hot. Remove the babka from the pan, and then use an offset spatula to smother the top with the cream cheese icing.

Cinnamon Filling

MAKES ENOUGH FOR 1 BABKA

104 grams (½ cup) packed dark brown sugar

1 teaspoon ground cinnamon

1½ teaspoons cornstarch

¼ teaspoon fine sea salt

44 grams (3 tablespoons) unsalted butter, at room temperature but not super soft

In a small bowl, whisk together the brown sugar, cinnamon, cornstarch and sea salt. Using a pastry cutter or your hands, add the butter and combine to create a cinnamon-sugar paste.

Cream Cheese Icing

MAKES 302 GRAMS (1 HEAPING CUP)

70 grams (5 tablespoons) cream cheese, at room temperature

70 grams (5 tablespoons) unsalted butter, at room temperature

¾ teaspoon vanilla bean paste or extract

½ teaspoon fresh lemon juice

6 grams (1 teaspoon) fine sea salt

165 grams (1½ cups) powdered sugar, sifted

In a small bowl, with a hand mixer, blend the cream cheese and butter together until combined and fluffy, about 2 minutes.

Add the vanilla, lemon juice, and salt and mix to combine.

Add the powdered sugar and starting off on low speed, begin to combine the powdered sugar into the mixture. Once you are not going to cause a sugar explosion, increase speed to high and whip until bright white.

If you make this ahead of time, I suggest whipping it again, right before using.

S'mores

Summertime just doesn't seem complete without a marshmallow roasting over a fire pit and s'mores following that. I did numerous tests of this recipe to make sure it had that campfire feel mixed with the right amount of chocolate and graham cracker. I finally landed on filling the babka with a torched meringue. I promise it's not as scary as it sounds to make and it is so worth it.

Makes 1 babka

Sweet Babka Dough (page 39) or Butter Blocked Dough (page 44), made with sweet dough

10 grams (1 tablespoon + 1 teaspoon) ground cinnamon

Chocolate Filling (recipe follows)

½ recipe Cinnamon Filling (recipe follows)

Softened butter, for the pan

All-purpose flour, for dusting

Simple Syrup (page 143), for generously brushing on after baking

Torched Marshmallow Cream (recipe follows)

Continued . . .

Make and chill the dough as directed, adding the cinnamon to the dry ingredients. Make the chocolate filling and cinnamon filling.

Butter an 8½ × 4½-inch loaf pan, using a pastry brush to get into the corners.

Lightly dust a work surface with flour and roll the dough to a 9 × 14-inch rectangle. Spread the cinnamon filling all over the rolled-out dough, followed by the chocolate filling, reaching the edges.

Roll up and cut the babka as directed on page 30.

Proof, bake, and cool as directed on page 34. Brush the babka generously with the simple syrup. Meanwhile, make the torched marshmallow cream.

Once the babka has cooled completely and right before you are ready to serve, take an 825 piping tip and create five holes along the bottom of the babka, making sure to insert the piping tip into the babka while rotating it.

Place the torched marshmallow cream into a piping bag fitted with an 802 piping tip and insert the piping bag all the way into each of the holes you just created. Squeeze from the back of the bag (so it does not come out that way!) and move the tip in different directions to make sure you have reached all areas inside the dough. If you begin to see filling coming out the top, that is your sign to stop.

Slice and serve!

Chocolate Filling

MAKES ENOUGH FOR 1 BABKA

114 grams (½ cup + 3 tablespoons) milk chocolate chips

114 grams (½ cup + 3 tablespoons) dark chocolate chips

32 grams (2½ tablespoons) unsalted butter

Make a double boiler: Fill a pot with 1 inch of water and find a heatproof bowl that can sit over the pot without touching the water. Bring the water to a boil without the bowl.

In the bowl, combine the chocolate chips and butter. Place the bowl on top of the pot and turn off the heat. Stir until melted. Remove the bowl from the pot. Let cool slightly before using.

Cinnamon Filling

MAKES ENOUGH FOR 1 BABKA

104 grams (½ cup) packed dark brown sugar

1 teaspoon ground cinnamon

1½ teaspoons cornstarch

¼ teaspoon of fine sea salt

44 grams (3 tablespoons) unsalted butter, at room temperature but not super soft

In a small bowl, whisk together the brown sugar, cinnamon, cornstarch and sea salt. Using a pastry cutter or your hands, add the butter and combine to create a cinnamon-sugar paste.

Torched Marshmallow Cream

MAKES 576 GRAMS (6 CUPS)

76 grams (⅓ cup) water

149 grams (¾ cup) sugar

234 grams (¾ cup) corn syrup or honey

3 large egg whites

½ teaspoon cream of tartar

1 teaspoon vanilla bean paste or extract

Double-check to make sure your mixer, mixing bowl, and whisk attachment are grease-free, as any grease here will cause your meringue to not whip up.

In a small saucepan, combine the water, sugar, and corn syrup. Bring to a boil over high heat. Once the mixture begins to boil, insert a candy thermometer into the liquid. Do not stir the liquid at all, as that will cause sugar crystals to form and will seize your meringue.

Place the egg whites and cream of tartar into the bowl of the stand mixer.

When the sugar mixture reaches 235°F, begin to whip your egg white mixture on medium-low, it should look like beer foam, 2 to 3 minutes.

Once the sugar mixture reaches 240°F, turn off the heat. Set your stand mixer on medium-high and very slowly and carefully pour the sugar syrup in a steady stream into the egg white mixture, making sure not to hit the side of the bowl or the whip too much.

Once all the sugar syrup is added, increase the mixer speed to high and whip. As the peaks begin to form, turn off the mixer and remove the bowl and whisk. Take a small kitchen torch and torch the top of the meringue until it is golden brown, just like you would a marshmallow. Return the bowl to the mixer and mix until incorporated. Repeat this step four or five more times until it tastes like a delicious roasted marshmallow.

Turn off the mixer and add the vanilla. Whip until incorporated and cool. You can test the thickness of the meringue by turning off the mixer, removing the whisk attachment, and holding the whisk upside down to see the peak formation. It should hold its form when put upside down and look like a mountain. It is very important not to under- or overwhip the meringue, though it is better for it to be slightly under than over, which causes your meringue to be more dry.

Use right away or store in an airtight container for 2 weeks at room temperature.

Note: If you have marshmallow cream left over, you can smear it on a peanut butter sandwich and make yourself a Fluffernutter! This is my favorite way of eating the leftovers.

Cannoli

Every time I go to New York City with my family we always make at least one stop at Ferrara Bakery on Grand Street. The dark wood, deep reds, and the waiters looking so dapper always filled me with awe as a kid. The one thing I will never forget is going to the pastry case with my dad and being allowed to choose whatever I wanted to try. My number one pick was always the same: a chocolate-dipped cannoli!

Makes 1 babka

Sweet Babka Dough (page 39) or Butter Blocked Dough (page 44), made with sweet dough

Cannoli Filling (recipe follows)

75 grams (⅓ cup) sugar

½ teaspoon grated orange zest

Softened butter, for the pan

All-purpose flour, for dusting

75 grams (6 tablespoons) unsalted butter, at room temperature

Simple Syrup (page 143), for generously brushing on after baking

Dark Chocolate Glazing Ganache (page 147)

Toasted pistachios, chopped

Continued . . .

Make and chill the dough as directed. Make the cannolli filling.

Create an orange sugar by mixing together the sugar and orange zest.

Butter an 8½ × 4½-inch loaf pan, using a pastry brush to get into the corners.

Lightly dust a work surface with flour and roll the dough to a 9 × 14-inch rectangle. Spread the 75 grams butter all over the rolled-out dough, reaching the edges. Sprinkle the orange sugar over the butter layer. Use a rolling pin to lightly press the sugar into the dough.

Roll up and cut the babka as directed on page 30.

Proof, bake, and cool as directed on page 34. Brush the babka generously with the simple syrup. Meanwhile, make the dark chocolate ganache.

Once the babka has cooled completely and right before you are ready to serve, take an 825 piping tip and create five holes along the bottom of the babka, making sure to insert the piping tip into the babka while rotating it.

Place the cannoli filling in a piping bag fitted with an 802 piping tip and insert the piping bag all the way into each of the holes you just created. Squeeze from the back of the bag (so it does not come out that way!) and move the tip in different directions to make sure you have reached all areas inside the dough. If you begin to see filling coming out the top, that is your sign to stop!

Place on a wire rack and glaze the top of the babka with the slightly cooled ganache, sprinkle with pistachios, and let set before moving to a serving dish.

Cannoli Filling

MAKES ENOUGH FOR 1 BABKA

225 grams (1 cup) whole-milk ricotta cheese (see Note)

225 grams (1 cup) mascarpone

70 grams (⅔ cup) powdered sugar

¼ teaspoon kosher salt

½ teaspoon ground cinnamon

½ teaspoon vanilla extract

The night before, place the ricotta in a fine-mesh sieve lined with cheesecloth. Set over a bowl to catch any liquid and place a small plate on top of it with a weight, such as a can or jar, to encourage the liquid to drain off. Refrigerate overnight.

The next day, in a food processor, combine the drained ricotta, mascarpone, powdered sugar, salt, cinnamon, and vanilla and blend until smooth. Refrigerate until ready to use.

Note: After the ricotta has strained overnight it will look grainy; don't worry, as it will smooth out once it is mixed with the other ingredients in the food processor.

Storage: This babka can be kept in the refrigerator for up to 2 days. Please note it will begin to stale in the refrigerator, so I recommend eating it all in one day.

Chocolate Peanut Butter

I couldn't have just one peanut butter babka in the book; I had to make sure I gave both classics a time to shine. This is my take on a peanut butter cup babka. I recommend using whatever peanut butter brand brings you back to childhood, as long as it is *not* an all-natural peanut butter as that will break; use a creamy variety.

Makes 1 babka

Chocolate Babka Dough (page 48)
Peanut Butter Filling (recipe follows)
Chocolate Filling (recipe follows)
Softened butter, for the pan
All-purpose flour, for dusting
Simple Syrup (page 143), for generously brushing on after baking
Peanut Butter Glaze (page 146)
½ cup roughly chopped peanut butter cups

Make and chill the dough as directed. Make the peanut butter and chocolate fillings.

Butter an 8½ × 4½-inch loaf pan, using a pastry brush to get into the corners.

Continued . . .

Lightly dust a work surface with flour and roll the dough to a 9 × 14-inch rectangle. Place the peanut butter filling in the microwave for 20 seconds, not to melt it but to soften it and make it a bit easier to spread. Spread the chocolate filling on the rolled-out dough, and then follow with the peanut butter filling, making sure both are to the edges.

Roll up and cut the babka as directed on page 30.

Proof, bake, and cool as directed on page 34. Brush the babka generously with the simple syrup. Meanwhile, make the peanut butter glaze and chop up the peanut butter cups.

Once cooled, take out of the pan and place the babka on a wire rack. Pour the glaze on top, sprinkle with chopped peanut butter cups, and let set before moving to a serving dish.

Peanut Butter Filling

MAKES ENOUGH FOR 1 BABKA

150 grams (½ cup) creamy peanut butter (I recommend Jif)

23 grams (3 tablespoons) powdered sugar, sifted

¼ teaspoon fine sea salt

Combine all the ingredients in a bowl with a spatula. Set aside until ready to use.

Chocolate Filling

MAKES ENOUGH FOR 1 BABKA

114 grams (½ cup + 3 tablespoons) milk chocolate chips

114 grams (½ cup + 3 tablespoons) dark chocolate chips

32 grams (2½ tablespoons) unsalted butter

Make a double boiler: Fill a pot with 1 inch of water and find a heatproof bowl that can sit over the pot without touching the water. Bring the water to a boil without the bowl.

In the bowl, combine the chocolate chips and butter. Place the bowl on top of the pot and turn off the heat. Stir until melted. Remove the bowl from the pot. Let cool slightly before using.

Apple Pie

I came up with this recipe for my dad—the man has never met a pie he does not like. To all my pie lovers out there, this one is for you.

Makes 1 babka

Sweet Babka Dough (page 39) or Butter Blocked Dough (page 44), made with sweet dough

---

200 grams (¾ cup) Apple Pie Puree (recipe follows)

---

30 grams (¼ cup) Candied Pumpkin Seeds (page 146)

---

56 grams (¼ cup) Oat Streusel (recipe follows)

Softened butter, for the pan

All-purpose flour, for dusting

Simple Syrup (page 143), for generously brushing on after baking

---

Make and chill the dough as directed. Make the apple pie puree, candied pumpkin seeds, and streusel.

Butter an 8½ × 4½-inch loaf pan, using a pastry brush to get into the corners.

Lightly dust a work surface with flour and roll the dough to a 9 × 14-inch rectangle. Spread the apple pie puree all over the rolled-out dough, reaching the edges. Sprinkle the candied pumpkin seeds and the oat streusel over the apple layer.

Roll up and cut the babka as directed on page 30.

Proof, bake, and cool as directed on page 34. Generously brush the babka with simple syrup.

Continued . . .

Apple Pie Puree

MAKES 513 GRAMS (1½ CUPS)

175 grams (6 ounces) ¼-inch diced and peeled Granny Smith apples (1½ cups)

175 grams (6 ounces) ¼-inch diced and peeled Gala apples (1½ cups)

50 grams (¼ cup) dark brown sugar

25 grams (2 tablespoons) granulated sugar

1 tablespoon apple pie spice

¼ teaspoon kosher salt

15 grams (1 tablespoon) bourbon or apple cider

½ tablespoon fresh lemon juice

In a medium pot, combine the apples, brown sugar, granulated sugar, apple pie spice, salt, bourbon, and lemon juice. Cook over low heat, stirring occasionally, until the apples are tender and the liquid has reduced by half. Taste and add more spices, sugar, or lemon to your liking.

Transfer the apple mixture to a food processor and process until almost smooth (don't feel like you have to make it look like applesauce; if it is a little chunky that is alright). Let cool and refrigerate until ready to use.

Oat Streusel

MAKES 325 GRAMS (2¼ CUPS)

100 grams (1 cup + 1 tablespoon) rolled oats

50 grams (¼ cup) dark brown sugar

86 grams (¾ cup) all-purpose flour

½ teaspoon ground cinnamon

½ teaspoon fine sea salt

65 grams (4½ tablespoons) unsalted butter, at room temperature

In a stand mixer fitted with the paddle, mix together the oats, brown sugar, flour, cinnamon, and sea salt on low until combined. Add the butter and mix on low until clumps begin to form. Set aside, at room temperature, until ready to use.

> **Note:** For a real apple pie à la mode experience, slice and toast your finished babka in butter in a skillet and top with ice cream!

Baklava

Visiting Israel opened me up to a whole new world of baklava. I was in awe of the flavor profiles and floral qualities. This recipe can be adapted to your flavor profile of choice. Feel free to switch out the nuts for others or add some orange blossom water.

Makes 1 babka

Sweet Babka Dough (page 39) or Butter Blocked Dough (page 44), made with sweet dough

Baklava Filling (recipe follows)

Softened butter, for the pan

All-purpose flour, for dusting

Honey Simple Syrup (page 143)

Make and chill the dough as directed. Make the baklava filling.

Butter an $8\frac{1}{2} \times 4\frac{1}{2}$-inch loaf pan, using a pastry brush to get into the corners.

Lightly dust a work surface with flour and roll the dough to a 9×14-inch rectangle. Spread the baklava filling all over the rolled-out dough, reaching the edges and making sure to be gentle as the nuts could rip through the dough if pressed down hard enough.

Roll up and cut the babka as directed on page 30.

Proof and bake as directed on page 34. Meanwhile, make the honey simple syrup.

Immediately after it comes out of the oven, generously brush the babka with the honey simple syrup. You want it *slightly* swimming in the syrup. Allow the babka to rest until cool, about 15 minutes, then remove from the pan and place on a wire rack.

Continued . . .

Baklava Filling

MAKES ENOUGH FOR 1 BABKA

86 grams (¾ cup) pistachios

86 grams (¾ cup) hazelnuts

86 grams (¾ cup) walnuts

11 grams (2¼ teaspoons) sugar

2 teaspoons ground cinnamon

1 teaspoon ground cloves

¼ teaspoon sea salt

114 grams (¼ cup + 4½ teaspoons) honey

3 drops of rose water

In a food processor, combine all the nuts and process until chopped to the size of small pieces of gravel. You do not want to pulverize the nuts and make them into butter. You also do not want ginormous pieces, which will make rolling up the babka and slicing it very difficult

Transfer the chopped nuts to a bowl and toss with the sugar, cinnamon, cloves, and salt. Drizzle the honey and rose water over the top and use a spatula to combine, making sure everything is well coated and evenly distributed. Adjust with more rose water, spices, or honey to taste. Set aside until ready to use.

Peach Cobbler

Summertime is not complete without a peach cobbler, especially when the Texas peaches are in season. I have driven out to the Hill Country numerous times to go and eat peach soft serve, peach jam, peach cider, you name it. If it has peaches in it, I am there. This is an ode to the peach cobblers I make in the summertime for my family and all those fun road trips to eat another great peach.

Makes 1 babka

Sweet Babka Dough (page 39) or Butter Blocked Dough (page 44), made with sweet dough

242 grams (¾ cup) Peach Preserves (recipe follows)

86 grams (⅓ cup) + 56 grams (¼ cup) Oat Streusel (recipe follows)

Softened butter, for the pan

All-purpose flour, for dusting

Simple Syrup (page 143), for generously brushing on after baking

Make the peach preserves and chill overnight.

Make and chill the dough as directed. Make the streusel.

Butter an 8½ × 4½-inch loaf pan, using a pastry brush to get into the corners.

Lightly dust a work surface with flour and roll the dough to a 9 × 14-inch rectangle. Spread the peach preserves all over the rolled-out dough, reaching the edges. Sprinkle 86 grams of the oat streusel over the peach layer. Use a rolling pin to gently push the streusel into the dough.

Roll up and cut the babka as directed on page 30.

Continued . . .

Proof the babka as directed on page 34.

Once the babka has been proofed, sprinkle the remaining 56 grams of the oat streusel on top and gently press in.

Bake and cool as directed on page 34. Brush the babka generously with the simple syrup.

Peach Preserves

MAKES 531 GRAMS (2 CUPS)

340 grams (12 ounces) peaches

250 grams (1¼ cups) + 14 grams (1 tablespoon) sugar

8 grams (½ tablespoon) fresh lemon juice

¼ teaspoon ground cinnamon

½ teaspoon salt

12 grams (1 tablespoon + 1 teaspoon) powdered pectin

Remove the pits of the peaches using clean needle-nose pliers by opening them to the approximate width of the pit, pushing into the center, and clamping down on the pit. Gently rotate the pit and remove. Peel the skins off the peaches with a vegetable peeler and chop into ¼-inch pieces.

Have a metal mixing bowl ready and set near the stove.

In a medium pot, combine the peaches, 250 grams of the sugar, the lemon juice, cinnamon, and salt. Use a potato masher or back of a wooden spoon to help break up the peaches further and to allow the ingredients to combine.

Bring to a boil over medium heat, stirring occasionally.

Meanwhile, in a small bowl, whisk together the remaining 14 grams sugar and the pectin.

Once the peaches are at a boil where it is bubbling rapidly in the center of the pot, whisk in the sugar and pectin mixture. Bring back to a rolling boil for 2 minutes, stirring constantly and being careful to scrape the bottom and corners of the pot so that nothing burns.

Pour the peach jam out into the metal mixing bowl, let cool to room temperature, then transfer to a lidded jar and refrigerate overnight to set.

Oat Streusel

MAKES 325 GRAMS (2¼ CUPS)

100 grams (1 cup + 1 tablespoon) rolled oats

50 grams (¼ cup) dark brown sugar

86 grams (¾ cup) all-purpose flour

½ teaspoon ground cinnamon

½ teaspoon fine sea salt

65 grams (4½ tablespoons) unsalted butter, at room temperature

In a stand mixer fitted with the paddle, mix together the oats, brown sugar, flour, cinnamon, and sea salt on low until combined. Add the butter and mix on low until clumps begin to form. Set aside at room temperature until ready to use.

Lemon, Basil, and Blueberry

I owned my own wedding cake business for seven years and this was my most popular flavor profile. I love the combination of tart, sweet, and herbaceous together; they play wonderfully. It may sound weird, but I promise that you will be very surprised at how much you like this combination. As for the extra blueberry basil jam you will end up with? Try spreading it on toast or dolloping over vanilla ice cream. It will change your mind about basil in baked goods.

Makes 1 babka

Lemon Curd (recipe follows)

200 grams (²⁄₃ cup) Blueberry Basil Jam (recipe follows)

Sweet Babka Dough (page 39) or Butter Blocked Dough (page 44), made with sweet dough

Softened butter, for the pan

All-purpose flour, for dusting

Simple Syrup (page 143), for generously brushing on after baking

Lemon Glaze (page 147)

Make the lemon curd and blueberry basil jam and chill overnight.

Make and chill the dough as directed.

Butter an 8½ × 4½-inch loaf pan, using a pastry brush to get into the corners.

Lightly dust a work surface with flour and roll the dough to a 9 × 14-inch rectangle. Spread the blueberry basil jam all over the rolled-out dough, reaching the edges.

Roll up and cut the babka as directed on page 30.

Proof, bake, and cool as directed on page 34. Generously brush the babka with simple syrup. Meanwhile, make the lemon glaze.

Once the babka has cooled completely and right before you are ready to serve, take an 825 piping tip and create five holes along the bottom of the babka, making sure to insert the piping tip into the babka while rotating it.

Fit the piping bag of lemon curd with an 802 piping tip and insert the piping bag all the way into each of the holes you just made from the back of the bag (so it does not come out that way!) and move the tip in different directions to make sure you have reached all areas inside the dough. If you begin to see filling coming out the top, that is your sign to stop!

Place on a wire rack and spoon the lemon glaze on top, allowing it to go over the edges. Let sit for 10 minutes to set before serving.

Continued . . .

Lemon Curd

MAKES 840 GRAMS (3½ CUPS)

2 sheets silver leaf gelatin (#170 bloom)

240 grams (1⅓ cups) sugar

2 teaspoons grated lemon zest

4 large eggs (200 grams)

160 grams (¾ cup) fresh lemon juice

300 grams (21 tablespoons) butter, cut into ½-inch cubes and cold

Set a fine-mesh sieve over the bowl of a stand mixer. Set a silicone spatula right next to it.

Place the gelatin in a bowl of ice-cold water, making sure all of it is submerged. Soak just until the gelatin is soft but still has some form. Check in 2 to 3 minutes. You should be able to take it out of the water, squeeze out the excess water, and place it on the table next to your pot. You don't want to overbloom the gelatin— it should not be a globby mess.

In a medium saucepan, combine the sugar, lemon zest, eggs, and lemon juice and whisk to combine. Set over medium heat and bring to a boil, whisking constantly and making sure your whisk is always in contact with the bottom of the pan.

Once the mixture is bubbling in the center, remove the saucepan from the heat and whisk in the gelatin completely.

Change out your whisk for the silicone spatula to put the lemon mixture through the sieve and into the mixer bowl.

Once all the mixture has been strained, remove the sieve. Set the bowl on the mixer and attach the paddle. Beat on medium to medium–high speed. You are looking to get the mixture moving but do not want to spray yourself and your kitchen with lemon curd, so use your judgment on how high the mixer speed should be.

Once you stop seeing steam coming out of the mixer, usually in 2 to 3 minutes, reduce the mixer to the lowest speed and begin to add the cubes of butter, a few at a time. Allow each addition to incorporate before adding more.

Once all the butter has been combined with the lemon mixture, stop the mixer and transfer to a heatproof container. Place plastic wrap directly on the surface of the lemon curd and then a lid on top, as this will stop a skin from forming. Refrigerate overnight to set before using.

Blueberry Basil Jam

MAKES 543 GRAMS (2 CUPS)

310 grams (2 cups) blueberries

250 grams (1¼ cups) + 14 grams (1 tablespoon) sugar

10 grams (2¼ teaspoons) fresh lemon juice

20 grams (2 tablespoons + 2 teaspoons) powdered pectin

1 tablespoon finely chopped fresh basil

Have a metal mixing bowl ready and set near the stove.

In a medium pot, combine the blueberries, 250 grams of the sugar, and the lemon juice. Place over low heat and mix until the sugar dissolves, making sure to keep the edges of the pot clean.

Once the sugar has dissolved, increase the heat to high and bring to a rolling boil, stirring occasionally.

Meanwhile, in a small bowl, combine the pectin and remaining 14 grams sugar.

Once the blueberries are at a boil, add the pectin/sugar mixture and bring back to a rolling boil. Boil for 2 minutes, while stirring.

Pour the jam out into the metal mixing bowl and let cool to room temperature. Transfer the jam to a container, mix in the basil, cover, and refrigerate overnight before using.

Storage: This babka can be kept in the refrigerator in an airtight container for up to 3 days. Please note it will begin to stale in the refrigerator, so I recommend eating it all in one day.

Nana's Fave

Nana Mary is the reason why this book exists, and I couldn't write it without having a recipe in here that was a play on one of her classic recipe cards. I came across a cake recipe with very similar components and I thought, why not use it in a babka? I had never heard of such a cake, but it sounded delicious and it worked even better in this format!

Makes 1 babka

Sweet Babka Dough (page 39) or
Butter Blocked Dough (page 44), made with sweet dough

160 grams (½ cup) Apricot Puree (recipe follows)

50 grams (⅓ cup) Soaked Golden Raisins (recipe follows)

50 grams (⅓ cup) pistachios, toasted and chopped (see Note)

1 recipe Meringue (follows)

Softened butter, for the pan

All-purpose flour, for dusting

Simple Syrup (page 143), for generously brushing on after baking

Continued . . .

Make and chill the dough as directed. Make the apricot puree, prepare the soaked raisins, and make the meringue.

Butter an 8½ × 4½-inch loaf pan, using a pastry brush to get into the corners.

Lightly dust a work surface with flour and roll the dough to a 9 × 14-inch rectangle. Spread the apricot puree all over the rolled-out dough, reaching the edges. Spread the meringue on top of that and sprinkle with the pistachios and raisins. Use a rolling pin to lightly press everything into the dough.

Roll up and cut the babka as directed on page 30.

Proof, bake, and cool as directed on page 34. Brush the babka generously with the simple syrup.

Note: To toast the pistachios, preheat the oven to 350°F. Spread the pistachios onto a sheet pan, and toast in the oven for 7 to 9 minutes, until they just begin to take on color. Remove from the oven and let cool.

Apricot Puree

MAKES 200 GRAMS (1 CUP)

170 grams (1¼ cups) dried apricots

227 grams (2 cups) hot water

Soak apricots in hot water, enough just to cover all of them, for 30 minutes or overnight.

Drain the apricots and pulse in a food processor until a smooth paste forms. Add water if necessary.

Soaked Golden Raisins

MAKES 125 GRAMS (½ CUP)

50 grams (⅓ cup) golden raisins, chopped if jumbo

60 grams (¼ cup) hot water

15 grams (1 tablespoon) amaretto

Place the raisins in a bowl with the hot water and amaretto and let soak until you are ready to use them, at least 30 minutes or overnight. When ready to use, drain off the liquid.

Meringue

MAKES ENOUGH FOR 1 BABKA

2 large egg whites

132 grams (⅔ cup + 1 tablespoon) sugar

In a stand mixer, whisk the egg whites until they look like beer foam. Add the sugar and whisk until stiff peaks form. Use immediately.

Mexican Chocolate Brownie

Growing up in Southern California and then moving to Central Texas has gifted me with so much exposure to Mexican cooking and baking. This recipe can be made without the ancho powder to create a regular brownie flavor profile.

Makes 1 babka

Chocolate Babka Dough (page 48)

Brownie Filling (recipe follows)

Softened butter, for the pan

All-purpose flour, for dusting

30 grams (3 tablespoons) dark chocolate chips, roughly chopped

30 grams (3 tablespoons) milk chocolate chips, roughly chopped

Simple Syrup (page 143), for generously brushing on after baking

Make and chill the dough as directed. Make the brownie filling.

Butter an 8½ × 4½-inch loaf pan, using a pastry brush to get into the corners.

Lightly dust a work surface with flour and roll the dough to a 9 × 14-inch rectangle. Spread the brownie mixture all over the rolled-out dough, reaching the edges. Sprinkle it with the chocolate chips.

Roll up and cut the babka as directed on page 30.

Proof, bake, and cool as directed on page 34. Brush the babka generously with the simple syrup.

Continued . . .

Brownie Filling

113 grams (8 tablespoons) unsalted butter

57 grams (⅓ cup) dark chocolate chips

2 large eggs (100 grams)

213 grams (1 cup) brown sugar

1 teaspoon vanilla bean paste or extract

72 grams (⅔ cup) all-purpose flour, sifted

½ teaspoon kosher salt

1¼ teaspoons ancho chile powder

1¼ teaspoons ground cinnamon

Place the butter and chocolate in a large microwave-safe bowl and heat for 10 seconds at a time, until both are melted. Whisk to combine.

In a separate bowl, whisk together the eggs, brown sugar, and vanilla.

Slowly add the eggs mixture to the chocolate mixture, whisking to combine. Add the flour, salt, ancho powder, and cinnamon, mixing just to combine.

Set aside until ready to use.

Miso Dulce de Leche

Miso adds just the right amount of salty sweet to anything,
and I find it is the perfect way to balance the sweetness of dulce de leche.

Makes 1 babka

Sweet Babka Dough (page 39) or Butter Blocked Dough (page 44), made with sweet dough

220 grams (1 cup) Miso Dulce de Leche (recipe follows)

Softened butter, for the pan

All-purpose flour, for dusting

100 grams (⅓ cup) raspberry jam

Simple Syrup (page 143), for generously brushing on after baking

Make and chill the dough as directed. Make the miso dulce de leche filling.

Butter an 8½ × 4½-inch loaf pan, using a pastry brush to get into the corners.

Lightly dust a work surface with flour and roll the dough to a 9 × 14-inch rectangle. Spread the miso dulce de leche filing all over the rolled-out dough, reaching the edges, then dollop on the raspberry jam and lightly spread that on top of the miso layer.

Roll up and cut the babka as directed on page 30.

Proof, bake, and cool as directed on page 34. Brush the babka generously with the simple syrup.

Continued . . .

Miso Dulce de Leche

MAKES 220 GRAMS ($^3/_4$ CUP)

---

210 grams ($^3/_4$ cup) dulce de leche, store-bought or homemade (see Note)

---

9 grams ($^1/_2$ tablespoon) red miso

---

1 teaspoon black sesame seeds

In a bowl, mix the dulce de leche, miso, and sesame seeds with a rubber spatula. Set aside until ready to use.

Note: To make your own dulce de leche, take a can of sweetened condensed milk, remove the label, and submerge in a pot of boiling water. Simmer for 2 to 3 hours. Remove, let cool, then open and use.

Stollen

In school my breads chef was from Germany and lucky for me, I took the class right before Christmas, when stollen is traditionally made. The bread is filled with dried fruit and marzipan, a perfect flavor combination for cozy weather.

Makes 1 babka

Sweet Babka Dough (page 39) or Butter Blocked Dough (page 44), made with sweet dough

---

75 grams (⅔ cup) Plumped Dried Fruit (recipe follows)

---

75 grams (⅓ cup) Spiced Sugar (recipe follows)

---

150 grams (½ cup) almond paste, chilled

Softened butter, for the pan

All-purpose flour, for dusting

---

75 grams (6 tablespoons) unsalted butter, at room temperature

---

Simple Syrup (page 143), for generously brushing on after baking

---

Powdered sugar, for dusting

Make and chill the dough as directed. Prepare the plumped dried fruit and spiced sugar.

In a food processor, process the almond paste until it looks like little crumbs.

Continued . . .

Butter an 8½ × 4½-inch loaf pan, using a pastry brush to get into the corners.

Lightly dust a work surface with flour and roll the dough to a 9 × 14-inch rectangle. Spread the 75 grams butter all over the rolled-out dough, reaching the edges. Sprinkle the almond paste, spiced sugar, and plumped dried fruit over the butter layer. Use a rolling pin to lightly press everything into the dough.

Roll up and cut the babka as directed on page 30.

Proof, bake, and cool as directed on page 34. Brush the babka generously with the simple syrup.

Once cooled, heavily dust with powdered sugar.

Plumped Dried Fruit

For the mixed fruit used in this recipe, get creative. What dried fruits do you enjoy together? I like to use apricots, figs, and dates. Other times I may use currants, raisins, and cherries. Create a mix that you love!

MAKES 183 GRAMS (1¼ CUPS)

75 grams (⅔ cup) dried cranberries, roughly chopped

75 grams (⅔ cup) dried mixed fruit, roughly chopped

½ teaspoon grated lemon zest

½ teaspoon grated orange zest

63 grams (¼ cup) fresh orange juice

In a small pan, simmer the cranberries, dried mixed fruit, lemon zest, orange zest, and orange juice until the fruit looks plump, about 5 minutes. Set aside to cool before using.

Spiced Sugar

MAKES 100 GRAMS (½ CUP)

100 grams (½ cup) sugar

1 teaspoon ground cinnamon

⅛ teaspoon ground nutmeg

⅛ teaspoon ground cloves

Place all ingredients in a bowl and mix with a whisk until combined.

Sweet Final Touches

Here are flavored simple syrups, glazes, and other fillings to finish your babka for the perfect additional pop of flavor.

Simple Syrup

MAKES 440 GRAMS (1½ CUPS)

240 grams (1 cup) water

200 grams (1 cup) sugar

Place the water and sugar into a pot and add the sugar on top. Give a quick stir and make sure no sugar is on the sides of the pot.

Bring to a boil over high heat and boil for 2 to 3 minutes, then turn off the heat. Let cool and set aside. Store in a sealed container in the refrigerator until ready to use.

Kirschwasser Simple Syrup

MAKES 205 GRAMS (⅔ CUP)

195 grams (⅔ cup) Simple Syrup

10 grams (2 teaspoons) Kirschwasser

Stir the cooled simple syrup and Kirschwasser together. Store in the refrigerator until ready to use.

Honey Simple Syrup

MAKES 134 GRAMS (⅓ CUP)

100 grams (⅓ cup) Simple Syrup, hot

34 grams (1½ tablespoons) honey

Pinch of ground cloves

Whisk the ingredients together. Store in the refrigerator until ready to use.

Whipped Cream

MAKES 2 CUPS

240 grams (1 cup) heavy cream

11 grams (1½ tablespoons) powdered sugar

½ teaspoon vanilla bean paste or extract

In a stand mixer, combine the heavy cream, powdered sugar, and vanilla and whip until stiff peaks form, 2 to 3 minutes. Use immediately.

Candied Pecans

Lemon Glaze

Candied Pumpkin Seeds

Whipped
Cream

Dark Chocolate
Glazing Ganache

Peanut Butter Glaze

MAKES 210 GRAMS (³⁄₄ CUP)

116 grams (1 cup) powdered sugar, sifted

68 grams (¼ cup) creamy peanut butter (I prefer Jif)

56 grams (¼ cup) whole milk

1 teaspoon vanilla bean paste or extract

½ teaspoon fine sea salt

In a bowl, whisk all the ingredients to combine. Set aside with either plastic wrap over the top or a lid until ready to use.

Candied Pecans

MAKES 160 GRAMS (1 CUP)

100 grams (½ cup) water

150 grams (¾ cup) sugar

150 grams (1 cup) pecans, chopped and toasted

Preheat the oven to 300°F. Line a sheet pan with a silicone baking mat or parchment paper. Set a fine mesh sleeve over a heatproof bowl. Have both near the stove.

In a pot, bring the water and sugar to a boil over high heat. Add the pecans, and once the mixture comes back up to a boil set a 14-minute timer.

Once the timer goes off, pour the nuts into the sieve to drain off the sugar syrup, then spread the nuts out on the sheet pan in an even layer.

Transfer to the oven and bake until they are not wet and are nicely toasted, 10 to 15 minutes. Make sure not to burn them.

I love to use the strained-off pecan syrup to brush over a sponge cake or in an old-fashioned cocktail.

Candied Pumpkin Seeds: Use 150 grams (1 cup) pumpkin seeds in place of the pecans.

Dark Chocolate Glazing Ganache

MAKES 380 GRAMS (1½ CUPS)

227 grams (1 cup) heavy cream

170 grams (1 cup) dark chocolate chips

Place the chocolate in a heatproof bowl large enough to accommodate the cream and chocolate together.

In a small pot, heat the cream over medium-low heat until bubbles form around the edges and it begins to climb up the walls of the pot.

Immediately pour the cream over the chocolate. Let sit undisturbed for 3 minutes. Using a whisk or a spatula, start with small circles in the center of your bowl, mixing the chocolate and cream together. Slowly begin to make your circles larger until you have married the chocolate and the cream into a homogenous mixture.

Let cool for 15 minutes before using. Keep in mind the longer this sits out the thicker it will get. If it gets too thick, you can place it over a double boiler to warm.

Basic Glaze

MAKES 125 GRAMS (⅓ CUP)

114 grams (1 cup) powdered sugar

¼ teaspoon fine sea salt

14 to 28 grams (1 to 2 tablespoons) milk, water, half-and-half, or any flavored liquid

Sift the powdered sugar and salt into a bowl. Add the liquid of choice and whisk until it comes together, adding more liquid if necessary. You want to make sure it is not too thin or thick. When you pick up your whisk and let the glaze fall from it back into the bowl, it should remain on top of the surface and then disappear within 15 seconds.

If you are not using it right away, cover the surface with plastic wrap to make sure it does not form a skin.

Lemon Glaze: Use lemon juice for the liquid and stir in 1 teaspoon grated lemon zest.

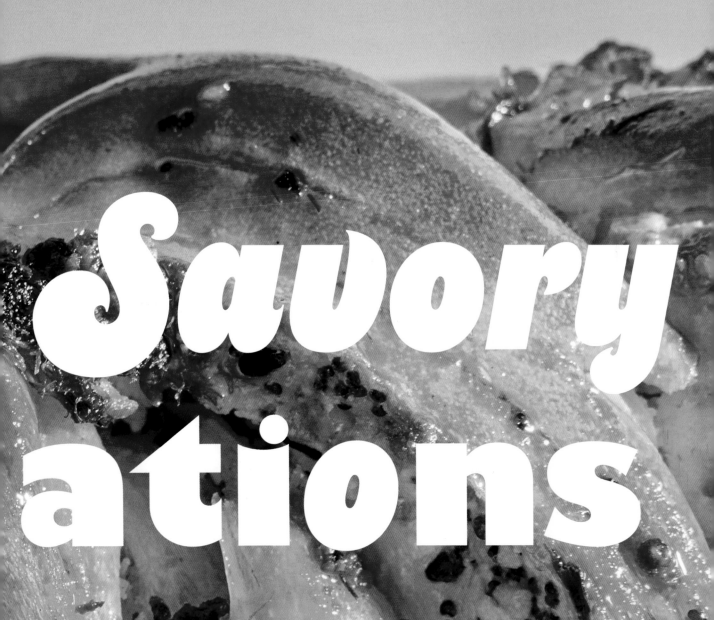

When I began writing this book, I told friends and family about all the fun flavor profiles I was creating and got the most crazy looks when I mentioned savory babka. I understand this is not a typical babka profile, but if you are a babka purist, I urge you to give it a try, at least once. All these savory babkas have a special place in my heart, and I hope you enjoy them as much as I do.

Savory ations

Ham and Cheese

This is the perfect babka to use for sandwich bread or to serve alongside a cheese platter.

Makes 1 babka

Savory Babka Dough (page 41) or Butter Blocked Dough (page 44), made with savory dough

---

1½ teaspoons fresh thyme, lightly chopped

Softened butter, for the pan

All-purpose flour, for dusting

---

43 grams (3 tablespoons) Dijon mustard

---

103 grams (3½ ounces) Gruyère cheese, shredded

---

150 grams (5 ounces) deli ham, thinly sliced

Olive oil, for generously brushing on after baking

Make the dough as directed, adding the chopped thyme to the mixing bowl right after adding the flour so the herbs are fully incorporated into the dough. Chill as directed.

Butter an 8½ × 4½-inch loaf pan, using a pastry brush to get into the corners.

Lightly dust a work surface with flour and roll the dough to a 9 × 14-inch rectangle. Spread the mustard on the rolled-out dough. Sprinkle the Gruyère on top and then the ham, doing your best to make sure the dough is mostly covered.

Roll up and cut the babka as directed on page 30.

Proof, bake, and cool as directed on page 34. Brush the babka generously with the olive oil.

Hatch Pimento Cheese

I loved the idea of creating a filling that resonated with Texas. Pimento cheese and Hatch chiles were the perfect combo.

Makes 1 babka

Savory Babka Dough (page 41) or Butter Blocked Dough (page 44), made with savory dough

---

Hatch Pimento Cheese (recipe follows)

---

85 grams (¼ cup) Caramelized Onions (page 182)

Softened butter, for the pan

All-purpose flour, for dusting

Olive oil, for generously brushing on after baking

Make and chill the dough as directed. Make the pimento cheese and caramelized onions.

Butter an 8½ × 4½-inch loaf pan, using a pastry brush to get into the corners.

Lightly dust a work surface with flour and roll the dough to a 9 × 14-inch rectangle. Spread the Hatch pimento cheese filling on the rolled-out dough. Follow with the caramelized onions, placing dollops of onions all over the dough and then spreading it out, making sure both are to the edges.

Roll up and cut the babka as directed on page 30.

Proof, bake, and cool as directed on page 34. Brush the babka generously with the olive oil.

Continued . . .

Hatch Pimento Cheese

MAKES 300 GRAMS (1½ CUPS)

1 to 2 fresh mild Hatch chiles (45 grams / ⅓ cup) (see Note)

227 grams (8 ounces) shredded Monterey Jack and Cheddar cheese blend

30 grams (¼ cup) minced yellow onion

120 grams (½ cup) mayonnaise (I prefer Duke's)

2 teaspoons fresh lemon juice

½ teaspoon garlic powder

¼ teaspoon paprika

⅛ teaspoon cayenne pepper

2 pinches of dried dill

¼ teaspoon salt

⅛ teaspoon freshly ground black pepper

Two methods for peeling the Hatch chiles:

a) Kitchen torch: Place the chiles on a metal wire rack over your sink. Using a kitchen torch, blister and burn the skin of the chiles, rotating with tongs to get all of it.

b) Gas stove: Turn a burner to high heat and, using tongs, hold the chiles over the flame, blistering and burning the skin.

Remove the skin of the chiles by placing them one at a time on a piece of paper towel and rubbing at the charred skin to remove it. Mince the chiles and add to a bowl.

To the bowl of chiles, add the cheese, onion, mayonnaise, lemon juice, garlic powder, paprika, cayenne, dill, salt, and pepper. Using a rubber spatula, mix together to make sure everything is evenly dispersed and combined. Transfer to a closed container and refrigerate until ready to use.

Note: If you don't have access to fresh Hatch chiles, you can use 45 grams (⅓ cup) canned, minced and drained very well.

Pesto, Mozzarella, and Sun-Dried Tomato

Makes 1 babka

Savory Babka Dough (page 41) or Butter Blocked Dough (page 44), made with savory dough

---

100 grams (½ cup) Pesto (recipe follows)

Softened butter, for the pan

All-purpose flour, for dusting

---

175 grams (¾ cup) sun-dried tomatoes, in oil, drained and pureed in a food processor

---

180 grams (6½ ounces) mozzarella cheese, shredded

Olive oil, for generously brushing on after baking

Make and chill the dough as directed. Make the pesto.

Butter an 8½ × 4½-inch loaf pan, using a pastry brush to get into the corners.

Lightly dust a work surface with flour and roll the dough to a 9 × 14-inch rectangle.

Spread the sun-dried tomato puree over the rolled-out dough. Follow with the pesto and then sprinkle the mozzarella on top, making sure all are to the edges.

Roll up and cut the babka as directed on page 30.

Proof, bake, and cool as directed on page 34. Brush the babka generously with the olive oil.

Continued . . .

Pesto

MAKES 320 GRAMS (1½ CUPS)

56 grams (scant 2 cups) fresh basil leaves (from about 113 g/4 ounces basil sprigs)

½ bunch (40 g) fresh flat-leaf parsley, leaves picked

2 garlic cloves, peeled

22 grams (2 tablespoons) pine nuts

16 grams (½ cup) freshly grated Parmesan cheese

Grated zest of ½ lemon

200 grams (1 cup) olive oil

½ teaspoon xanthan gum

Kosher salt

Fill a bowl with ice and water and have it near the sink. Place a colander in the sink. Bring a small pot of water to a boil. Add the basil and the parsley and boil for 90 seconds. Drain and immediately place into the ice water to cold-shock.

Remove the herbs from the ice bath and squeeze hard to wring out all excess moisture. Transfer the herbs to a blender, making sure to break them up so it is not one big clump. Add the garlic, pine nuts, Parmesan cheese, lemon zest, and olive oil. Blend until smooth. Blend in the xanthan gum and salt to taste.

Transfer to an airtight container and store in the refrigerator until ready to use. It will keep for up to 1 week.

Everything Bagel

This is an homage to eating everything bagels with smoked fish spreads—a break-fast Yom Kippur tradition shared by many Jewish families and a favorite of mine.

Makes 1 babka

Savory Babka Dough (page 41) or Butter Blocked Dough (page 44), made with savory dough

---

125 grams (4 ounces) cream cheese, at room temperature

Softened butter, for the pan

All-purpose flour, for dusting

---

50 grams (1⅓ cup) hot-smoked salmon, shredded

---

14 grams (4½ teaspoons) everything bagel seasoning

Olive oil, for generously brushing on after baking

Make and chill the dough as directed.

In a stand mixer fitted with the paddle, beat the cream cheese until soft and spreadable.

Butter an 8½ × 4½-inch loaf pan, using a pastry brush to get into the corners.

Lightly dust a work surface with flour and roll the dough to a 9 × 14-inch rectangle. Spread the cream cheese onto the rolled-out dough. Follow with the smoked salmon and then sprinkle the everything bagel seasoning on top, making sure all are to the edges.

Roll up and cut the babka as directed on page 30.

Proof, bake, and cool as directed on page 34. Brush the babka generously with the olive oil.

Grilled Cheese

This is one of those choose-your-own-adventure babkas—I have given you the road map to what my ideal grilled cheese looks like, but please get creative and make it your own. Some ideas: Add Brie and some apple butter, or add some garlic butter before sprinkling with cheese.

Makes 1 babka

Savory Babka Dough (page 41) or Butter Blocked Dough (page 44), made with savory dough

Infused Olive Oil (page 185), for brushing

Softened butter, for the pan

All-purpose flour, for dusting

174 grams (6 ounces) American cheese, shredded

99 grams (3½ ounces) Cheddar cheese, shredded

150 grams (5¼ ounces) Muenster cheese, shredded

Make and chill the dough as directed. Make the infused olive oil.

Butter an 8½ × 4½-inch loaf pan, using a pastry brush to get into the corners.

Lightly dust a work surface with flour and roll the dough to a 9 × 14-inch rectangle. Mix all the cheeses together and sprinkle over the dough in an even layer.

Roll up and cut the babka as directed on page 30.

Proof and bake as directed on page 34.

As soon as the babka comes out of the oven, brush with the infused olive oil.

Bacon and Beer Jam

My husband and I worked at a restaurant in Austin together. This is an ode to the beer bread that we served with some of my own tweaks and fun edits added.

Makes 1 babka

200 grams (1¼ cups) Bacon Jam (recipe follows)

175 grams (¾ cups) Caramelized Onions (page 182)

Beer Jam (recipe follows), for serving

Savory Babka Dough (page 41) or Butter Blocked Dough (page 44), made with savory dough

Softened butter, for the pan

All-purpose flour, for dusting

Olive oil, for generously brushing on after baking

Make the bacon jam, caramelized onions, and beer jam and chill overnight.

Make and chill the dough as directed.

Butter an 8½ × 4½-inch loaf pan, using a pastry brush to get into the corners.

Lightly dust a work surface with flour and roll the dough to a 9 × 14-inch rectangle. Spread the bacon jam over the rolled-out dough. Follow with the caramelized onions, making sure both are to the edges.

Roll up and cut the babka as directed on page 30.

Proof, bake, and cool as directed on page 34. Brush the babka generously with the olive oil.

Serve with a side of beer jam for dipping or spreading.

Continued . . .

WITH LOVE AND BABKA

Bacon Jam

MAKES 260 GRAMS (1⅔ CUPS)

150 grams (5 ounces) bacon, minced

30 grams (2 tablespoons) apple cider vinegar

5 grams (1 teaspoon) balsamic vinegar

30 grams (2 tablespoons) brown sugar

10 grams (1 tablespoon) granulated sugar

Cook the bacon in a skillet over medium heat until crispy, about 10 minutes. Strain the bacon from the fat. (Save the fat to cook a pork chop or some potatoes—it's delicious!)

In a saucepan, combine the bacon, apple cider vinegar, balsamic vinegar, and both sugars and bring to a boil. Reduce to a simmer and cook the mixture until thick, about 5 to 7 minutes. You should be able to take your spatula and run it through the center of the jam in the saucepan and it will come back together. You are looking for a jammy consistency, not concrete.

Remove from heat. If your bacon jam is looking a bit too chunky, place in a food processor and lightly process.

Let cool before storing in an airtight container in the refrigerator.

Beer Jam

MAKES 475 GRAMS (2 CUPS)

16 grams (1 tablespoon) Sure-Jell no sugar/low sugar fruit pectin

37 grams (2½ tablespoons) + 150 grams (¾ cup) sugar

1 (12 ounces) bottle West Coast or Imperial IPA (I used Tupps)

¼ teaspoon kosher salt

In a small bowl, combine the pectin and 37 grams of the sugar.

Pour the beer into a 4-quart soup pot and whisk in the pectin-sugar mixture to combine. Bring to a boil and add the remaining 150 grams sugar and the salt. Return to a boil and whisk constantly for 1 minute. The mixture will bubble up, and the faster you whisk, the more it will deflate.

Remove from the heat and pour into a heatproof container. Let cool before covering and refrigerating for at least 24 hours before using.

Reuben

This one's for all of the Reubens my husband and I have shared throughout the years, my favorite being the one from Katz's Delicatessen in New York City.

1½ teaspoons caraway seeds

Savory Babka Dough (page 41) or Butter Blocked Dough (page 44), made with savory dough

---

1 tablespoon neutral oil

---

206 grams (2 cups) sauerkraut

Kosher salt and freshly ground black pepper

---

114 grams (4 ounces) pastrami, shredded

---

74 grams (2½ ounces) Swiss cheese, shredded

Softened butter, for the pan

All-purpose flour, for dusting

Olive oil, for generously brushing on after baking

Continued . . .

Before making the babka dough, lightly toast the caraway seeds in a skillet over medium heat for about 2 minutes.

Make the dough as directed, adding the caraway seeds to the mixing bowl right after adding the flour so the seeds are fully incorporated into the dough. Chill the dough.

Meanwhile, in a saucepan, heat the neutral oil over medium heat. Drain the sauerkraut and once the oil is shiny, add it to the pan (be careful as it might pop and get a little messy). Cook until a golden color is achieved. Season with salt and pepper. The sauerkraut will have shrunk by about half after being cooked. Measure out 103 grams (1 cup) of the sauerkraut and set aside to cool completely. If you have any sauerkraut left, place in a lidded jar in the refrigerator and you can eat it as a snack later.

In a bowl, stir together the shredded pastrami, shredded Swiss cheese, and cooled sauerkraut.

Butter an 8½ × 4½-inch loaf pan, using a pastry brush to get into the corners.

Lightly dust a work surface with flour and roll the dough to a 9 × 14-inch rectangle. Sprinkle the pastrami mixture over the dough and gently press down with a rolling pin to adhere to the dough, being gentle to make sure no tears occur.

Roll up and cut the babka as directed on page 30.

Proof, bake, and cool as directed on page 34. Brush the babka generously with the olive oil.

Pizza

My mom made a pizza roll when I was growing up, so I thought: Why not make a babka pizza roll?! This is the perfect babka to bring to a party with a side of tomato sauce. Add your favorite fillings to the middle, or make it all white with ricotta and lemon and serve it with pesto (page 157). The possibilities are endless and delicious.

Makes 1 babka

Savory Babka Dough (page 41) or Butter Blocked Dough (page 44), made with savory dough
Softened butter, for the pan
All-purpose flour, for dusting
75 grams (½ cup) sliced pepperoni
200 grams (7 ounces / 3½ cups) mozzarella cheese, shredded
Freshly grated Parmesan cheese
Olive oil, for generously brushing on after baking
Tomato sauce, for dipping

Make and chill the dough as directed.

Butter an 8½ × 4½-inch loaf pan, using a pastry brush to get into the corners.

Lightly dust a work surface with flour and roll the dough to a 9 × 14-inch rectangle. Shingle the pepperonis over the babka dough, covering the entire dough and creating two layers of pepperoni. Sprinkle the mozzarella over the top and then grate Parmesan over that, to your liking.

Roll up and cut the babka as directed on page 30.

Proof, bake, and cool as directed on page 34. Generously brush the babka with the olive oil.

Once cooled, slice the babka and heat up some tomato sauce.
Dip and enjoy like a pizza roll.

BEC

The classic New York breakfast: bacon, egg, and cheese on a kaiser roll. The poppy seeds in the dough resemble the kaiser roll, and the filling is meant to bring up those memories of eating a hot breakfast sandwich on the New York City subway. This one is the perfect breakfast bread, served with scrambled eggs on top or eaten by itself.

Makes 1 babka

Savory Babka Dough (page 41) or Butter Blocked Dough (page 44), made with savory dough

---

1½ teaspoons poppy seeds

Neutral oil

---

3 large eggs (150 grams)

Kosher salt and freshly ground black pepper

---

100 grams (3½ ounces) yellow American cheese, cut into ¼-inch pieces

---

32 grams (⅓ cup) bacon, cut into ¼-inch pieces

Softened butter, for the pan

All-purpose flour, for dusting

Olive oil, for generously brushing on after baking

Continued . . .

Make the dough as directed, adding the poppy seeds to the mixing bowl right after adding the flour so the seeds are fully incorporated into the dough. Chill as directed.

Heat 2 tablespoons of neutral oil in a skillet over medium-high heat to shimmering. Depending on the size of your pan and how experienced you are with frying eggs, decide if you would like to fry one at a time or two or three. Crack as many eggs as you are going to fry at once into a bowl. Once the oil begins to shimmer, add the eggs to the pan. Once one side of the egg is a golden brown, about 2 minutes, flip to cook the other side for about 2 minutes. You want to make sure the eggs are getting crispy and will be cooked over hard—so no runny yolk. Season with salt and pepper and continue with the rest of the eggs.

Once all the eggs are cooked, let cool in the refrigerator for about 20 minutes. Crumble up the eggs and mix them with the American cheese and bacon. Season with salt and pepper to taste. You want this mixture to be heavily seasoned so it shines through in the babka. Store in an airtight container in the refrigerator until ready to use.

Butter an 8½ × 4½-inch loaf pan, using a pastry brush to get into the corners.

Lightly dust a work surface with flour and roll the dough to a 9 × 14-inch rectangle. Spread the egg mixture in an even layer over the rolled-out dough, then use a rolling pin to push the filling lightly into the dough.

Roll up and cut the babka as directed on page 30.

Proof, bake, and cool as directed on page 34. Generously brush the babka with the olive oil.

Summer Symphony

This babka just reminds me of summer: Fresh sweet corn, Cheddar cheese, and garlic all play so beautifully together.

Makes 1 babka

Savory Babka Dough (page 41) or Butter Blocked Dough (page 44), made with savory dough

---

163 grams (1⅔ cups) Corn Puree (recipe follows)

---

38 grams (2 tablespoons + 2 teaspoons) Golden Garlic Butter (page 186)

Softened butter, for the pan

All-purpose flour, for dusting

---

97 grams (3½ ounces / scant 1 cup) Cheddar cheese, shredded

Olive oil, for generously brushing on after baking

Make and chill the dough as directed. Make the corn puree and garlic butter.

Butter an 8½ × 4½-inch loaf pan, using a pastry brush to get into the corners.

Lightly dust a work surface with flour and roll the dough to a 9 × 14-inch rectangle. Spread the garlic butter in an even layer over the rolled-out dough. Follow with the corn puree. You want this to be a thicker layer than the garlic butter (remember garlic is a strong flavor profile). Sprinkle the Cheddar cheese over the top.

Roll up and cut the babka as directed on page 30.

Proof, bake, and cool as directed on page 34.
Brush the babka generously with the olive oil.

Continued . . .

Corn Puree

MAKES 325 GRAMS (3 CUPS)

595 grams (2⅔ cups) whole milk

320 grams (2 cups) frozen sweet yellow corn kernels

13 grams (1 tablespoon) + 10 grams (2 teaspoons) olive oil

20 grams (2 tablespoons) shallot, sliced paper thin

19 grams (1½ tablespoons) unsalted butter

½ teaspoon kosher salt, plus more as desired

Pinch of xanthan gum

In a saucepan, combine the milk and corn kernels and cook over medium heat until the milk is almost all gone, 15 to 20 minutes. You should have about 1 tablespoon of liquid remaining.

Meanwhile, heat 13 grams of the olive oil in a skillet over medium heat until hot. Add the shallot and cook until tender and just beginning to brown, about 3 minutes. Remove from the heat.

Transfer the corn mixture to a blender and add the shallot, butter, and 10 grams olive oil. Blend and add more milk if the mixture is too thick. You want to form a vortex in the blender so you get a smooth puree, but you do not want to add too much liquid and get a soup.

Add salt to taste, starting with ½ teaspoon. As with all babka fillings, you want to season this mixture well so that the flavor comes through in the babka. Don't be afraid of the salt. Add the xanthan gum at the end and make sure it is well combined. This will help make sure the puree does not break when baking in the dough.

Let the puree cool and then store in an airtight container in the refrigerator until ready to use.

The Garden

Being married to a chef has completely changed the way I view the food I eat and where it comes from. This is an ode to all the farmers out there. If you have a farm stand near you, I highly recommend getting the carrots from them; it will make a world of difference in the flavor of this babka. Support your local farmers and enjoy this babka.

Makes 1 babka

Savory Babka Dough (page 41) or Butter Blocked Dough (page 44), made with savory dough

1½ teaspoons fresh dill, chopped

138 grams (½ cup) Carrot Puree (recipe follows)

Softened butter, for the pan

All-purpose flour, for dusting

57 grams (2 ounces / ⅓ cup) goat cheese, crumbled

Olive oil, for generously brushing on after baking

Honey, for drizzling

Continued . . .

Make the dough as directed, adding the dill to the mixing bowl right after adding the flour so it is fully incorporated in the dough. Chill as directed. Make the carrot puree.

Butter an 8½ × 4½-inch loaf pan, using a pastry brush to get into the corners.

Lightly dust a work surface with flour and roll the dough to a 9 × 14-inch rectangle. Spread the carrot puree in an even layer over the rolled-out dough. Sprinkle the goat cheese over the top of the carrot puree.

Roll up and cut the babka as directed on page 30.

Proof and bake as directed on page 34. Once the babka comes out of the oven, generously brush it with olive oil and then brush and drizzle with honey.

Carrot Puree

MAKES 270 GRAMS (2 CUPS)

265 grams (9½ ounces / 1⅓ cups) carrots, peeled and chopped

Water or vegetable stock

57 grams (4 tablespoons) butter, cubed and at room temperature

Kosher salt

Pinch of xanthan gum

In a saucepan, combine the carrots with enough water or vegetable stock to cover and bring to a simmer over medium-low heat. Cook until the carrots are fork-tender and all the liquid has been absorbed, about 10 to 15 minutes.

Transfer the carrots to a blender, add the butter, and puree. If needed, add some more liquid to the blender until a vortex forms. You want to add enough liquid to get the puree moving but not so much that it turns into a soup.

Add salt to taste, starting with ½ teaspoon. As with all babka fillings, you want to season this mixture well so that the flavor comes through in the babka. Don't be afraid of the salt. Add the xanthan gum at the end and make sure it is well combined. This will help make sure the puree does not break when baking in the dough.

Let the puree cool and then store in an airtight container in the refrigerator until ready to use.

Savory

This chapter contains the final steps before your babka is complete. I brush all my savory babkas with olive oil to give them a beautiful shine, and here you will find different ideas for infusing olive oils as well as a recipe for a delicious golden garlic butter.

uches

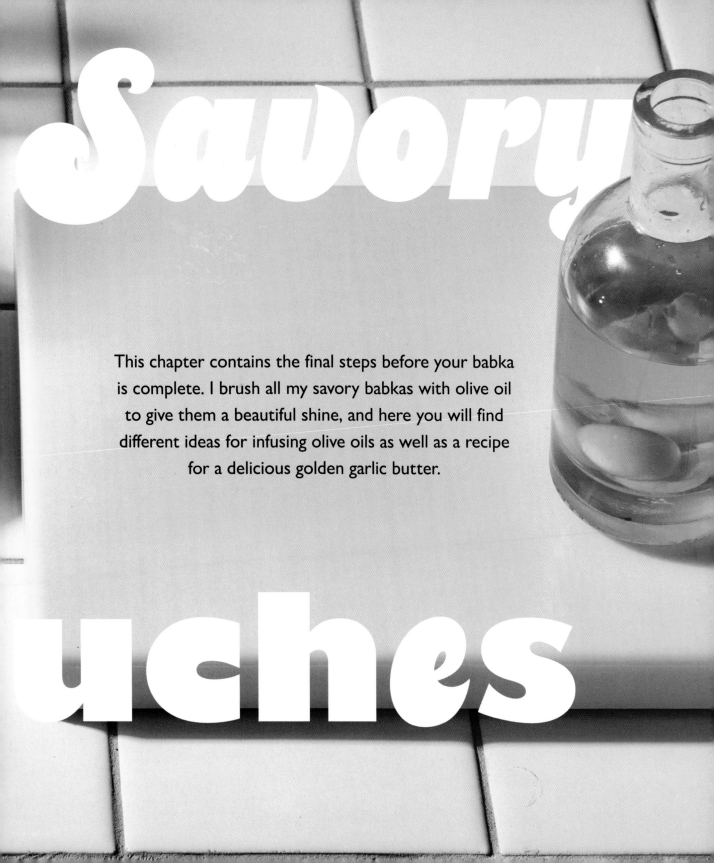

Caramelized Onions

MAKES 125 GRAMS (½ CUP)

25 grams (2 tablespoons) clarified butter

350 grams (2½ cups) finely diced yellow onion

20 grams (1½ tablespoons) Calvados

¼ teaspoon dried thyme

Place a saucepan over medium heat, get a hot, and then add in the clarified butter and melt. Add the onion, increase the heat to medium-high, and cook, stirring every minute or so, until the onion begins to foam and turn golden, about 20 minutes.

Once golden, reduce the heat to low and mix every minute. Once the onion has reached that perfect golden brown, add a splash of water to the pot and bring the heat back up to high for 30 seconds to caramelize once more.

Reduce the heat to medium and add the Calvados and thyme. Mix constantly for 2 minutes.

Let cool, then transfer to an airtight container and store in the refrigerator until ready to use.

Infused Olive Oil

MAKES 400 GRAMS (2 CUPS)

400 grams (2 cups) high-quality olive oil

Infusion Options:

Fresh herbs: 5 sprigs rosemary, 7 sprigs thyme

Dried herbs: 2 tablespoons dried oregano

2 tablespoons Italian seasoning (2 teaspoons dried oregano, 2 teaspoons dried thyme, 2 teaspoons dried basil)

Garlic: 1 head garlic, peeled

Lemon: 1 lemon, zested, use only the zest

In a small saucepan, combine the olive oil with your choice of infusion. Heat over low heat to 165°F. Remove from the heat and let steep for 5 minutes. Strain out the add-in, pour into a bottle, and let cool to room temperature. Cover and store in the refrigerator.

Golden Garlic Butter

MAKES 400 GRAMS (1½ CUPS)

4 heads garlic, cloves separated, peeled, and minced

200 grams (¼ cup) olive oil, or as needed

227 grams (16 tablespoons) unsalted butter, at room temperature

Kosher salt

In a small saucepan, combine the minced garlic with just enough olive oil to cover. Bring to a simmer over low heat, stirring constantly. Cook until the garlic turns golden brown, about 30 to 40 minutes.

Strain the garlic from the oil and let cool for about 10 minutes (save the oil to use as a garlic oil for the babka or other dishes). Transfer the cooled garlic to a food processor, add the butter, and pulse to combine. Add salt to taste.

Transfer to a container and store in the refrigerator until ready to use. If making ahead, bring the butter to room temperature before using.

Index